Ext.NET Web Application Development

A guide to building Rich Internet Applications
with Ext.NET using ASP.NET Web Forms and
ASP.NET MVC

Anup Shah

[PACKT]

PUBLISHING

BIRMINGHAM - MUMBAI

Ext.NET Web Application Development

First published: November 2012

Production Reference: 1121112

Published by Packt Publishing Ltd.

Livery Place

35 Livery Street

Birmingham B3 2PB, UK.

ISBN 978-1-84969-324-0

www.packtpub.com

Cover Image by Geoffrey McGill (geoff@ext.net)

Credits

Author
Anup Shah

Reviewers
Geoffrey McGill

Daniil Veriga

Vladmir Shcheglov

Acquisition Editor
Usha Iyer

Lead Technical Editor
Kedar Bhat

Technical Editors
Vrinda Amberkar

Devdutt Kulkarni

Worrell Lewis

Project Coordinator
Vishal Bodwani

Proofreaders
Clyde Jenkins

Linda Morris

Indexer
Tejal Soni

Graphics
Aditi Gajjar

Production Coordinator
Nilesh R. Mohite

Cover Work
Nilesh R. Mohite

About the Author

Anup Shah has been a professional software and web developer since 1997. After graduating from Manchester University with a First Class Honors degree in Computing and Information Systems, he got a job in the United States. There, he soon headed the web development for a rapidly growing dot com, experiencing both the highs and lows of the first dot com bubble.

After a number of years there he moved back to England where he grew up and joined a small dynamic software company working as a consultant, architect, and web developer for some high profile retail e-commerce websites, including some of the world's largest.

Around 2007, while at the same company, he changed focus from a consulting role to a product development role, responsible for the user interface of a complex retail web application product. It was at this time he came across Ext.NET (or Coolite as it was known back then) and rapidly adopted it and introduced it into the company's product.

Anup can be found on the Ext.NET forums, and contacted via his blog, http://www.onenaught.com.

I would like to thank a number of people for their direct or indirect role in producing this book. First, there is my wife Kajal, without whom none of this would be possible. Her support has been second to none, especially after what she has endured this year. Thank you. I also wish to thank my work colleagues — past and present — for their support and encouragement in various ways over the years (I dare not list names as I will certainly miss some out but you know who you are!) I must also thank all at Packt for giving me this opportunity, as well as having patience and understanding during some difficult times. And, of course, there is the Ext.NET team. They have not only created an amazing framework (that stopped me quitting ASP.NET development altogether!) but their professionalism, dedication, and support has been amazing and I have learned a lot both professionally and personally along the way. Geoffrey, Daniil, Vladimir: This book would not be possible without you. Finally, I dedicate this book to the loving memory of my baby twins, Preetam and Bhaav.

About the Reviewers

Geoffrey McGill is the founder of Ext.NET and a 10+ year veteran of ASP.NET, C#, and JavaScript development. Geoffrey is responsible for overseeing the technical and strategic direction of Ext.NET.

As an early adopter of Ext JS (originally yui-ext), the benefit to ASP.NET developers was obvious, although how to integrate into the ASP.NET life cycle was not. This is where the idea for Ext.NET was born.

As a passionate advocate for free and open-source software, Geoffrey has contributed code to many projects, including as the creator of DateJS (`http://datejs.com/`) which has been downloaded more than 2,000,000 times.

Daniil Veriga was born in 1985. As a young man, he enjoyed programming and won prizes in school competitions on programming. His interest in programming predetermined his path. He graduated from the Department of Computer Systems and Programming of the Saint-Petersburg State University Of Aerospace Instrumentation with honors. He started his career as a Software Engineer in a company developing industrial automation systems. He got great experience designing and implementing high performance real-time systems and solving challenging tasks. But later, he got interested in web technologies and was eventually hired to work for `Ext.NET` in 2010. His main skills and experience are C#, .NET, ASP. NET, ASP.NET MVC (Web Form and Razor engines), SQL, Visual Studio, JavaScript, HTML, CSS, ExtJS, and (obviously) Ext.NET, which this book is about. In his spare time, Daniil likes reading, swimming, skiing, biking, exercising on horizontal bars, and arm-wrestling.

First of all I would like to thank my chiefs and colleagues – Geoffrey McGill and Vladimir Shcheglov, as well as my brother – Leonid Veriga. They truly helped my professional development in the programming and web technologies area. Also, I thank my family and all my friends. All of them made a certain contribution to my professional growth! And, finally, I thank Anup Shah for his efforts to write this book and, respectively, for popularizing Ext.NET. I think we all did a good job!

Vladimir Shcheglov graduated from Saint-Petersburg State University of Aerospace Instrumentation with a Master's degree in Computer Science. He began his IT career as a Delphi developer (industrial control). Since 2005, he has been a C#/ASP.NET developer.

Vladimir started to learn ExtJS from Version 1.1 and tried using it in an ASP.NET context. He received an invite to participate in the Coolite framework (former name of Ext.Net) development after creating and sharing the first prototype of Visual Studio designers and ASP.NET controls.

Vladimir is the lead Software Engineer on the Ext.NET team.

www.PacktPub.com

Support files, eBooks, discount offers and more

You might want to visit www.PacktPub.com for support files and downloads related to your book.

Did you know that Packt offers eBook versions of every book published, with PDF and ePub files available? You can upgrade to the eBook version at www.PacktPub.com and as a print book customer, you are entitled to a discount on the eBook copy. Get in touch with us at service@packtpub.com for more details.

At www.PacktPub.com, you can also read a collection of free technical articles, sign up for a range of free newsletters and receive exclusive discounts and offers on Packt books and eBooks.

http://PacktLib.PacktPub.com

Do you need instant solutions to your IT questions? PacktLib is Packt's online digital book library. Here, you can access, read and search across Packt's entire library of books.

Why Subscribe?

- Fully searchable across every book published by Packt
- Copy and paste, print and bookmark content
- On demand and accessible via web browser

Free Access for Packt account holders

If you have an account with Packt at www.PacktPub.com, you can use this to access PacktLib today and view nine entirely free books. Simply use your login credentials for immediate access.

Table of Contents

Preface

This book will show how to use Ext.NET 2 to create sophisticated and highly interactive web applications whether you use ASP.NET Web Forms or ASP.NET MVC. The chapters will go through setting up and exploring various controls that Ext.NET provides. It will look at the sophisticated AJAX and data-handling options available while also providing tips and guidance for creating reusable and maintainable components.

The list of components that Ext.NET covers and the variety of ways in which you can use them are immense. It would be beyond the scope of this book to detail all of them, so this book will cover the most common and/or interesting ones, but importantly it will also empower you with the ability to learn and explore the rest in your own time.

What this book covers

Chapter 1, Getting Started with Ext.NET, provides an overview of what Ext.NET is and how it is related to Ext JS and ASP.NET. In addition, this chapter covers how you can obtain and set up your development environment ready for Ext.NET development.

Chapter 2, Ext.NET Controls Overview, introduces various types of controls available in Ext.NET. Using the Button control, we introduce many concepts common throughout the Ext.NET control suite. We also look at how client-side and server-side events can be set up. This chapter also introduces other more common components including Panels, Toolbars, Menus, Windows, and Tooltips. We also get a glimpse of some of the complex UIs that are possible by reusing these components.

Chapter 3, Layout with Ext.NET, covers the numerous layout options available in Ext.NET to help you organize your web applications. Topics covered include the Viewport, and specific layouts such as Border, Accordion, Fit, HBox, VBox, and more.

Chapter 4, AJAX with Ext.NET, looks at the powerful AJAX options Ext.NET supports. We cover the powerful DirectEvents and DirectMethods features, as well as AJAX options specific to certain controls. This is a powerful chapter that lays the foundation for slick and usable applications that are responsive to user interactions.

Chapter 5, Working with Data, looks at the powerful data handling techniques available in Ext.NET. We cover XTemplates, which allows you to define HTML templates to bind data to, and we explain the Stores, Models, and Proxies architecture that allows for powerful data-binding reuse across many Ext.NET components. The ComboBox and DataView are introduced as examples of controls that reuse this architecture.

Chapter 6, Introducing GridPanels, covers the popular and highly sophisticated GridPanel control. It is another control that reuses the Stores, Models, and Proxies architecture, but is given its own chapter. We look at various features of the GridPanel such as paging, filtering, sorting, grouping, column summaries, row expanding, and selection models. We also look at how grid editing can be enabled, including in-line grid editing at the row or cell level. As large as this chapter is, there are many other GridPanel capabilities that we have not been able to fit into this book, so many links to further examples and resources are also provided.

Chapter 7, Forms and Validation, looks at the numerous form controls available in Ext. NET, how to lay them out, and how to enable client and remote validation. We also look at how custom validators can be created. Lastly, we also see how Ext.NET's data-binding capabilities can also be reused with forms.

Chapter 8, Trees and Tabs with Ext.NET, introduces the popular TreePanel and TabPanel controls. Due to limited space in the book, we cannot cover all the sophisticated possibilities that these controls offer, but we do provide an overview of how tree nodes can be loaded asynchronously and how to reuse the Store, Models, and Proxies architecture to bind data to trees. We also look at various ways TabPanels can be configured, including how to load content on-demand using various AJAX techniques supported by Ext.NET.

Chapter 9, Extending Ext.NET Controls – Custom Controls and Plugins, is perhaps the most powerful chapter in this book. It shows you how to extend Ext.NET controls in a variety of ways to support both ASP.NET Web Forms and ASP.NET MVC Razor templates, enabling you to create highly reusable components. Most of the chapter looks at how controls can be extended, but we also look at how you can use the available plugin mechanisms to reuse functionality across different types of components.

Chapter 10, Troubleshooting and Debugging, looks at how to debug your Ext.NET applications. In particular, we look at how to enable debug versions of Ext.NET and Ext JS JavaScript and what tools to use for cross-browser troubleshooting. This chapter also provides important tips on how to request help in the Ext.NET forums in a way that will increase your chances of receiving a quick response.

What you need for this book

Chapter 1, Getting Started with Ext.NET will explain prerequisites further. But as a summary, you will need Visual Studio 2008 or later (the book uses Visual Studio 2010). In addition to Internet Explorer, it is recommended to also use Chrome and Firefox (with the Firebug plugin installed) to test the examples.

Who this book is for

This book is for anyone who wants to use ASP.NET to create sophisticated applications, whether you have used Ext JS directly with ASP.NET before or not.

As a .NET based component framework, Ext.NET code can be written in any supported .NET language, but this book will use C#. As such, familiarity with C# and ASP.NET is assumed. It is also assumed that the reader will have some basic knowledge of HTML, CSS, and JavaScript.

Although it is not essential to know Ext JS upfront, it would be highly beneficial. That being said, some Ext JS code will naturally be used in various examples, where necessary. Such code will be explained appropriately and references for further Ext JS related information will also be provided, where needed.

Conventions

In this book, you will find a number of styles of text that distinguish between different kinds of information. Here are some examples of these styles, and an explanation of their meaning.

Code words in text are shown as follows: "When normally developing ASP.NET applications, you add controls to the container's `Controls` collection."

A block of code is set as follows:

```
<pages>
  <controls>
    <add tagPrefix="ext" namespace="Ext.Net" assembly="Ext.Net"/>
  </controls>
</pages>
```

When we wish to draw your attention to a particular part of a code block, the relevant lines or items are set in bold:

```
<ext:Viewport runat="server" Layout="Border">
  <Items>
    <ext:UserControlLoader Path="WestPanel.ascx" />
    <ext:Panel Region="Center" />
  </Items>
</ext:Viewport>
```

Any command-line input or output is written as follows:

```
Install-Package Ext.NET.MVC
```

New terms and **important words** are shown in bold. Words that you see on the screen, in menus or dialog boxes for example, appear in the text like this: "Right-click on the file and select **View in Browser** and you will see a page similar to the following".

> Warnings or important notes appear in a box like this.

> Tips and tricks appear like this.

Reader feedback

Feedback from our readers is always welcome. Let us know what you think about this book—what you liked or may have disliked. Reader feedback is important for us to develop titles that you really get the most out of.

To send us general feedback, simply send an e-mail to feedback@packtpub.com, and mention the book title via the subject of your message.

If there is a topic that you have expertise in and you are interested in either writing or contributing to a book, see our author guide on www.packtpub.com/authors.

Customer support

Now that you are the proud owner of a Packt book, we have a number of things to help you to get the most from your purchase.

Downloading the example code

You can download the example code files for all Packt books you have purchased from your account at `http://www.PacktPub.com`. If you purchased this book elsewhere, you can visit `http://www.PacktPub.com/support` and register to have the files e-mailed directly to you.

Downloading the color images of this book

We also provide you a PDF file that has color images of the screenshots used in this book. You can download this file from `http://www.packtpub.com/sites/default/files/downloads/3240OT_Images.pdf`.

Errata

Although we have taken every care to ensure the accuracy of our content, mistakes do happen. If you find a mistake in one of our books—maybe a mistake in the text or the code—we would be grateful if you would report this to us. By doing so, you can save other readers from frustration and help us improve subsequent versions of this book. If you find any errata, please report them by visiting `http://www.packtpub.com/support`, selecting your book, clicking on the **errata submission form** link, and entering the details of your errata. Once your errata are verified, your submission will be accepted and the errata will be uploaded on our website, or added to any list of existing errata, under the Errata section of that title. Any existing errata can be viewed by selecting your title from `http://www.packtpub.com/support`.

Piracy

Piracy of copyright material on the Internet is an ongoing problem across all media. At Packt, we take the protection of our copyright and licenses very seriously. If you come across any illegal copies of our works, in any form, on the Internet, please provide us with the location address or website name immediately so that we can pursue a remedy.

Please contact us at copyright@packtpub.com with a link to the suspected pirated material.

We appreciate your help in protecting our authors, and our ability to bring you valuable content.

Questions

You can contact us at questions@packtpub.com if you are having a problem with any aspect of the book, and we will do our best to address it.

Getting Started with Ext.NET

1

This chapter will introduce you to Ext.NET and how it fits into ASP.NET-based development. It will then guide you through installing and setting up Ext.NET on your local development machine. In particular, we cover the following topics:

- An overview of Ext.NET
- Choosing the right Ext.NET license
- Downloading Ext.NET
- Compiling Ext.NET
- Creating a simple ASP.NET project with Ext.NET enabled
- Creating a simple ASP.NET MVC Razor Project with Ext.NET enabled

An overview of Ext.NET

As mentioned on Ext.NET's official website (`http://ext.net`):

> *Ext.NET is an open source ASP.NET (WebForm + MVC) component framework integrating the cross-browser Sencha Ext JS JavaScript Library.*

Sencha's official website (`http://www.sencha.com/products/extjs/`) describes Ext JS (pronounced *eee-ecks-tee*) as a JavaScript framework for rich apps in every browser.

In other words, Ext.NET is an ASP.NET framework, or a set of controls and classes, that typically generates JavaScript (though HTML and CSS are generated wherever needed). And, the JavaScript it generates is based on the Ext JS framework, from Sencha.

Ext.NET also includes components that are not found in Ext JS, and extends various Sencha Ext JS classes wherever needed, thus providing its own JavaScript layer on top of Ext JS.

Ext.NET is a good abstraction over Ext JS. The abstraction is not leaky or restrictive—you can also write Ext JS-based JavaScript directly, as well as in conjunction with Ext.NET. This flexibility importantly allows you to tap into the wider Ext JS community of plugins and components that you might want to incorporate into your Ext.NET applications.

This means that knowing the underlying Ext JS library can really help you understand Ext.NET, and will open you to more options when building complex applications.

The other way of thinking about it is that Ext.NET is a great bridge between Ext JS on the client side and ASP.NET on the server side.

Ext.NET and its relationship with ASP.NET Web Forms and ASP.NET MVC

A great thing about Ext.NET is that it works with both ASP.NET Web Forms and ASP.NET MVC. If you are integrating Ext.NET into a legacy application built with ASP.NET Web Forms, or if you simply prefer ASP.NET Web Forms, Ext.NET will work very well and provide enhanced HTML5 functionality.

The newer ASP.NET MVC framework is a powerful and well-architected MVC framework, designed to avoid the Post Back model that ASP.NET Web Forms is based on and allow better access for developers to the underlying HTML, JavaScript, and CSS.

The choice of using ASP.NET MVC or Web Forms is not important for the scope of this book. Examples of both will be shown from time to time, though most of these will be based on ASP.NET Web Forms.

Ext JS

Many ASP.NET developers, especially those using ASP.NET MVC may be more familiar with jQuery or other JavaScript frameworks. It is, therefore, worth explaining Ext JS a bit further.

Comparing with other JavaScript libraries such as jQuery

Although Ext JS is a reasonably popular JavaScript framework (especially in the enterprise and in the Java world), there are other more popular JavaScript frameworks, such as the excellent jQuery.

However, as popular as jQuery may be (Microsoft includes it by default in their MVC framework, for example), there is a significant difference between Ext JS and libraries such as jQuery, Prototype, and MooTools.

Libraries such as jQuery attempt to solve common problems for web developers and designers by providing cross-browser compatible ways to navigate and manipulate the DOM. They provide standard event, AJAX and other capabilities. Their UI components, such as jQuery UI are typically designed to work in a progressive enhancement way (i.e. the web page will work with and without JavaScript; JavaScript in that context, when structured properly, is used to enhance the base functionality of a web document to add further behavior and improved user experience, but the absence of JavaScript allows search engines and users of lower-grade browsers to still access the page and use it).

Ext JS's goal, however, is to provide a complete UI framework for building complex web-based applications. Ext JS also provides a full and extensible object-oriented UI component framework, in addition to providing cross-browser abstractions in the similar ways that other JavaScript frameworks do. (Ext.NET mimics this component hierarchy on the server side quite closely, which makes for easier learning of both frameworks).

In that regards, it is more appropriate to compare jQuery UI with Ext JS, and in that context, Ext JS is far richer in capability.

All that being said, the use of Ext JS—and, therefore, Ext.NET—does not preclude the use of other frameworks. For example, you can include jQuery on the same page as an Ext.NET application.

From a web developer's point of view

Progressive enhancement and web standards are excellent principles for building websites. However, Ext JS is not about progressive enhancement. The problem space it addresses is different; it is intended for much richer applications where a dependency on JavaScript can be mandated. A back-office application in a corporate or intranet setting is one example. Another may be a public application but where search engine visibility is not required. In such scenarios typically, JavaScript is the starting point for the application; the HTML-based web page then becomes a container to load and initialize the JavaScript-based application.

It is possible to use Ext JS on top of HTML and get it to replace say an HTML table with a powerful Ext JS grid, but that is not considered the optimal way to use Ext JS.

All is not lost from a web standards perspective, however! You should still test on modern browsers, such as Chrome, Firefox, and Opera, first and then work backwards. It is well established that this way of working with web technologies will reduce (though not eliminate) the number of workarounds you need for older web browsers, in a maintainable way. For many components, Ext JS and Ext.NET will also let you override the underlying HTML it uses to generate its components. In addition, Ext JS is also increasing its HTML5 and ARIA accessibility standards support in its numerous widgets.

From a CSS point of view, complete themes are provided. These also include resets of default styles to normalize them across browsers as much as possible. The default themes may be quite suitable for many Ext JS-based applications, which also means less time may be required working with CSS on Ext.NET-based applications. You can also create your own themes but this will be beyond the scope of this book. You can find various tutorials on the Web, as well as on Sencha's official website.

Ext.NET from an ASP.NET application developer's point of view

If you are used to creating ASP.NET applications using ASP.NET controls or using vendor controls that follow ASP.NET controls closely (for example, using the Post Back model where most of the control state is maintained on the server via ViewState) then Ext.NET may initially appear quite similar, but behind the scenes, there are some useful enhancements and considerations, for example:

- ViewState is typically not required for Ext.NET controls and is turned off by default (but is on if you use FormsAuthentication, which requires it). This can save a lot of bandwidth. In one case, a roughly 1.5 MB page (mostly due to ViewState) during an AJAX request became a mere 500 bytes using one of Ext.NET's AJAX approaches.

- An ASP.NET Web Forms application requires a single ASP.NET `<form runat="server">`, which contains all the controls, ViewState, event arguments, and so on. With Ext.NET it is optional as later chapters will show. Furthermore, you can choose to have multiple HTML `form` tags if you require and Ext.NET will happily work with that.

- When normally developing ASP.NET applications, you add controls to the container's `Controls` collection. With Ext.NET, you typically add child Ext.NET controls to an Ext.NET component's `Items` collection. This is important to bear in mind. This helps generate more optimized Ext.NET JavaScript and lets you take advantage of additional Ext.NET features such as Layout which we will see in *Chapter 3, Layout with Ext.NET*.

It is worth focusing on the point about ViewState for a moment. In a traditional ASP. NET Web Forms application, ViewState and the associated Post Back Model are the keys to recreating complex controls in the state the user expects them to be. With Ext. NET's approach, however, control state does not typically need to be maintained on the server; this usually flies against conventional ASP.NET Web Forms applications, but rich Internet applications are becoming more and more AJAX-oriented, which means less (sometimes no) browser page reloads. As such, the control state management normally associated with page reloads and post backs is less prominent and helps simplify code.

For the client side, Ext.NET's JavaScript and the underlying Ext JS framework handles most complexities of control management such as instantiation, destruction, layout management, and redrawing components. This also means the client-side code needed to maintain the state is also very minimal, if anything; Ext JS components will handle most of the internal state for you and if you need more, the API is flexible enough for you to introduce your own code as needed.

Because Ext.NET uses Ext JS's built-in AJAX capabilities, mixing different server-side toolkits — while not impossible — can limit the flexibility and performance you can get out of Ext.NET. For example, if you have a mix of components on your page, and the other non-Ext.NET components rely on ASP.NET Web Form's Post Back and ViewState, Ext.NET will still work with that, but you won't be able to take advantage of some of Ext.NET's more sophisticated capabilities, as frequently.

At the same time as being a complete UI framework, you can always by-pass Ext. NET on the server side and do something directly using Ext JS or Ext.NET's own JavaScript, if that proves more optimal. This flexibility makes the Ext.NET server-side abstraction more flexible and less "leaky".

From an ASP.NET development perspective, the main thing to take away is that as powerful as ASP.NET is, Ext.NET enhances and integrates client and server coding much more completely and gives you the flexibility to get your hands dirty with JavaScript, if you so wish.

> To get the most out of Ext.NET, it is strongly recommended to spend time learning more about Ext JS as well.

Ext.NET and Ext JS versions

With Ext.NET's integration of Ext JS the versions are important to understand.

The latest version of Ext JS, as of writing, is 4.1. It is an impressive evolution of the previous version (Ext JS 3.4) which is still widely used.

Ext.NET targets specific Ext JS versions:

- Ext.NET 1.x works with Ext JS 3.x
- Ext.NET 2.x works with Ext JS 4.x

> This book covers Ext.NET 2.1 which is the latest version as of writing. However, note that the Ext.NET team works to produce updates as frequently as they can. If Ext.NET 2.2 or later has been produced, most principles and techniques from this book will still apply.

This is important to note if ever consulting the Ext.NET or Ext JS documentation online.

Prerequisites

Ext.NET 2 will work with the following:

- Visual Studio 2010 or 2012
- Visual Web Developer Express 2010 or 2012
- .NET Framework 4.0 and 4.5

In this book, code examples will be created using Visual Studio 2010 Service Pack 1 and .NET Framework 4.

Ext JS and Ext.NET support all the major modern browsers such as Chrome, Firefox, IE9, Opera, and Safari) as well as older versions of Internet Explorer (also referred to as IE) — IE8, IE7, and IE6. As of writing, IE10 has only just come out, so is not officially supported, but we can expect both Ext.NET and Ext JS to provide maintenance releases to support IE10, as they have done with IE9 in the past.

> Keep an eye on the Ext.NET website, `http://ext.net`, because new versions of the .NET framework and Visual Studio are being released as of writing, and browser manufacturers are frequently releasing newer versions of their software.

When to use ExtJS/Ext.NET and when not to

With all the benefits that Ext.NET may offer, why might you consider not using it?

The following points are just guidelines as there will always be exceptions, but the main consideration is that Ext.NET is based on Ext JS, which is a JavaScript framework.

If you have a website where search engine visibility is crucial, progressive enhancement is important, and full control over every bit of HTML and CSS is important, Ext JS (and therefore Ext.NET) may not be for you. This may include public-facing consumer websites such as blogs and e-commerce sites. You can certainly use Ext JS (and Ext.NET) on these sites, but it would not be the main or intended use cases.

However, if you are building complex applications, such as business/intranet applications or a public-facing site where JavaScript dependency can be an accepted pre-requisite, then Ext JS/Ext.NET can be an excellent choice.

If you are looking to build a sophisticated application, the user interface, the usability, and interaction design principles may also differ to what you would follow for websites. There is certainly a lot of overlap, but additional principles such as those described in the authoritative *About Face 3: The Essentials of Interaction Design* by *Alan Cooper* et al is highly recommended.

Getting Ext.NET

We will now look at what is involved in downloading the Ext.NET framework.

Choosing the right Ext.NET license

The first thing to note is that Ext.NET is dual licensed and you can choose between the following:

- **Ext.NET Pro**: For commercial closed-source projects
- **Ext.NET Community**: For open source AGPL licensed projects

The differences between the two are very minimal. In the Ext.NET Pro release there is an option to render resources (JavaScript, CSS, and images) from a global Content Delivery Network. The Community version does not have this option. The Pro version also does some license checking. Other than that, the code is the same.

If your own project is licensed with the AGPL license, then you can use the Community license. If you are producing a closed source project, then you should purchase an Ext.NET Pro license. The Pro license includes a license to the underlying Ext JS framework so you do not have to purchase both. The Pro license also comes with a license key that can be added to `Web.config` or `Global.asax` without which you would see a message appearing on any web pages that are not running locally. This message warns about the software being unlicensed. The FAQs at Ext.NET's download page, `http://ext.net/download/`, has further details and can help you decide which license is suitable for your project.

Downloading Ext.NET

There are a number of ways you can download Ext.NET:

From the Ext.NET download site: `http://ext.net/download/`

- From GitHub: `https://github.com/extnet/`
- From SVN, if you have a Premium Support Subscription: `http://ext.net/store/`
- As a NuGet Package: `http://nuget.org/packages/Ext.NET`

All these options, except the NuGet option, include the full source code so you can choose whether to build the solution yourself or use the supplied assemblies. Downloading the source code is useful to at least explore how Ext.NET has been put together. The SVN option will include a pre-release source code if you want bug fixes more quickly than official releases.

NuGet is a popular Visual Studio extension to manage packages for you and will install the Ext.NET binaries to your web project's `bin` folder. The download from Ext. NET is a ZIP file. The DLLs that you will find are as follows:

- `Ext.Net.dll`: The Main Ext.NET assembly
- `Ext.Net.pdb`: The debugging symbols
- `Ext.Net.xml`: The IntelliSense help text for the assembly when you are coding
- `Ext.Net.Utilities.dll`: Additional utilities from the Ext.NET framework
- `Ext.Net.Utilities.xml`: IntelliSense help text
- `NewtonSoft.Json.dll`: The Json.NET framework that Ext.NET uses
- `NewtonSoft.Json.xml`: The Json.NET IntelliSense
- `Transformer.NET.dll`: A .NET template parsing and transformation library
- `Transformer.NET.xml`: The Transformer.NET IntelliSense

Json.NET is itself a popular open source .NET library for working with JSON. It is extremely effective at serializing .NET into JSON and deserialization from JSON to .NET. So much so that Microsoft itself has started using it instead of some of its own JSON serializers. More information about Json.NET can be found at its website: `http://james.newtonking.com/pages/json-net.aspx`.

In addition to the DLLs, the following text files are also available and worth reading:

- `README.txt`
- `CHANGELOG.txt`
- `LICENSE.txt`

Compiling (if needed)

If you have opted for the Ext.NET Premium Support Subscription service, amongst other benefits, you get access to their latest source code. So, for example, any bug fixes or feature requests reported by you or others in the community that have recently been implemented are available immediately for you to compile and use.

If you go for this option, Ext.NET will send you instructions on how to connect to the public SVN code repository to download the latest code. You can then open the Visual Studio solution file and compile the code manually. If you then look in the Ext.Net project's `bin\Debug` or `bin\Release` directory (depending on which mode you want) you will find the same DLLs as above.

You can then include the output assemblies in your own solution. This means you do not need to compile their source code every time you compile your own solution; only when you update your local Ext.NET code from their SVN repository.

A walkthrough – creating a simple ASP. NET project with Ext.NET enabled

We will use the simplest and quickest approach to get you ready and playing with Ext.NET. Although the following steps and screenshots assume Visual Studio 2010 Service Pack 1, similar steps can be performed with Visual Studio 2012.

Creating the project and enabling Ext.NET

The quickest way to get going in just a few seconds is to use NuGet. First, ensure you have the latest version of NuGet installed and then perform the following steps:

1. In Visual Studio, create a new **ASP.NET Empty Web** project.
2. Once it is created, open the Package Manager Console in Visual Studio.
3. Enter the following NuGet command:

   ```
   Install-Package Ext.NET
   ```

4. Once installed, compile your project and you are done!

> You can also run the NuGet command on an existing web project and it will add the new references and update your Web.config with its new additions for you.

Running the sample Ext.NET page

Following the above steps, the project will include a new page called Ext.NET.Default.aspx.

Right-click on the file and select **View in Browser** and you will see a page similar to the following:

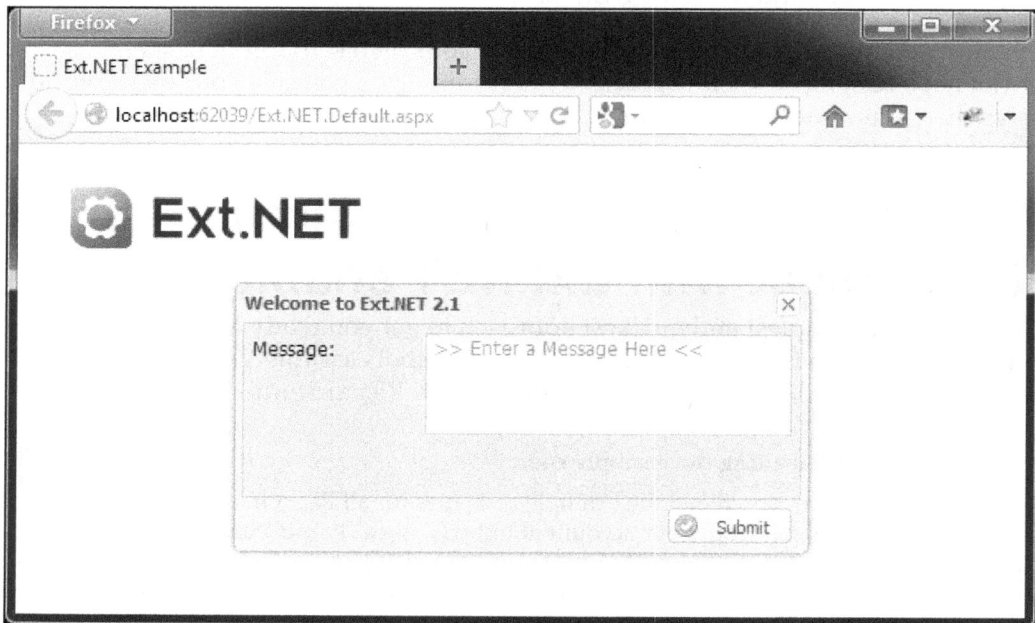

The above page renders a simple Ext.NET Window in the center of the page with a message textbox.

But it is not a static page; go ahead, type a short message, and click on **Submit**.

An AJAX request will be made to the server and a message notification will slide up from the lower-right side of the browser window, then slide-out and disappear after a few seconds:

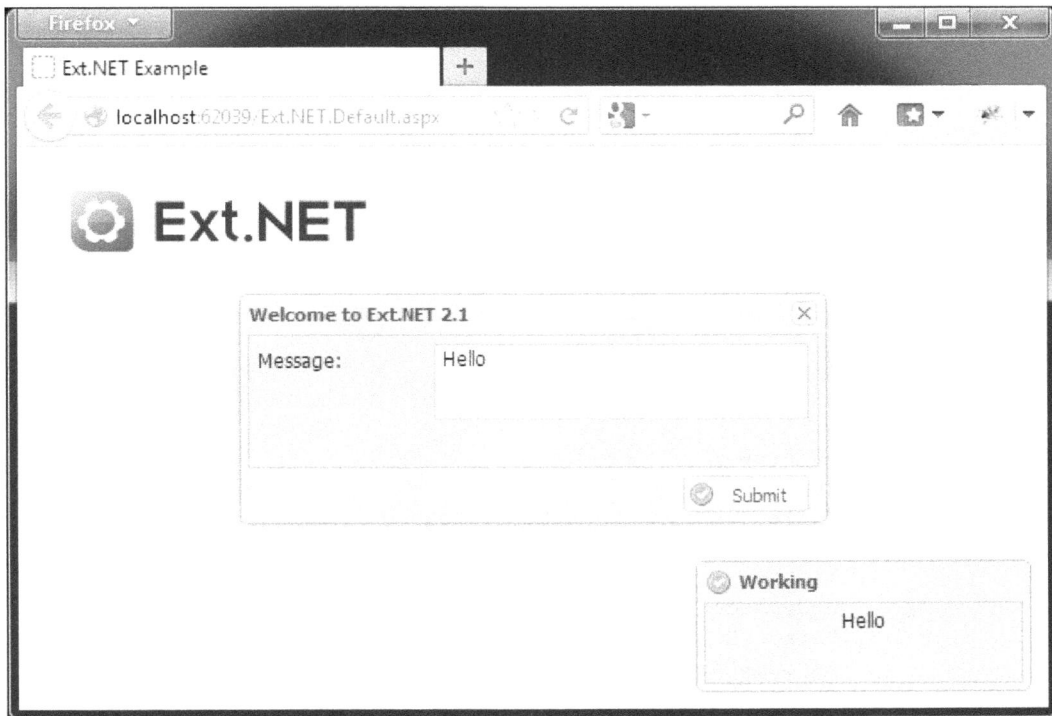

What the sample page does

This very simple example does many things for you

- It loads the required JavaScript and CSS resources
- It generates the necessary client-side initialization script, which renders the Ext. NET Components, such as the Window, TextArea, and Button, to the browser
- When the message is submitted, an AJAX request is posted to the server
- The server responds with a snippet of JavaScript to pop up the Ext.NET Notification

The code for the sample page is quite minimal. Here is the full ASPX code:

```
<%@ Page Language="C#" %>

<script runat="server">
    protected void Button1_Click(object sender, DirectEventArgs e)
    {
        X.Msg.Notify(new NotificationConfig {
            Icon  = Icon.Accept,
            Title = "Working",
            Html  = this.TextArea1.Text
        }).Show();
    }
</script>

<!DOCTYPE html>
<html>
<head runat="server">
    <title>Ext.NET Example</title>
</head>
<body>
    <form runat="server">
        <ext:ResourceManager runat="server" Theme="Gray" />

        <ext:Window
            runat="server"
            Title="Welcome to Ext.NET 2.1"
            Height="215"
            Width="350"
            BodyPadding="5"
            DefaultButton="0"
            Layout="AnchorLayout"
            DefaultAnchor="100%">
            <Items>
                <ext:TextArea
                    ID="TextArea1"
                    runat="server"
                    EmptyText=">> Enter a Message Here <<"
                    FieldLabel="Test Message"
                    Height="85"
                    />
            </Items>
            <Buttons>
                <ext:Button
                    runat="server"
                    Text="Submit"
                    Icon="Accept"
```

```
                OnDirectClick="Button1_Click"
                    />
            </Buttons>
        </ext:Window>
    </form>
</body>
</html>
```

The key things happening in the preceding code are as follows:

- All the Ext.NET components are registered from the Ext.NET assembly using the ext tag prefix.

- In the HTML, inside the form, is ext:ResourceManager. It is responsible for including the required JavaScript and CSS resources. In the above code, the theme has been set to the Gray theme. If this is not set, you get the default theme which is currently Blue.

- Next, an Ext.NET Window component is placed on the screen and inside that, is a TextArea and a Button component.

- The button, when clicked, will invoke an Ext.NET DirectEvent. A DirectEvent is Ext.NET's mechanism for doing server side calls in such a way it looks like a remote procedure call and the details of making the AJAX request and handling it on the server are all taken care of for you. (*Chapter 4, AJAX with Ext.NET*, will cover this in a bit more detail.)

- The Button1_Click server-side event handler is defined near the top of the ASPX page. It simply calls the Notify method on the Msg property of the X class, which creates the Ext.NET Notification widget in the browser's corner using the supplied configuration options for the title, title icon, and the main text which is the value picked up from the TextArea.

The X class contains many Ext.NET utilities and properties.

All the components and techniques used in the above code will be expanded upon in subsequent chapters. A key thing to note at this point is that overall, this looks much like a regular ASP.NET button-click handler in terms of the code you write. However, the significant difference is that this is not doing a full page post back; it is a light-weight AJAX request, with an even lighter AJAX response.

Here is the full response from the server to the browser:

```
{script:"Ext.net.Notification.show({title:\"Working\",html:\"Hello Wor
ld!\",iconCls:\"#Accept\"});"}
```

It is just 100 bytes of JSON which Ext.NET's JavaScript will handle and process for you. Had this been an ASP.NET traditional post back, the response would have been a full HTML page. In a real application these kinds of responses can save a lot of server resources and improve the user experience considerably.

Let's take moment to go back to the project we created and see what other project artifacts we now have after the NuGet package installed Ext.NET for us.

Ext.NET in the ASP.NET project

In addition to creating `Ext.NET.Default.aspx`, the only other things that were done to the project were the following:

- Four new references were added, to Ext.Net, Ext.Net.Utilities, Newtonsoft. Json and Transformer.NET
- `Web.config` was updated to include a few additional settings (discussed in the next section)
- A folder called `App_Readme` with useful Ext.NET files such as a change log, readme files, and license information were added
- A `packages.config` file was also added (by NuGet) to list the added components

Ext.NET and Web.config

`Web.config` is an important file in ASP.NET and for Ext.NET too. The bare minimum `Web.config` that is created is as follows:

```xml
<?xml version="1.0" encoding="utf-8"?>
<configuration>
  <configSections>
    <section name="extnet" type="Ext.Net.GlobalConfig"
requirePermission="false" />
  </configSections>
  <system.web>
    <compilation debug="true" targetFramework="4.0" />
    <httpHandlers>
      <add path="*/ext.axd" verb="*" type="Ext.Net.ResourceHandler"
validate="false" />
    </httpHandlers>
    <httpModules>
      <add name="DirectRequestModule" type="Ext.Net.
DirectRequestModule, Ext.Net" />
```

```
          </httpModules>
       </system.web>
       <extnet theme="Default" />
       <system.webServer>
          <validation validateIntegratedModeConfiguration="false" />
          <modules>
             <add name="DirectRequestModule" preCondition="managedHandler"
type="Ext.Net.DirectRequestModule, Ext.Net" />
          </modules>
          <handlers>
             <add name="DirectRequestHandler" verb="*" path="*/ext.axd"
preCondition="integratedMode" type="Ext.Net.ResourceHandler" />
          </handlers>
       </system.webServer>
       <runtime>
          <assemblyBinding xmlns="urn:schemas-microsoft-com:asm.v1">
             <dependentAssembly>
                <assemblyIdentity name="Newtonsoft.Json" publicKeyToken="30ad4
fe6b2a6aeed" />
                <bindingRedirect oldVersion="0.0.0.0-4.5.0.0"
newVersion="4.5.0.0" />
             </dependentAssembly>
          </assemblyBinding>
       </runtime>
    </configuration>
```

The above configuration uses both system.web and system.webServer to support
IIS6 and IIS7+ to set up the AJAX handlers that Ext.NET will be using, as well as
defining the custom section called extnet. This important configuration setting
doesn't look like much by default:

```
<extnet theme="Default" />
```

However, it is where global settings can be applied to determine how Ext.NET will
behave across all pages in your application. The above example sets a global setting
to tell the Ext.NET ResourceManager to use the default theme when rendering out
the Ext.NET pages. As we saw in the sample page, we can also set the theme on the
ResourceManager on the page itself.

> **The extnet configuration has many more options**
>
> The configuration can take many other parameters which the accompanying README in the project lists and explains. Useful options include a `scriptMode` property which can be set to `Release` or `Debug` (we will look at this in a later chapter to help troubleshoot your application), a property on whether to gzip your resources or not, and many more. The *Examples Explorer* page on Ext.NET's website has a full list of the configuration options and is worth studying:
>
> ```
> http://examples.ext.net/#/Getting_Started/
> Introduction/README/
> ```

If you have purchased an Ext.NET Pro license, then the license key should have been sent to you by the Ext.NET team. That key can be put in the `licenseKey` property of the `extnet` configuration section. Without this key, if your site is accessed remotely (for non-development purposes) each page will get a notification pop up saying the software is not licensed.

Ext.NET controls are registered in Web.config for you

In the earlier code for `Ext.NET.Default.aspx`, there was no explicit registration of the Ext.NET components (using a `<%@Register` line). Instead, the NuGet installation process adds the following into the `system.web` section of your `Web.config` file:

```
<pages>
  <controls>
    <add tagPrefix="ext" namespace="Ext.Net" assembly="Ext.Net"/>
  </controls>
</pages>
```

As a result, none of your ASPX pages require the `<%@ Register` line.

> If you do not use the NuGet install method, then you can add the above code manually into `Web.config`.

As an aside, the NuGet package used above does not have MVC support built into it, which means you can use it against a .NET 3.5 solution, if you require, though .NET 4 would usually be recommended. Ext.NET's MVC support is for MVC 3 including the popular Razor engine so .NET 4 is, therefore, needed then. Conveniently, Ext. NET provides a separate NuGet package for this, which we turn to next.

A walkthrough – creating a simple ASP.NET MVC Project with Razor and Ext.NET enabled

Ext.NET also supports ASP.NET MVC with both the default view template engine, as well as the popular Razor engine. Although the majority of this book will mostly show examples using ASP.NET Web Forms, there will be some examples showing MVC and Razor usage.

Creating an MVC project and enabling Ext.NET

To get MVC support, there is a similar NuGet package, called `Ext.Net.MVC`. So, you can follow the earlier steps, but instead do the following:

1. Create a new **ASP.NET MVC 3 Web Application** project.

2. Use the following NuGet command:

    ```
    Install-Package Ext.NET.MVC
    ```

The changes will be the same as before. `Web.config` will be updated for you as needed, and `Global.asax` will have an additional route registered to handle Ext.NET resources.

> The following Ext.NET forum post is worth looking at to see how to manually apply the configuration changes to an existing project (because you can always use ASP.NET Web Forms and ASP.NET MVC in one project if you wish):
>
> http://forums.ext.net/showthread.php?16920

The sample Ext.NET page using MVC and Razor

To get a feel of how Ext.NET looks in MVC/Razor, here is a similar example as earlier, but using the MVC/Razor syntax. First, the View:

```
<!DOCTYPE html>
<html>
<head>
    <title>Ext.NET Example</title>
</head>
```

```
<body>
    @Html.X().ResourceManager().Theme(Theme.Gray)

    @(Html.X().Window()
        .Title("Welcome to Ext.NET 2.1")
        .Height(215)
        .Width(350)
        .Layout(LayoutType.Fit)
        .Items(Html.X().FormPanel()
            .Layout(LayoutType.Anchor)
            .DefaultAnchor("100%")
            .Border(false)
            .BodyPadding(5)
            .Items(Html.X().TextArea()
                .ID("message")
                .EmptyText(">> Enter a Message Here <<")
                .FieldLabel("Text Message")
                .Height(85)
            )
            .Buttons(
                Html.X().Button()
                    .Text("Submit")
                    .Icon(Icon.Accept)
                    .DirectClickAction("Notify", "ExtNET")
            )
        )
    )
</body>
</html>
```

And next, the Controller:

```
using System.Web.Mvc;
using Ext.Net;
using Ext.Net.MVC;
using Controller = System.Web.Mvc.Controller;

namespace ExtNet2Mvc.Controllers
{
    public class DirectEventExampleController : Controller
    {
        //
        // GET: /DirectEventExample/
        public ActionResult Index()
        {
            return View();
        }
```

```
        //
        // GET: /DirectEventExample/Notify/
        public ActionResult Notify(string message)
        {
            var config = new NotificationConfig
            {
                Icon = Icon.Accept,
                Title = "Working",
                Html = message
            };

            X.Msg.Notify(config).Show();

            return this.Direct();
        }
    }
}
```

The code does the same thing as the ASP.NET Web Forms example, earlier. We have defined two actions in the same controller. The Index, or default action when browsing /DirectEventExample/ will simply return the View. The View creates the same components as before, but using Razor syntax and Ext.NET's MVC helper methods.

The button's Click DirectEvent is slightly different; the associated controller action, Notify, takes a string parameter. To set that parameter, the Click DirectEvent adds it as an extra parameter getting the value via a small bit of client-side JavaScript code (which gets the value of the client-side representation of the text area).

To handle the event on the server side, the Notify action creates an Ext.NET Notification object and shows it. The Direct() method generates a DirectResult which is a subclass of ActionResult. It is a class created by Ext.NET and handles the script generation so that the Notification object appears on the user's browser.

These techniques will, of course, be expanded upon in this book, so don't worry about the inner workings in too much detail for now! The key points to take away for MVC Razor is that it generally follows the standard ASP.NET MVC Razor patterns and Ext.NET components come with their own helper methods to help configure the controls as needed. There will be additional features specific to MVC that Ext.NET is building even as this book goes to print so there will be more capabilities to expect that cannot be covered in this book, including Data Annotations support, Model Binding support, specialized Ext.NET action results, and more.

Summary

In this chapter we looked at what Ext.NET is and how it integrates both the Ext JS JavaScript framework and the ASP.NET server-side web framework. We also saw how you can set up Ext.NET on your development environment. We saw a variety of ways that Ext.NET can be added to your project, depending on your needs.

Using NuGet is perhaps the quickest way to get started with using Ext.NET. We created an empty ASP.NET Web Application project and installed Ext.NET via NuGet.

This gave us a simple Ext.NET ready project with a sample Ext.NET page. With very little code we saw a component that could talk to the server via AJAX and result in an AJAX response that interacted with the user.

We also got a glimpse of how Ext.NET can be used with an ASP.NET MVC 3 project that uses a Razor template engine.

In the next chapter we will look at various controls that Ext.NET provides.

2
Ext.NET Controls Overview

Ext.NET provides a rich and vast set of UI controls that extends the already versatile set provided by Ext JS. Given the extensiveness of the set of controls, it won't be possible to cover them all in detail in this book. Instead, in this chapter we look at some of the more basic—but still powerful—controls, such as buttons, toolbars, menus, panels, and more. This will help to introduce Ext.NET syntax and conventions, showing how the server side and the client side (JavaScript) can integrate together. Subsequent chapters will explore more complex controls, such as various layout controls and more advanced controls like grids and trees. At the end of this chapter, you will also get a glimpse of some complex controls that we will not be able to cover in this book, just so you get an idea of the possibilities that Ext. NET offers.

By the end of this chapter you will understand:

- The type of controls in Ext.NET
- Common features of most controls
- Handling events on the client side and server side
- Using Container components, such as Menus, Toolbars, Panels, Windows, and Tooltips
- How complex controls can come about from these concepts

Control overview

Ext.NET provides a vast array of controls. We can broadly group the controls by their main functionality as follows:

Functionality Area	Examples
Data visualization	DataView, GridPanel, PropertyGrid, TreePanel, Chart, and Calendar
Data handling	Store, Proxies, Model, Reader/Writer, and Associations
Containers	Container, Panel, Window, ButtonGroup, Toolbar, ViewPort, TabPanel, and Menu
Special containers	Desktop and Portal
Control elements	Various types of buttons (such as Button, SplitButton, and LinkButton), pickers (such as ColorPicker and DatePicker), Slider, ProgressBar, Image, and Editor
Layouts	Accordion, Anchor, Border, HBox, VBox, and many more
Form and fields	FormPanel, FieldContainer, TextField, NumberField, ComboBox, CheckBoxField, DateField, DropdownField, FileUploadField, HyperLink, Label, MultiSelect, SpinnerField, TimeField, TriggerField, and many more
Utilities and helpers	DragDrop, KeyMap, KeyNav, XTemplate, TaskManager, Selection Models, and XScript

This list is not a complete list, but it gives you an idea of the types of controls Ext.NET provides in these areas. Some of these controls such as the GridPanel, TreePanel, and others are extremely sophisticated themselves. In addition, some of these are covered in dedicated chapters later in this book. However, it would be impossible to cover all of them in detail in this one book alone! This chapter attempts to give you a sufficient overview in the hope that it will enable you to know how to learn and explore these more quickly.

> All these controls, and more, are demonstrated in the Ext.NET Examples Explorer. It is the best online resource to see all the controls in action. For each example, you can see the source code, to see how it was put together: http://examples.ext.net.

The base class for most controls in Ext.NET is Component. All components can be shown/hidden and enabled/disabled, and can take part in sophisticated Ext.NET component registration and internal management. The class model is a close mirror of the client side, with Component being the base class for most Ext JS components, which provides some familiarity regardless of which way you look at the framework.

Common to most visual controls is the ability to set dimensions, provide a class attribute, handle core events (on the client side and via AJAX requests), and so on.

Container components additionally let you contain other components (recursively). Containers can also be defined with a layout, allowing you to arrange those contained components in numerous ways to help you bring about an application-type look and feel.

In this chapter, we will use the humble Button to demonstrate various features common to most Ext.NET controls. We will then introduce the mechanisms Ext. NET provides for setting up client-side and server-side events. Following that, we will look at Container components, such as Toolbar, Panel, and Window to get an introduction to how Container components work.

The following chapter will then be dedicated to a variety of layout options for flexible component arrangement.

Later chapters will cover other types of controls, such as DataView, GridPanel, TreePanel, TabPanel, various form controls, and more.

> Ext.NET provides many controls and capabilities over what the underlying Ext JS provides. Ext.NET also extends many Ext JS components to enhance functionality or provide better integration with the server side of Ext.NET.
>
> As a result, it can be very valuable to learn about Ext JS. However, it is beyond the scope of this book to go into the Ext JS component hierarchy as well. Sencha's own blogs and documentation are quite detailed and growing quickly. Their own examples explorer is also very rich. Here are some suggested resources:
>
> *Ext JS 4 First Look, Loiane Groner, PACKT Publishing, 2011*
>
> *Ext JS 4 Web Application Development Cookbook, Stuart Ashworth, Andrew Duncam, PACKT Publishing, 2012*
>
> Ext JS code, documentation and examples:
> `http://www.sencha.com/products/extjs/`

Buttons

A number of Ext.NET features and capabilities will be introduced alongside these seemingly simple components. Examples of features that are common to many components include:

- Setting icons
- Client-side (JavaScript) event handlers
- Server-side (via DirectEvents) event handlers

There are many others, and these will be introduced in the following examples. AJAX event handling will also be covered in its own chapter later, but you will get a taste of it here.

A simple button

If you are using regular HTML, you can create buttons using either the `<button>` element or the `<input type="button">` element (or you can create your own that behaves like buttons, though for accessibility and other reasons that is often not advised). These buttons are functional and work, and are crucial to many websites.

Desktop applications on the other hand, have many variations of buttons, such as SplitButtons, MenuButtons, and more. Ext JS, being a rich application framework, therefore offers similarly versatile buttons which Ext.NET exposes and augments with their own (for example, LinkButton, which is similar to ASP.NET's LinkButton except that Ext.NET's version is fully integrated into the rest of Ext.NET).

> I strongly recommend the book, *About Face 3: The Essentials of Interaction Design*, by usability expert *Alan Cooper, John Wiley & Sons, 2007* for detailed insight into numerous widgets such as these button variations and when best to use them.

Creating a new ASPX page (without code-behind for demonstration purposes), is all that is needed to show a simple button:

```
<%@ Page Language="C#" %>
<!DOCTYPE html>
<html>
  <head runat="server">
    <title>A simple button</title>
  </head>
  <body>
    <ext:ResourceManager runat="server" Theme="Gray" />
```

```
    <ext:Button runat="server" Text="Click Me!" />
  </body>
</html>
```

The highlighted section is all that is needed to create the button. It does not do much, but will render like this:

Click Me!

> Note that the ID attribute is optional for most components; if you do not supply one, Ext.NET will create one for you. We will see later where it can be quite useful to supply one so you can refer to it inside Ext.NET event handlers.

You can also create the same from code-behind. Here is a C# example:

```
protected void Page_Load(object sender, EventArgs e)
{
   var button = new Ext.Net.Button {Text = "Click me!"};

   Controls.Add(button);
}
```

> In the first chapter, we noted that Ext.NET controls are added to other Ext.NET controls via the Items collection, not the Controls collection. The exception is when a control is added directly to the page, as shown in the previous example. In other words, because the button is not being added to another Ext.NET control, we use the Controls collection of the Page instance itself.

Button with icon

Ext.NET provides an Icon enumeration which can be added to many controls. Here is how it is added to an Ext.NET Button:

```
<ext:Button runat="server" Text="Click Me!" Icon="Add" />
```

This will be rendered as:

Click Me!

> The `Icon` enumeration provides around 1700 icons from the popular FamFamFam Silk icon set, from Mark James, and covers most needs. More information on this icon set can be found here: `http://www.famfamfam.com/lab/icons/silk/`
>
> If you want to use your own icon, you can use the `IconCls` attribute instead of the `Icon` attribute and with CSS you can load the appropriate background image using `background-image`. All the other CSS rules will be ready to provide the appropriate space for the icon, typically 16x16 pixels. You can find out more here: `http://examples.ext.net/#/Miscellaneous/Icon/Icon_Summary/`

Note that when defined in markup, the `Icon` attribute value is a string, but this string value is from the `Icon` enumeration found in the Ext.Net namespace. So, if setting the `Icon` property in code-behind, you would use something like this:

```
MyButton.Icon = Icon.Add;
```

Button with menu

At times you may want to present secondary options via a menu. This is a technique commonly seen on desktop applications, such as Microsoft Word. With Ext.NET, many controls can take an optional `Menu` configuration:

```
<ext:Button runat="server" Text="Change case">
  <Menu>
    <ext:Menu>
      <Items>
        <ext:MenuItem Text="Lower case" Icon="TextLowercase" />
        <ext:MenuItem Text="Upper case" Icon="TextUppercase" />
        <ext:MenuSeparator />
        <ext:MenuItem Text="Title case" />
      </Items>
    </ext:Menu>
  </Menu>
</ext:Button>
```

The output of this code will appear as:

Change case ▾

Notice the arrow to the right-hand side of the button. When clicked, the menu will appear:

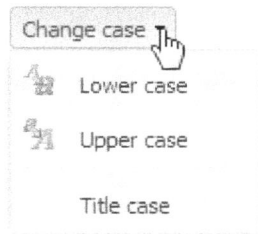

> Note that `runat="server"` has not been added to the nested Ext.NET Controls. Generally speaking, `runat="server"` is only needed for Ext.NET Controls added directly to a page. Any Ext.NET Control added as a child of another Ext.NET Control does not need it (unless it needs to be accessed from the server, in which case the `ID` also needs to be set).

Split button

A variation of the menu button is the SplitButton. The difference here is that the button itself can be selected as the default action, while the menu offers other options that may be used less frequently, but can still be hidden for most cases. A classic example of this is seen in Microsoft Office's Ribbon interface. Here is an example using Ext.NET:

```
<ext:SplitButton ID="SplitButtonExample" runat="server" Text="Paste"
Icon="PastePlain">
    <Menu>
    <ext:Menu>
      <Items>
        <ext:MenuItem Text="Paste Plain Text" />
        <ext:MenuItem Text="Paste with Merge" />
        <ext:MenuSeparator />
        <ext:MenuItem Text="Paste Special..." />
      </Items>
    </ext:Menu>
  </Menu>
</ext:SplitButton>
```

This code will produce the following output:

The difference between the earlier button with menu example is that the **Paste** button itself can be pressed, as the default action:

Or, you can press the arrow button to get more advanced options:

Other button options

There are many options you can apply to buttons. Here is just one example of setting a custom icon class, scaling it to be larger than normal (usually for a 32x32 pixel icon), and aligning the icon above the text while the arrow is positioned at the bottom:

```
<ext:SplitButton runat="server" Text="Paste" IconCls="icon-paste-
large" Scale="Large" IconAlign="Top" ArrowAlign="Bottom" Width="64">
  <Menu>
    <ext:Menu>
      <Items>
        <ext:MenuItem Text="Paste Plain Text" />
        <ext:MenuItem Text="Paste with Merge" />
        <ext:MenuSeparator />
        <ext:MenuItem Text="Paste Special..." />
      </Items>
    </ext:Menu>
  </Menu>
</ext:SplitButton>
```

The corresponding CSS for the previous `IconCls` may be something like this:

```
.icon-paste-large {
    background-image: url(images/iconPasteLarge.png);
}
```

The result is as follows:

This is what you get when you expand it:

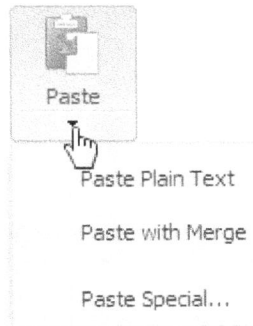

If that is not enough, there are further button options such as:

- `Button` with the attribute `EnableToggle` set to `true` to make the button stay pressed
- `CycleButton` (similar to a split menu where the menu selection replaces the default visible menu option)
- `ButtonGroup` (which allows you to group buttons together to place on a toolbar, for example)
- `LinkButton`, similar to ASP.NET's `LinkButton`, but with all the additional capabilities that Ext.NET offers
- `ImageButton` to provide your own look and feel

Visit the Ext.NET Examples Explorer to see these and a lot more at `http://examples.ext.net`

Events in Ext.NET

Ext.NET supports a number of different event mechanisms. For example, there are client-side events, AJAX events, and general publish/subscribe event patterns that are available. Different controls in Ext.NET support different types of events. Buttons, LinkButtons, and similar controls will support a click event when the control is clicked. Other specialized controls will have more events. For example, most container controls have events related to when items are added or removed from a container, and so on. We will continue using the Button control to demonstrate how you can subscribe to and handle events.

Listeners – client-side events

Ext JS provides a vast event-handling framework for its components, which Ext.NET exposes quite elegantly. Ext JS lets you subscribe to an event through the use of listeners. So, here is an example of a simple click handler for a button:

```
<ext:Button runat="server" Text="Click Me!">
  <Listeners>
    <Click Handler="alert('clicked');" />
  </Listeners>
</ext:Button>
```

In its simplest form, the previous code shows a listener for the click event being added to the button. When the click event occurs, the handler will execute the JavaScript provided. However, the event handler options are more sophisticated.

For example, rather than using a `Handler`, you can point to an already defined function, which can aide with reuse or code organization, for example:

```
<ext:Button runat="server" Text="Click Me!">
  <Listeners>
    <Click Fn="MyApp.onButtonClick" />
  </Listeners>
</ext:Button>
```

With the previous code, we have changed `Handler` to `Fn` and the value of the property is now a JavaScript function `pointer`. The JavaScript code for onButtonClick may look something like this:

```
var MyApp = {
  onButtonClick: function (button, event) {
    console.log(this, button, event);
  }
};
```

Notice that the function receives a button and an event argument. The example just uses the Console API (built into most modern browsers, and also available in the popular Firebug extension to Firefox) to simply write those values out to the JavaScript console, as well as the `this` object. The console will be looked at further in *Chapter 10, Troubleshooting and Debugging*. You can also look at the Console API on the Firebug team's wiki at `https://getfirebug.com/wiki/index.php/Console_API`.

> **Determining event handler arguments**
>
> Using the Ext JS documentation, you can find out what arguments are passed to any event handler. Different controls and different events will naturally have different arguments, so it is worth consulting the detailed documentation for further insights by going to `http://docs.sencha.com/ext-js/4-1`.
>
> You can also test it by defining your function without any arguments and doing `console.log(arguments);` as `arguments` is a keyword available inside any JavaScript method and will be an array of arguments to that method.

In this next example, we have added the scope under which this function will be invoked. In JavaScript, whenever a function is running, it has a scope; it is either in the context of a class that it is part of or ultimately the global container (the `window` object when in a browser).

```
<ext:Button runat="server" Text="Click Me!">
  <Listeners>
    <Click Fn="MyApp.onButtonClick" Scope="window" />
  </Listeners>
</ext:Button>
```

If you run the previous code, the same handler will get invoked as before, but the console will show that the `window` object is logged as the first item.

Another possibility with event handlers is to make them run only once, as the next example shows, using the `Single="true"` option:

```
<ext:Button runat="server" Text="Click Me!">
  <Listeners>
    <Click Fn="MyApp.onButtonClick" Single="true" />
  </Listeners>
</ext:Button>
```

There are many other event handler options available, and the Ext JS documentation explains them quite well and is worth looking into:

```
http://docs.sencha.com/ext-js/4-1/#!/api/Ext.EventManager-method-
addListener
```

Passing the component ID around on the client side

In ASP.NET, controls have both an `ID` attribute and a `ClientID` attribute. The former is the server-side identifier, while the latter is what will be sent to the web page as HTML ids must be unique. To ensure uniqueness, ASP.NET has typically combined the IDs of all containing controls with the ID of the current control to ensure it is unique. While unique, this has often caused difficulties on the client side (JavaScript and CSS, even attempts at automated testing become quite brittle and overexposed to refactoring and layout changes). So, in more recent versions of ASP. NET, .NET has introduced the ability to determine how ClientIDs are generated. For example, they can be explicitly fixed to the value you give it, they can carry on using the old mechanism, or you can have some variations. For more information on this see MSDN:

```
http://msdn.microsoft.com/en-us/library/system.web.ui.clientidmode.
aspx and http://www.asp.net/whitepapers/aspnet4/breaking-changes
```

On the client side, Ext JS and Ext.NET's JavaScript works with component ids. On the server side, Ext.NET creates an id for you if you do not provide one. You can also set your own id. Either way, to be sure you are accessing the correct id on the client side, Ext.NET provides a useful syntax enhancement in their event handlers. Consider this contrived example of two buttons, which, when clicked, will update the text of the other button:

```
<ext:Button ID="ButtonA" runat="server" Text="Change Button B">
  <Listeners>
    <Click Handler="MyApp.changeButtonText(#{ButtonB}, this);" />
  </Listeners>
</ext:Button>
<ext:Button ID="ButtonB" runat="server" Text="Change Button A">
  <Listeners>
    <Click Handler="MyApp.changeButtonText(#{ButtonA}, this);" />
  </Listeners>
</ext:Button>
```

Here is the associated JavaScript for `changeButtonText`:

```
var MyApp = {
  changeButtonText: function (target, source) {
    target.setText('Text changed by ' + source.id);
  }
};
```

> Notice the special identifier syntax, #{ButtonB}, or more generally #{ComponentId}, where ComponentId is the ID set for any Ext.NET component. During server-side generation of the Ext.NET JavaScript, any Ext.NET controls that have string properties using the identifier syntax will have it replaced by the ClientID equivalent. The reason there are no quotes surrounding it is that it corresponds to an instance on the client side (in Ext.NET's App namespace), so there is no need to make it a string and look it up again unnecessarily.

Setting custom values on components.

Consider a variation of the button text changing example:

```
<ext:Button ID="ButtonC" runat="server" Text="Change Button D">
  <Listeners>
    <Click Handler="MyApp.changeButtonText(#{ButtonD}, this);" />
  </Listeners>
  <CustomConfig>
    <ext:ConfigItem Name="whoAmI" Value="Button C" Mode="Value" />
  </CustomConfig>
</ext:Button>
<ext:Button ID="ButtonD" runat="server" Text="Change Button C">
  <Listeners>
    <Click Handler="MyApp.changeButtonText(#{ButtonC}, this);" />
  </Listeners>
  <CustomConfig>
    <ext:ConfigItem Name="whoAmI" Value="Button D" Mode="Value" />
  </CustomConfig>
</ext:Button>
```

In this code, we have added a new `CustomConfig` section and created a dynamic property just for that *instance* of the button.

> **Use of camelCase per JavaScript conventions**
>
> If you used uppercase for the first letter, Ext.NET will convert it to lowercase for you to match the typical JavaScript naming conventions.

- The `ConfigItem` has a `Value` property. This is the value that will be used in JavaScript. The `Mode` property helps control how this value will be serialized. Although JavaScript is quite flexible in this regards, using the right data types can help with performance and other operations, so `Mode` is therefore important to consider. `Mode` is an enum of type `ParameterMode`. It has three options:Auto: Let Ext.NET work out whether the value will be converted to a string, number, boolean, or serialized without quotes. For example, `Value="5" Mode="Auto"` will mean JavaScript number 5 will be generated, not the string 5. Similarly this can help create JavaScript boolean values of `true` or `false`, not the string `true` or `false`.

- `Raw`: Ensures the `Value` property is serialized without quotes (that is, it will not become a string). Sometimes `Auto` cannot detect the difference between a string and say a reference to another object or functions. In these cases, `Raw` is what you would use.

- `Value`: Ensures the `Value` property is serialized into a string (that is surrounded by quotes).

JavaScript is a dynamically typed language. This makes adding custom configuration properties to any Ext JS component really easy. It is worth seeing what JavaScript is generated by the previous code at this point to see how the `whoAmI` property is available. Here is the snippet generated for `ButtonC`:

```
Ext.create("Ext.button.Button", {
    id: "ButtonC",
    whoAmI: "Button C",
    renderTo: "App.ButtonC_Container",
    text: "Change Button D",
    listeners: {
        click: {
            fn: function (item, e) {
                MyApp.changeButtonText(App.ButtonD, this);
            }
        }
    }
});
```

In the previous code, the Ext JS `create` factory method creates an instance of a `Button` (in the `Ext.button` namespace). The custom configuration property is added as just another property to this button instance. This works fine in JavaScript because it is a dynamically typed language. The `changeButtonText` listener function can then be slightly tweaked to take advantage of that custom property:

```
changeButtonText: function(target, source) {
    target.setText('Text changed by ' + source.whoAmI);
}
```

Notice that custom configuration values can be set on any instance of a component (not just buttons) using the `CustomConfig` collection.

Ext.NET also provides a number of alternative ways to achieve the previous Ext JS. If you are instantiating a component via code-behind, then you can use the same `CustomConfig` collection as shown in the earlier markup example. Ext.NET also takes advantage of dynamic properties, so you can also do this in code-behind: `ButtonC.Configs.whoAmI = "Button C"`. Another option in markup, which can help create terser code, is to simply add a property to the component. If it is not a defined property of the component, then Ext.NET will add it as a custom configuration. So the previous example could be shortened to this:

```
<ext:Button ID="ButtonC" runat="server" Text="Change Button D"
WhoAmI="Button C">
  <Listeners>
    <Click Handler="MyApp.changeButtonText(#{ButtonD}, this);" />
  </Listeners>
</ext:Button>
<ext:Button ID="ButtonD" runat="server" Text="Change Button C"
WhoAmI="Button D">
  <Listeners>
    <Click Handler="MyApp.changeButtonText(#{ButtonC}, this);" />
  </Listeners>
</ext:Button>
```

Using this approach, the first letter of the custom property will be converted to lowercase to match the naming conventions typically used in JavaScript. Ext.NET is also smart enough to convert boolean and numeric values to their boolean and numeric equivalents in JavaScript, so if a property such as `IsMyFirstButton="True"` was added, the JavaScript output would be `isMyFirstButton: true` rather than the string `"True"` surrounded by quotes.

Direct Events – server-side handlers for client-side events

Along with client-side event handling we can also have server-side handling. This is similar to how traditional ASP.NET Web Forms work, but Ext.NET takes advantage of full AJAX requests, which we briefly saw in the first chapter.

Chapter 4, AJAX with Ext.NET, will cover server-side event handling in further detail, but for the moment, here is an overview:

```
<ext:Button runat="server" Text="Click Me">
  <DirectEvents>
    <Click OnEvent="Button_Click">
      <ExtraParams>
        <ext:Parameter Name="Item" Value="My param" />
      </ExtraParams>
      <EventMask ShowMask="true" />
    </Click>
  </DirectEvents>
</ext:Button>
```

In the previous code, we invoke the server-side method – Button_Click, using an Ext.NET DirectEvent. This packages the request into an appropriate AJAX request, and the server unwraps the request and calls the appropriate method. Additional data can also be passed through using the ExtraParams' Parameter collection. While the AJAX request is occurring, an EventMask has been set to provide a **Loading...** mask, which covers the page to show the user that something is happening.

The server-side click handler method looks similar to a regular ASP.NET control event handler, except the type of the event arguments parameter is an Ext.NET DirectEventArgs instance:

```
protected void Button_Click(object sender, DirectEventArgs e)
{
  X.Msg.Alert("DirectEvent", string.Format("Item - {0}",
e.ExtraParams["Item"])).Show();
}
```

In this example, the handler is simply creating an Ext JS message alert box with the title of **DirectEvent** and a message showing the parameter that was received.

> DirectEvent handlers can be defined to use System.EventArgs instead of DirectEventArgs. In that case, you would not have access to specialized properties such as ExtraParams.

It is important to note that for the event to be handled on the server in this way, the Ext.NET control has to be recreated on the server first, just like you do with ASP.NET controls in a traditional ASP.NET Post Back model.

However, unlike traditional ASP.NET Post Back, this similar looking code is fully AJAX enabled, providing a far superior user experience. In terms of performance, the HTTP traffic of a DirectEvent is orders of magnitude smaller and leaner than the traditional Post Back or even the ASP.NET UpdatePanel approach to AJAX.

DirectEvents and other techniques for AJAX requests will be looked at in more detail in *Chapter 4, AJAX with Ext.NET*.

MessageBus – inter-component messaging

MessageBus is a new feature to Ext.NET 2. It provides a publish/subscribe mechanism for components to notify or react to various events. Components can publish events (or broadcast, in Ext.NET speak) and other components on the page can choose to subscribe to them (via listeners in Ext.NET) if they want. Ext.NET also supports broadcasting events to a page from within an HTML iframe and from an iframe page to the containing page. Broadcasters and listeners of events do not need to know about each other. This helps create a flexible and loosely coupled component architecture, making code more reusable and manageable. Ext.NET also makes this seamless between server and client.

An example where this can be useful is, if you have reusable components that can be used in different areas of a page or many pages, you may just want to broadcast when your component has entered a different state. Then listeners can do what they want. For example, if you are providing an app with a global toolbar running along the top, you may want to enable/disable various menus or toolbar buttons based on what components broadcast. As another example, when components broadcast certain messages, you may have a global subscriber that can log these or even queue them up to then make an AJAX request to the server to log it there, and so on.

This also gives you more choice on how you want to arrange code: use controls, master templates, custom components that extend existing Ext.NET classes, can all use the MessageBus.

For example, we can provide a simple logger that will just log events to the screen:

```
<ext:Panel
  runat="server"
  Title="MessageBus Event Logger"
  Width="200"
  Height="150"
  AutoScroll="true">
```

```
      <MessageBusListeners>
        <ext:MessageBusListener
          Name="App.*"
          Handler="this.body.createChild({
            html: 'Received event from ' + data.item.id,
            tag: 'p'
          });" />
      </MessageBusListeners>
      <Buttons>
        <ext:Button ID="Button1" runat="server" Text="Publish event 1">
          <Listeners>
            <Click BroadcastOnBus="App.event1" />
          </Listeners>
        </ext:Button>
        <ext:Button ID="Button2" runat="server" Text="Publish event 2">
          <Listeners>
          <Click Fn="DoSomething" />
          </Listeners>
        </ext:Button>
      </Buttons>
  </ext:Panel>
```

In this markup, we have a simple Panel (which is a container which will be looked at, in further detail, later in this chapter). It has a `MessageBusListener` property, which will watch for any events that match the `Name` property. In the example above, `App.*` means it will watch for any event starting with `App.` and when such an event is received, the JavaScript code defined in the `Handler` property will be executed. In this case, it will create a child element with some HTML content and add it to the body of the Panel. In effect, this Panel is acting like a simple logging tool.

A Panel can have a `Buttons` collection, which is one way to add buttons that are associated with a Panel. These buttons have `Click` listeners. For the first button, rather than using a `Handler` or a `Fn` to handle the event, we use the `BroadcastOnBus` property to say that when this button is clicked we want to broadcast `App.event1`. As it starts with `App`, it will be caught by the MessageBus listener and logged into the Panel body.

For the second button, we show a variation whereby we use the `Click` listener's `Fn` function pointer. In this case, it points to the following JavaScript function:

```
function DoSomething() {
  // run some code
  Ext.net.Bus.publish('App.event2', { item: this });
}
```

The JavaScript function allows you to run your own code before or after the JavaScript call to Ext.NET's client-side bus API. In this case, we simply call the publish singleton method, which takes two arguments: the event being published and additional data. This data can be anything you want, because our `MessageBusListener` is expecting a component in the `item` property, we create an object to match it passing this, which is the button that caused this event. As the following screenshot shows, both approaches work with the `MessageBusListener`:

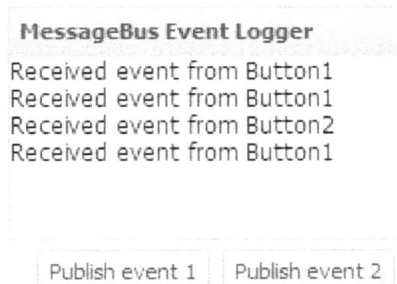

MessageBus Event Logger

Received event from Button1
Received event from Button1
Received event from Button2
Received event from Button1

Publish event 1   Publish event 2

The previous explanation only scratches the surface. The example shown here demonstrates just one `MessageBusListener` looking for a specific event, but you can have many listeners on a page looking for different MessageBus events, as you require.

In addition, you will also see examples of how you can handle the event on the server side using a `MessageBusDirectListener`. You can also use `MessageBusDirectEvents` to have your MessageBus automatically handled on the server as well as, or instead, on the client if you wish.

> It is highly recommended to study the following examples from the Ext.NET Examples Explorer further as they demonstrate these capabilities of MessageBus:
>
> `http://examples.ext.net/#/MessageBus/Basic/Simple/`
>
> `http://examples.ext.net/#/MessageBus/Basic/Complex/`

Container components

Container components allow you to add other components (and containers) to it. Container components can also be configured with a layout to help control how its items are presented, which will be covered in the next chapter, dedicated to layouts. In this chapter, we will look at some core examples, such as the Container, Toolbar, Panel, and Window. Tooltips are also containers, so we will have a quick look at that. Other chapters will cover the popular and powerful GridPanel, TreePanel, and TabPanel.

Container

A Container is the most basic of, well, Containers! It simply acts as a lightweight container without any fancy or sophisticated options compared to its various subclasses, such as Toolbar, Panel, Window, Tooltip, and more. The Container is often used in conjunction with a layout, which we will look at in the next chapter.

Toolbars and menus

The button examples showed a number of features of Ext.NET. Toolbars and menus are additional controls that may feature in Ext JS-based web applications. Creating them, like buttons, is quite simple. We already saw some button examples earlier that had menus, so here are a few more examples that can help create toolbars.

Toolbars with various buttons

This first example combines a number of different buttons we saw earlier, such as the button with menu, a split button, and buttons with icons into a toolbar. The code may seem long, but it is a really quick toolbar declaration with our previous buttons as its items:

```
<ext:Toolbar runat="server">
  <Items>
    <ext:SplitButton Text="Paste" Icon="PastePlain">
      <Menu>
        <ext:Menu>
          <Items>
            <ext:MenuItem Text="Paste Plain Text" />
            <ext:MenuItem Text="Paste with Merge" />
            <ext:MenuSeparator />
            <ext:MenuItem Text="Paste Special..." />
          </Items>
        </ext:Menu>
      </Menu>
    </ext:SplitButton>
    <ext:Button Tooltip="Cut" Icon="Cut" />
    <ext:Button Tooltip="Copy" Icon="PageWhiteCopy" />
    <ext:ToolbarSeparator />
    <ext:Button Text="Change case">
      <Menu>
        <ext:Menu>
          <Items>
            <ext:MenuItem Text="Lower case" Icon="TextLowercase" />
            <ext:MenuItem Text="Upper case" Icon="TextUppercase" />
            <ext:MenuSeparator />
            <ext:MenuItem Text="Title case" />
          </Items>
```

```
        </ext:Menu>
      </Menu>
    </ext:Button>
  </Items>
</ext:Toolbar>
```

The output of the code will be the following:

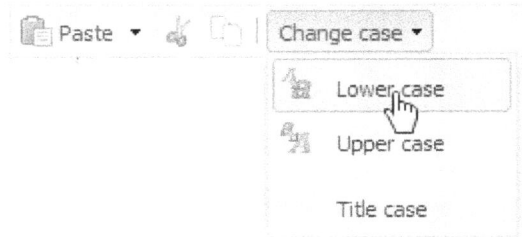

As all the menus are contained inside the toolbar, opening another menu (the **Paste** menu, in the previous example) will automatically take care of closing any other opened menus (the **Change case** menu, in the previous screenshot) for you.

> The book, *About Face 3: The Essentials of Interaction Design,*
> *John Wiley & Sons* by usability expert Alan Cooper has a
> great section on menus and toolbar best practices.

Overflowing toolbars

Toolbars can also be set to overflow if their contents don't fit the available area. To show this we will put a toolbar inside a Window. A Window is a floating container Panel which we will look at in more detail in a moment. As a Window, it can be optionally resized, and as a subclass of Panel, it can contain toolbars as the following example shows:

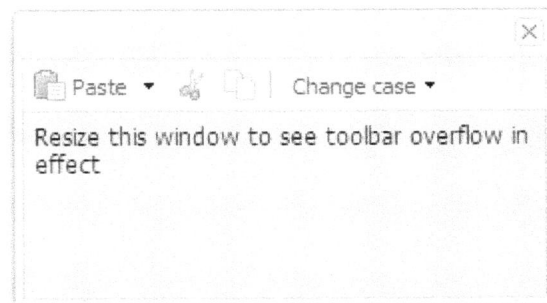

If the previous Window is resized small enough, the toolbar will show an overflow marker:

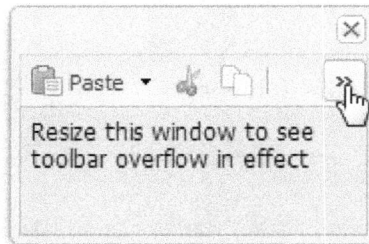

Clicking the overflow marker will bring up the hidden menu items:

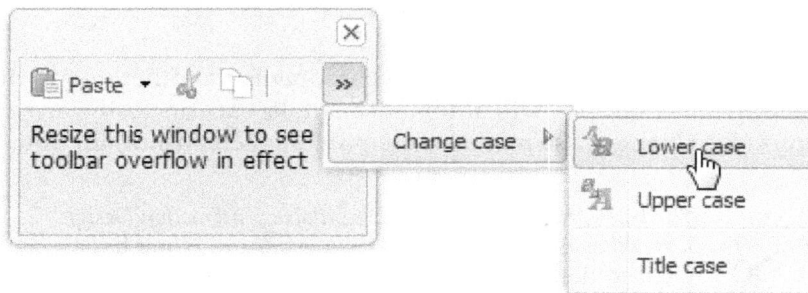

The code to achieve the previous result is relatively simple. Shown here is just the introduction of the Ext.NET Window, which wraps the Toolbar we used earlier, that now also has overflow enabled. The toolbar items are the same as the earlier example, so are omitted for brevity:

```
<ext:Window runat="server" Resizable="true" Width="300" Height="200"
BodyPadding="5">
  <TopBar>
    <ext:Toolbar EnableOverflow="true">
      <Items>
        <!-- same items as earlier -->
      </Items>
    </ext:Toolbar>
  </TopBar>
  <Content>
    <p>Resize this window to see toolbar overflow in effect</p>
  </Content>
</ext:Window>
```

Nested menus

Sometimes you may need to further nest your menus. Menu items, as we used earlier, in our buttons with menus can themselves contain menus, allowing you a recursive definition. The toolbar and menu handling code from Ext JS takes care of rendering it appropriately.

In our previous Window example, we can add one more button to the toolbar's Item collection:

```
<ext:Button runat="server" Text="More options">
  <Menu>
    <ext:Menu runat="server">
      <Items>
        <ext:MenuItem runat="server" Text="Theme">
          <Menu>
            <ext:Menu runat="server">
              <Items>
                <ext:CheckMenuItem
                  Text="Black"
                  Group="theme"
                  CheckHandler="MyApp.onItemCheck" />
                <ext:CheckMenuItem
                  Text="Gray"
                  Group="theme"
                  Checked="true"
                  CheckHandler="MyApp.onItemCheck" />
                <ext:CheckMenuItem
                  Text="Blue"
                  Group="theme"
                  CheckHandler="MyApp.onItemCheck" />
              </Items>
            </ext:Menu>
          </Menu>
        </ext:MenuItem>
      </Items>
    </ext:Menu>
  </Menu>
</ext:Button>
```

In this code, we have introduced `CheckMenuItem` component, which is a subclass of `MenuItemBase`, which is also the parent class for `MenuItem`. With the use of the `Group` attribute, you can achieve a menu option where you select one item:

The code sample for just that one button looks a bit long, because each `CheckMenuItem` has its attributes on new lines for formatting purposes.

Although the nesting in the previous code does look quite deep, the collection based approach helps with reusability as other types of items can also be added, as the following demonstrates.

We can add the following two `MenuItem` examples into the **More Options** menu's `Items` collection that we created earlier:

```
<ext:MenuItem Text="Choose a Date" Icon="Calendar">
  <Menu>
    <ext:DateMenu>
      <Picker/>
      <Listeners>
        <Select Handler="alert(Ext.String.format('You chose {0}.',
Ext.util.Format.date(date, 'M j, Y')));" />
      </Listeners>
    </ext:DateMenu>
  </Menu>
</ext:MenuItem>
<ext:MenuItem Text="Choose a Color" Icon="ColorSwatch">
  <Menu>
    <ext:ColorMenu>
      <Listeners>
        <Select Handler="alert(Ext.String.format('You chose {0}.',
color));" />
      </Listeners>
    </ext:ColorMenu>
  </Menu>
</ext:MenuItem>
```

In this code example, there are a number of things introduced. We have used a `DateMenu` to enable a date picker from the menu itself, and a `ColorMenu` to enable a color palette to let users choose a color:

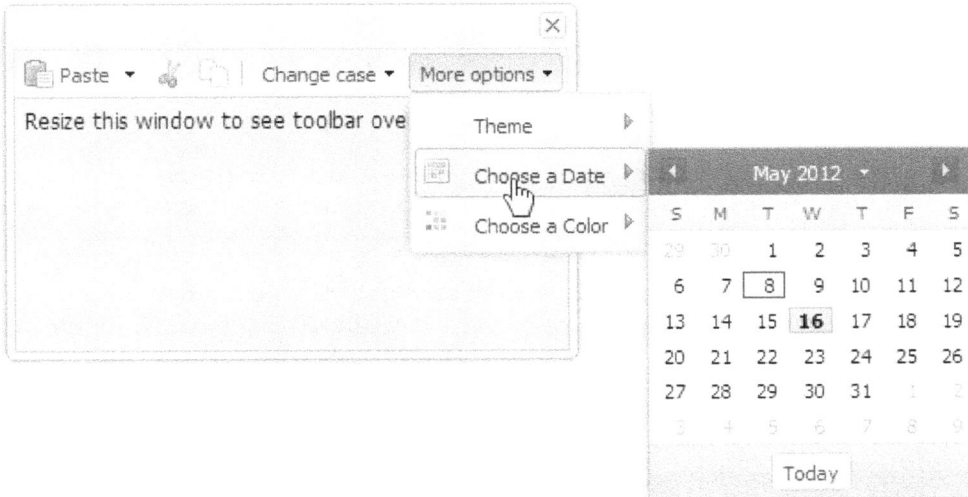

The date picker is quite versatile, and we will revisit it in the *Chapter 7, Forms and Validation*.

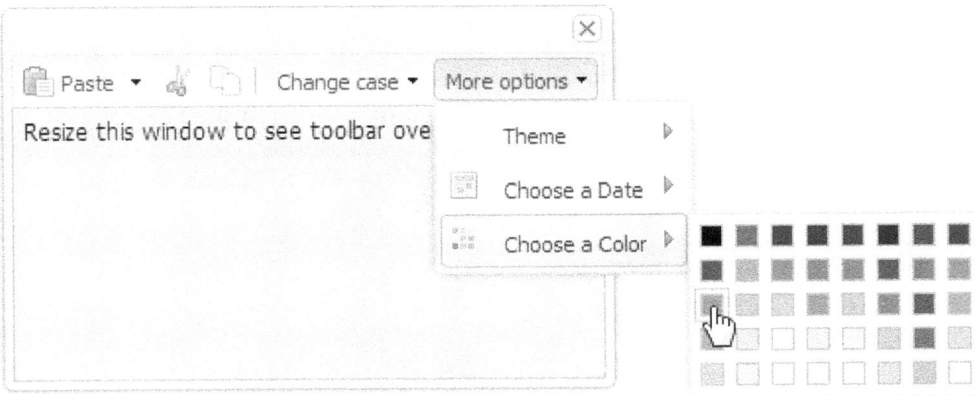

What this shows is that any subclass of `MenuItemBase`, by definition, can be used as a menu item, such as the check menu item. Any subclass of `MenuBase` can also be used to create custom menus, such as the date picker and color picker examples shown before. You could create your own subclasses if you wanted too, and the Sencha web site has examples of how you can do this. In a later chapter, we will also look at extending and creating custom components.

How did we know to use the date and color arguments in the select handlers?

If you notice the JavaScript handlers for the `Select` listeners, we had access to a `date` and `color` variable, respectively. How did we know that?

Ext.NET provides a handy example in their Examples Explorer:

`http://examples.ext.net/#/Events/Listeners/Arguments/`

This link will help you pick an Ext.NET component and the event for which you wish to find the arguments and give you a function signature. This is a really useful way to get going quickly.

As Ext.NET uses Ext JS, you can also consult the Ext JS documentation for more on each of the arguments. For the date menu class, we can see the documentation for the `Select` listener here:

`http://docs.sencha.com/ext-js/4-1/#!/api/Ext.menu.DatePicker-event-select`

However, be aware that Ext.NET enhances and extends many Sencha components so sometimes the names of event parameters may not exactly match or Ext.NET may provide other capabilities. With that in mind, the Sencha documentation can often be a useful place to learn more details about some of these event parameters.

Menus and form fields

Interestingly, menus do not need to contain just buttons and submenus. That's because a `Toolbar` is a `Container`; it can contain any other component, including form fields like textboxes and comboboxes. This, for example, is how Ext JS grids have pager toolbars with textboxes and buttons. Here is a quick demonstration of some possibilities.

First, a TextField inside a toolbar:

```
<ext:Toolbar runat="server">
  <Items>
    <ext:Button Icon="PastePlain" />
    <ext:Button Icon="Cut" />
    <ext:Button Icon="PageCopy" />
    <ext:ToolbarSeparator />
    <ext:TextField FieldLabel="Search" LabelAlign="Right"
LabelWidth="50" />
    <ext:Button runat="server" Icon="Find" />
  </Items>
</ext:Toolbar>
```

Next to the button, after the separator we add a text field and an additional button to give us this:

Where it gets more interesting is that other components, such as a full-on Panel, can also be presented inside a menu:

The output in the previous screenshot can be achieved by simply inserting the following next to the find button:

```
<ext:ToolbarSeparator />
<ext:Button Text="Action">
  <Menu>
    <ext:Menu>
      <Items>
        <ext:Panel
          Title="Mega dropdown!"
          Icon="ApplicationForm"
          Width="200"
          Height="100" />
      </Items>
    </ext:Menu>
  </Menu>
</ext:Button>
```

This example shows how easy it can be to provide sophisticated user interfaces.

A Panel is just the beginning; panels can load content via AJAX. Panel subclasses such as `GridPanels` or `TabPanels` or complex layout panels are all options as well, depending on the need (and suitability). There are more examples on this in the Ext.NET Examples Explorer: `http://examples.ext.net/#/Toolbar/Menu/Controls_In_Menu/`

Dynamically inserting menus and buttons

There will be times where you cannot know the full set of menu items upfront, or you may be populating a toolbar via some configuration or other information in the system. As with most ASP.NET controls, you can create the same thing from code-behind. Although later chapters will show more examples of this, here is an example just to introduce the concept, whereby the `Window` is declared on the markup, but the Toolbar buttons are added in code-behind.

First the ASPX markup:

```
<%@ Page Language="C#" AutoEventWireup="true" CodeBehind="Tool
barFromCodeBehind.aspx.cs" Inherits="ControlsOverview.Toolbars.
ToolbarFromCodeBehind" %>
<!DOCTYPE html>
<html>
  <head>
    <title>Toolbar loaded from code-behind</title>
    <script>
      var MyApp = {
        onDateSelected: function (item, date) {
          alert(Ext.String.format('You chose {0}.', Ext.util.Format.
date(date, 'M j, Y')));
        }
      };
    </script>
  </head>
  <body>
    <ext:ResourceManager runat="server" Theme="Gray" />
    <ext:Window ID="Window1" runat="server" />
  </body>
</html>
```

Notice, we have set the ID for `Window`, as we will refer to it in the code-behind:

```
using System;
using System.Web.UI;
using Ext.Net;

namespace ControlsOverview.Toolbars
{
  public partial class ToolbarFromCodeBehind : Page
  {
    protected void Page_Load(object sender, EventArgs e)
    {
      Window1.TopBar.Add(new Toolbar
      {
        EnableOverflow = true,
```

```
        Items =
        {
          new Button
          {
            Text = "More options",
            Menu = { GetMoreOptionsMenu() }
          }
        }
    });
}

private Menu GetMoreOptionsMenu()
{
  return new Menu
  {
    Items = { GetDateChooser() }
  };
}

private MenuItem GetDateChooser()
{
  return new MenuItem
  {
    Text = "Choose a Date",
    Icon = Icon.Calendar,
    Menu = { GetDateMenu() }
  };
}

private DateMenu GetDateMenu()
{
  return new DateMenu
  {
    Listeners =
    {
      Select =
      {
        Fn = "MyApp.onDateSelected"
      }
    }
  };
}
  }
}
```

Notice the `using` statement to bring in the Ext.Net classes. On `Page_Load`, we are simply using C# object initializers to create the same menu option as in the previous example (though limiting ourselves to just the **More Options** menu option).

Also note that in the earlier example, the GetDateMenu method sets up a Fn pointer instead of a Handler. In cases where you have a JavaScript library of functions that can be accessed as singletons; this can help prevent the need to create an anonymous function wrapper just to call such a method.

Although the earlier C# code could have been written inside one combined object initializer, splitting it into methods this way can help with readability, but can also help you create more flexible (and unit testable) code when combined with various other refactoring and object-oriented programming techniques.

Panels

Some earlier examples have introduced a Panel. But barely! The Ext JS documentation for Panel describes it as:

> *a container that has specific functionality and structural components that make it the perfect building block for application-oriented user interfaces.*

Some of the structural components that come with a Panel include a top toolbar, a bottom toolbar, a title area with optional tool buttons, built in expand/collapse, and more.

Here is an example with some of those elements being used:

```
<ext:Panel runat="server" Title="My Panel" Icon="UserHome"
BodyPadding="10" Width="300" Height="150" AutoScroll="true">
  <Items>
    <ext:Label Html="<p>Some text</p>" />
    <ext:Label Html="<p>Some text</p>" />
    <ext:Label Html="<p>Some text</p>" />
    <ext:Label Html="<p>Some text</p>" />
    <ext:Label Html="<p>Some text</p>" />
    <ext:Label Html="<p>Some text</p>" />
  </Items>
  <TopBar>
    <ext:Toolbar>
      <Items>
        <ext:Button Icon="Add" Text="Do something">
          <Menu>
            <ext:Menu>
              <Items>
                <ext:MenuItem Text="Something more" />
              </Items>
            </ext:Menu>
```

```
          </Menu>
        </ext:Button>
      </Items>
    </ext:Toolbar>
  </TopBar>
  <BottomBar>
    <ext:StatusBar DefaultText="Ready" BusyText="Please wait...">
      <Items>
        <ext:ToolbarFill />
        <ext:Button Text="About" />
      </Items>
    </ext:StatusBar>
  </BottomBar>
  <Tools>
    <ext:Tool Type="Gear" Fn="MyApp.showOptions" Qtip="View options"
/>
    <ext:Tool Type="Help" Fn="MyApp.showHelp" />
  </Tools>
</ext:Panel>
```

Here is the JavaScript for handling the Tool clicks:

```
var MyApp = {
  showHelp: function() {
    alert('showing help');
  },

  showOptions: function() {
    alert('showing options');
  }
};
```

This is the end result:

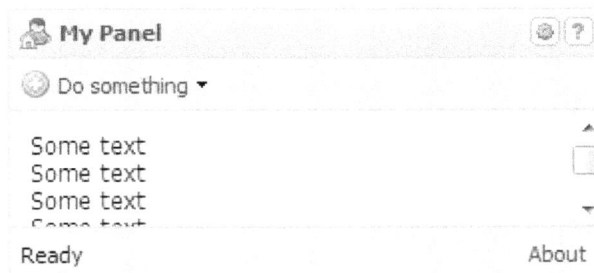

We've introduced a few new things in the previous code:

- A top and bottom bar.

- A `StatusBar` inside the bottom bar – similar to a `Toolbar`, but has some options for showing different text in different situations. See `http://examples.ext.net/#/Toolbar/StatusBar/Overview/` for more information and examples.

- Tools that will appear in the upper-right corner of a panel – like mini-icons.

- Instead of using `<Content>`, we have used `<Items>`. This allows more efficient initialization of components through a technique known as *lazy instantiation* (also known as on-demand). Only Ext-based components can go into an `Items` collection, whereas `Content` can contain any HTML. The items we chose to add were some labels, but it could be any complex component, including panels that have sophisticated layout settings, as we will see in the next chapter.

- We have enabled `AutoScroll` so that the panel contents will show a scroll bar if necessary.

The earlier example uses an explicit top and bottom bar and is very useful. But it is also limited to just having those two bars. In Ext JS 4, Sencha extended this further to provide any number of docked items, so you could stack multiple toolbars on top of each other if you needed to, or even dock them to the left and right. Ext.NET exposes this very nicely, as this modified version of the earlier example demonstrates:

```
<ext:Panel runat="server" Title="My Panel" Icon="UserHome"
BodyPadding="10" Width="300" Height="200" AutoScroll="true">
  <Items>
    <ext:Label Html="<p>Some text</p>" />
    <ext:Label Html="<p>Some text</p>" />
    <ext:Label Html="<p>Some text</p>" />
    <ext:Label Html="<p>Some text</p>" />
    <ext:Label Html="<p>Some text</p>" />
    <ext:Label Html="<p>Some text</p>" />
    <ext:Label Html="<p>Some text</p>" />
    <ext:Label Html="<p>Some text</p>" />
  </Items>
  <Tools>
    <ext:Tool Type="Gear" Fn="MyApp.showOptions" Qtip="View options"
/>
    <ext:Tool Type="Help" Fn="MyApp.showHelp" />
  </Tools>
  <DockedItems>
    <ext:Toolbar Dock="Top">
      <Items>
        <ext:Button Icon="Add" Text="Do something">
          <Menu>
```

```
            <ext:Menu>
              <Items>
                <ext:MenuItem Text="Something more" />
              </Items>
            </ext:Menu>
          </Menu>
        </ext:Button>
      </Items>
    </ext:Toolbar>
    <ext:StatusBar DefaultText="Ready" BusyText="Please wait..."
  Dock="Bottom">
      <Items>
        <ext:ToolbarFill />
        <ext:Button Text="About" />
      </Items>
    </ext:StatusBar>
    <ext:Toolbar Dock="Bottom">
      <Items>
        <ext:Button Icon="Disk" Text="Save" />
        <ext:Button Icon="Delete" Text="Cancel" />
      </Items>
    </ext:Toolbar>
    <ext:Toolbar Dock="Left">
      <Items>
        <ext:Button Icon="UserAdd" />
        <ext:Button Icon="UserDelete" />
        <ext:ToolbarSeparator />
        <ext:Button Icon="TimeAdd" />
      </Items>
    </ext:Toolbar>
  </DockedItems>
</ext:Panel>
```

This code produces the following:

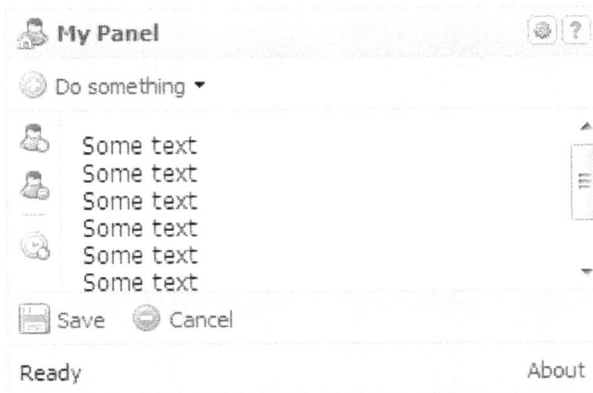

In the previous code, we have not only used the docked items, but we have stacked two sets of components on the bottom dock; a status bar and a button bar. Furthermore, we have now also been able to dock a toolbar to the left.

Windows

A `Window`, as we have seen, is a subclass of `Panel`. It is used as a window on a desktop windowing system would be: they are floated, resizable, and draggable by default, but you can also configure them to maximize and fill the viewport, restore to their prior size, and minimize. You can also make them modal or non-modal, as well as close them and hide them. (Closing destroys the object from memory on the browser while hiding just hides it from view while staying in memory and allowing you to reopen it later).

As a subclass of `Panel`, defining a `Window` should be quite familiar. Here is an example very similar to the first Panel example earlier:

```
<ext:Window runat="server" Title="My Panel" Icon="UserHome"
BodyPadding="10" Width="300" Height="150" AutoScroll="true">
  <Items>
    <ext:Label Html="<p>Some text</p>" />
    <ext:Label Html="<p>Some text</p>" />
    <ext:Label Html="<p>Some text</p>" />
    <ext:Label Html="<p>Some text</p>" />
    <ext:Label Html="<p>Some text</p>" />
    <ext:Label Html="<p>Some text</p>" />
  </Items>
  <Tools>
    <ext:Tool Type="Gear" Fn="MyApp.showOptions" Qtip="Options" />
    <ext:Tool Type="Help" Fn="MyApp.showHelp" />
  </Tools>
  <DockedItems>
    <ext:Toolbar Dock="Top">
      <Items>
        <ext:Button Icon="Add" Text="Do something" />
      </Items>
    </ext:Toolbar>
  </DockedItems>
  <Buttons>
    <ext:Button Icon="Disk" Text="Save" />
    <ext:Button Icon="Cancel" Text="Cancel" />
  </Buttons>
</ext:Window>
```

The previous code is very similar, except we have moved the buttons from being inside a toolbar to being inside a Window's own `Buttons` collection. This code would produce the following:

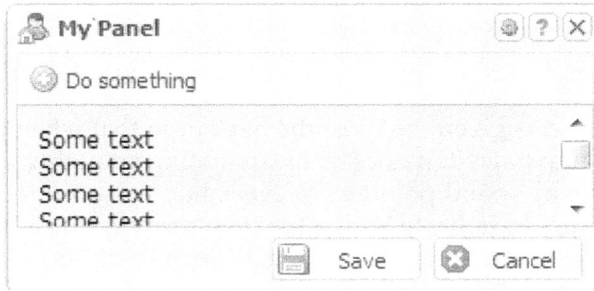

`Window` is a subclass of `Pane`; this is why you get all the Panel features plus the additional window-specific ones.

Here is an example of a full ASPX page with just a window and a button. The window starts of closed and the button shows the window:

```
<%@ Page Language="C#" %>
<!DOCTYPE html>
<html>
  <head>
    <title>Ext.NET Window example</title>
  </head>
  <body>
    <ext:ResourceManager runat="server" Theme="Gray" />
    <ext:Button ID="Button1" runat="server" Text="Show Window">
      <Listeners>
        <Click Handler="#{Window1}.show();" />
      </Listeners>
    </ext:Button>

    <ext:Window
      ID="Window1"
      runat="server"
      AnimateTarget="Button1"
      CloseAction="Destroy"
      Height="200"
      Hidden="true"
      Icon="ApplicationCascade"
      Maximizable="true"
      Minimizable="true"
      Modal="true"
      Title="My Window"
      Width="300">
```

```
        <Listeners>
          <Minimize Handler="this.hide();" />
        </Listeners>
      </ext:Window>
    </body>
  </html>
```

This example, although simple, introduces a number of window features:

- `AnimateTarget` is given the ID of the button, so that when the window is minimized/maximized, it does so by animating smoothly to and from the button. This may sound pointless or eye candy only, but it can be a useful usability feature to indicate with what item the window is associated. (The `AnimateTarget` can be any element on the web page.)

- `CloseAction` can be set to close the window or hide the window. (`Destroy` destroys it so it is not available again, whereas `Hide` lets you reopen it because it is hidden off screen).

- `Maximizable` and `Minimizable` create two new icons in the upper-right corner. Maximize will take up the whole screen, but minimize is not implemented by default. So we have added a listener to listen for the `Minimize` event. At that time, we simply hide the window (the `this` object is the window in the event handler).

- `Modal` is set to `true` so that when the window is shown, a semi-transparent mask is shown behind it so you cannot access items without first closing the window.

This is what the window looks like after clicking the button to show it:

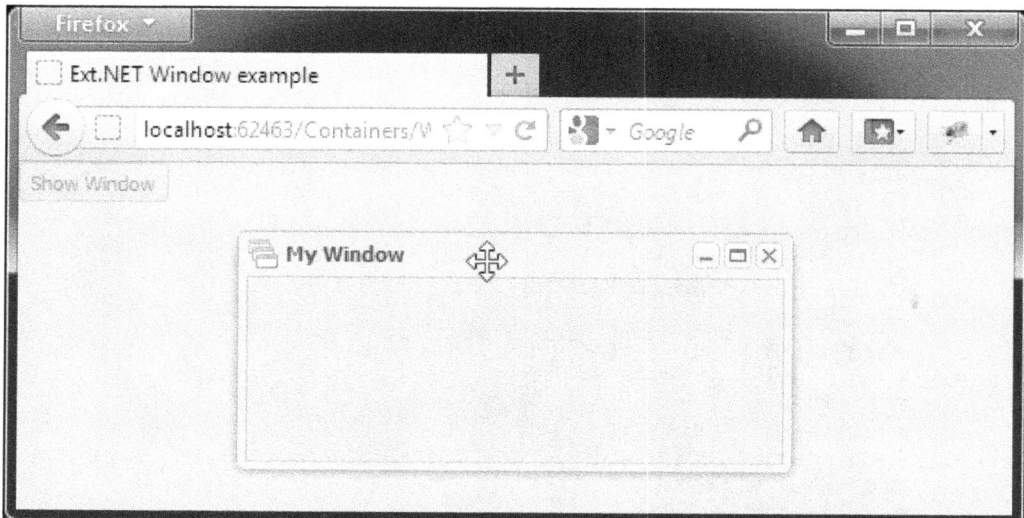

Notice the mouse cursor now indicates the window is draggable when hovering over the title area of the window. The moving of windows can also be constrained using `Constrain="true"` or `ConstrainHeader="true"` on the window declaration.

Tooltips

In HTML, almost every element can have a tool tip via the `title` attribute. With Ext JS, almost every component has the option to show *rich* tool tips. The richness comes in the ability to define the delay before the tool tip disappears, whether it auto-disappears or whether a user has to close it explicitly, a title for the tool tip, HTML for the tool tip body (so you can include links and images for example), whether there is a small arrow/call-out like style from a side of the tool tip, whether to track the mouse movement, and more.

Many components have a simple `Tooltip` attribute where you can set the HTML string to display as the tool tip:

```
<ext:Button runat="server" Text="Hover over me" ToolTip="Tooltip text"
/>
```

This code will produce the following output:

It doesn't look too fancy, other than being themed consistently with the rest of the Ext.NET controls. However, more advanced options also exist using the `Tooltip` control available on most components:

```
<ext:Button runat="server" Text="Hover over me">
  <ToolTips>
    <ext:ToolTip
      Anchor="right"
      Width="318"
      Title="My title"
      ConstrainPosition="true"
      Cls="my-custom-class"
      AutoHide="false"
      MinWidth="318"
      Closable="true">
      <Content>
```

```
        <p>Html including <a href="http://ext.net">links</a> and
images:</p>
        <p><img src="<%= ResolveUrl("~/images/rotary-phone.jpg") %>"
alt="Not so long ago...!" height="240" width="305" /></p>
      </Content>
    </ext:ToolTip>
  </ToolTips>
</ext:Button>
```

In this code, a single `Tooltip` instance can be added with additional behavior, such as, a title, whether to constrain it to the visible area, preventing it from hiding automatically after a delay, and showing a close icon instead. In addition, rich HTML content, including links and images have been added and have been styled using the `Cls` property for custom control over the appearance. In this example, the corresponding CSS is simply the following:

```
.my-custom-class p { line-height:1.6; }
.my-custom-class a { color:#00f; }
```

As a reminder, the default themes provide CSS reset of default values to standardize styles across browsers. Hence, some simple styles, such as that used for the link in this example, may be needed for custom displays. (The previous example shows the link being styled to blue, but remember to apply the usual best practice for CSS links and define the `:link`, `:active`, `:hover`, and `:focus` styles as well!)

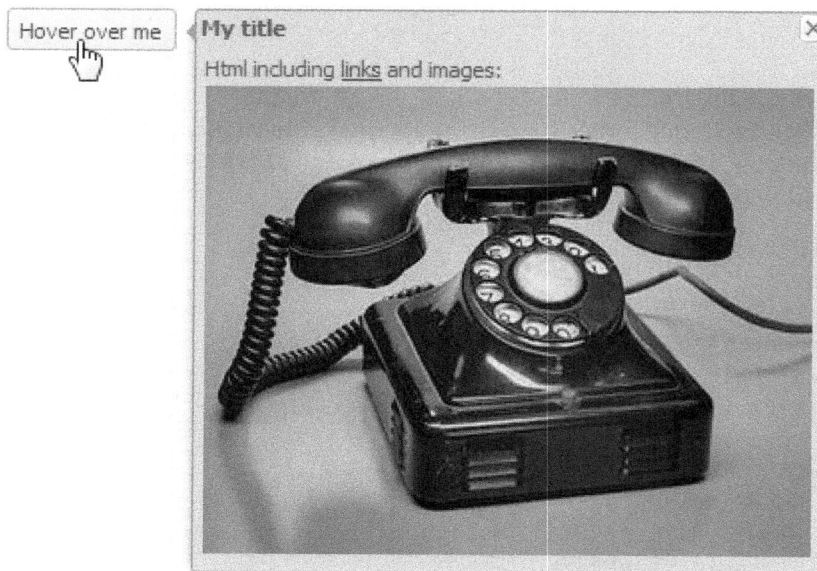

While this is quite useful, it gets even more powerful to be able to load the tool tip on-demand, via AJAX requests, if needed. This is possible without much effort, because tool tip inherits from an Ext JS panel so it gets the AutoLoad behavior of Panels. We will see an example of this in the AJAX chapter.

Note that the tool tip does not have to be declared only inside a control like we have seen so far. For example, if you have the following button declared:

```
<ext:Button runat="server" Id="Btn1" Text="Hover over me" />
```

You can declare a tool tip on its own and target the Button using the `Target` attribute:

```
<ext:ToolTip runat="server" Html="My Tip" Target="#{Btn1}" />
```

Similarly, Ext.NET tool tips can be applied to any HTML on the page, not just Ext. NET controls. For example, if you have the following HTML code:

```
<div id="my-div">Some content</div>
```

You can target that `div` with a standalone tool tip:

```
<ext:ToolTip runat="server" Target="my-div" Html="My tip" />
```

There are many other useful options in the Ext.NET Examples Explorer:

```
http://examples.ext.net/#/search/tooltip
```

Tool tips, as simple as they seem, are good for improving user experience when used appropriately. For example, if you have an application with a save button there may be times where the save button is disabled. Applying a tool tip to explain why it is disabled can be useful. Changing that tool tip when the save button becomes enabled can also be an option. The examples linked to earlier also show how you can update tool tips.

Complex components

Ext.NET is incredibly vast, and this book is constrained such that many controls cannot be described in detail here. While later chapters look at important, popular, and common controls, such as GridPanel, DataView, XTemplate, TreePanel, TabPanel, and various form controls, it is worth bearing in mind that there are many other rich controls that cannot be covered here simply due to lack of space. However, it is highly recommended to spend time browsing the Examples Explorer at `http://examples.ext.net`. But to just give you a hint of some of the possibilities, consider these sophisticated component:

Desktop

This is an example of how many Ext.NET components can all come together to provide a powerful desktop-like effect. Components such as Windows and Toolbars play an important part when put together like this!

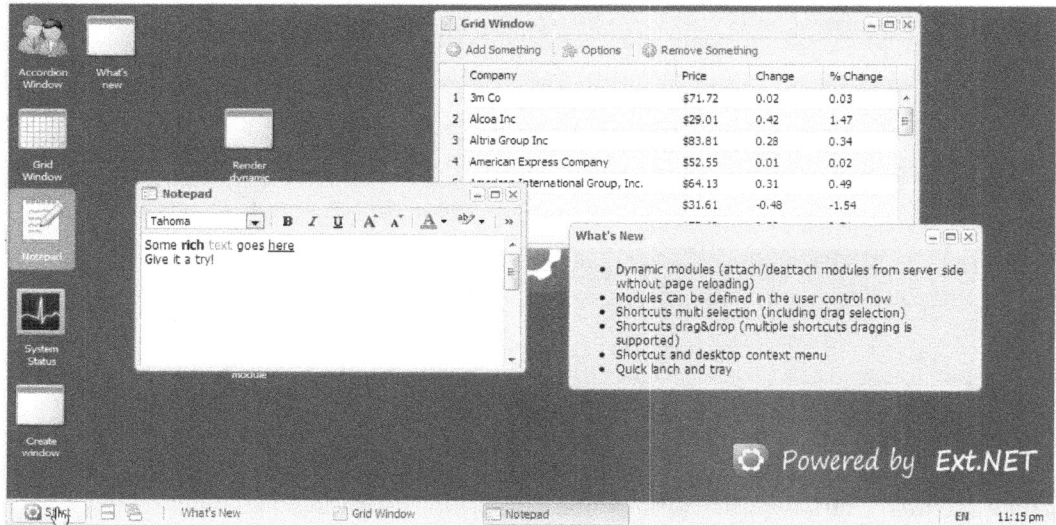

If your application is complex enough, you may consider creating a desktop within your browser! You can put this kind of look and feel together through the use of components, such as Desktop, DesktopModule, DesktopConfig, StartMenu, TaskBar, and more. For details, refer to this example: http://examples.ext.net/#/Desktop/Introduction/Overview/.

Charts

Ext.NET incorporates Ext JS's powerful charting mechanisms but also integrates the powerful Store architecture so that data binding is as familiar as binding data to grids and other data bound components in Ext.NET.

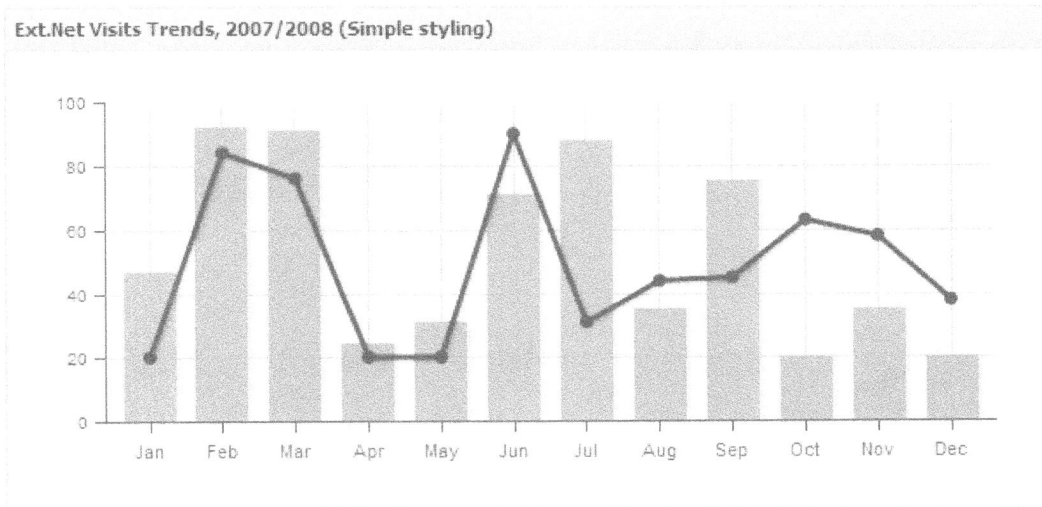

Charts are possible through the use of the Chart components, which have various capabilities to provide interactivity, live data, and different chart types (line, pie, bar, radar, gauge, column, and more). Refer to the Examples Explorer under the Chart section for many examples: `http://examples.ext.net/#/search/chart`.

Calendars

Another very powerful component is the Calendar. Like Charts, it also reuses the powerful Store data architecture, but presents information in a highly sophisticated calendar view.

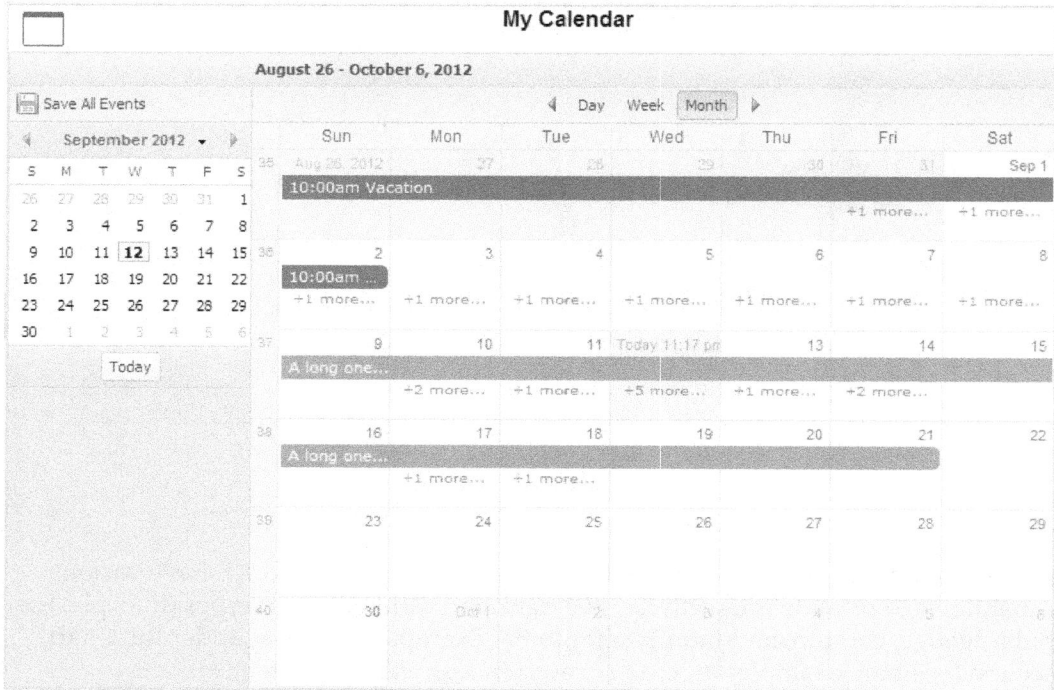

Using components such as Calendar and EventWindow you can create interactive calendars. See `http://examples.ext.net/#/Calendar/Overview/Basic/` for more details.

Even more!

Ext.NET provides many utilities as well, from utility classes to helper controls, such as progress bars, task managers, keyboard handlers, and more. These can be seen in the Examples Explorer: `http://examples.ext.net`.

Summary

In this chapter, we saw that although components can be building blocks, such as buttons and various form controls, we can also have Container components which additionally have the ability to contain other components and provide layout capabilities.

Using the humble Button various features common to many components were introduced, such as the ability to set icons, and add menus. Variations of the Button, such as SplitButtons, were also covered. We also saw common features, such as event handling and setting custom configuration properties on various controls.

Container controls were also introduced. These are more sophisticated, being able to contain yet other controls. The toolbars showed that many controls, not just menus and buttons, can be contained. Panels, Windows, and Tooltips were also introduced as other variations of container controls to demonstrate some important building blocks for applications.

Some initial AJAX capabilities were described, but a lot more will be covered in the AJAX chapter. As an introductory chapter, many more advanced capabilities, such as organizing these components were also left out. That is covered in the next chapter on layouts.

3
Layout with Ext.NET

Web applications often require rich and sophisticated layouts. Ext.NET provides a comprehensive set of layout options which we will look at in this chapter, focusing in particular on the following:

- The Viewport, which helps to make the whole page feel like an application
- Common layouts such as Border, Accordion, Fit, HBox, VBox, and many more
- Different ways to create layouts (with markup, code, and a mix, as well as using explicit layout components or flexible but terser Panel properties)

Viewport

A Viewport isn't a layout strictly speaking. It is a special type of container to represent the entire viewable area (the *viewport*) of the web browser window.

On a web page, the Viewport sits at the top-most level, rendering to the document body (or to the ASP.NET form if it is present on the page). From there it can automatically size itself to fill the browser viewport and resize when the browser window size changes. Therefore, there is only one Viewport in a page.

A benefit of the Viewport is that you can contain the whole user interface of the application inside this Viewport. Unlike a traditional web page where you may scroll beyond the page, the Viewport makes your application look more like, well, an application! You never scroll beyond the page (components contained inside a Viewport, of course, can have their own scrolling if needed). This means, for example, you can have a fixed menu or toolbar at the top that will always remain there, or if you have buttons at the bottom to save or discard changes, for example, they can always remain visible. The Viewport can, therefore, play an important part in the user's overall experience with your application.

A Viewport can be given a layout so that it can manage its immediate child items, which can be any component, typically Panels or their subclasses. This way you start the beginnings of a responsive application that can size to your browser's viewport. Nested Panels, which may have their own layout settings, also benefit from the window size management that the Viewport does.

There isn't a useful example of a Viewport on its own so we will look at different layouts and see examples of Viewport in action that way.

Note, that it is not mandatory for a page to start with a Viewport. As examples in earlier chapters have shown components can be placed anywhere and container components, like Panel, can contain many other components, and as long as the height and width are set they can also provide application behavior. The Viewport, however, gives flexibility in taking up the full browser viewport available and, therefore, can be less restrictive.

Border layout

The Border layout is perhaps one of the more popular layouts. While quite complex at first glance, it is popular because it turns out to be quite flexible to design and to use. It offers common elements often seen in complex web applications, such as an area for header content, footer content, a main content area, plus areas to either side. All are separately scrollable and resizable if needed, among other benefits. In Ext speak, these areas are called **Regions**, and are given names of North, South, Center, East, and West regions.

Only the Center region is mandatory. It is also the one without any given dimensions; it will resize to fit the remaining area after all the other regions have been set. A West or East region must have a width defined, and North or South regions must have a height defined. These can be defined using the Width or Height property (in pixels) or using the Flex property which helps provide ratios. We will look at Flex later when looking at HBox.

Each region can be any Ext.NET component; a very common option is Panel or a subclass of Panel. There are limits, however: for example, a Window is intended to be floating so cannot be one of the regions. This offers a lot of flexibility and can help avoid nesting too many Panels in order to show other components such as GridPanels or TabPanels, for example.

Here is a screenshot showing a simple Border layout being applied to the entire page (that is, the viewport) using a 2-column style layout:

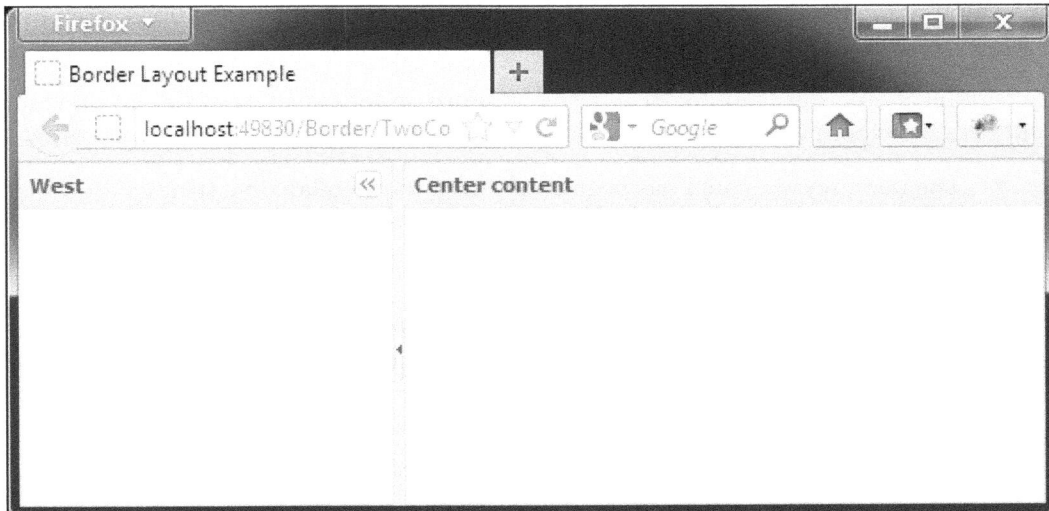

We have configured a Border layout with two regions; a West region and a Center region. The Border layout is applied to the whole page (this is an example of using it with Viewport. Here is the code:

```
<%@ Page Language="C#" %>

<!DOCTYPE html>
<html>
  <head runat="server">
    <title>Border Layout Example</title>
  </head>
  <body>
    <ext:ResourceManager runat="server" Theme="Gray" />
    <ext:Viewport runat="server" Layout="border">
      <Items>
        <ext:Panel Region="West"
          Split="true" Title="West" Width="200"
          Collapsible="true" />
        <ext:Panel Region="Center"
          Title="Center content" />
      </Items>
    </ext:Viewport>
  </body>
</html>
```

The code has a `Viewport` configured with a Border layout via the `Layout` property. Then, into the `Items` collection two Panels are added, for the `West` and `Center` regions.

The value of the `Layout` property is case insensitive and can take variations, such as `Border`, `border`, `borderlayout`, `BorderLayout`, and so on.

As regions of a Border layout we can also configure options such as whether you want split bars, whether Panels are collapsible, and more. Our example uses the following:

- The `West` region Panel has been configured to be collapsible (using `Collapsible="true"`). This creates a small button in the title area which, when clicked, will smoothly animate the collapse of that region (which can then be clicked again to open it).

- When collapsed, the title area itself can also be clicked which will float the region into appearance, rather than permanently opening it (allowing the user to glimpse at the content and mouse away to close the region). This floating capability can be turned off by using `Floatable="false"` on the Panel.

- `Split="true"` gives a split bar with a collapse button between the regions.

This next example shows a more complex Border layout where all regions are used:

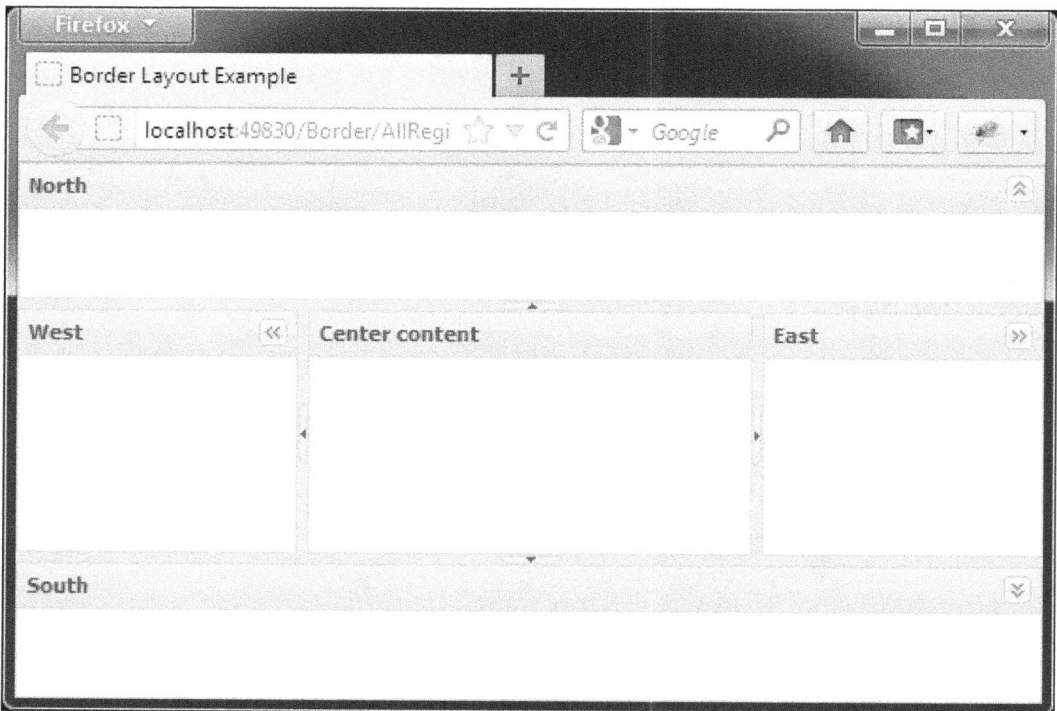

The markup used for the previous is very similar to the first example, so we will only show the Viewport portion:

```
<ext:Viewport runat="server" Layout="border">
  <Items>
    <ext:Panel Region="North" Split="true" Title="North" Height="75"
Collapsible="true" />
    <ext:Panel Region="West" Split="true" Title="West" Width="150"
Collapsible="true" />
    <ext:Panel runat="server" Region="Center" Title="Center content"
/>
    <ext:Panel Region="East" Split="true" Title="East" Width="150"
Collapsible="true" />
    <ext:Panel Region="South" Split="true" Title="South" Height="75"
Collapsible="true" />
  </Items>
</ext:Viewport>
```

Although each Panel has a title set via the `Title` property, it is optional. For example, you may want to omit the title from the `North` region if you want an application header or banner bar, where the title bar could be superfluous.

Different ways to create the same components

The previous examples were shown using the specific `Layout="Border"` markup. However, there are a number of ways this can be marked up or written in code. For example,

- You can code these entirely in markup as we have seen
- You can create these entirely in code
- You can use a mixture of markup and code to suit your needs

Here are some quick examples:

Border layout from code

This is the code version of the first two-panel Border layout example:

```
<%@ Page Language="C#" %>

<script runat="server">
  protected void Page_Load(object sender, EventArgs e)
  {
    var viewport = new Viewport
    {
      Layout = "border",
```

```
          Items =
          {
            new Ext.Net.Panel
            {
              Region      = Region.West,
              Title       = "West",
              Width       = 200,
              Collapsible = true,
              Split       = true
            },

            new Ext.Net.Panel
            {
              Region = Region.Center,
              Title  = "Center content"
            }
          }
        };

        this.Form.Controls.Add(viewport);
      }
</script>

<!DOCTYPE html>
<html>
  <head runat="server">
    <title>Border Layout Example</title>
  </head>
<body>
    <form runat="server">
        <ext:ResourceManager runat="server" Theme="Gray" />
    </form>
</body>
</html>
```

There are a number of things going on here worth mentioning:

- The appropriate panels have been added to the Viewport's `Items` collection
- Finally, the Viewport is added to the page via the form's `Controls` Collection

If you are used to programming with ASP.NET, you normally add a control to the `Controls` collection of an ASP.NET control. However, when Ext.NET controls add themselves to each other, it is usually done via the `Items` collection. This helps create a more optimal initialization script. This also means that only Ext.NET components participate in the layout logic. There is also the `Content` property in markup (or `ContentControls` property in code-behind) which can be used to add non-Ext.NET controls or raw HTML, though they will not take part in the layout. It is important to note that configuring Items and Content together should be avoided, especially if a layout is set on the parent container. This is because the parent container will only use the `Items` collection. Some layouts may hide the Content section altogether or have other undesired results. In general, use only one at a time, not both because the Viewport is the outer-most control; it is added to the `Controls` collection of the form itself.

Another important thing to bear in mind is that the Viewport must be the only top-level visible control. That means it cannot be placed inside a `div`, for example it must be added directly to the body or to the `<form runat="server">` only. In addition, there should not be any sibling controls (except floating widgets, like Window).

Mixing markup and code

The same 2-panel Border layout can also be mixed in various ways. For example:

```
<%@ Page Language="C#" %>

<script runat="server">
  protected void Page_Load(object sender, EventArgs e)
  {
    this.WestPanel.Title       = "West";
    this.WestPanel.Split       = true;
    this.WestPanel.Collapsible = true;

    this.Viewport1.Items.Add(new Ext.Net.Panel
    {
      Region = Region.Center,
      Title  = "Center content"
    });
  }
</script>

<!DOCTYPE html>
<html>
  <head runat="server">
    <title>Border Layout Example</title>
  </head>
```

```
<body>
  <ext:ResourceManager runat="server" />
  <ext:Viewport ID="Viewport1" runat="server" Layout="Border">
    <Items>
      <ext:Panel ID="WestPanel" runat="server" Region="West"
Width="200" />
    </Items>
  </ext:Viewport>
</body>
</html>
```

In the previous example, the Viewport and the initial part of the West region have been defined in markup. The Center region Panel has been added via code and the rest of the West Panel's properties have been set in code-behind. As with most ASP. NET controls, you can mix and match these as you need.

Loading layout items via User Controls

A powerful capability that Ext.NET provides is being able to load layout components from User Controls. This is achieved by using the UserControlLoader component. Consider this example:

```
<ext:Viewport runat="server" Layout="Border">
  <Items>
    <ext:UserControlLoader Path="WestPanel.ascx" />
    <ext:Panel Region="Center" />
  </Items>
</ext:Viewport>
```

In this code, we have replaced the West region Panel that was used in earlier examples with a UserControlLoader component and set the Path property to load a user control in the same directory as this page. That user control is very simple for our example:

```
<%@ Control Language="C#" %>
<ext:Panel runat="server" Region="West" Split="true" Title="West"
Width="200" Collapsible="true" />
```

In other words, we have simply moved our Panel from our earlier example into a user control and loaded that instead. Though a small example, this demonstrates some useful reuse capability. In *Chapter 9, Extending Ext.NET–Custom and Plugins* we will look at some more advanced re-use capabilities, such as creating custom controls by subclassing various Ext.NET components.

Also note, that although we used the UserControlLoader in this Border layout example, it can be used anywhere else as needed, as it is an Ext.NET component.

The containing component does not have to be a Viewport

Note also that the containing component does not have to be a Viewport. It can be any other appropriate container, such as another Panel or a Window. Let's do just that:

```
<ext:Window runat="server" Layout="Border" Height="200" Width="400"
Border="false">
  <Items>
    <ext:Panel Region="West" Split="true" Title="West" Width="150"
Collapsible="true" />
    <ext:Panel Region="Center" Title="Center content" />
  </Items>
</ext:Window>
```

The container has changed from a Viewport to a Window (with dimensions). It will produce this:

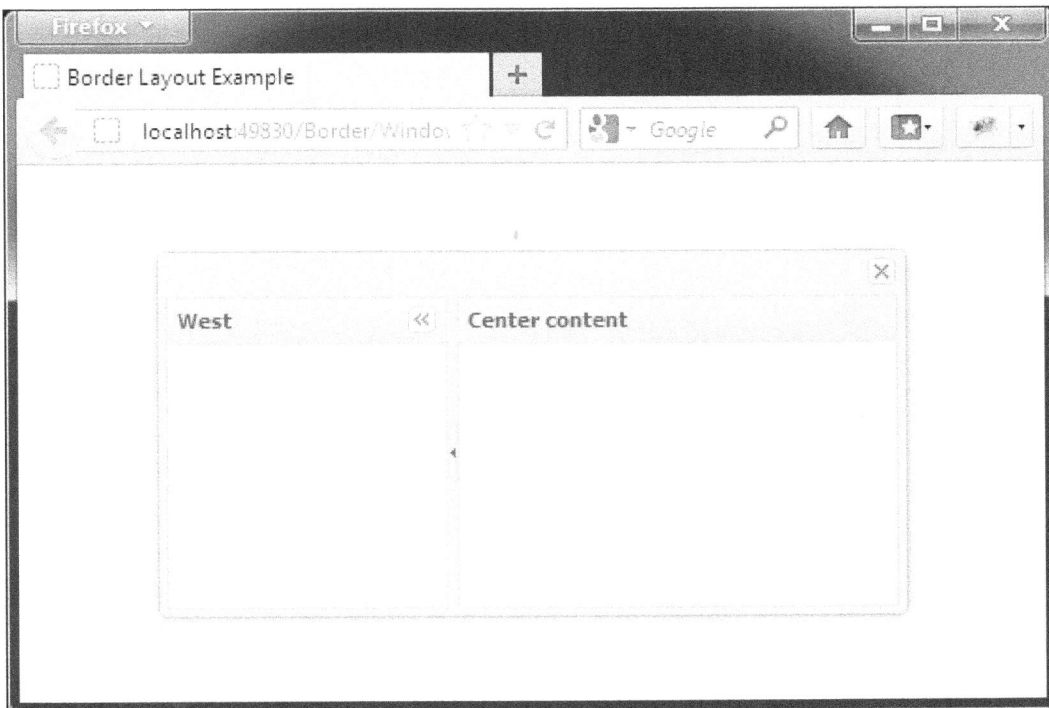

More than one item with the same region

In previous versions of Ext JS and Ext.NET you could only have one component in a given region, for example, only one North region Panel, one West region Panel, and so on. New to Ext.NET 2 is the ability to have more than one item in the same region. This can be very flexible and improve performance slightly. This is because in the past if you wanted the appearance of say multiple West columns, you would need to create nested Border layouts (which is still an option of course). But now, you can simply add two components to a Border layout and give them the same region value.

Nested Border layouts are still possible in case the flexibility is needed (and helps make porting from an earlier version easier). First, here is an example using nested Border layouts to achieve three vertical columns:

```
<ext:Window runat="server" Layout="Border" Height="200" Width="400"
Border="false">
  <Items>
    <ext:Panel Region="West" Split="true" Title="West" Width="100"
Collapsible="true" />
    <ext:Panel Region="Center" Layout="Border" Border="false">
      <Items>
        <ext:Panel Region="West" Split="true" Title="Inner West"
Width="100" Collapsible="true" />
        <ext:Panel Region="Center" Title="Inner Center" />
      </Items>
    </ext:Panel>
  </Items>
</ext:Window>
```

This code will produce the following output:

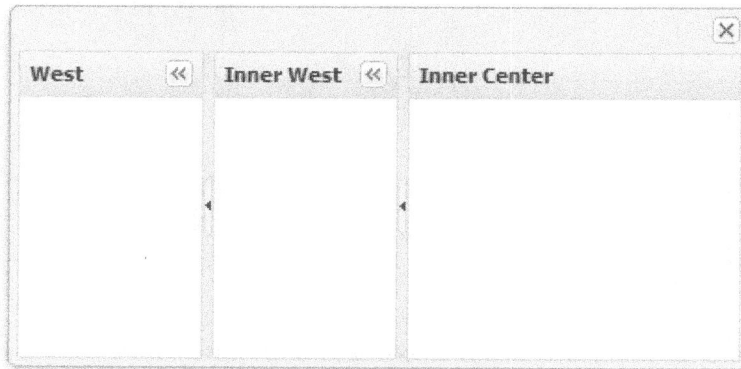

The previous code is only a slight variation of the example preceding it, but has a few notable changes:

- The Center region Panel has itself been given the layout as Border. This means that although this is a Center region for the window that it is a part of, this Panel is itself another Border layout.

- The nested Border layout then has two further Panels, an additional West region and an additional Center region.

- Note, the Title has also been removed from the outer Center region so that when they are rendered, they line up to look like three Panels next to each other.

Here is the same example, but without using a nested border Panel and instead, just adding another West region Panel to the containing Window:

```
<ext:Window runat="server" Layout="Border" Height="200" Width="400"
Border="false">
  <Items>
    <ext:Panel Region="West" Split="true" Title="West" Width="100"
Collapsible="true" />
    <ext:Panel Region="West" Split="true" Title="Inner West"
Width="100" Collapsible="true" />
    <ext:Panel Region="Center" Title="Center content" Border="false"
/>
  </Items>
</ext:Window>
```

Regions are not limited to Panels only

A common problem with layouts is to start off creating more deeply nested controls than needed and the example earlier shows that it is not always needed. Multiple items with the same region helps to prevent nesting Border Layouts unnecessarily. Another inefficiency typical with the Border layout usage is using too many containing Panels in each region. For example, there may be a Center region Panel which then contains a TabPanel. However, as TabPanel is a subclass of Panel (we will cover TabPanels in their own chapter separately, later) it can be given a region directly, therefore avoiding an unnecessary Panel to contain the TabPanel:

```
<ext:Window runat="server" Layout="Border" Height="200" Width="400"
Border="False">
  <Items>
    <ext:Panel Region="West" Split="true" Title="West" Width="100"
Collapsible="True" />
    <ext:TabPanel Region="Center">
      <Items>
```

```
        <ext:Panel Title="First Tab" />
        <ext:Panel Title="Second Tab" />
      </Items>
    </ext:TabPanel>
  </Items>
</ext:Window>
```

This code will produce the following output:

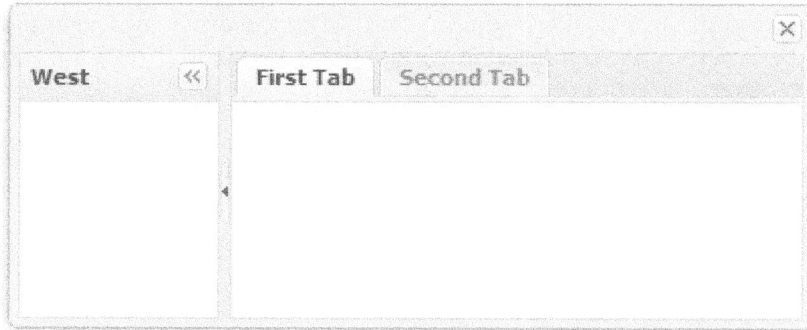

The differences with the nested Border layout example shown earlier are:

- The outer Center region has been changed from Panel to TabPanel.
- TabPanels manage their own items' layout so Layout="Border" is removed.
- The TabPanel also has Border="false" taken out (so it is true by default).
- The inner Panels have had their regions, Split, and other border related attributes taken out. This is because they are not inside a nested Border layout now; they are tabs.

Other Panels, such as TreePanel or GridPanel, can also be used as we will see.

> Something that can be fiddly from time to time is knowing which borders to take off and which ones to keep when you have nested layouts and controls like this. There is a logic to it, but sometimes a quick bit of trial and error can also help figure it out! As a programmer this sounds minor and unimportant, but usually you want to prevent the borders becoming too thick, as aesthetically it can be off-putting, whereas just the right amount of borders can help make the application look clean and professional. You can always give components a class via the Cls property and then in CSS you can fine tune the borders (and other styles of course) as you need.

Weighted regions

Another feature new to Ext.NET 2 is that regions can be given weighting to influence how they are rendered and spaced out. Prior versions would require nested Border layouts to achieve this. To see how this works, consider this example to put a South region only inside the Center Panel:

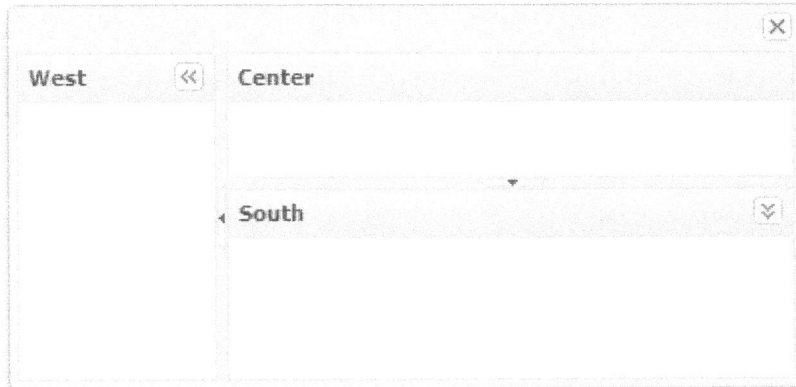

To achieve this output, if we used the old way — the nested Border layouts — we would do something like this:

```
<ext:Window runat="server" Layout="Border" Height="200" Width="400"
Border="false">
  <Items>
    <ext:Panel Region="West" Split="true" Title="West" Width="100"
Collapsible="true" />
    <ext:Panel Region="Center" Layout="Border" Border="false">
      <Items>
        <ext:Panel Region="Center" Title="Center" />
        <ext:Panel Region="South" Split="true" Title="South"
Height="100" Collapsible="true" />
      </Items>
    </ext:Panel>
  </Items>
</ext:Window>
```

In the preceding code, we make the Center region itself be a Border layout with an inner Center region and a South region. This way the outer West region takes up all the space on the left. If the South region was part of the outer Border layout, then it would span across the entire bottom area of the window.

But the same effect can be achieved using weighting. This means you do not need nested Border layouts; the three Panels can all be items of the containing window, which means a few less objects being created on the client:

```
<ext:Window runat="server" Layout="Border" Height="200" Width="400"
Border="false">
  <Items>
    <ext:Panel Region="West" Split="true" Title="West" Width="100"
Collapsible="true" Weight="10" />
    <ext:Panel Region="Center" Title="Center" />
    <ext:Panel Region="South" Split="true" Title="South" Height="100"
Collapsible="true" />
  </Items>
</ext:Window>
```

The way region weights work is that the region with the highest weight is assigned space from the border before other regions. If more than one region has the same weight as another, they are assigned space based on their position in the owner's Items collection (that is first come, first served). In the preceding code, we set the Weight property to 10 to the West region only, so it is rendered first and, thus, takes up all the space it can before the other two are rendered. This allows for many flexible options and Ext.NET has an example where you can configure different values to see the effects of different weights:

http://examples.ext.net/#/Layout/BorderLayout/Regions_Weights/

As the previous examples show, there are many ways to define the layout, offering you more flexibility, especially if generating from code-behind in a very dynamic way.

Knowing that there are so many ways to define the layout, we can now speed up our look at many other types of layouts.

Accordion layout

This popular layout lets you stack Panels (or its subclasses) on top of each other and expand and view just one at a time. From a usability perspective this helps group common functionality together while hiding parts the user is not interested in, simplifying what the user is seeing at any one time. Here is an example of a very simple Panel:

The code to achieve it:

```
<ext:Window runat="server" Layout="Accordion" Width="150" Height="200"
Border="false">
  <Items>
    <ext:Panel Title="Panel 1" />
    <ext:Panel Title="Panel 2" />
    <ext:Panel Title="Panel 3" />
  </Items>
</ext:Window>
```

Key aspects of this code include the following:

- A `Window` acting as the container is configured with the layout as `Accordion`
- The `Items` collection of the `Window` contains Ext.NET components that the `Accordion` layout will manage for you

By default, the collapsing and expanding of Panels is animated for you. If you need to turn that off, you can add a `LayoutConfig` configuration as a property of the window:

```
<LayoutConfig>
  <ext:AccordionLayoutConfig Animate="false" />
</LayoutConfig>
```

Using `LayoutConfig` means you do not need to set the `Layout` property explicitly, either. There are many more configuration options for the Accordion layout using `AccordionLayoutConfig`. For example you can configure where the first item should be collapsed by default or not (using the `CollapseFirst` property), or you can prevent the opening of one item to close the previously opened one (using the `Multi` property), and so on. For further details, please refer to the Ext JS documentation site: `http://docs.sencha.com/ext-js/4-1/#!/api/ Ext.layout.container.Accordion`

Panel subclasses as Accordion items

As various subclasses of Panel can be used, we'll quickly introduce a TreePanel example, although *Chapter 8, Trees and Tabs with Ext.NET* will look at TreePanels further:

```
<ext:Window runat="server" Title="PIM" Layout="Accordion" Width="200"
Height="225" Icon="ApplicationTileVertical">
  <Items>
    <ext:TreePanel Title="Folders" Icon="Email" AutoScroll="true"
RootVisible="false">
      <Root>
        <ext:Node>
          <Children>
            <ext:Node Text="Inbox (100)" Expanded="true">
              <Children>
                <ext:Node Text="Important (5)" Icon="Exclamation"
Leaf="true" />
                <ext:Node Text="Saved searches (6)" Icon="Magnifier"
Leaf="true" />
              </Children>
            </ext:Node>
            <ext:Node Icon="EmailStop" Text="Outbox" Expanded="false"
Leaf="true" />
            <ext:Node Icon="EmailGo" Text="Sent items (300)"
Expanded="false" Leaf="true" />
            <ext:Node Text="Private" Expanded="False" Leaf="true" />
          </Children>
        </ext:Node>
      </Root>
    </ext:TreePanel>
    <ext:Panel Title="Calendar" Icon="Date" />
    <ext:Panel Title="Contacts" Icon="Group" />
  </Items>
</ext:Window>
```

The previous code will give:

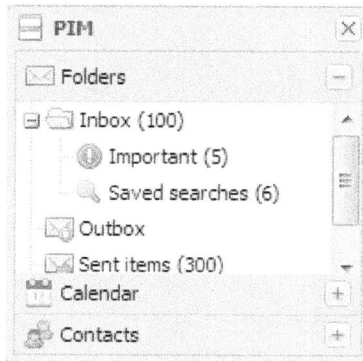

Other than the use of `TreePanel`, everything else has used standard features of Panels, such as `Title` and `Icon`. The TreePanel, like any other Panel can also have `AutoScroll`. This has been added to the TreePanel to show that only its contents can be scrolled (if needed). The Accordion layout has added the *plus* and *minus* icons to the right of the panel bar to provide the expand/collapse effect required to bring the Accordion to life.

Layout combinations

To highlight the flexibility of layouts further, consider this example:

```
<ext:Viewport runat="server" Layout="Border">
  <Items>
    <ext:Panel Region="West" Split="true" Title="West" Width="200"
Collapsible="true" Layout="Accordion">
    <Items>
      <ext:TreePanel Title="Folders" Icon="Email" AutoScroll="true"
RootVisible="false">
        <Root>
          <ext:Node>
            <Children>
              <ext:Node Text="Inbox (100)" Expanded="true">
                <Children>
                  <ext:Node Text="Important (5)" Icon="Exclamation"
Leaf="true" />
                  <ext:Node Text="Saved searches (6)" Icon="Magnifier"
Leaf="true" />
                </Children>
              </ext:Node>
              <ext:Node Icon="EmailStop" Text="Outbox"
Expanded="false" Leaf="true" />
              <ext:Node Icon="EmailGo" Text="Sent items
(300)"Expanded="false" Leaf="true" />
              <ext:Node Text="Private" Expanded="false" Leaf="true" />
            </Children>
          </ext:Node>
        </Root>
      </ext:TreePanel>
      <ext:Panel runat="server" Title="Calendar" Icon="Date" />
      <ext:Panel runat="server" Title="Contacts" Icon="Group" />
    </Items>
  </ext:Panel>
    <ext:TabPanel Region="Center">
      <Items>
        <ext:Panel Title="First Tab" />
```

```
            <ext:Panel Title="Second Tab" />
        </Items>
      </ext:TabPanel>
    </Items>
  </ext:Viewport>
```

The previous code produces this:

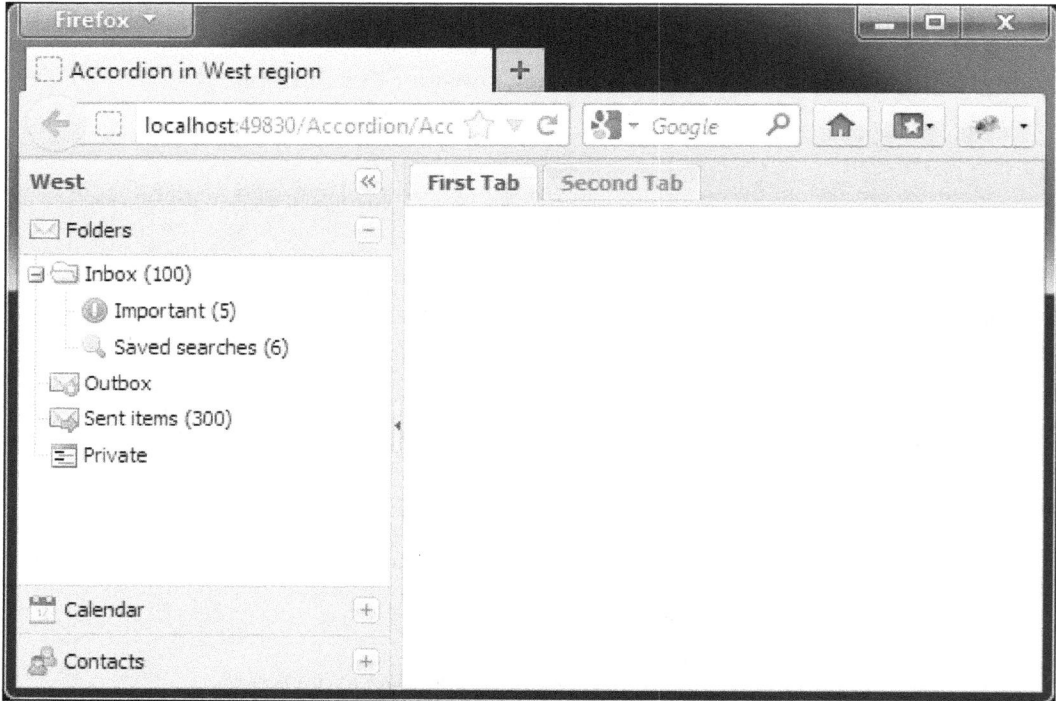

What happens here is as follows:

- The Viewport is given a Border layout
- The West region item is itself given an Accordion layout so its own items behave like an accordion
- The Center region itself is a TabPanel, thus getting tab behavior for its own items

Many more permutations and combinations are, of course, possible.

Fit Layout

A Fit layout can be very useful to fit an item into all the available space of its container (for example a Viewport or a Window, or another Panel). In this example, a `Window` is given a Fit layout so that the Panel takes up the full space of the `Window`:

```
<ext:Window runat="server" Layout="Fit" Width="200" Height="200">
  <Items>
    <ext:Panel Title="Fitted panel" AutoScroll="true" Border="false">
      <BottomBar>
        <ext:StatusBar>
          <Items>
            <ext:Button Text="Click Me!" />
          </Items>
        </ext:StatusBar>
      </BottomBar>
    </ext:Panel>
  </Items>
</ext:Window>
```

When rendered, it will look like this:

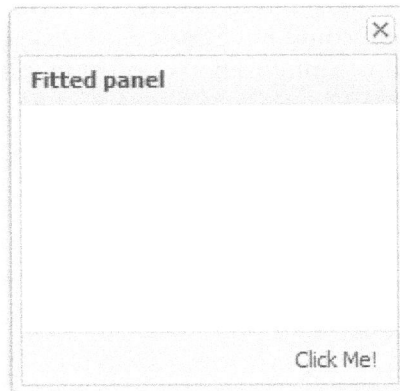

The bottom bar has been added just for demonstration purposes. If we did not use a Fit layout in the previous example, the Panel would have been only as high as its contents (unless explicit width and height dimensions were added to the Panel itself) and the bottom bar would have been flush under the title bar (because there is no content in the previous example). The Fit layout has distributed the full width and height so the bottom bar appears at the bottom as desired.

HBox layout

The HBox layout is a powerful layout option that arranges items horizontally across a container. You can divide the space between child items in various ways giving you powerful layout options. Consider the following screenshot:

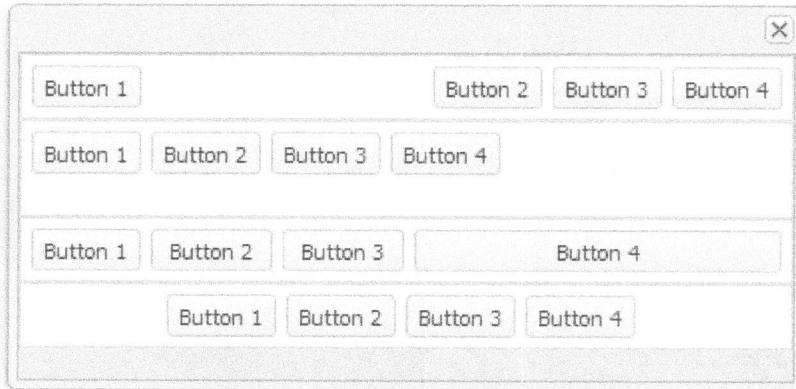

In this screenshot, we have four different Panels, each with four buttons (though any components, including Panels could have been used instead of buttons). Each Panel, however, has a different HBox configuration applied to it to achieve the different horizontal layouts.

Let's look at each one in turn, starting from the top-most Panel of buttons and working our way down:

```
<ext:Panel runat="server" Layout="HBox" BodyPadding="5"
DefaultMargins="0 5 0 0">
  <Items>
    <ext:Button Text="Button 1" />
    <ext:Panel BaseCls="x-plain" Flex="1" />
    <ext:Button Text="Button 2" />
    <ext:Button Text="Button 3" />
    <ext:Button Text="Button 4" Margins="0" />
  </Items>
</ext:Panel>
```

In the previous code, we have inserted a flexible Panel (using `Flex="1"`) to take up all the space between its adjacent items.

Note, the use of `DefaultMargins` is a shortcut to using the following:

```
<Defaults>
  <ext:Parameter Name="margins" Value="0 5 0 0" Mode="Value" />
</Defaults>
```

The use of `Defaults` (or the shorthand) is a useful way to provide default values to all *child* items in a container. Generally speaking, Ext.NET can use properties starting with *Default* and they will be serialized to the same as if you used the `Defaults` property and added parameters explicitly. Of course, you can use the longhand if you need to control whether the value has quotes around it when serialized to JavaScript or not (via the `Mode` property) which is explained further in *Chapter 4, AJAX with Ext.NET*.

The second example is very similar:

```
<ext:Panel runat="server" Layout="HBox" Height="50" BodyPadding="5"
DefaultMargins="0 5 0 0">
  <LayoutConfig>
    <ext:HBoxLayoutConfig Align="Top" />
  </LayoutConfig>
  <Items>
    <ext:Button Text="Button 1" />
    <ext:Button Text="Button 2" />
    <ext:Button Text="Button 3" />
    <ext:Button Text="Button 4" />
  </Items>
</ext:Panel>
```

In the previous code, we have added a height of 50 pixels to the Panel for demonstration of the `Align="Top"` configuration that aligns all the child items to the top. Other possible values for the `Align` attribute are:

- Bottom
- Stretch to fill the full height
- StretchMax to equalize heights of all child items to the tallest ones

In the third example, powerful flexing options are available:

```
<ext:Panel runat="server" Layout="HBox" BodyPadding="5"
DefaultMargins="0 5 0 0">
  <Items>
    <ext:Button Text="Button 1" />
    <ext:Button Text="Button 3" Flex="1" />
    <ext:Button Text="Button 2" Flex="1" />
    <ext:Button Text="Button 4" Flex="3" Margins="0" />
  </Items>
</ext:Panel>
```

Notice the differences in the Panels:

- Button 1 has no flex (width will be determined by the button text)
- Button 2 and 3 have a flex of 1
- Button 4 has a flex of 3

So how does HBox work out the widths?

- All flex values are totaled (in this case, 5).
- Any item without a flex is ignored.
- Knowing the remaining width (after accounting for non-flexed items), the flex values are apportioned out.
- For example, if the remaining widths for Buttons 2, 3, and 4 are 500 pixels, then Flex of 1 will mean a ratio of 1 out of 5 (the flex total). This gives us 100 pixels for Buttons 2 and 3. Button 4 will, therefore, be 300 pixels.

Finally, the fourth example shows how the entire *pack* of child items can be positioned:

```
<ext:Panel runat="server" Layout="HBox" BodyPadding="5"
DefaultMargins="0 5 0 0">
  <LayoutConfig>
    <ext:HBoxLayoutConfig Pack="Center" />
  </LayoutConfig>
  <Items>
    <ext:Button Text="Button 1" />
    <ext:Button Text="Button 2" />
    <ext:Button Text="Button 3" />
    <ext:Button Text="Button 4" />
  </Items>
</ext:Panel>
```

The example shows a `Pack` with value `Center` to center all the child items. Other values for `Pack` could be:

- `Start` to show all the items grouped to the left
- `End` to show all the items grouped to the right

The examples shown previously have all involved buttons, but many other components can be used. This next example shows a common requirement: equal height columns. In addition, we've made some of the columns collapsible/expandable:

```
<ext:Window runat="server" Width="400" Height="200">
  <LayoutConfig>
    <ext:HBoxLayoutConfig Align="Stretch" DefaultMargins="2 0" />
  </LayoutConfig>
  <Items>
```

```
        <ext:Panel Flex="1" Title="Panel 1" CollapseDirection="Left" />
        <ext:BoxSplitter runat="server" Collapsible="true"
CollapseTarget="Prev" />

        <ext:Panel Flex="1" Title="Panel 2" CollapseDirection="Left" />
        <ext:BoxSplitter Collapsible="true" CollapseTarget="Prev" />

        <ext:Panel Flex="1" Title="Panel 3" />

        <ext:BoxSplitter Collapsible="true" />
        <ext:Panel Flex="1" Title="Panel 4" CollapseDirection="Right" />

        <ext:BoxSplitter Collapsible="true"  />
        <ext:Panel ID="Panel5" Flex="1" Title="Panel 5"
CollapseDirection="Right" />
    </Items>
</ext:Window>
```

This code will produce:

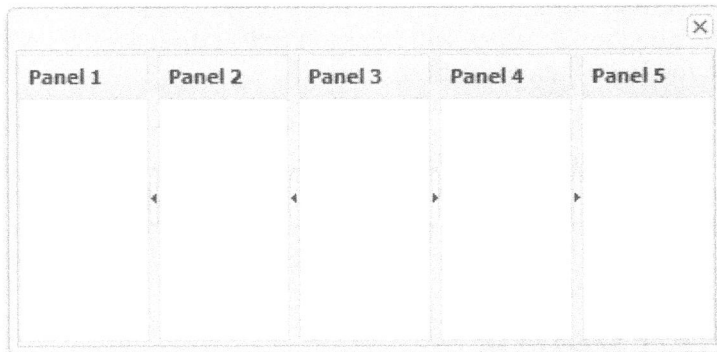

If we collapse say the first and second Panel, it would produce this:

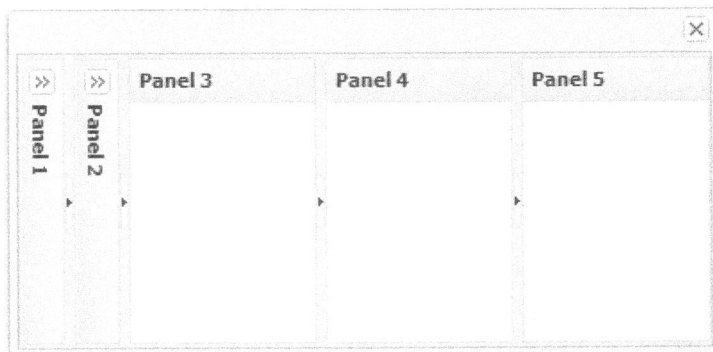

How this is achieved:

- Using `Align="Stretch"` means we fill the full height of the container giving us equal height columns.

- Panels can have a collapse direction set to either `Left`, `Right`, `Top`, or `Bottom`. For `HBox` layouts, `Left` and `Right` make sense. `VBox` layout is similar to `HBox` except that it works against the vertical, where using `Top` or `Bottom` for collapse direction would make sense.

- We also introduce another control here, the `BoxSplitter`. A `BoxSplitter` is added as a sibling to the Panel that it will control the resizing of. Using `CollapseTarget`, you can set it to `Prev` or `Next` (the latter being the default). This tells the splitter which sibling to collapse.

VBox layout

As with HBox, the VBox layout is a powerful layout option that lets you arrange items vertically across a container using a variety of ways that match HBox (of course, some directional values will refer to vertical directions for VBox, as noted earlier in the HBox layout section).

Due to space constraints in this book we won't look at the exact same concepts as HBox here. Armed with the knowledge of HBox, earlier, you can study this example in the Examples Explorer: `http://examples.ext.net/#/Layout/VBoxLayout/Basic/`. Although the name of the page implies a basic overview of VBox, it is quite rich and thorough! For this chapter, we will instead look at a couple of useful tips:

Reordering Panels

A useful plugin that comes with VBox is the ability to reorder items inside a container. Consider this example markup:

```
<ext:Window runat="server" Width="250" Height="200">
  <LayoutConfig>
    <ext:VBoxLayoutConfig Align="Stretch" />
  </LayoutConfig>
  <Items>
    <ext:Panel Flex="1" Title="Panel 1" />
    <ext:Panel Flex="1" Title="Panel 2" />
    <ext:Panel Flex="1" Title="Panel 3" />
  </Items>
  <Plugins>
    <ext:BoxReorderer />
  </Plugins>
</ext:Window>
```

This markup produces three vertical Panels contained in a Window. But with the reorder plugin added, it allows the user to move the Panels around if they want:

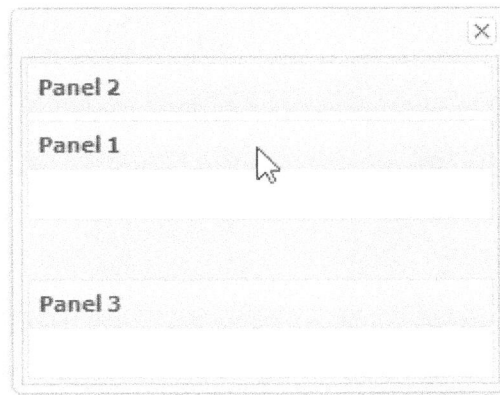

In the screenshot when **Panel 1** is being dragged down and **Panel 2** has automatically slid up to fill the space.

The same `BoxReorderer` plugin can be used on an HBox layout to move components arranged horizontally. See the following for an example: `http://examples.ext.net/#/Layout/HBoxLayout/Reordering/`.

Centering a component

We can combine VBox and HBox layouts to center an element on the screen:

```
<ext:Viewport runat="server" Layout="HBoxLayout">
  <LayoutConfig>
    <ext:HBoxLayoutConfig Pack="Center" Align="Stretch" />
  </LayoutConfig>
  <Items>
    <ext:Container Layout="VBoxLayout">
      <LayoutConfig>
        <ext:VBoxLayoutConfig Pack="Center" />
      </LayoutConfig>
      <Items>
        <ext:Panel Title="Centered Panel" Height="200" Width="200" />
      </Items>
    </ext:Container>
  </Items>
</ext:Viewport>
```

In this example, we have centered a Panel on the entire screen:

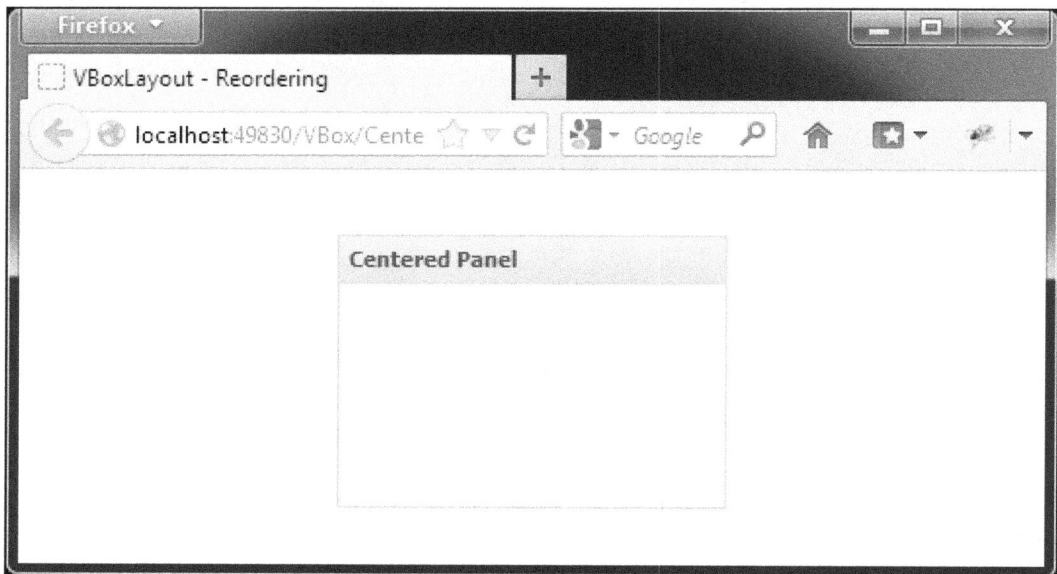

How is this achieved?

- The Viewport is configured with an HBoxLayout and the HBoxLayoutConfig is set to pack things into the center using the Pack property.

- The Viewport HBoxLayoutConfig is also set to align its child items using the value Stretch. As noted earlier in the section on HBox, this will stretch the children to the full height of the container. Notice, there is only one child item of the Viewport: a container.

- The container is a good choice here as it is lightweight compared to a Panel, and we are not going to use it other than to give it a VBoxLayout, so its contents can be packed into the center using the Pack property of the VBoxLayoutConfig.

- So this means that Viewport will center things horizontally and its single child will center things vertically. This just leaves the real content, in our example, a Panel which requires explicit dimensions for this to work.

- In this way if you resize the browser, the Panel remains centered on the page.

Of course, you can use any other container not just the Viewport to start your centering from. So, this means if you have a complex layout, one of your items can center its own contents in the middle of its area, regardless of where it fits into the larger layout.

Many other layouts

Ext.NET provides many other layouts and it would be beyond the scope of this book to describe them all. However, the previously mentioned layouts are among the most widely used ones and cover most of the techniques that the other layouts would also employ. But here is a brief list of other layouts:

- **Absolute Layout** positions an item using specific x/y coordinates.
- **Anchor Layout** anchors items across the four sides of its containers in various ways to achieve automatic stretching as the container is resized.
- **Card Layout** stacks components on top of each other. It is the developer's responsibility to programmatically hide and show the right component. The TabPanel is an extension of this idea, hiding specific tabs as needed. You can also use a Card layout to create a wizard-style effect.
- **Column Layout** supports multi-column formatted layouts.
- **Form Layout** is a simple way to lay out form controls one on top of each other but in a way that will stretch to its container's width. Other layout options with forms will be looked at in *Chapter 7, Forms and Validation*.
- **Table Layout** to achieve a table-like layout with row spanning and column spanning possibilities as seen in the old days of HTML table-based layout.

Further resources and examples

These are described in more detail and with more examples at the Ext.NET website:

```
http://examples.ext.net/
```

In particular, see the Layout section for more layout examples.

In addition, the documentation for Ext JS at the Sencha website provides further details and as the underlying JavaScript framework, is worth getting familiar with as it can help understand and appreciate what Ext.NET is doing for you. It can also help you troubleshoot any problems that may arise. This documentation can be found at:

```
http://docs.sencha.com/ext-js/
```

In particular, look for the documentation subsection on layouts.

Summary

In this chapter we had a look at how Ext.NET and Ext JS provide layout capabilities. While Ext.NET provides many layouts we saw a few in detail here:

- Border layout
- Accordion layout
- Fit layout
- HBox layout
- VBox layout

The Border layout demonstrated both the power of that particular layout but also the flexibility in Ext.NET in terms of how to define and use it. We saw that we can also nest Border layouts, and when we looked at the Accordion layout we also saw that a combination of layouts is easily possible. The Fit layout demonstrated how you can get something to fit the container and stretch with it whenever the container is resized. With HBox and VBox layouts we saw powerful options to configure items in numerous ways horizontally and vertically. In addition, we saw they could be combined to help center a component which is quite a popular thing to do.

We also looked at the Viewport as another example of a container which is frequently used in conjunction with a layout to create an application look and feel for your web page. But we also saw that layouts can be applied to other containers, such as Panels and Windows. Finally, we noted that Panels are not the only items taking part in layout. Other components such as TabPanel and TreePanel can be directly used in place of a Panel (as they are subclasses of Panel) which helps create more reusable and lean applications, instead of embedding and deeply nesting Panels everywhere. Another powerful Panel subclass is a GridPanel which can also be used directly instead of a Panel. But before we look at the GridPanel we will introduce some other powerful features of Ext.NET. The next chapter looks at how AJAX works with Ext.NET.

4
AJAX with Ext.NET

Modern web applications will invariably need to make heavy use of **Asynchronous JavaScript and XML (AJAX)**. Some of the preceding chapters have hinted at, or given some examples of, AJAX capabilities available in Ext.NET. In this chapter, we look at those again, comparing it to other mechanisms available in ASP.NET.

By the end of this chapter, you will gain an understanding of the various ways AJAX operations can be performed, understanding the pros and cons of each approach.

AJAX with ASP.NET

ASP.NET has a number of ways to do AJAX. They include, though are not limited to, AJAX Control Toolkit, page methods, ASMX, and WCF Web Services that can be called directly from JavaScript, `UpdatePanel`, ASHX generic handlers, WCF Data Services, MVC Controller actions, and more. For the purpose of this book, we'll just have a brief look at two of these, to compare and contrast.

The first is `UpdatePanel`, which is generally out of favor now, but demonstrates the benefits of clean AJAX over excessive abstraction, which is important to keep in mind.

The second example is the page method (or `WebMethods`), which is similar to one of the AJAX options that Ext.NET includes, which we will look at in depth later.

Later examples will show how we can take advantage of existing ASP.NET features, such as ASHX generic handlers, ASMX Web Services, and more.

UpdatePanel

Although `UpdatePanel` is out of favor compared to other AJAX methods in ASP. NET, it is still supported. In addition, for lots of intranet business applications (where Ext.NET is a good fit), many applications may still be using `UpdatePanel`, so if it comes round to porting such applications to Ext.NET then understanding its limitations may be useful.

Consider this snippet of ASP.NET markup:

```
<asp:ScriptManager runat="server" />
<asp:UpdatePanel runat="server">
  <ContentTemplate>
    <asp:Panel ID="MyPanel" runat="server" Visible="false">
      <asp:Literal ID="MyLiteral" runat="server" />
    </asp:Panel>
    <asp:Button runat="server" OnClick="ShowMyPanel" Text="Click Me"
/>
  </ContentTemplate>
</asp:UpdatePanel>
```

Here is the corresponding ASP.NET click event handler, `ShowMyPanel`:

```
protected void ShowMyPanel(object sender, EventArgs e)
{
  this.MyLiteral.Text = "Time on server: " + DateTime.Now;
  this.MyPanel.Visible = true;
}
```

This code simply posts back to the server on the click of the button. But the server ends up sending back a huge chunk of HTML. This is how it looks in Firebug:

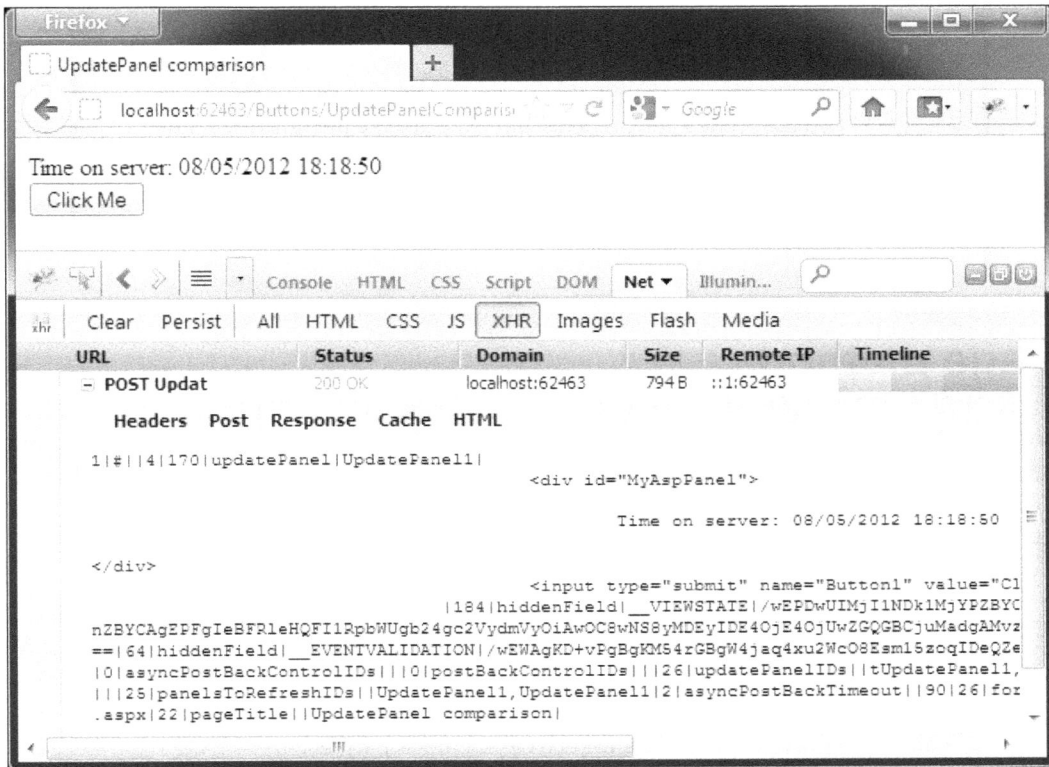

The key point here is that although this is an AJAX request, the way it is done is quite expensive: ASP.NET intercepts the normal form post and runs through the full page lifecycle of control loading and event handling. Updated HTML is sent back, and the control is re-rendered entirely, rather than just updating affected parts. But it was useful in the early days of ASP.NET to provide a clever way to *AJAXify* existing pages that used the standard control suite and full page Post Back model.

Also note as mentioned in *Chapter 1, Getting Started with Ext.NET*, Ext.NET doesn't require an ASP.NET form tag on the page. However, for the UpdatePanel example to work (or any other ASP.NET controls), the form tag is needed. When Ext.NET makes a proper AJAX request, Ext.NET request can prevent the entire form from being submitted back to the server. As a result, in addition to the already smaller response, the request to the server is also reduced in terms of size.

Although Ext.NET components will render and function when placed inside an `UpdatePanel`, `UpdatePanel` itself is not recommended, because it will often re-render HTML and associated scripts. This can lead to very unsightly screen repaints, which may affect the user experience. Ext.NET's approach to AJAX is far more efficient and lightweight. Generally speaking, `UpdatePanel` (which is increasingly outdated anyway) should not be needed if Ext.NET is being used.

Page methods

In .NET 2, ASP.NET introduced page methods — these are similar to calling normal web services from JavaScript, but are defined as methods on the web page itself. This offers a nicer, more concise way of doing what looks like a remote procedure call; like `UpdatePanel`, the AJAX request is abstracted away, but in a way that is more optimal. Take this code snippet for example:

```
public partial class Test : System.Web.UI.Page
{
  [WebMethod]
  public static string GetCurrentDate()
  {
    return DateTime.Now.ToShortDateString();
  }
}
```

This can be invoked from JavaScript, and it looks like a regular method call. The interaction with the server is taken care of for you seamlessly:

```
<script type="text/javascript">
  var GetDateFromServer = function () {
    PageMethods.GetCurrentDate(OnSuccess, OnError);
    return false;
  }

  var OnSuccess = function (response) {
    alert(response);
  }

  var OnError = function (error) {
    alert(error);
  }
</script>
```

The full response will be a **JSON** string, for example:

```
{"d":"10/04/2012 19:25:47"}
```

(The d is ASP.NET's way of putting the data in the d property.)

This is far superior to the UpdatePanel in terms of bandwidth. It also more closely reflects what AJAX is all about; calling a server resource and getting back the bare minimum data needed, which can then be handled on the client side.

> You can call page methods either directly in JavaScript, or using most modern frameworks, such as jQuery, that have AJAX capabilities. This means you can also use Ext JS's own AJAX methods to call page methods. Ext.NET provides similar approaches, such as DirectMethods, which can often be more appropriate, which we will see shortly.

Other approaches in .NET

Other approaches, such as using ASMX Web Services or using generic ASHX handlers are all very good options for hosting services that can be accessed via an AJAX request. As web-based services, they are usually operations that return data structure such as JSON or XML (it can also be HTML or other text-based formats if you want).

How this relates to Ext.NET

Broadly speaking, AJAX requests can be of two types:

- In-page AJAX requests
- Off-page AJAX requests

In-page requests involve calling some kind of AJAX-based methods on the same page from which the current page was rendered. Off-page requests call a different page, or an additional web service, on the server where you normally specify the URL and know something about the data to send and receive.

Ultimately, in-page requests are nothing more than off-page requests that happen to call the same page. More importantly, many server-side frameworks such as ASP. NET and Ext.NET, try to provide an extra layer of abstraction to make the request much easier and seamless, so that some of the details of making the round trip are taken care of for you.

Page methods is one way ASP.NET achieves this. You can still use page methods in an Ext.NET based application. However, you will then also need to include the ASP. NET ScriptManager, which will load unnecessary JavaScript and ASP.NET AJAX resources, adding bloat to the page. So instead of page methods, Ext.NET offers a far more integrated and sophisticated set of AJAX-based approaches for in-page AJAX:

- DirectEvents (event handling on the server)
- DirectMethods (calling methods on the server)

As we saw in *Chapter 2, Ext.NET Controls Overview*, there is also the MessageBus mechanism that supports ways to publish and subscribe to events via AJAX using the MessageBusDirectEvents. Off-page ASP.NET techniques are also available via DirectEvents, DirectMethods, and JavaScript. For example, you can make an AJAX request to a generic ASHX handler, to a web service, or even calling a simple ASPX page that returns the appropriate data in the required MIME type (typically application/json, text/javascript, text/html, and so on). All these approaches also expose different abilities and have their own pros and cons.

DirectEvents

Simply put, DirectEvents are server-side event handlers for events triggered on the client side. DirectEvents can be applied to Ext.NET Controls, ASP.NET controls, and even any HTML elements on the page. Off-page services can also be invoked by DirectEvents. As mentioned in *Chapter 2, Ext.NET Controls Overview*, it is important to note that for a DirectEvent to work, the Ext.NET control has to be recreated on the server first, just like you do with ASP.NET controls in a traditional ASP.NET Post Back model using the full page lifecycle. If the ASP.NET Web Forms page has a form with runat="server", then that entire form will be submitted by default.

DirectEvents on Ext.NET Controls

In *Chapter 2, Ext.NET Controls Overview*, we saw how various controls can raise events that can be handled on the client side using JavaScript event handlers. We also saw a quick example of handling events on the server side instead. We will revisit this here. Consider this snippet of Ext.NET:

```
<ext:Panel ID="MyExtPanel" runat="server" Title="My Panel"
Hidden="true">
  <Items>
    <ext:Label ID="MyExtLabel" runat="server" />
  </Items>
</ext:Panel>
<ext:Button runat="server" Text="Click Me"
            OnDirectClick="ShowPanel" />
```

The previous code renders a Panel control and a Button control. The Button's `Click` event will fire *on the server* and invoke the `ShowPanel` method, defined as follows:

```
protected void ShowPanel(object sender, DirectEventArgs e)
{
    this.MyExtLabel.Text = "Time on server: " + DateTime.Now;
    this.MyExtPanel.Show();
}
```

The response after clicking this button is as follows:

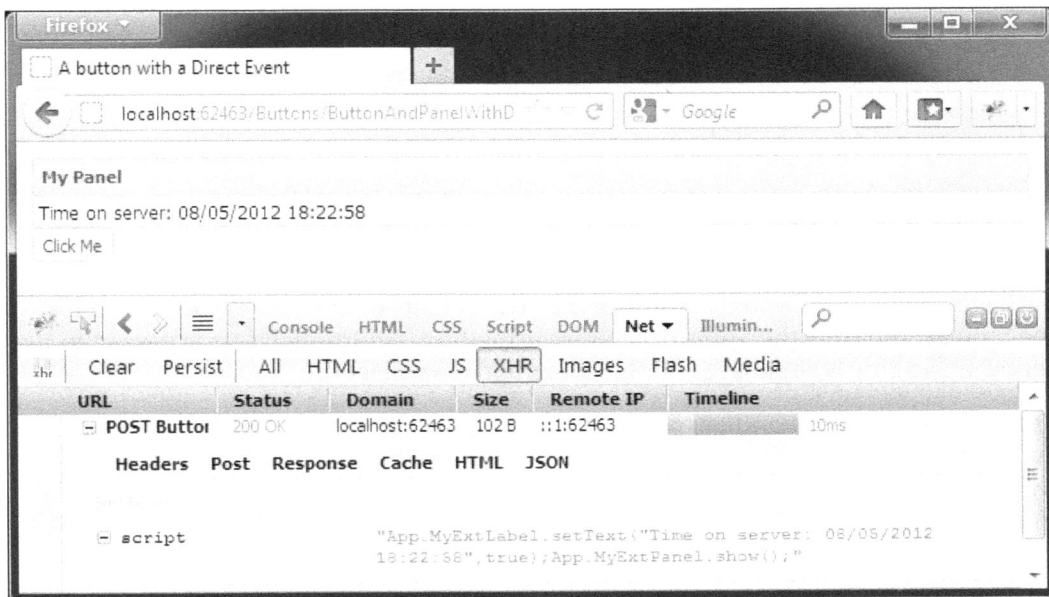

The response is a mere 102 bytes. The reason for such a low page size is because of the way we defined the markup; Ext.NET created the Panel on the initial page load, so it is already there as a JavaScript object but hidden. On the AJAX response, all that needs to be returned is the text to display and the instruction to show it. Ext.NET does this by generating the appropriate JavaScript which is sent in the response and interpreted by Ext.NET's client-side handlers for DirectEvents.

Notice that we used the `OnDirectClick` property of the Button. It is a shortcut to this:

```
<ext:Button runat="server" Text="Click Me">
  <DirectEvents>
    <Click OnEvent="ShowPanel" />
  </DirectEvents>
</ext:Button>
```

The use of the `DirectEvents` property is needed if you want to define additional configuration properties for the Click event or if you want to use other DirectEvents.

Passing additional parameters to the event

Custom parameters can also be passed to the server. In *Chapter 2, Ext.NET Controls Overview* we got a glimpse of DirectEvents. In this chapter, we will delve into the details a bit further, starting with the following example:

```
<ext:Button runat="server" Text="Click Me">
  <DirectEvents>
    <Click OnEvent="Button_Click">
      <ExtraParams>
        <ext:Parameter Name="Item" Value="My param" />
      </ExtraParams>
    </Click>
  </DirectEvents>
</ext:Button>
```

In the preceding code, we invoke the server-side method, `Button_Click`, using a DirectEvent. Ext.NET does this via its client-side extensions to Ext JS, which packages the request into the appropriate AJAX request. The server then unwraps the request and calls the appropriate server method. Additional data is passed to the server by adding a `Parameter` to the `ExtraParams` collection.

The server-side click handler method looks similar to a regular ASP.NET control event handler, except the type of the event arguments parameter is an Ext.NET `DirectEventArgs` instance:

```
protected void Button_Click(object sender, DirectEventArgs e)
{
  X.Msg.Alert("DirectEvent", string.Format("Item - {0}",
e.ExtraParams["Item"])).Show();
}
```

In this example, the handler is simply creating an alert box with the title of `DirectEvent` and a message showing the parameter that was received.

Note that the Parameter has been set using the `Name` and `Value` properties. You can further control the serialization process of the value using the `Mode` property, which an enum of type `Ext.Net.ParameterMode`. This enum supports three values:

- **Auto**: Ext.NET will detect that if your value is numeric or boolean, it will not put double quotes around the value. If your value is a DateTime, then it will convert it to a JavaScript date. Otherwise, it will put quotes around strings. This can be quite efficient for numeric, Boolean, and date values in JavaScript to prevent additional string conversions. This is the default `Mode`, if not set explicitly.

- **Raw**: This forces Ext.NET to send the value as is, without putting double quotes around the value. This can be useful, if for example, you have a string value that actually refers to another JavaScript object or method, which you do not want quotes around. For example, `<ext:Parameter Name="currentUrl" Value="window.location.href" Mode="Raw" />`.

- **Value**: This forces Ext.NET to put double quotes around the value so it is treated as a string.

For some examples of how you can dynamically add extra parameters to a DirectEvent see these Ext.NET forum thread posts:

`http://forums.ext.net/showthread.php?14903`

`http://forums.ext.net/showthread.php?12972`

Also note that we have used `DirectEventArgs`. If we don't need to access the `ExtraParams` collection, we can just use `System.EventArgs`. Also `DirectEventArgs` has other properties that can be useful. For example:

- `ExtraParamsResponse` lets you set additional data to pass back to the client (which we will see an example of in the next section).

- The `Success` property lets you set whether the handling of the event should be considered successful or not. This will help invoke the correct success or failure JavaScript handler. If `Success` is set to `false`, then no script is sent back to the client; only the `Success` indicator and the `ErrorMessage` is sent.

- `ErrorMessage` can be used when `Success` is `false` to provide a message back to the client (which could be shown to the user).

- `Name` is used by the MessageBus to indicate what events to catch.

- `Token` is also used by the MessageBus to represent the published event.

Sending custom data back to the client

In the previous example we have seen the server update the client-side Ext.NET Controls. The server can also send back additional response data, which can then be handled by custom client-side code. For example:

```
<ext:Button runat="server" Text="Click Me">
  <DirectEvents>
    <Click
     OnEvent="DoSomething" Success="onAfterServerDidSomething" />
  </DirectEvents>
</ext:Button>
```

In the previous code, we will handle the successful completion of the server event with a JavaScript method. The server-side event handler can do something like this:

```
protected void DoSomething(object sender, DirectEventArgs e)
{
  e.ExtraParamsResponse.Add(new Ext.Net.Parameter("paramName",
"response value"));
  X.Msg.Notify("Done", "Done").Show();
}
```

In the preceding code, along with issuing a notification message (which shows a little *popup toast* style notification in the bottom corner of the page), this method has also added some data to the `ExtraParamsResponse` collection of the `DirectEventArgs` event. This allows custom data to be passed back to the client side, which can access the extra response parameters as follows:

```
var onAfterServerDidSomething = function (response, result) {
  console.log(result.extraParamsResponse.paramName);
}
```

In this JavaScript snippet, the result parameter has the `extraParamsResponse` property, which will contain `paramName` as one of the properties, and its value will be what was set on the server side, in this case `response value`. In this way, an event can be handled by both client and server, if needed.

There are also many other properties for each DirectEvent, in addition to the `Success` and `ExtraParams` properties seen so far:

DirectEvent Property	Description
After	This is called immediately after the DirectEvent is fired, and before the response is returned from the server.
Before	This is called before the DirectEvent is fired.
Buffer	A time in milliseconds to delay the request to the server (so if the event is requested again, for example the button with this is clicked again within the time period, then the first event is not sent, only the last one is sent).
CleanRequest	This can be used when calling a different URL (see later) to submit the parameters related to this event only and not any other form controls.
Complete	This is called after the DirectEvent completes (successfully or with a server error), and the response is parsed on the client side.

DirectEvent Property	Description
Delay	This sets an invocation delay in milliseconds (defaults to 20).
DisableCaching	Ensures the server response is fresh and not a browser cached response (defaults to true). It does this by adding a unique cache-buster parameter to the GET request or URL in the case of a form POST.
DisableCaching Param	If DisableCaching is used, this lets you set the name of the cache-busting parameter to send. It defaults to _dc.
EventMask	To show the user a mask while loading to indicate something is happening while they wait (discussed further below).
Failure	Is called if a DirectEvent fails. This can happen if there is an unhandled server exception or if the Success property of DirectEventArgs is set to false.
FormID	The ID of the form to submit. If this.ParentForm is not null, then this.ParentForm.ClientID is used, else if FormID is empty (which is the default) then Page.Form.ClientID is used, else it will try to find an HTML form or an Ext.NET FormPanel up the hierarchy.
HtmlEvent	The HTML event type to which to attach. Used by the CustomDirectEvents property of ResourceManager. Defaults to Click.
IsUpload	true if the form object is a file upload or download (false by default). Note, for this to work, a form is required.
Json	true to format the request parameters as JSON data and set it as the HTTP POST body. Any additional parameters set in the ExtraParams will be appended to the URL. Defaults to false.
Method	The HTTP method to use. Defaults to HttpMethod.POST if ExtraParams are present, or HttpMethod.GET if not.
ShowWarning OnFailure	Shows a warning if the request fails by default. It can be set to false to turn it off. If a Failure handler exists, then this handler will be called instead of showing a warning.
Target	Is the target to which to attach this DirectEvent. The target can be an ID, an ID token (#{Button1}), or a CSS selector token using the ${div.box} syntax. It is used by the CustomDirectEvents property of ResourceManager.
Timeout	The timeout in milliseconds for the request (defaults to 30000).
Type	The type of DirectEvent to perform. The value can be either Submit or Load. Submit means it will POST the entire form. Load means the form is ignored, and only the parameters for this DirectEvent are submitted. Defaults to Submit.

DirectEvent Property	Description
Url	The default URL to be used for requests to the server. (defaults to ` `)
ViewStateMode	An enum of `Inherit`, `Enabled`, or `Disabled`. The global default behavior is to disable ViewState. ViewState may be passed back to the server if it is part of a submitted form, but will be returned.

Event masks

It is also possible to add an event mask—an interstitial that masks the page with a loading indicator—so the user knows something is happening (as the server might take some time to respond). This is useful from a usability perspective. Consider the following example:

```
<ext:Button runat="server" Text="Click Me">
    <DirectEvents>
        <Click OnEvent="Button_Click">
            <EventMask ShowMask="true" />
        </Click>
    </DirectEvents>
</ext:Button>
```

This code would produce a mask that says **Loading...** by default, and covers the whole page which a semi-transparent mask:

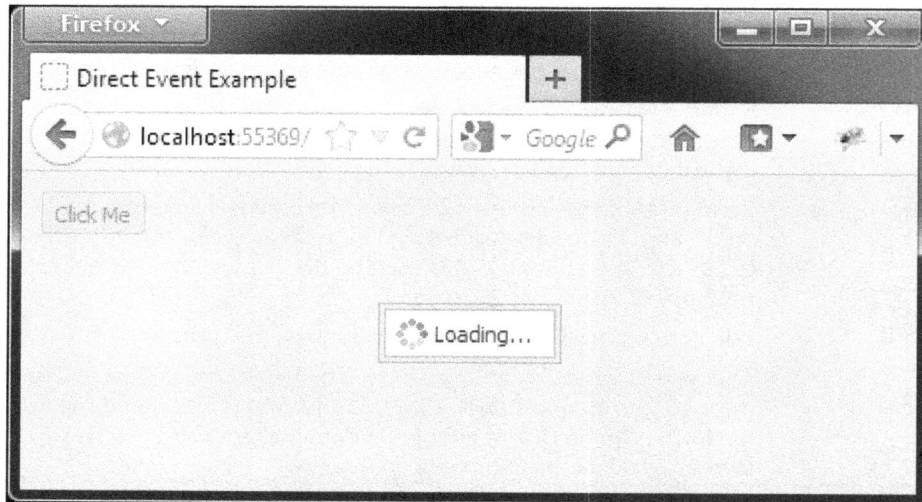

You can control where the mask appears. By default, as above it is the entire page, but as the next example shows, it covers just the `Window`:

```
<ext:Window ID="Window1" runat="server" Title="Window with Button"
Width="200" Height="150">
    <Buttons>
        <ext:Button runat="server" Text="Click Me">
            <DirectEvents>
                <Click OnEvent="ShowPanel">
                    <EventMask
                        ShowMask="true"
                        Target="CustomTarget"
                        CustomTarget="Window1"
                        />
                </Click>
            </DirectEvents>
        </ext:Button>
    </Buttons>
</ext:Window>
```

By setting `Target` to `CustomTarget`, the `CustomTarget` property can then be set to `ID` of a client-side object, in this case `Window1`. This will put the loading mask only on the Window:

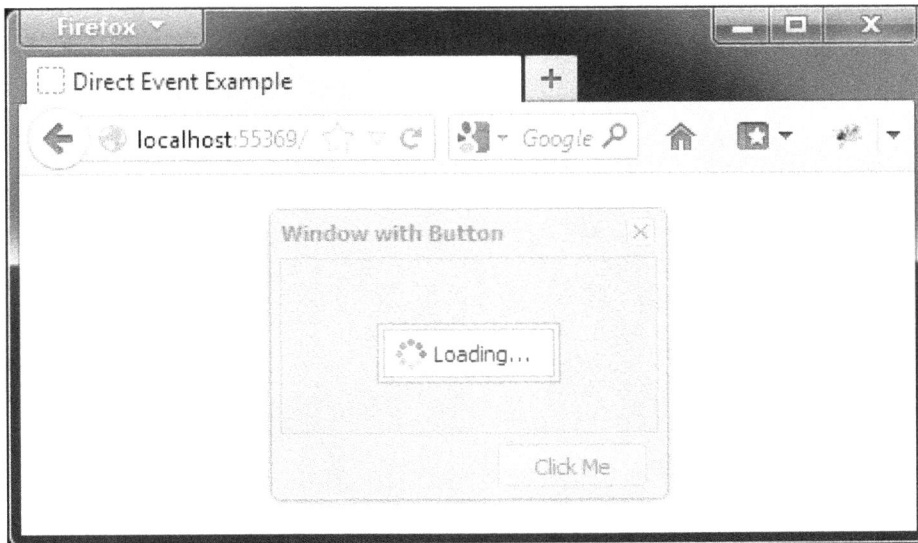

Notice how the **Click Me** button that initiated this is also masked. As the custom target can be any DOM element or JavaScript object, we can target the body property of the Ext.NET Window object on the client side, which represents the main content area:

```
<ext:Window ID="Window1" runat="server" Title="Window with Button"
Width="200" Height="150">
    <Buttons>
        <ext:Button runat="server" Text="Click Me">
            <DirectEvents>
                <Click OnEvent="ShowPanel">
                    <EventMask
                        ShowMask="true"
                        Target="CustomTarget"
                        CustomTarget="App.Window1.body"
                        />
                </Click>
            </DirectEvents>
        </ext:Button>
    </Buttons>
</ext:Window>
```

This time the mask is almost as before, but just covers the Window body, so the **Click Me** button is not masked:

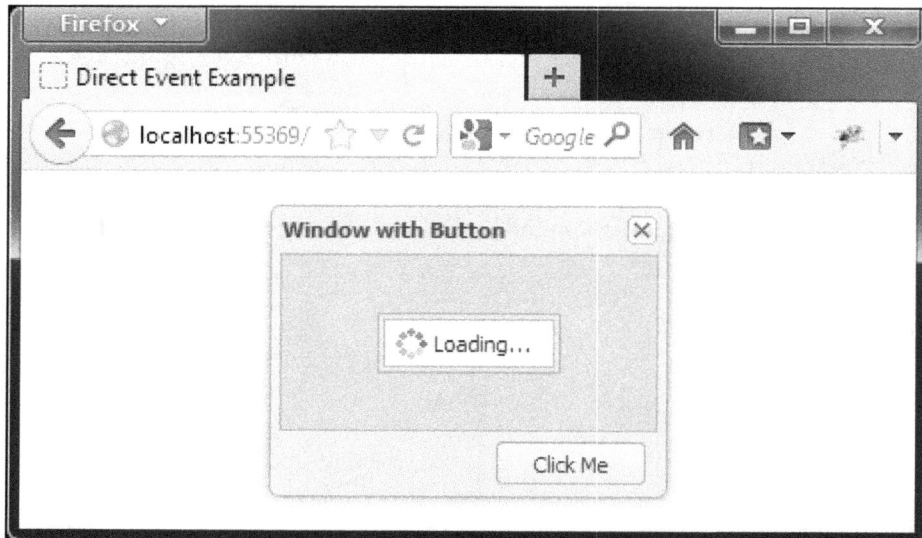

You can also make the target any HTML element. In this next example, the CustomTarget property has been set to custom-div, which is the ID of a div that has been styled to look like a big box. Note the mask only covers that div:

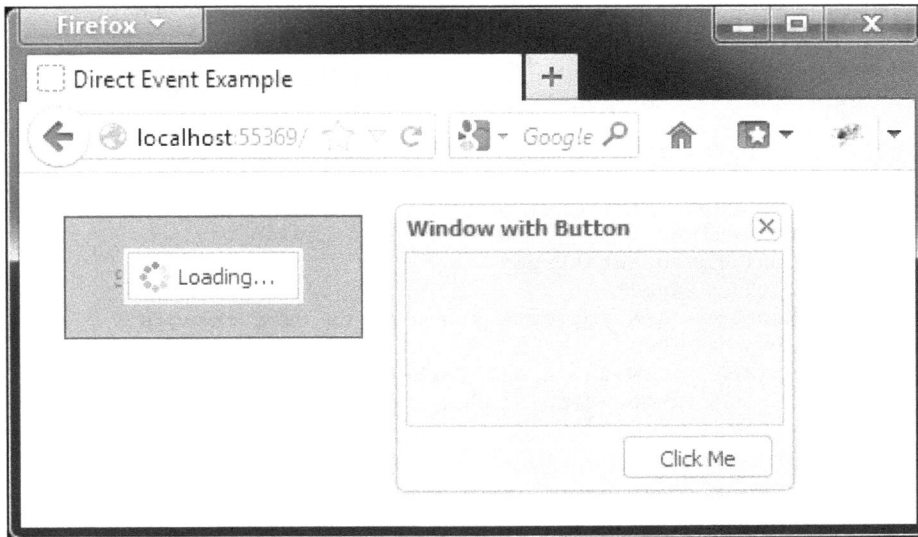

The App client-side namespace

Notice an earlier example used `App.Window1.body` instead of `Window1` as the `CustomTarget`. `App` is a JavaScript object created by Ext.NET to act as a namespace or a container for Ext.NET generated controls. Because our Window was given the ID of `Window1`, it will be found as `App.Window1` on the client.

Ext.NET parses the `CustomTarget` value to determine which object is being used. So `Window1` from the earlier example will be found. Using `App.Window1.body` as the value of `CustomTarget` means there is less parsing of the value to do as one of the early tests checks if the value is an object that exists and if so, to use it. By comparison, it can take longer to determine what the string `Window1` is.

Note, we could have also used `#{Window1}.body` as an alternative to `App.Window1.body`. As explained in *Chapter 2, Ext.NET Controls Overview*, the `#{}` syntax is special to Ext.NET and will convert it into the correct client-side `id` for you.

By default, if the `ID` property is not set on an Ext.NET Control, an instance is not added to the client-side `App` namespace. In general, it's considered good practice to not set the `ID` property of Ext.NET Controls unless they are explicitly required for your application. The `ID` property can be safely removed in many scenarios.

The client-side rendering of `ID` values can be further refined by configuring the `IDMode` property. The `IDMode` property can be set globally within the `Web.config`, or `Global.asax` files, at the page level using the ResourceManager, or at the individual component level, such as on a Viewport.

Event confirmation

You can also pop up a confirmation dialog to get confirmation from the user before performing the task. For example:

```
<ext:Button ID="Button1" runat="server" Text="Click Me" Icon="Disk">
  <DirectEvents>
    <Click OnEvent="ShowPanel">
      <Confirmation
          ConfirmRequest="true"
          Title="Save?"
          Message="Are you sure you want to save changes?"
          />
      <EventMask ShowMask="true" Target="CustomTarget"
          CustomTarget="App.Window1.body" />
    </Click>
  </DirectEvents>
</ext:Button>
```

In this code, a confirmation is added, which will show before the event is submitted to the server (and before the event mask appears):

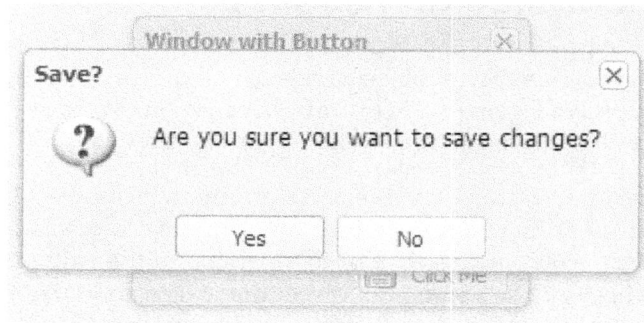

> You can optionally also use the BeforeConfirm property inside Confirmation. This is a function handler. In here, you can invoke JavaScript, which could return true or false as to whether or not you want the confirmation message to show first. Note, returning false does not cancel the entire DirectEvent request; it just determines whether to show the confirmation dialog first, or not. There is also the Cancel property, which is another function handler that will be invoked if you press **No** inside the Confirmation dialog. These are both optional. Inside BeforeConfirm, you can set the message to appear, allowing you to construct a message dynamically. For example, BeforeConfirm="config.confirmation.message = 'Message';".

DirectEvents on ASP.NET Controls

DirectEvents can also be applied to ASP.NET controls. This is achieved by using the `CustomDirectEvents` collection of the `ResourceManager` to add items to watch:

```
<ext:ResourceManager runat="server">
  <CustomDirectEvents>
    <ext:DirectEvent Target="Btn1" OnEvent="MyServerMethod">
      <EventMask ShowMask="true" />
    </ext:DirectEvent>
  </CustomDirectEvents>
</ext:ResourceManager>

<form runat="server">
  <asp:Button ID="Btn1" runat="server" Text="Click Me" />
</form>
```

In the above example, the Ext.NET `ResourceManager` has a `DirectEvent` added to it, with the `Target` set to the ID of the ASP.NET Button control's ID. We've also added an event mask. Although we have used a class ASP.NET control, we do not need to include the ASP.NET ScriptManager for this; it is all handled by Ext.NET for you.

Note, in addition, Ext.NET has provided a very useful extension method to the classic ASP.NET Controls, named `Update`. This will let you update those controls during a DirectEvent. For example, if we have the following ASP.NET Panel on our page:

```
<asp:Panel ID="Panel1" runat="server">
  <p>Some initial content</p>
</asp:Panel>
```

And if we invoke a DirectEvent with this Ext.NET Button:

```
<ext:Button runat="server" Text="Click Me"
            OnDirectClick="CreatePanel" />
```

Notice also the use of the shorthand `OnDirectClick`. We can now update the ASP.NET Panel in our DirectEvent, for example:

```
protected void CreatePanel(object sender, DirectEventArgs e)
{
  var literal = new Literal { Text = "<p>From server</p>" };
  Panel1.Controls.Clear();
  Panel1.Controls.Add(literal);
  Panel1.Update();
}
```

Note that you could leave out the `Panel1.Controls.Clear()` line if you want to append content to the Panel rather than replacing it.

DirectEvents on HTML Elements

Although the previous example showed an ASP.NET Button control being used, unless you are migrating a legacy application from ASP.NET controls to Ext.NET, normally for usability and design consistency, the advice would be to replace an `<asp:Button>` with an `<ext:Button>` button.

But the principle is what is of importance here; using the same syntax and techniques, you can target any HTML element on the page with a DirectEvent. We can extend the above example to add more `DirectEvents` to the `CustomDirectEvents` collection:

```
<ext:ResourceManager runat="server">
  <CustomDirectEvents>
    <ext:DirectEvent Target="Btn1" OnEvent="MyServerMethod">
      <EventMask ShowMask="true" />
    </ext:DirectEvent>
    <ext:DirectEvent Target="MyDiv" OnEvent="MyServerMethod"/>
    <ext:DirectEvent Target="${.box}" OnEvent="MyServerMethod2" />
  </CustomDirectEvents>
</ext:ResourceManager>
```

This code shows that `Target` can be a custom CSS selector to find HTML elements through means other than just their IDs (in this case using `.box` surrounding by `${ }`).

Also note that DirectEvent has a property called `HtmlEvent`. This lets you set the name of an HTML-based event handle (rather than the default `Click` event) to invoke the DirectEvent. For example, you could set `HtmlEvent` to the value `MouseOver`, and if the HTML element corresponding to the `Target` is hovered over, the DirectEvent will fire at that point, instead of when that HTML element is clicked. The `OnEvent` shows that different `DirectEvents` can be handled by different methods if needed.

DirectEvents dynamically generating new Ext. NET Components

In the earlier example, we saw that during a DirectEvent an Ext.NET Panel that had already been rendered was updated. But you can create completely new components too. For example, consider this code:

```
<ext:Button runat="server" Text="Click Me" OnDirectClick="ShowTime" />
```

When this Button is pressed, the following DirectEvent code will run on the server.

```
protected void ShowTime(object sender, DirectEventArgs e)
{
  new Window("Server time", Icon.Time)
  {
    ID   = "MyWindow",
    Html = DateTime.Now.ToString()
  }.Render();
}
```

It will produce a new Window that will render to the screen, showing the server time. This is very powerful and flexible, because by creating parts of the UI screen on demand, your initial page can load much more quickly. Note also, if you want to render a new control inside an existing Ext.NET Container, you can do that, too. For example, suppose we have the following Ext.NET Container somewhere on the page:

```
<ext:Container ID="Container1" runat="server" />
```

And if we had a Button with a DirectEvent pointing to a method called `ShowPanel`, we could implement that as follows:

```
protected void CreatePanel(object sender, DirectEventArgs e)
{
  var panel = new Ext.Net.Panel
  {
    Title = "Created during DirectEvent",
    Html  = DateTime.Now.ToString()
  };
  panel.AddTo(this.Container1);
}
```

Using the Panel's `AddTo` method, we can add this newly generated Panel into an existing Container. This can get more advanced. For example, instead of a Container, suppose you have a TabPanel (which will be covered in more detail in a later chapter). You could have some tabs that are already loaded when the page has been loaded, but other tabs could be generated on demand. For example, consider this TabPanel with just one tab:

```
<ext:TabPanel ID="TabPanel1" runat="server" Height="100">
  <Items>
    <ext:Panel Title="Created on page load" Html="Content"/>
  </Items>
</ext:TabPanel>
```

Now if we have a DirectEvent that wants to add a brand new tab, generated on demand, we can have a DirectEvent handler like this:

```
protected void CreateTab(object sender, DirectEventArgs e)
{
    var panel = new Ext.Net.Panel
    {
        Title = "Created during DirectEvent",
        Html = DateTime.Now.ToString()
    };
    panel.AddTo(this.TabPanel1);
    this.TabPanel1.SetActiveTab(panel);
}
```

This is very much the same code as the preceding example, except we have used the TabPanel's SetActiveTab method to also switch to the newly added tab. Ext.NET generates all the relevant JavaScript for these actions, even though they are occurring on the server. TabPanel will be covered in more detail in *Chapter 8, Trees and Tabs with Ext.NET* but the key point is that this technique gives a hint at the possibilities of very dynamic applications. It is also possible to generate Ext.NET Controls like this when DirectEvents invoke off-page resources, which we look at next.

DirectEvents invoking web services

DirectEvents are extremely powerful, as we have just seen. The examples up to this point have been in-page AJAX requests, relying on the presence of various Ext.NET Controls that first created the page, so that the event handlers on the server can update them.

But you can also make DirectEvents be sent to another URL on the same server. For example, you can invoke and reuse your own web services.

Consider the following WebMethod which simply returns the current server time:

```
[WebService(Namespace = "http://tempuri.org/")]
[WebServiceBinding(ConformsTo = WsiProfiles.BasicProfile1_1)]
public class ServerTimeService : WebService
{
    [WebMethod]
    public DirectResponse GetServerTime()
    {
        X.Js.Alert("Server time is " + DateTime.Now);

        return new DirectResponse();
    }
}
```

This service will return a `DirectResponse` instance so that Ext.NET's client-side proxy can easily work with it.

> Notice the use of `X.Js`. This is a very useful property on the Ext.NET `X` class, which also has the more general purpose `AddScript` method to add any JavaScript code as part of the overall response. In addition, there is the `Call` method which lets you call specific JavaScript functions with parameters if needed. When scripts are set this way, they are returned as part of the response using `DirectResponse` (as shown previously), or using `this.Direct()` in MVC Controllers, of which we will see an example shortly.

Here is how the WebMethod might be invoked:

```
<ext:Button runat="server" Text="Get Server Time">
  <DirectEvents>
    <Click
      Url="ServerTimeService.asmx/GetServerTime"
      Type="Load"
      Method="POST"
      />
  </DirectEvents>
</ext:Button>
```

This example shows the DirectEvent click handler `URL` property explicitly set to the URL of the ASMX Web Service. In addition, the `Type` of this event request is set to `Load`, which means the DirectEvent will not submit any form data, only ExtraParams if defined. If the `Type` is set to `Submit`, it would submit the HTML form instead, which would result in a lot more data being posted back. To use the `Method` of `GET`, ensure the `HttpGet` protocol is enabled as explained by MSDN: `http://msdn.microsoft.com/en-us/library/b2c0ew36%28v=vs.100%29.aspx`.

The result of clicking this Button is simply a browser alert prompt as per the ASMX Web Service response above.

DirectEvents invoking web services with parameters

Putting an alert statement into the web service itself may not be very maintainable. So instead, we can have the ASMX service return the data and let the client alert it to the browser. We can demonstrate that by adding another WebMethod (which will also take a parameter):

```
[WebMethod]
public DirectResponse GetRelativeServerTime(int hours)
{
    return new DirectResponse
    {
        ExtraParamsResponse = JSON.Serialize(new
        {
            relativeTime = DateTime.Now.AddHours(hours)
        })
    };
}
```

In the preceding code, we return additional parameters with the response. They can then be used by having the button invoke a JavaScript handler when the DirectEvent finishes:

```
<ext:Button runat="server" Text="Get server time 5 hours from now">
  <DirectEvents>
    <Click
        Success="showServerResponse(result);"
        Url="ServerTimeService.asmx/GetRelativeServerTime"
        Type="Load"
        Method="POST">
        <ExtraParams>
          <ext:Parameter Name="hours" Value="5" />
        </ExtraParams>
    </Click>
  </DirectEvents>
</ext:Button>
```

In the previous example, we pass parameters to the web service using the ExtraParams collection. In addition, to deal with the response, we use a Success property to specify the JavaScript to run after the DirectEvent has succeeded. When the previous code runs, the following JavaScript will be executed:

```
var showServerResponse = function (result) {
  var params = result.extraParamsResponse || {};
```

```
    if (params.relativeTime) {
        alert(params.relativeTime);
    }
};
```

When the Ext.NET client-side proxy has received the response, it converts it to the appropriate JavaScript representation and passes it to the success handler, in this case as the `result` parameter. The `extraParamsResponse` represents the parameters added by the server, and the `relativeTime` parameter contains the value added by the web service.

DirectEvents invoking web services that return new Ext.NET components

In both the previous examples, very simple data is returned (the server time or a server time with some hours added to it). Although they demonstrate some different abilities of DirectEvent requests, we can also create new Ext.NET components on-demand, as we saw with the in-page DirectEvent handlers, earlier. This powerful capability comes from realizing that ultimately the response has a script or additional parameters in it. We can use this to our advantage to create far more complex scripts on demand.

Consider this next example using a WebMethod:

```
[WebService(Namespace = "http://tempuri.org/")]
[WebServiceBinding(ConformsTo = WsiProfiles.BasicProfile1_1)]
public class ServerTimeService : WebService
{
  [WebMethod]
  public DirectResponse GetServerTimeWindow()
  {
    new Window("Server time", Icon.Time)
    {
        ID = "MyWindow",
        Html = DateTime.Now.ToString()
    }.Render();

    return new DirectResponse();
  }
}
```

The previous example is generating and returning an entire Ext.NET control during the web service request. An Ext.NET `Window` is being created, with the title set to **Server time**, along with an icon next to it. The `Html` property is set to display the current server time. Finally, we call the `Render` method on the Window. This means that when the final step to return a `DirectResponse` instance is called, any JavaScript needed for creating the Window will be returned to the client.

> **What ID to assign to components generated on the fly?**
>
> If you use a fixed ID as per the previous example, and if you invoke the DirectEvent again, the previous window will be replaced by this new one. If that is not your intent, then you can omit the ID entirely (Ext.NET will autogenerate a unique one each time). Alternatively, if you require an ID, but you also want a new window, you should create your own unique ID. There are many ways to do this. For example, you could use a GUID. Other options (which will also help in creating an easier to read and debug identifier compared to a GUID), include using .NET's built-in `Interlocked.Increment()` method or Ext.NET's `BaseControl.GenerateID()` method.

You can use these techniques in other web service options, for example ASHX generic handlers and MVC Controllers. You can also create controls in this way using DirectMethods, which we will cover shortly.

DirectEvents invoking generic ASHX handlers

Here we have the previously mentioned service implemented using an ASHX handler:

```
<ext:Button runat="server" Text="Get Server Time">
  <DirectEvents>
    <Click
        Url="ServerTimeHandler.ashx"
        Type="Load"
        Method="POST"
        />
  </DirectEvents>
</ext:Button>
```

The corresponding ASHX handler would now look like this:

```
public class ServerTimeHandler : IHttpHandler
{
    public void ProcessRequest(HttpContext context)
    {
        new Window("Server time", Icon.Time)
```

```
        {
            ID = "MyWindow",
            Html = DateTime.Now.ToString()
        }.Render();

        new DirectResponse().Return();
    }

    public bool IsReusable
    {
        get { return false; }
    }
}
```

Apart from the differences between writing an ASHX generic handler and an ASMX Web Service, the core code is almost identical to the earlier ASMX service. The subtle difference here is that the `DirectResponse` instance's `Return()` method is explicitly invoked, so it can set correct server response headers.

DirectEvents invoking ASP.NET MVC Controllers

Here is an example of a Controller configured to generate a Window control similar to the earlier examples:

```
public class ServerTimeController : Controller
{
    //
    // GET: /ServerTime/
    public ActionResult Index()
    {
        return View();
    }

    //
    // GET: /ServerTime/GetTime
    public ActionResult GetTime()
    {
        new Window("Server time", Icon.Time)
        {
            ID = "MyWindow",
            Html = string.Format("Server time is {0}", DateTime.Now)
        }.Render();

        return this.Direct();
    }
}
```

This Controller has two actions – `Index` and `GetTime`. Index will just show a page with a button. `GetTime` is the second action. It will be invoked when that button is clicked. It will create a Window, as earlier examples did. However, note the way it returns is by calling `this.Direct()` (an extension method of .NET's Controller). Like DirectResponse, this will ensure the response is generated correctly. The View for the first action is this Razor template:

```
<!DOCTYPE html>
<html>
<head>
  <title>Get Server Time</title>
</head>
  <body>
    @Html.X().ResourceManager()

    @(Html.X().Button()
        .Text("Get Server Time")
        .DirectClickAction("GetTime")
    )
  </body>
</html>
```

Note, there is a longer form alternative to `DirectClickAction` used in the previous code which would also be used if you need to set other properties:

```
.DirectEvents(directEvents => directEvents.Click.Url = Url.
Action("GetTime")
```

In addition, because a View and Controller are not coupled together, we can invoke the Controller from an ASP.NET Web Forms page too:

```
<%@ Page Language="C#" %>
<!DOCTYPE html>
<html>
  <head>
    <title>Get Server Time</title>
  </head>
  <body>
    <ext:ResourceManager runat="server" />

    <ext:Button runat="server" Text="Get Server Time">
      <DirectEvents>
        <Click Url="/ServerTime/GetTime" />
      </DirectEvents>
    </ext:Button>
  </body>
</html>
```

The behavior will be the same as calling the ASMX Web Services.

Best server option? ASMX, ASHX, MVC, ASPX, WCF?

Given the variety of ways we can call the server, is there a recommended best practice for what type of server page to use when calling off-page AJAX resources? There's no clear-cut answer; each option has its pros and cons.

For example, ASHX responses are in JSON format, whereas the ASMX responses, by default, are in XML which generally involves a larger HTTP response size. While the ASMX response can also be made into JSON, the response is slightly different to, and larger than, the generic ASHX handler approach.

An ASP.NET MVC Controller will also be JSON, and its response will be identical to an ASHX equivalent. In a way, an MVC Controller looks more like REST whereas ASMX looks more like a Remote Procedure Call (though MVC actions can also be made to look like RPC, too). MVC Controllers have better facilities for unit testing more easily.

You can even use an ASPX Web Forms page and set its response type to be JSON, but this will likely be the most expensive option because the full page lifecycle gets invoked.

Although not shown here, a WCF service can also be an option. However, both ASMX and WCF may have some JSON serialization issues, as discussed later in this chapter.

An ASHX handler by-passes much of the web page or web service lifecycle that ASMX, ASPX, MVC Controllers, and so on will require, thus reducing server overhead and therefore may be the most optimal for performance. However, you may lose some of the conveniences that an MVC Controller or web service can offer which may affect maintainability, so the trade-offs between the two should be carefully considered for a given situation. You could certainly refactor code inside an ASHX handler for easier unit testing, and common boiler plate code could certainly be factored into a handler class hierarchy to reduce repeated code in different handlers. Lastly, there is nothing stopping you from using different options for different purposes, of course.

DirectMethods

As we have seen, DirectEvents are very powerful; they are attached to an Ext.NET control and called when that event fires and invokes a server method. As powerful as they are, you may want to call a server method at your own choosing, directly from within your own JavaScript function—similar to invoking ASP.NET's own page methods. As we noted earlier, DirectEvents require the control to be recreated on the server as part of the page lifecycle. A DirectMethod, however, doesn't require a control instance on the server (unless it is defined inside a user control). Furthermore, if you use a static DirectMethod, it won't even require the full page lifecycle. Otherwise, most things possible with DirectEvents are possible with DirectMethods. Here are a few examples.

Basic DirectMethod

On the server side, a DirectMethod looks very similar to an ASP.NET page method. Consider the following example:

```
[DirectMethod]
public void AddToServerTime(int hours)
{
    var date = DateTime.Now.Add(new TimeSpan(hours, 0, 0));
    this.Label1.Text = date.ToString();
}
```

The `DirectMethod` attribute tells Ext.NET to create a client-side proxy for it so that it can be called from JavaScript. The method itself is updating a control during the AJAX request. When the method finishes, all the operations applied to the Ext.NET Controls are converted into their corresponding JavaScript and sent as the response, which is then executed on the browser.

> Unlike ASP.NET page methods, DirectMethods do not have to be static. Static DirectMethods do give the best performance, as the full page lifecycle is not executed, but it also means you cannot access controls.

So how are these methods invoked? Because Ext.NET makes the DirectMethod available on the client side via a proxy (that enabled an RPC-style method call), you simply invoke the proxy. For example, consider this button:

```
<ext:Button runat="server" Text="Update" Icon="ArrowRefresh">
  <Listeners>
    <Click Handler="doUpdate(5);" />
  </Listeners>
</ext:Button>
```

This Button has a client-side listener for the client-side `Click` event, which will be handled by a JavaScript function, doUpdate, defined as the following:

```
var doUpdate = function (hours) {
    App.direct.AddToServerTime(hours);
};
```

The JavaScript function calls AddToServerTime with the parameter 5. The AddToServerTime it is calling is the proxy method that Ext.NET has generated, and it is this proxy method that will internally make the AJAX request to the actual DirectMethod on the server.

You can also change the JavaScript namespace for DirectMethods. On the JavaScript side, DirectMethod proxies are added to the App.direct namespace by default. You can change the namespace in a few ways.

If you want to change it site-wide, you can add the directMethodNamespace property to the `<extnet>` configuration in `Web.config`, for example:

```
<extent directMethodNamespace="MyApp.DirectMethods" />
```

Alternatively, you can set it on the ResouceManager for the page, for example:

```
<ext:ResourceManager runat="server" DirectMethodNamespace="MyApp.
DirectMethods" />
```

Or you can use the Namespace property on the DirectMethod attribute of a DirectMethod, for example:

```
[DirectMethod(Namespace="MyApp.DirectMethods")]
```

Then the JavaScript call to the above method would be:

```
MyApp.DirectMethods.AddToServerTime(5);
```

The preceding snippets can be shown all together in this fully self-contained sample:

```
<%@ Page Language="C#" %>
<script runat="server">
[DirectMethod]
public void AddToServerTime(int hours)
{
  var date = DateTime.Now.Add(new TimeSpan(0, hours, 0));
  this.Label1.Text = date.ToString();
}
</script>
<!DOCTYPE html>
<html>
  <head runat="server">
    <title>DirectMethod Example</title>
```

```
    <script>
      var doUpdate = function (hours) {
        App.direct.AddToServerTime(hours);
      };
    </script>
  </head>
  <body>
    <ext:ResourceManager runat="server" />
    <ext:Window runat="server" Title="My Window" Width="250"
                Height="150">
      <Items>
       <ext:Label ID="Label1" runat="server" Text="Initial text"/>
      </Items>
      <TopBar>
        <ext:Toolbar>
          <Items>
            <ext:Button Text="Update" Icon="ArrowRefresh">
              <Listeners>
                <Click Handler="doUpdate(5);" />
              </Listeners>
            </ext:Button>
          </Items>
        </ext:Toolbar>
      </TopBar>
    </ext:Window>
  </body>
</html>
```

As you can see, a client-side DirectMethod is simply a JavaScript function that acts as a proxy for its server-side counterpart. Being a regular JavaScript function, it can be invoked directly on the client side. This also means you can run custom code before or after the method is invoked. But because of the asynchronous nature of the DirectMethod, care must be taken when running code after a DirectMethod is invoked, which we turn to next.

Running JavaScript after the DirectMethod is invoked

What does it mean to invoke code after the method is invoked? Suppose we have a couple of console.log lines in our JavaScript:

```
var doUpdate = function (hours)  {
    console.log("Before");
    App.direct.DirectMethods.AddToServerTime();
    console.log("After");
};
```

You might expect `After` to be logged after the server event has been invoked and updated the label. But instead it will appear after the server event is invoked, but *before* the label is updated. The reason is the server method is an AJAX call, which is *asynchronous* by default. So although the console will show **After** after the server method is invoked, it will write to the console *before* the server method has *completed*.

To invoke code that runs after the server method has *completed*, you have to use the appropriate callback. Ext.NET lets you supply one via a DirectMethod configuration object, which is an optional last parameter to the JavaScript DirectMethod proxy.

Here is an example of that by modifying the call to the DirectMethod:

```
var doUpdate = function () {
    console.log("Before");
    App.direct.AddToServerTime(5, {
        success: onSuccess,
        failure: onFailure,
        eventMask: { showMask: true }
    });
    console.log("After");
}
```

Notice the last parameter to `AddToServerTime()` is a JavaScript object literal with three properties:

- A success handler to call if the method returns successfully
- A failure callback and
- An event mask (with options similar to those seen with DirectEvents)

And here are the callbacks:

```
var onSuccess = function (result) {
    console.log("onSuccess", result);
}

var onFailure  = function (errorMessage) {
    Ext.Msg.alert('Failed', errorMessage);
}
```

The `onSuccess` handler is your opportunity to run custom code after the server has returned. In this case, it is simply logging the result to the console. The result parameter is the result of the method call (in this case a string, matching the return type defined in the DirectMethod). The failure handler receives an error message string, which in this case is output via an Ext JS alert box.

Putting that altogether, here is the Firebug console output showing the order in which things are logged:

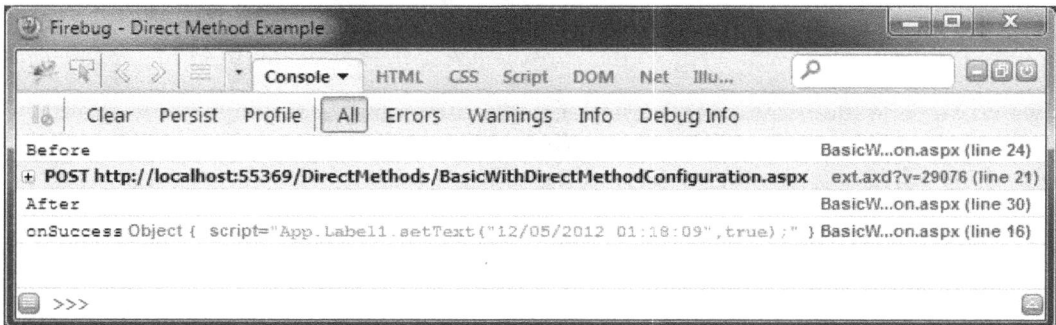

Notice, how **After** is logged after the server method is invoked, but before the server has responded and invoked the success handler.

If you want to force your DirectMethod call to be synchronous instead (which would not normally be recommended!), you can set the Async property (true by default) to false in the DirectMethod Attribute. For example:

```
[DirectMethod(Async=false)]
public static void MyMethod()
{
}
```

Static DirectMethods for best performance

In the earlier examples, DirectMethod updated Label1 directly. This can be immensely powerful and flexible because you can call many other Ext.NET methods on client components during a server AJAX method. However, it comes at a cost; the client has to send various control states back to the server, and the server must also go through the full page lifecycle and recreate various controls again in order to update them.

In cases where very simple operations are being performed, or just raw data needs returning, then static DirectMethods would be preferable. With the previous example, we would modify the DirectMethod as follows:

```
[DirectMethod]
public static string AddToServerTime(int hours)
{
    return DateTime.Now.Add(new TimeSpan(hours, 0,
                                        0)).ToString();
}
```

Two important things to note in the preceding code: the `static` declaration and the return of the raw data, rather than setting the Label from the server.

This means the client will need to handle raw data as follows:

```
var onSuccess = function (result) {
    App.Label1.setText(result);
}
```

Handling raw data like this can also mean the effort of the server is reduced. Of course, in each case there is a balance to consider between client and server performance, developer convenience, and maintainability.

Returning custom types

The previous example showed `DirectMethod` returning a basic type, a string. But we can return custom objects too—Ext.NET will serialize it to JSON for you.

Consider this server-side class:

```
public class GroceryItem
{
    public string Name { get; set; }
    public double WeightKgs { get; set; }
}
```

And a `DirectMethod` that returns a List of these objects:

```
[DirectMethod]
public static List<GroceryItem> GetItems()
{
    return new List<GroceryItem>
    {
        new GroceryItem { Name = "Apples", WeightKgs = 1.5 },
        new GroceryItem { Name = "Pears", WeightKgs = 0.5 },
    };
}
```

If this method is now invoked from the client, the .NET `List<GroceryItem>` will be serialized into its JSON equivalent—an array of JSON objects. We can update our earlier Button handler like this:

```
<ext:Button runat="server" Text="Update" Icon="ArrowRefresh">
    <Listeners>
        <Click Fn="getItems" />
    </Listeners>
</ext:Button>
```

And `getItems` might be defined like this:

```
var getItems = function () {
    App.direct.GetItems({
        Success: onSuccess,
        eventMask: { showMask: true }
    });
}

var onSuccess = function (items) {
    var buffer = [Ext.String.format("<p>Got {0} items:</p><ul>",
items.length)],
        window = Ext.getCmp('Window1');

    Ext.each(items, function (item) {
        buffer.push(Ext.String.format("<li>{0} kilos of {1}</li>",
item.WeightKgs, item.Name));
    });

    buffer.push("</ul>");

    window.removeAll();
    window.update(buffer.join(""));
}
```

In the preceding code, the success handler's items parameter is now an array. If we inspect the JSON that is returned from the server, it looks like this:

```
{
    result: [{
        "Name": "Apples",
        "WeightKgs": 1.5
    }, {
        "Name": "Pears",
        "WeightKgs": 0.5
    }]
}
```

Ext.NET's DirectMethod simply passes the `result` property to the success handler. The success handler loops through each item in the array (using the `Ext.each` function) and lists the items returned, resulting in a window that looks like this:

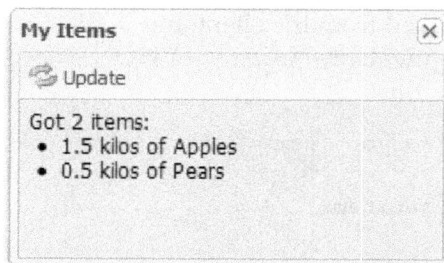

> The previous example created HTML in a rather crude way, just to demonstrate and focus on the DirectMethod instead. Far more maintainable, elegant and powerful techniques to generate HTML, such as using XTemplates, will be shown in *Chapter 5, Working with Data*, when we start to look at data.

Handling exceptions

When discussing DirectEvents, we briefly saw that you can handle `success`, `failure`, and `complete` events, and we touched upon how the DirectEvent can send a response. We will look at this further with DirectMethods.

In .NET, a typical best practice pattern in exception handling is to only have catch blocks if you can actually handle the exception. Otherwise, you let the exception bubble up to the next layer, and so on until you hit the boundary of your service or application. At that boundary level you typically want to catch unhandled exceptions, so you have a chance to handle it and inform the user or code that invokes this service in a more graceful way.

In a way, a DirectMethod is at the boundary layer of your server; it is the entry point for your JavaScript method call. So how do you handle exceptions and inform the user? The browser is not .NET, and what would happen if an unhandled exception went through?

Consider this contrived example that will cause a divide-by-zero exception:

```
<%@ Page Language="C#" %>
<script runat="server">
  [DirectMethod]
  public static int Divide(int number1, int number2)
  {
    return number1 / number2;
  }
</script>
<!DOCTYPE html>
<html>
  <head runat="server">
    <title>DirectMethod Example</title>

      <script>
        var doDivision = function () {
          App.direct.Divide(5, 0);
        };
      </script>
  </head>
```

```
<body>
  <ext:ResourceManager runat="server" />
  <ext:Button runat="server" Text="Do Divide">
    <Listeners>
      <Click Fn="doDivision" />
    </Listeners>
  </ext:Button>
</body>
</html>
```

If we click this Button we, of course, get a divide-by-zero error. If we do not handle it, we get Ext.NET's default request failure handler that shows detailed stack trace information. This is great for debugging. When running in Release mode, you won't get a stack trace, but it will still have the general purpose request failure window, and you may not want your users to see that.

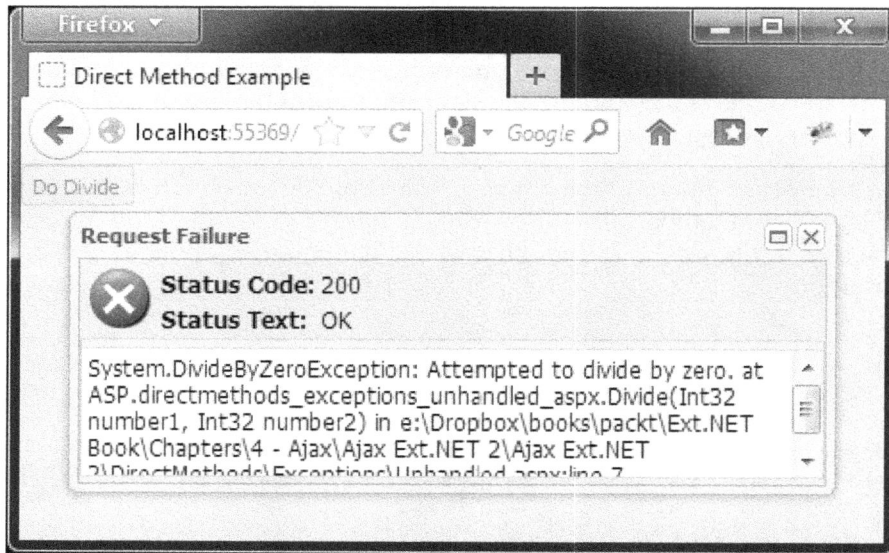

One way to deal with this is to use the `failure` callback on the DirectMethod configuration object. So to do that we could define our Button handler like this:
var doDivision = function () {

```
    App.direct.Divide(5, 0, {
        failure: directMethodFailed
    });
};

var directMethodFailed = function (msg) {
    Ext.Msg.alert('Failed', msg);
};
```

In this code, a DirectMethod configuration is passed as the last parameter of the DirectMethod call. The `failure` handler will create an alert message if the request fails:

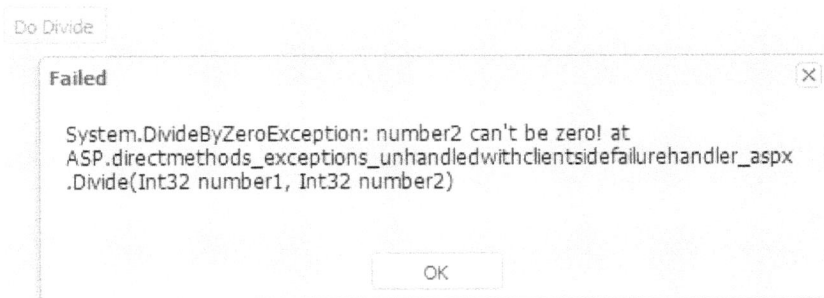

```
Do Divide

Failed                                                    ×

System.DivideByZeroException: number2 can't be zero! at
ASP.directmethods_exceptions_unhandledwithclientsidefailurehandler_aspx
.Divide(Int32 number1, Int32 number2)


                            OK
```

Again, this is not much of an improvement. Fortunately there is another option:

```
[DirectMethod]
public static int Divide(int number1, int number2)
{
    if (number2 == 0)
    {
        ResourceManager.AjaxSuccess = false;
        ResourceManager.AjaxErrorMessage = "number2 can't be zero!";

        return 0;
    }

    return number1 / number2;
}
```

Ext.NET has a `ResourceManager` object with some static properties, `AjaxSuccess` and `AjaxErrorMessage`. These can be set as shown (or in a general `try`/`catch` block), and the `return` value is ignored. In its place, the failure handler on the client side is invoked. With no other change, this is what you would get:

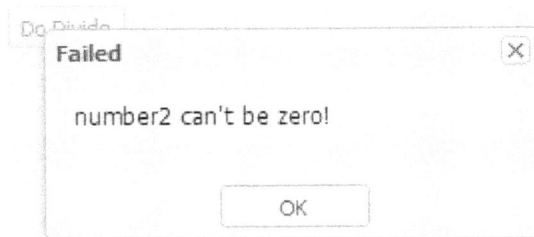

```
Do Divide

Failed                                      ×

number2 can't be zero!


                      OK
```

This is slightly better; all the inner details are now omitted.

> It seems to be a bit of a limitation that the `failure` handler is only a string message. But you could always construct a JSON string object and return that, and manually convert it to a real JavaScript object using `Ext.JSON.decode` in JavaScript and do more sophisticated error handling if needed.

Note, if you did not set a client-side error handler (that is, did not pass a DirectMethod configuration object) you would get the default Ext.NET error-handler Window:

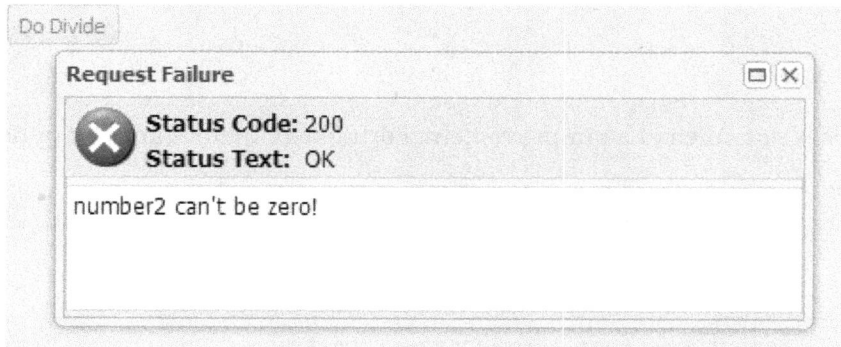

Finally, also note a more realistic pattern for a more complex `DirectMethod` would be to call into a business layer object, and handle any exception not already handled inside the business layer, something like this:

```
[DirectMethod]
public static void DoSomething()
{
  try
  {
    // call through to your business logic layer
  }
  catch (Exception e)
  {
    ResourceManager.AjaxSuccess = false;
    ResourceManager.AjaxErrorMessage = GetFriendlyMessage(e);

    // Do any logging and other operations here
  }
}
```

This gives you a chance to try and provide something friendlier to your end user, and also log further information or perform other operations as needed. Notice also that Ext.NET will swallow DirectMethod exceptions on the server side (they will still be presented on the client side of course, as we have shown). This means that on the server side, you will not catch the exception in the application global error handler (`global.asax`). However, you can set the `RethrowException` property to `true` inside the `DirectMethod` attribute for a particular `DirectMethod` if you wish. Or you can set it for all DirectMethods on a page by setting the same property in the `ResourceManager`, or set it globally in `Web.config` in the `<extnet>` configuration.

Global AJAX operation handlers

There may be times where you want to perform common operations for each AJAX request. For example, suppose you have a web application that uses a status bar. This status bar can be updated to have an indicator to signal that an operation is taking place.

Let's take an admittedly over-simplified example to illustrate this. Suppose we have a similar application as earlier that divides two numbers, and for some reason it does the division on the server. We will let the user input two numbers and then submit them to and update a field with the result. We will put the fields inside a Panel and use an Ext.NET `StatusBar` to put appropriate messages there when the time comes:

```
<ext:Panel runat="server" Title="My Panel" Width="300"
          BodyPadding="4">
  <Items>
    <ext:NumberField ID="Number1" runat="server"
                     FieldLabel="Divide this" />
    <ext:NumberField ID="Number2" runat="server"
                     FieldLabel="By this" />
    <ext:Button runat="server" Text="And you get">
      <Listeners>
        <Click Fn="MyApp.doDivision" />
      </Listeners>
    </ext:Button>
    <ext:DisplayField ID="Answer" runat="server"
                      FieldLabel="Answer" />
  </Items>
  <BottomBar>
    <ext:StatusBar ID="StatusBar1" runat="server"
                   DefaultText="Ready" />
  </BottomBar>
</ext:Panel>
```

This will start off like:

My Panel		
Divide this:		⌃⌄
By this:		⌃⌄
And you get		
Answer:		
Ready		

So far, nothing special. We will look at fields, such as NumberFields, DisplayFields, and more in *Chapter 7, Forms and Validation*.

The listener for the Button calls the JavaScript function doDivision, which is defined in the MyApp namespace:

```
var MyApp = {
    doDivision: function () {
        var field1 = App.Number1.getValue(),
            field2 = App.Number2.getValue(),
            answer = App.Answer;

        App.direct.Divide(field1, field2, {
            success: function (result) {
                answer.setValue(result);
            }
        });
    }
};
```

The code so far is straight forward; we pick out the two NumberFields and the **Answer** label. We call the DirectMethod, Divide, and update the **Answer** field with the result.

The DirectMethod is defined like this:

```
[DirectMethod]
public static decimal Divide(decimal number1, decimal number2)
{
  try
  {
    return number1/number2;
```

```
    }
  catch (DivideByZeroException)
    {
    ResourceManager.AjaxSuccess = false;
    ResourceManager.AjaxErrorMessage = "Number2 can't be zero!";
    return 0;
    }
}
```

We use a decimal here to capture an attempt to divide by zero, and if that happens, we will send back a DirectMethod error response that can be handled by the client. In order for the C# code to compile, the `catch` block needs to return a decimal, so it has been set to `zero` here (as there is no representation for infinity). However, as the `AjaxSuccess` property of `ResourceManager` is `false`, the `return` value will be ignored.

The examples so far have shown success and failure handlers passed as DirectMethod configuration objects when the method is called. But global handlers are possible too.

In our example, we will make the decision that during any AJAX request we want to update the status bar with a **Loading...** indicator, and remove it once the request is complete (with or without failure). If the request fails (divide by zero) we will show the error message from the server. To achieve this, Ext.NET provides the ability to define global listeners on the page for three AJAX stages:

1. Before an AJAX request is made.

2. When an AJAX request is completed.

3. When an AJAX request has failed.

As with listeners for other Ext.NET Controls, you can define these using the `Listeners` collection, this time of the Ext.NET `ResourceManager` itself:

```
<ext:ResourceManager runat="server" ShowWarningOnAjaxFailure="false">
  <Listeners>
    <BeforeAjaxRequest Fn="MyApp.Ajax.onBeforeAjaxRequest"/>
    <AjaxRequestComplete Fn="MyApp.Ajax.onRequestComplete"/>
    <AjaxRequestException Fn="MyApp.Ajax.onRequestException"/>
  </Listeners>
</ext:ResourceManager>
```

Notice that we have turned off the default AJAX error message window using Show WarningOnAjaxFailure="false". The three listeners are handled by corresponding JavaScript methods in our MyApp namespace (within an Ajax sub-namespace). So our entire JavaScript would now look like this:

```
var MyApp = {
  doDivision: function () {
    var field1 = App.Number1.getValue(),
        field2 = App.Number2.getValue(),
        answer = App.Answer;

    App.direct.Divide(field1, field2, {
      success: function (result) {
        answer.setValue(result);
      }
    });
  },

  Ajax: {
    onBeforeAjaxRequest: function () {
      var statusBar = App.StatusBar1;
        statusBar.showBusy();
    },

    onRequestComplete: function () {
      MyApp.Ajax.clearStatus();
    },

    onRequestException: function (response, result) {
      MyApp.Ajax.clearStatus();

      Ext.Msg.alert("Could not divide", result.errorMessage);
    },

    clearStatus: function () {
      App.StatusBar1.clearStatus({ useDefaults: true });
    }
  }
};
```

Before any AJAX request is made, we are invoking the showBusy() method on the status bar, which by default will show the **Loading...** indicator as per the next screenshot:

In the screenshot, notice the **Loading...** indicator in the status bar. This will appear until the server comes back with a response. This is an alternative to using the EventMask we saw earlier, depending on the desired effect you want to achieve.

Once the server has responded, the onRequestComplete method is eventually invoked, which clears the status. We do this via a helper method, MyApp.Ajax.clearStatus(). If an error occurs instead, the onRequestException method can also reset the status bar with the same code.

Here is what would happen once the previous example returns without error:

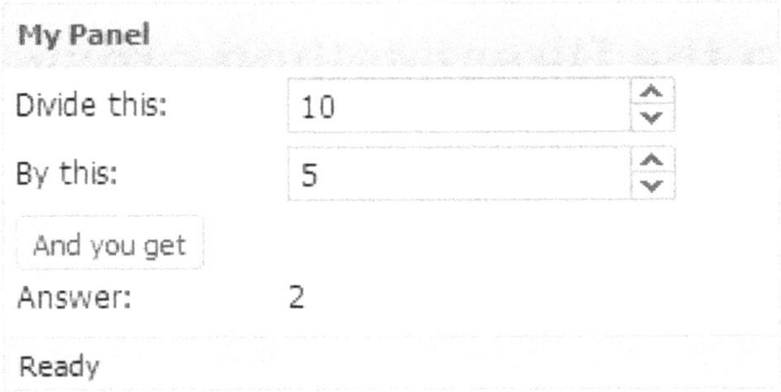

Answer is updated with the result (**2** in this case). If we attempt to divide by zero, however, we can now do our own error handling by inspecting the response and in this case, alerting a message to the user:

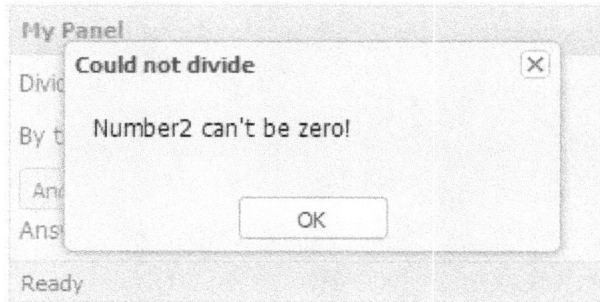

Of course, the example used here is very superficial. In a real application, the global handlers can help provide reusability and interaction consistency in your application. For example, you can provide a consistent appearance while an operation is occurring, and if there are exceptions, you can provide a consistent way to notify the end user.

You can also mix things up; each call to a DirectMethod can still use its own DirectMethod configuration object to define specific handlers for success or failure. You can use the local configuration object to deal with specific issues, while leaving any global ones to deal with truly global application consistency things, for example.

By-passing the DirectMethod proxy

As described earlier, the DirectMethod proxy lets you call a DirectMethod from JavaScript seamlessly. If we look into this further, we can see how the proxy is set up and therefore see what else we can do. Consider the simplistic `Divide` method used earlier:

```
[DirectMethod]
public static decimal Divide(decimal number1, decimal number2)
{
    return number1 / number2;
}
```

On the page running this example, if we look at the JavaScript that Ext.NET generates, we can see how the DirectMethod proxy is generated and how it calls the server. To do this, if we view the source of the page, find the Ext.NET initialization script and pretty print it, we see the relevant snippet for DirectMethod declarations:

```
Ext.apply(App.direct, {
    Divide: function (number1, number2, config) {
        Ext.net.DirectMethod.request(
            "Divide",
            Ext.applyIf(config || {}, {
                params: {
                    number1: number1,
                    number2: number2
                },
                specifier: "static",
                url: "/DirectMethods/DivideExample.aspx"
            })
        );
    }
});
```

In other words, using the Ext JS method, `Ext.apply`, App is extended with a `Divide` function. This `Divide` function, when invoked with parameters `number1` and `number2` (plus any additional DirectMethod configuration object), will call the underlying `Ext.net.DirectMethod.request` method that makes the AJAX request.

The configuration object passed to the request method and all the possible options are documented in Ext.NET's overview of DirectMethods (see *Example 6, Disable the DirectMethod ClientProxy Creation*): `http://examples.ext.net/#/Events/DirectMethods/Overview/`.

> **Why use Ext.NET's DirectMethods instead of Ext JS's own Ext. data.Connection.request or Ext.Ajax.request?**
>
> It is a reasonable question to wonder why bother using DirectMethods if `Ext.Ajax.request` or `Ext.data.Connection.request` from Ext JS can be called directly instead? The main benefits of using DirectMethods are simply consistency and re-using the extensive response building and handling code that Ext.NET has built around DirectMethods (and DirectEvents) which include proper encoding, minification, gzip compression, and client-side execution of any return scripts. The additional capabilities, such as confirmation dialogs, event masking, global request, and exception handling via the ResourceManager are also available to use. That being said, Ext. NET does not stop you from using `Ext.Ajax.request` or `Ext.data.Connection.request` if you have to.

How does this help us? We can set a custom URL to invoke an off-page service. This can be to any type of web service, such as an ASMX Web Service, generic ASHX handler, another ASPX page, a WCF Web Service, or an ASP.NET MVC Controller that returns JSON. As a general AJAX security limitation implemented by all browsers, the request has to be to a service on the same domain as the web page. Here are some examples.

DirectMethods calling an ASP.NET MVC Controller

Earlier we saw an example of calling an ASP.NET MVC Controller via a DirectEvent. The same service can be invoked as a DirectMethod request. Consider this Button:

```
<ext:Button runat="server" Text="Get Server Time">
  <Listeners>
    <Click Fn="MyApp.getServerTime" />
  </Listeners>
</ext:Button>
```

And the corresponding client-side Click handler:

```
var MyApp = {
    getServerTime: function () {
        Ext.net.DirectMethod.request({
            url: "/ServerTime/GetTime"
        });
    }
};
```

This code simply invokes the service we saw earlier that creates the Window with the time set to the body of the Window. If we had data coming back from the request, we could use the success handler to deal with it.

DirectMethods calling web services

Another option, which requires more discussion, is using ASMX Web Services. Consider this very simple (and not very useful in real life!) example service that simply echoes what it is passed in:

```
[WebMethod]
public string Echo(string something)
{
  return something;
}
```

To invoke it from JavaScript, we do not need a DirectMethod proxy. Instead, we can call the DirectMethod directly by setting the URL and other configuration settings:

```
var showRelativeServerTime = function () {
  Ext.net.DirectMethod.request({
    url: "EchoService.asmx/Echo",
    cleanRequest: true,
    params: {
      something: "Hello world!"
    },
    success: function (result) {
      alert(Ext.DomQuery.selectValue("string", result, ""));
    }
  });
}
```

Notice, that the success handler is using standard Ext JS functionality to extract an XML node named `string` from the result and show it in an `alert` prompt. The reason for this is that by default ASMX Web Services are configured to return XML.

XML is not usually as efficient as JSON when being handled directly by JavaScript. Fortunately, as a standard feature of ASMX Web Services, you can add the `ScriptService` attribute to the entire service, to configure it to return JSON instead.

The full web service definition would then look like this:

```
[WebService(Namespace = "http://tempuri.org/")]
[WebServiceBinding(ConformsTo = WsiProfiles.BasicProfile1_1)]
[ScriptService]
public class EchoService : WebService
{
  [WebMethod]
  public string Echo(string something)
  {
    return something;
  }
}
```

In that case, we need to modify the `DirectMethod` request to indicate we are expecting JSON. In addition, the success handler result will be JSON instead of XML, so in our example we would be getting a string value:

```
var showRelativeServerTime = function () {
    Ext.net.DirectMethod.request({
        url: "EchoService.asmx/Echo",
        cleanRequest: true,
        json: true,
```

```
            params: {
                something: "Hello world!"
            },
            success: function (result) {
                alert(result); // result is the echoed value
            }
        });
}
```

JSON Serialization considerations with ASMX Web Services

ASMX Web Services—especially when returning JSON—have a few considerations of which to be aware. Earlier in the DirectEvent examples, we saw an ASMX Web Service to request the server time, offset by a specified number of hours. It returned a `DirectResponse` which contained the result. Here is the same service, but now simplified and with the entire service configured as a `[ScriptService]` as below:

```
[WebService(Namespace = "http://tempuri.org/")]
[WebServiceBinding(ConformsTo = WsiProfiles.BasicProfile1_1)]
[ScriptService]
public class ServerTimeServiceAsJson : WebService
{
  [WebMethod]
  public DateTime GetRelativeServerTime(int hours)
  {
    return DateTime.Now.AddHours(hours);
  }
}
```

We can invoke the service using the following:

```
var showRelativeServerTimeJson = function () {
  Ext.net.DirectMethod.request({
    url: "ServerTimeServiceAsJson.asmx/GetRelativeServerTime",
    cleanRequest: true,
    json: true,
    params: {
      hours: 5
    },
    success: function (result) {
      alert(result);
    }
  });
};
```

If we looked at the result, we would see something odd-looking, for example, /Date(1335752521448)/.

If the response from the server was a string, or a number, there'd be no problems here. Dates from ASMX Web Services, however, are a bit more involved.

Unfortunately, JSON doesn't specify a standard way to represent dates, while strings and numbers are fine. The JSON serialization used by ASMX services (DataContractJsonSerializer) creates a date using a pattern that was initially designed to be consumed by its own client-side AJAX library.

However, we are using Ext.NET and Ext JS, so we would have to handle this difficult-to-debug format manually. We can use Ext JS's client-side Date formatting API, for example, Ext.Date.parseDate("/Date(1335752521448)/", 'MS') which will give you back a JavaScript date object.

Alternatively, you could configure your service to return the date as a string that can be parsed when needed. Unfortunately, there is still no one way for JSON to agree and handle dates but at least there are some options here.

> See also these explanations from Dave Ward:
>
> http://encosia.com/how-i-handle-json-dates-
> returned-by-aspnet-ajax/
>
> http://encosia.com/jquery-asp-net-web-api-and-
> json-net-walk-into-a-bar/

You can also return a custom object and ASMX Web Services will serialize into JSON for you.

> Be aware that the JSON serialization that ASMX Web Services (and WCF by default) use is the DataContractJsonSerializer. This is different from Ext.NET, which uses the popular and very efficient open source library, Json.NET (Microsoft is also thinking of incorporating this into their upcoming versions of ASP.NET to overcome various issues with their own one).

For example, consider this service that returns a scorecard for browsers based on their HTML5 support. The simple scorecard might be defined like this in C#:

```
public enum BrowserGrade
{
  Poor,
  Okay,
```

```
   Good
};

public class Browsers
{
  public string Name { get; set; }
  public int Version { get; set; }
  public BrowserGrade Grade { get; set; }
}
```

And we might return it in an ASMX Web Service as follows (showing only some browsers for brevity):

```
[WebMethod]
public List<Browsers> GetHtml5BrowserScoreCard()
{
  return new List<Browsers>
  {
    new Browsers {Name = "IE", Version = 6, Grade = BrowserGrade.
Poor},
    new Browsers {Name = "IE", Version = 9, Grade = BrowserGrade.
Okay},
    new Browsers {Name = "IE", Version = 10, Grade = BrowserGrade.
Good}
  };
}
```

We can then call it as a DirectMethod from JavaScript as the following shows:

```
var showHtml5BrowserScoreCard = function () {
  Ext.net.DirectMethod.request({
    url: "ServerTimeServiceAsJson.asmx/GetHtml5BrowserScoreCard",
    json: true,
    success: function (result) {
        console.log(result);
    }
  });
}
```

The success handler is simply writing out the result to the console. The result is the array that the service returns (although it is a List<T> in the .NET side, it is serialized to an array on the JavaScript side).

The JSON response from the web service is worth commenting on. Here is what the server would send to the browser before being passed to the previous success handler:

```
{
    "d": [{
        "__type": "Ajax.DirectMethods.WebServices.ServerTimeServiceAsJ
son+Browsers",
```

```
            "Name": "IE",
            "Version": 6,
            "Grade": 0
    }, {
            "__type": "Ajax.DirectMethods.WebServices.ServerTimeServiceAsJ
    son+Browsers",
            "Name": "IE",
            "Version": 9,
            "Grade": 1
    }, {
            "__type": "Ajax.DirectMethods.WebServices.ServerTimeServiceAsJ
    son+Browsers",
            "Name": "IE",
            "Version": 10,
            "Grade": 2
    ]
}
```

It is worth noting the following:

- The d object is Microsoft's AJAX convention for JSON serialized responses. The value of this d object is the `result` in the preceding JavaScript code example.

- Microsoft's JSON serialization also adds a `__type` property to each item in the array which can add to the response size if that information is not needed.

- The enums are also just numbers, which might be a bit harder to deal with than if it were the string name of the enum instead.

As noted earlier, if we had dates, they are also a bit fiddly with which to deal. Combined, these can be irritations to varying degrees, depending on your situation. However, if you already have existing services you want to reuse quickly, ASMX is certainly an option.

DirectMethods calling generic ASHX handlers

If you want finer grained control to overcome some of the issues described with ASMX Web Services, an ASHX handler is one way to do it. This option can also give you good performance (by passing various ASP.NET lifecycle stages).

Here is a similar request to get the HTML 5 browser scorecard. First, the ASHX handler:

```
public void ProcessRequest(HttpContext context)
{
  context.Response.ContentType = "application/json";

  var scoreCard = new List<Browsers>
  {
```

```
    new Browsers {Name = "IE", Version = 6, Grade = BrowserGrade.
Poor},
    new Browsers {Name = "IE", Version = 9, Grade = BrowserGrade.
Okay},
    new Browsers {Name = "IE", Version = 10, Grade = BrowserGrade.
Good}
  };

  context.Response.Write(JSON.Serialize(scoreCard));
}
```

Note that as an ASHX, we have a bit more raw power, which therefore also comes with a bit more responsibility! For example, we have to set the content type manually, and also serialize the result manually.

But this also gives us flexibility; we get to serialize our object using whichever JSON serializer we wish. This means we have an opportunity to overcome issues with the ASMX approach that we saw earlier, and use the same JSON serializer that Ext.NET uses itself, that is Json.NET.

JSON.Serialize in the example above is part of the Ext.NET namespace. Ext.NET's JSON class provides convenience wrappers over Json.NET for you and is available for you to use yourself (to avoid inconsistency issues in serialization).

To call it as a DirectMethod, it is almost identical to the earlier example that calls the ASMX version:

```
var showHtml5BrowserScoreCardFromHandler = function () {
    Ext.net.DirectMethod.request({
        url: "Handler.ashx",
        success: function (result) {
            console.log(result);
        }
    });
}
```

There are just two differences:

1. The URL simply points to the ASHX handler.
2. There is no need to set json:true.

Here is the JSON response we would now get from the server:

```
[{
    "Name": "IE",
    "Version": 6,
    "Grade": "Poor"
}, {
```

```
        "Name": "IE",
        "Version": 9,
        "Grade": "Okay"
    }, {
        "Name": "IE",
        "Version": 10,
        "Grade": "Good"
    }]
```

Compared to the JSON returned by the similar ASMX service, note:

- The response is also an array (as expected) but without the need for an additional d property
- There is no __type property
- The enum is an easier to understand string value

> As we have seen with DirectEvents, you are not limited to just returning data. You can return an entire set of Ext.NET Controls. This lets you create parts of your UI on demand. The exact same ASHX handlers can be invoked from DirectMethods, as well as DirectEvents, giving you more power and flexibility.

DirectMethods on user controls

User controls can be a convenient way to reuse ASP.NET code. Ext.NET therefore supports defining DirectMethods on user controls, too. This is something ASP.NET does not support with page methods.

Consider this very simple user control:

```
<%@ Control Language="C#" %>

<script runat="server">
  protected void Page_Load(object sender, EventArgs e)
  {
    if (!X.IsAjaxRequest)
    {
        this.Button1.Text = "UserControl: " + this.Name;
    }
  }

  [DirectMethod]
  public void GetName()
  {
```

```
      X.MessageBox.Alert("Name", this.Name).Show();
   }

   public string Name { get; set; }
</script>

<ext:Button ID="Button1" runat="server">
   <Listeners>
     <Click Handler="#{DirectMethods}.GetName();" />
   </Listeners>
</ext:Button>
```

In this code, the user control is simply creating a Button that when clicked, will invoke the `GetName` DirectMethod. The user control has a `Name` property, so the page (or another user control) that uses this can set it. That `Name` property is then used during the `Page_Load` phase to set the Button text.

Two new features to note here are:

`#{DirectMethods}` is a shortcut to create a client-side namespaced reference to the namespace where the DirectMethod proxies will be created. This doesn't work in all cases (for example, if there are nested master pages or user controls, where you can sometimes get the wrong reference). In that case, you can use the `DirectMethodProxyIDMode` attribute as described in: `http://examples.ext.net/#/Events/DirectMethods/ID_Mode/` and `http://forums.ext.net/showthread.php?18853`.

The use of `X.IsAjaxRequest`: `IsAjaxRequest` is a useful method on Ext.NET X object that lets you know whether the code is running as part of an AJAX request or not. Much like how ASP.NET has the `IsPostBack` method on the page instance, this is useful to help avoid re-running various initialization code when an AJAX request comes back to the same page.

Here is a snippet for a simple use of the user control on a page:

```
<uc:GetName ID="ucGetName1" runat="server" Name="Joe" />
<uc:GetName ID="ucGetName2" runat="server" Name="Bob" />
```

Clicking either Button will result in the user control's Button being invoked and showing the alert with the correct name.

So far, so good. However, because a user control can be used more than once on a page, how does Ext.NET ensure the correct user control instance's method gets invoked? The best way to answer this is to have a look at the JavaScript generated by Ext.NET for the previous page and user control combination. Using the browser's view source and pretty printing the output, here is the snippet that represents the Buttons:

```
new Ext.Button({
    id: "ucGetName1_Button1",
    renderTo: "ucGetName1_Button1_Container",
    text: "UserControl: Joe",
    listeners: {
        click: {
            fn: function (item, e) {
                App.direct.ucGetName1.GetName();
            }
        }
    }
});
new Ext.Button({
    id: "ucGetName2_Button1",
    renderTo: "ucGetName2_Button1_Container",
    text: "UserControl: Bob",
    listeners: {
        click: {
            fn: function (item, e) {
                App.direct.ucGetName2.GetName();
            }
        }
    }
});
```

Notice how the code, #{DirectMethods} is converted to the namespace of the DirectMethods (by default App.direct) but in addition, there is a further subsection for each instance of the user control. These names correspond to the ClientID of the user controls that were declared on the page.

This means you can of course call a user control's DirectMethod from elsewhere on your page. For example, the page (or containing user control) could do something like this:

```
<ext:Button runat="server" Text="Call UserControl DirectMethod (Joe)">
    <Listeners>
        <Click Handler="App.direct.ucGetName1.GetName();" />
    </Listeners>
</ext:Button>
```

Because it is calling the DirectMethod of the first instance of the user control, it will show the name **Joe**.

This code, of course, assumes you can predict the ClientID of the user control so that you can call the DirectMethod that will be created for it. Nested user controls can result in quite a complex or hard-to-predict ClientID. One option is to use the `DirectMethodProxyIDMode` attribute approach on your DirectMethod as noted earlier, or you can try to either use ASP.NET 4's `ClientIdMode` properties on a control, or Ext.NET's own `IDMode` on your Ext.NET Controls inside your user control, which has a few more options.

One limitation to bear in mind is that DirectMethods on user controls cannot be static. As well as defining DirectMethods on user controls, they can also be defined in custom controls that extend Ext.NET Controls (and they too have to be non-static). *Chapter 9, Extending Ext.NET – Custom Controls and Plugins* will cover extending components.

DirectMethods on ASP.NET MVC Controllers

DirectMethods can also be defined on MVC Controllers. To do this, you add a DirectControllerAttribute to your `Controller` class. Then, inside your Controller, any action you want to be a DirectMethod, simply use the DirectMethodAttribute. Extending the MVC Controller example shown much earlier, we can simply update it as follows:

```
[DirectController]
public class ServerTimeController : Controller
{
    // Other Controller Actions as before

    [DirectMethod]
    public ActionResult GetServerTime()
    {
        var label = this.GetCmp<Label>("Label1");
        label.Text = DateTime.Now.ToLongTimeString();

        return this.Direct();
    }
}
```

This new Controller action, GetServerTime, simply gets the label defined as Label1 in the view and updates its Text property to the current server time. This approach lets your Controller contain both your original actions as well as the DirectMethod actions, keeping functionality together. The view's Razor template declaration for this label and a Button to invoke the DirectMethod is as follows:

```
@(Html.X().Button().Text("Update")
    .Handler("App.direct.GetServerTime();"))

@Html.X().Label().ID("Label1").Text("Updated from server")
```

There are many more capabilities such as being able to indicate if a DirectMethod belongs to a particular Area and configuring how the proxy is generated. These are shown and explained on the dedicated MVC Examples Explorer, in particular the Direct Method examples: http://mvc.ext.net/#/search/directmethod.

Turning off the ID mode for DirectMethods

Master pages, like user controls, can also have DirectMethods on them. In terms of the ClientID prediction challenge if you want to call the DirectMethod, you have another option that is more practical for DirectMethods than for user controls; turn off the ID creation inside the DirectMethod namespace altogether. This then makes the DirectMethods on the master pages look like they belong to the page you are on, creating a more consistent look (and also avoiding issues of predicting master page ids when they are nested). To achieve this, consider this master page code-behind:

```
[DirectMethod(IDMode = DirectMethodProxyIDMode.None)]
public partial class DirectMethodExample : MasterPage
{
  [DirectMethod]
  public void HelloMasterPage()
  {
    X.Msg.Alert("Message", "Hello from MasterPage").Show();
  }
}
```

In this example, we can use the DirectMethodProxyID attribute on the master page's subclass itself. Here we have set the IDMode to None. This means when we try to call the method from a page or JavaScript, it will be called using App.direct. HelloMasterPage() without any control ID in between.

Controlling the rendering of dynamically generated controls

DirectEvents and DirectMethods both support a number of ways to generate controls during an AJAX request. We have seen DirectEvents rendering controls. In the following example, we will see a DirectMethod rendering a control but also determining where and how a control is rendered:

```
<ext:Button runat="server" Text="Click Me"
            OnClientClick="onClickMe" />

<ext:TabPanel ID="TabPanel1" runat="server" Height="100">
  <Items>
    <ext:Panel Title="Initially created" />
  </Items>
</ext:TabPanel>
```

The `OnClientClick` JavaScript function is defined as follows:

```
var onClickMe = function () {
    Ext.net.DirectMethod.request({
        url: "GenerateComponent.ashx",
        cleanRequest: true,
        params: {
            container: "TabPanel1"
        }
    });
};
```

Notice that the previous code is making a DirectMethod request to an ASHX, passing an extra parameter in the `params` property. This is the container to which to generate the component. The ASHX handler looks like this:

```
public void ProcessRequest(HttpContext context)
{
    var panel = new Panel { Title = "Hello" };

    string container = context.Request["container"];

    panel.AddTo(container)

    new DirectResponse().Return();
}
```

In the preceding code, we are dynamically creating a simple Panel. Using the AddTo method, we can add this Panel as a new item of the passed in container. Similarly, we can use methods like InsertTo to insert it into a specific position (using 0 to make it the first item of the container rather than the last). There is also the Replace method that will take in a component (not a container) to replace. For additional flexibility, there is also the Render method. This has a number of overloads, but the main difference is that is can also take an enum named RenderMode. So, for example, instead of using panel.AddTo() you could use this:

```
panel.Render(container, RenderMode.AddTo);
```

Other options of the RenderMode enum include InsertTo and Replace, which correspond to the methods of the same name we just saw. There is also RenderTo, which renders the control into a DOM object, not as an item of the Ext.NET Container. Why use Render with the RenderMode enum if methods exist for each option? Sometimes you may have other code passing in the RenderMode to you, and this can save a few lines of if/else or switch statements.

AJAX options specific to certain controls

Some controls, by their very nature, have their own additional AJAX options and capabilities. Data Stores (used by many data bound components such as GridPanels, Charts, and ComboBoxes) as well as TreePanels (that can load nodes dynamically) warrant their own chapters so AJAX options for them will be covered there. Here we will look at some loading options that are supported by Panels.

Loading content with Panels

AbstractComponent, the base class for all Ext.NET components has a feature named **Loaders** (known as AutoLoad in previous versions), which can load in content from another URL or DirectMethod. It can be merged into the current page, or be presented in isolation by loading it inside an HTML iframe.

Loading inside an iframe has the drawback of loading an entire page, as it is not AJAX. If that page is on your own server that you control, then it is not always optimal because using an iframe can be quite expensive because the browser is managing an entire page, and all Ext.NET resources have to be loaded again, so use with care. On the other hand, this may be a useful option if you are migrating an existing application towards Ext.NET and have to do it iteratively. This approach also lets you load external URLs, which could be useful at times.

Here is an example of auto-loading a child page, where you can also pass custom parameters via the query string:

```
<ext:Panel runat="server" Title="AutoLoad" Height="200" Width="500">
  <Loader Url="Child.aspx" Scripts="true">
    <Params>
      <ext:Parameter Name="param1" Value="Value1" />
      <ext:Parameter Name="param2" Value="Value2" />
    </Params>
  </Loader>
</ext:Panel>
```

The use of `Params` allows various values to be passed via the query string. The child page is a full ASPX page in its own right; not a user control. It would typically come with its own CSS, scripts (which are only processed if `Scripts` is set to `true` and by default it is `false`), and more. However, in the preceding code, the `Mode` property of Loader has not been set, so it defaults to `Html`, which is parsed and handled by Ext. NET for you.

If you set the `Mode` to `Frame`, the same content would be loaded in an HTML `iframe`. Also, if the `Url` starts with `http`, it will automatically go into `Frame` mode. The interaction between the child page and the client page could be limited, would involve inter-frame JavaScript communication typically, and generally would not perform as well.

As a result the `Frame` option, although available, isn't as ideal or flexible as using DirectMethods and DirectEvents which can also dynamically generate controls. As such, we won't dwell on this further here, but the Ext.NET Examples Explorer shows more options for loader: `http://examples.ext.net/#/search/loader`.

Component loader

Ext.NET also provides a way to load components straight into another component, such as a Panel. This is similar to how we create components in ASHX and ASMX Web Services but uses the Loader capabilities, so that what is returned is a configuration object which Ext.NET will then load for you.

Also note that subclasses of Panel, such as Window and TabPanel, can also use Loader. By default, the `Render` event of Ext.NET Controls is used to execute auto-loading. This render event fires as soon as the control is being rendered. By default, tab rendering is deferred to the first time the tab is activated (because TabPanel has a property, `DeferredRender`, which is `true` by default). This helps to load tabs on demand, and only if needed. We will explore TabPanels in a separate chapter, but here is a quick example to illustrate:

```
<ext:TabPanel runat="server" Width="300" Height="200">
  <Items>
    <ext:Panel Title="First"
      Html="Activate 2nd panel to see contents on demand"/>
    <ext:Panel Title="Second" Layout="Accordion">
      <Loader Url="LoadComponent.ashx" Mode="Component">
        <LoadMask ShowMask="true" />
      </Loader>
    </ext:Panel>
  </Items>
</ext:TabPanel>
```

In this code, we have used a Loader configured to run in Component mode. This will tell Ext.NET to make the server request and pass the resulting component to Ext.NET's Loader to load the components in for you. The first tab will have some content, but the second tab will only load if the user goes there (on demand). This is more efficient for the user (who gets the initial user interface more quickly) and for the server (to do minimal work). If the user does want the second tab, we also enable a loading mask to compensate for making them wait just that bit longer! Here is what a handler might return:

```
public void ProcessRequest(HttpContext context)
{
  context.Response.ContentType = "application/json";

  ComponentLoader.Render(new List<AbstractComponent>
  {
    new Panel { Title="Item 1", Icon = Icon.UserBrown },
    new Panel { Title="Item 2", Icon = Icon.UserGray },
    new Panel { Title="Item 3", Icon = Icon.UserGreen }
  });
}
```

Notice that the ComponentLoader.Render method is being given a list of components. Unlike our earlier ASHX and ASMX examples, we didn't explicitly call .Render(). This is because if we look at Firebug, we can see what is being sent to the browser (line breaks added for readability):

```
[
  {xtype:"panel",title:"Item 1",iconCls:"#UserBrown"},
  {xtype:"panel",title:"Item 2",iconCls:"#UserGray"},
  {xtype:"panel",title:"Item 3",iconCls:"#UserGreen"}
]
```

It is a JSON array of configuration items (xtypes are Ext JS's way of defining components to lazy load, via configuration rather than explicit instantiation). Notice also that this is unlike the DirectResponses we saw earlier, where the JSON response only has one property; the script to execute. Instead, this is pure JSON configuration being generated; Ext.NET's Loader script will then load these into the tab producing this:

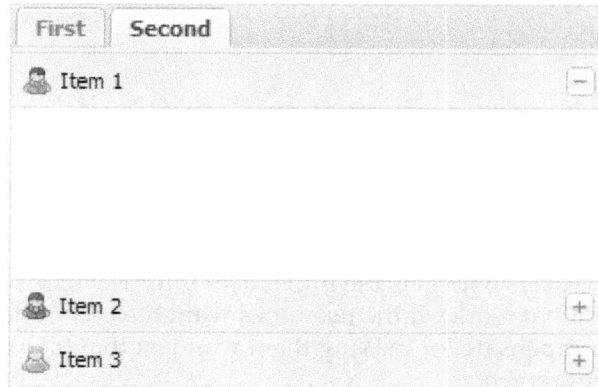

> Notice how this example did not return a *Panel* that contained the three accordion Panels; that would have created an unnecessary additional nested Panel to go inside the tab, which itself is already a Panel. Avoiding such additional nesting where possible helps with overall performance, and on complex apps, it can improve rendering and reduce memory usage.

Another option for loading components is to use a DirectMethod invocation from the Loader, using the DirectMethod property on the Loader. Although space in this book is quite limited and prevents all possibilities from being demonstrated here, fortunately this useful technique is highlighted well in this Ext.NET Examples Explorer example: http://examples.ext.net/#/Loaders/Component/Direct_Method/.

Ultimate performance option: avoid AJAX!

It might be odd in a chapter on AJAX to say avoid it, but with the seamlessness and power that Ext.NET offers, it might be tempting to code everything in C# and avoid client-side coding. But excessive HTTP requests this causes would affect performance.

However, as an Ext.NET developer has noted, it may be worth trying to minimize the amount of DirectEvents and DirectMethods that are invoked, especially in the cases where the same effect can be achieved purely by JavaScript code, because that will avoid the HTTP roundtrip overhead, thus providing a better user experience.

Of course, many important operations will need to get data and interact with the server, but for other cases, if it can be done on the client side, try to do so. It is therefore worth repeating what was said at the beginning of the book: it is beneficial to invest time learning client-side Ext JS library in addition to Ext.NET to get the best of both worlds and ensure that your Ext.NET app has trade-offs based on as much information available as possible.

Summary

Ext.NET offers many ways to make AJAX requests including:

- DirectEvents
- DirectMethods
- Loader

We saw how seamless DirectEvents are, and how flexible DirectMethods can be to create a Remote Procedure Call like experience with minimal effort. We also saw that DirectMethods can be made static, which can boost performance. You can also create Ext.NET components during an AJAX request, on demand, which is very powerful for dynamic and responsive applications.

For even more flexible options, we noted that requests can be configured to use other services on your server by explicitly changing the URL. In doing so, we saw that some options, such as calling an ASMX service, can be flexible but has some caveats to consider. Calling ASHX-based services offers good performance but lacks the conventions that calling an ASMX or MVC Controller may provide. In addition, we saw that DirectMethods can be defined on User Controls and Master Pages, which offers further flexibility and reuse.

We also learned the Loader can load content remotely given a URL, and Ext.NET is able to handle whether it is another website or the same server being requested.

Finally, we noted that while these are all excellent and powerful options at your disposal, the ultimate performance consideration for AJAX requests may be to not make one; if you do not need server resources during an AJAX request and the operation can be performed all on the client side, then it is worth doing so to help improve your end user's experience. Ext.NET offers the ability to manipulate its client controls on the server during an AJAX request, and this is incredibly powerful. But this can also increase the temptation to do too much on the server and avoid using client-side JavaScript when appropriate. It can be a difficult balance, but generally very simple actions that can be done on the client side could ideally be left in JavaScript, for example, showing a Window. Sometimes benefits such as compilation or code maintenance of running things on the server may be a trade-off to consider. Of course, for any serious web application, AJAX requests are going to require many server resources, such as getting data. So the next chapter looks into this in more detail.

5
Working with Data

Web application toolkits aren't too useful if they don't support handling data! Fortunately, Ext.NET covers this very well, providing various components to separate the structure of data, how it is retrieved and updated, and how it is displayed. This lets many components reuse common data handling features such as XTemplates, Stores, and Models.

In this chapter, we will look at how the DataView and ComboBox components use the templating mechanism, XTemplates, to provide rich views of data. In addition, we will see how these components make use of Stores, Models, and Proxies to separate presentation from the data model and underlying storage/retrieval mechanisms. This chapter will, therefore, go through these features in the following order:

- XTemplates
- Stores
- Models
- Proxies
- DataView
- ComboBox

By the end of this chapter, you will gain an understanding of the different ways in which you can bind data to various controls.

XTemplates

XTemplate is a mechanism to support templated content. In other words, you define
an HTML snippet, or template, using special markers for data items to appear in the
right place. The XTemplate is then populated with data at the right time. XTemplates
support both single data and repeated data templates. The data is typically a JSON
structure and the JSON structure is not limited to a flat list of properties and their
values; it can be hierarchical. We will have a quick look at a basic XTemplate using
a single data structure, and then see how we can apply XTemplates to lists of
repeated data.

Basic XTemplates

Consider the following simple Panel:

```
<ext:Panel ID="Panel1" runat="server" Width="300" Height="200">
  <Tpl runat="server">
    <Html>
      <div class="info">
        <p>First Name: {FirstName}</p>
        <p>Last Name: {LastName}</p>
        <p>Info1: {Info1}</p>
        <p>Info2: {Info2}</p>
      </div>
    </Html>
  </Tpl>
  <BottomBar>
    <ext:Toolbar>
      <Items>
        <ext:Button Icon="Reload" Text="Reload">
          <Listeners>
            <Click Handler="updatePanel(#{Panel1});" />
          </Listeners>
        </ext:Button>
      </Items>
    </ext:Toolbar>
  </BottomBar>
</ext:Panel>
```

In the preceding example, we have introduced the template property of Panel, `Tpl`.
Inside that we have an `Html` property. This is where the template is defined. Here we
have a simple scenario. We display a first and last name, plus some other properties,
called `Info1` and `Info2`. As a template, we have placeholders for the values, denoted
by braces, `{}`. So `{FirstName}`, `{LastName}`, and so on, will be the properties from a
JSON object that will be used to fill in the values when needed.

We will populate this template on the page load and then show how fresh data can be obtained (via the `Reload` button's `Click` handler as defined in the preceding example). First, let's define a simple class in C# that will serialize into JSON, as follows:

```
public class TemplateData
{
    public string FirstName { get; set; }
    public string LastName { get; set; }
    public string Info1 { get; set; }
    public string Info2 { get; set; }
}
```

And when the page is loading:

```
protected void Page_Load(object sender, EventArgs e)
{
    Panel1.Data = new TemplateData
    {
        FirstName = "Joe",
        LastName = "Blogs",
        Info1 = "Hello",
        Info2 = "World"
    };
}
```

We can use the `Data` property of `Panel1` to assign the supplied data to the Panel. The instance of `TemplateData` is given some initial values to produce the following:

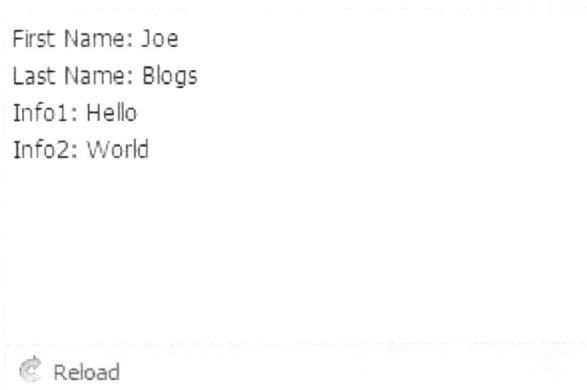

First Name: Joe
Last Name: Blogs
Info1: Hello
Info2: World

Reload

(For the preceding screenshot, the `info` class defined in the template was used to create CSS styles to subtly increase the line height in order to space out the four lines. This is done because the HTML by default has Ext JS's reset stylesheet applied, which essentially strips off all the default browser styles, as all browsers have subtly different defaults. This then allows more specific CSS to be applied that increases consistency across browsers. Example CSS for this will be shown a bit later.)

So far so good. Now, what if we want to reload this Panel with updated data from the server? As we saw in the previous chapter, there are numerous ways to interact with the server. In the preceding code, we defined a `Click` handler for the **Reload** button. We can make a `DirectMethod` request to get new data from the server, as shown in this example:

```
var updatePanel = function (panel) {
    Ext.net.DirectMethod.request({
        success: function (response) {
            panel.update(response);
        },
        url: 'DataUpdater.ashx',
        cleanRequest: true,
        eventMask: { showMask: true }
    });
}
```

The ASHX handler called by the preceding code returns new data as follows:

```
public class DataUpdater : IHttpHandler
{
    public void ProcessRequest(HttpContext context)
    {
        var data = new TemplateData
        {
            FirstName = "Joe",
            LastName = "Bloggs1",
            Info1 = DateTime.Now.ToLongDateString(),
            Info2 = DateTime.Now.ToLongTimeString()
        };

        new DirectResponse { Result = data }.Return();
    }

    public bool IsReusable { get { return false; } }
}
```

In the preceding code, we have used the `DirectResponse` class introduced in *Chapter 4, AJAX with Ext.NET*. We assign our data to the `Result` property and call `Return`, which ends the request and sets the appropriate response headers for you. The success handler then simply updates the Panel with the response, which is the data we returned from the server. The updated Panel would look like the following screenshot:

First Name: Joe
Last Name: Bloggs1
Info1: 13 May 2012
Info2: 17:32:37

Reload

Basic XTemplates with repeated data

We may want to show a list of the preceding data, repeatedly. In that case, we simply update our ASHX to return an instance of `List<T>` where `T` is our `TemplateData` class, and this will be serialized into a JSON array. We then need to update our template definition to loop through the array.

For demonstration purposes we will extend our contrived example. It will still show just a single instance to start with, but on pressing **Reload**, we will show a list of new items in its place. This will let us introduce another feature in Ext.NET, the `XTemplate` control.

In our first example, we defined an XTemplate inline via the `Tpl` property of the Panel. But you can also define one standalone (which allows other components on the page to reuse it if needed, for example). The earlier template could be modified to work with repeated data, but we will add an XTemplate onto the page just to show both can be used:

```
<ext:XTemplate ID="XTemplate1" runat="server">
    <Html>
        <tpl for=".">
            <div class="info">
                <p>Item Number: {#}</p>
```

```
            <p>First Name: {FirstName}</p>
            <p>Last Name: {LastName}</p>
            <p>Info1: {Info1}</p>
            <p>Info2: {Info2}</p>
        </div>
      </tpl>
    </Html>
  </ext:XTemplate>
```

The only difference with this template and the inline one is the template keyword, `for`. This is Ext JS's way to allow you to loop through each object. In this case, because the JSON object to loop through is an array `"."` denotes each `TemplateData` object in the array. More generally, the `"."` points to the root node of the data passed in. If the data in the root node happens to be an array, then the template will repeatedly apply for each item in the array. The ASHX handler can now return a list of `TemplateData` instances:

```
public void ProcessRequest(HttpContext context)
{
    var items = new List<TemplateData>();

    for (int i = 1; i < 11; i++)
    {
        items.Add(new TemplateData
        {
            FirstName = "First Name " + i,
            LastName = "Last Name " + i,
            Info1 = "Info 1." + i,
            Info2 = "Info 2." + i
        });
    }

    new DirectResponse { Result = items }.Return();
}
```

The preceding code is returning 10 items in an array. We can now slightly modify the `success` handler to pass the new data to the external template rather than the inline one, which can only handle one item at a time:

```
<ext:Button runat="server" Icon="Reload" Text="Reload">
  <Listeners>
    <Click Handler="updatePanel(#{Panel1}, #{XTemplate1});"/>
  </Listeners>
</ext:Button>
```

We have passed a second parameter to our JavaScript `updatePanel` function which now looks like the following code:

```
var updatePanel = function (panel, template) {
    Ext.net.DirectMethod.request({
        success: function (response) {
            template.overwrite(panel.body, response);
        },
        url: 'DataUpdaterMultiple.ashx',
        cleanRequest: true,
        eventMask: { showMask: true }
    });
}
```

It is virtually the same as the initial example, except it takes in a template as a second argument and we use the template's `overwrite` method to apply the response to the template and put that applied template into the Panel body.

> We could have used `App.XTemplate1` to access the template so it doesn't have to be passed in. While that is a workable option for this trivial example, in reality you may want to reduce the assumptions and dependencies your JavaScript has to make. Passing control references in is more reusable.

When we click on **Reload**, we now get a list of items rendered, as the following shows:

Item Number: 1
First Name: First Name 1
Last Name: Last Name 1
Info1: Info 1.1
Info2: Info 2.1

Item Number: 2
First Name: First Name 2
Last Name: Last Name 2

 Reload

We have used `AutoScroll="true"` in our Panel so we get scrollbars automatically. In the CSS we have simply added a bottom border to the `info` class. But you are free to style it how you wish, for example, consider this small amount of CSS:

```
.info {
    margin: 10px 1% 0 2%;
    padding: 4px;
    display: inline-block;
    width: 30%;
    border: 1px solid #ddd;
    border-radius: 4px;
    box-shadow: 2px 2px 2px #999;
}
.info:nth-child(odd) { background-color: #eee; }
.info p { line-height: 1.6; }
```

The preceding CSS makes each `info` display as an inline block level element. The `width` and `margin` settings mean each element will cover one-third of a line. Every alternating element is styled with a light gray background. We also add a soft shadow and rounded corners (for browsers that support them). (We could also add `float:left` for IE6 and IE7 to work here, but have left it out for conciseness as their margin calculations also need adjusting, and CSS, while interesting is mostly beyond the scope of this book). Increasing the Panel's width and height to demonstrate, the result will be the following:

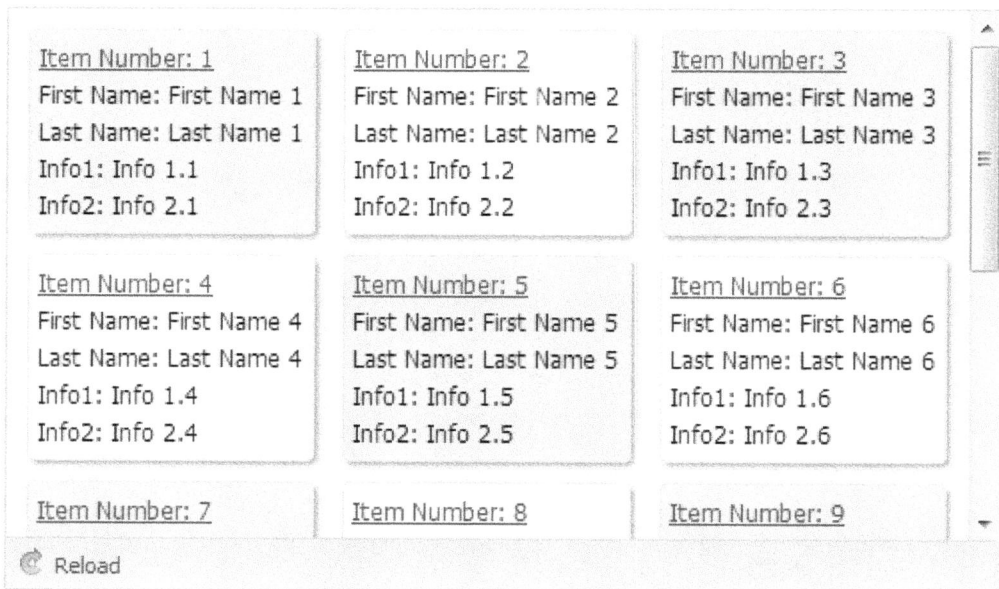

Note, you can also repeat the use of placeholders and use them in HTML attributes, too. For example, we converted each **Item Number** in the preceding example into a link to a details page by modifying the template to look like the following code:

```
<tpl for=".">
    <div class="info">
        <p><a href="/Details/{#}">Item Number: {#}</a></p>
        <p>First Name: {FirstName}</p>
        <p>Last Name: {LastName}</p>
        <p>Info1: {Info1}</p>
        <p>Info2: {Info2}</p>
    </div>
</tpl>
```

In the preceding example {#} is used twice, once for constructing the URL to a details page, and then as part of the display text as we had earlier.

More XTemplate rendering options

XTemplates are quite rich and this book is limited in space to discuss the other features in detail, but it is worth knowing the types of things that are possible, for example:

- There are mechanisms to support comparisons and conditional operators such as the `if` and `switch` statements
- Built-in template variables are also available to access the current item and related information
- Basic math operators are also possible
- You can also define your own custom functions and invoke them from within the template

You will also find that XTemplates are used in many parts of Ext.NET. For example, we have seen the `Tpl` property in Panel. In the previous chapter we looked at Loader and some of the modes that can be used. It can also have a mode of `Data`, which can be used in conjunction with XTemplates as demonstrated at `http://examples.ext.net/#/Loaders/Data/Overview/`.

You can also create your own components using `Component` and the `RenderTpl` property which is described at `http://examples.ext.net/#/Miscellaneous/Render_Template/Basic/`.

Much more is possible as detailed on both the Sencha Ext JS XTemplates documentation at `http://docs.sencha.com/ext-js/4-1/#!/api/Ext.XTemplate` and Ext.NET's Examples Explorer at `http://examples.ext.net/#/search/template`.

XTemplates are very powerful. But we may want to do a bit more. For example, we may want to return a limited amount of data, rather than an entire list (that is a page worth of data). Or we may want to use it to format autocomplete pickers in various ways. Such capabilities expose us to more sophisticated data handling components, such as Stores, Models, and data access Proxies. So, we will take a look at what these are and then expand our earlier example to have paged results.

Stores

A **Store** is a component that manages data for you on the client. It is typically used with grids and repeating lists of data, but also with hierarchical data such as TreePanels, as we will see in a later chapter. A Store manages features such as sorting and filtering data (locally or remotely). To achieve this, a Store has two important aspects to it as follows:

- A Model, to define the items in the Store, their data types, validation requirements, and so on
- A Proxy, to help retrieve and synchronize any changes back from the original data source

> Ext JS 4 has various subclasses for the Store component, such as `ArrayStore`, `JsonStore`, `JsonPStore`, `BufferStore`, and `XmlStore`. These stores are very simple subclasses that simply instantiate the corresponding proxy for you. When Ext.NET generates an Ext JS Store for you, all the various proxies that Ext JS defines are created appropriately, so Ext.NET itself doesn't need explicit classes corresponding to these Store subclasses.

Models

A **Model** defines the items that the Store will manage. It is new to Ext.NET 2 and Ext JS 4. In earlier versions of Ext JS and Ext.NET, the `Record` class served a similar purpose (some of the client-side API methods still refer to `Record` when using Model data).

A Model lets you declare the data you are expecting from the data source. You can set its type and any validation that goes along with each field.

Proxies

Proxies are used by Stores to handle the retrieval and modification of data. A **Proxy** hides the details of the underlying storage mechanism, thus providing a familiar abstraction over different storage possibilities, and allowing for expansion to roll your own.

Proxies come in the following two types:

- Client-side Proxies
- Server-side Proxies

Client-side Proxies include the following:

- `MemoryProxy`
- `LocalStorageProxy`
- `SessionStorageProxy`

Server-side Proxies include the following:

- `AjaxProxy`
- `DirectProxy`
- `JsonPProxy`
- `PageProxy`
- `RestProxy`

`MemoryProxy` is a simple Proxy that stores data on the browser's page and will be lost when the page is reloaded. `LocalStorageProxy` and `SessionStorageProxy` use newer HTML5 storage features that come in newer browsers. Generally speaking, IE6 and IE7 will not work with those Proxies as they do not support these HTML5 features.

For the server-side Proxies, `AjaxProxy` is a general purpose AJAX request Proxy. If you are going to call back to the page that has loaded your components, `PageProxy` will likely be what you need and will allow you to wire server-side event handlers, that are familiar to most ASP.NET developers. If you want to use a REST API, then `RestProxy` is available. `DirectProxy` is like `AjaxProxy` except it uses Ext JS `Ext.Direct` requests, and `JsonPProxy` allows for cross-domain AJAX-like requests.

Separation of concerns and loose coupling

The Store/Model/Proxy architecture is loosely coupled. Models and Proxies can be defined inline in a Store. Alternatively, a Proxy can be defined inside a Model because a Model itself can manipulate data separately from a Store. (When a Model is defined separately from a Store, the Model's Name property can be set allowing you to then set the ModelName property on a Store pointing to this Model. This allows you to potentially reuse the same Model on many stores if you wish.)

That being said, it is quite common to define a Model and Proxy inside a Store, as can be seen in the following diagram:

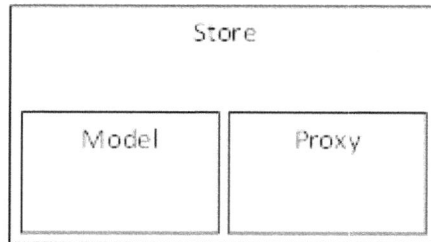

By separating out and encapsulating the data structure (that is, the Model) from how it is obtained or updated (that is, the associated Proxy), the Store provides a common abstraction for a component to work with, thus separating it from the presentation of the data. This makes Stores very much reusable between numerous data-bound components, if needed. Any data-bound component (that implements the IStore<Store> interface, such as a GridPanel, a DataView, a ComboBox, and many others) will, therefore, typically have a Store property that you can set.

This separation of concerns, therefore, gives us flexibility. For example, there are Proxies that can work with data purely on the client browser, as well as Proxies for storing data on the server. They all have a common interface so that the Model is not coupled to a particular way of storing and retrieving that information.

This means the user interface component does not have to worry too much about where the data came from, just that it has to show it. Whether paging, sorting, filtering, and other features are AJAX based or not, it is typically taken care of for you by the Store and its underlying Proxy.

In the following sections, we will look at how some different UI components can make use of the same Store architecture. We will start with the DataView, which builds upon our earlier XTemplate examples. Then we will look at ComboBoxes.

DataView

A **DataView** is one of the many data-bound controls that can use Stores and Models. It uses XTemplates to render data making it quite versatile.

Our first attempt

Let us make a variation of our earlier XTemplate example to show a few more capabilities. Suppose we want to show a list of employees (and quite a strange-looking bunch they are too!) similar to the following screenshot:

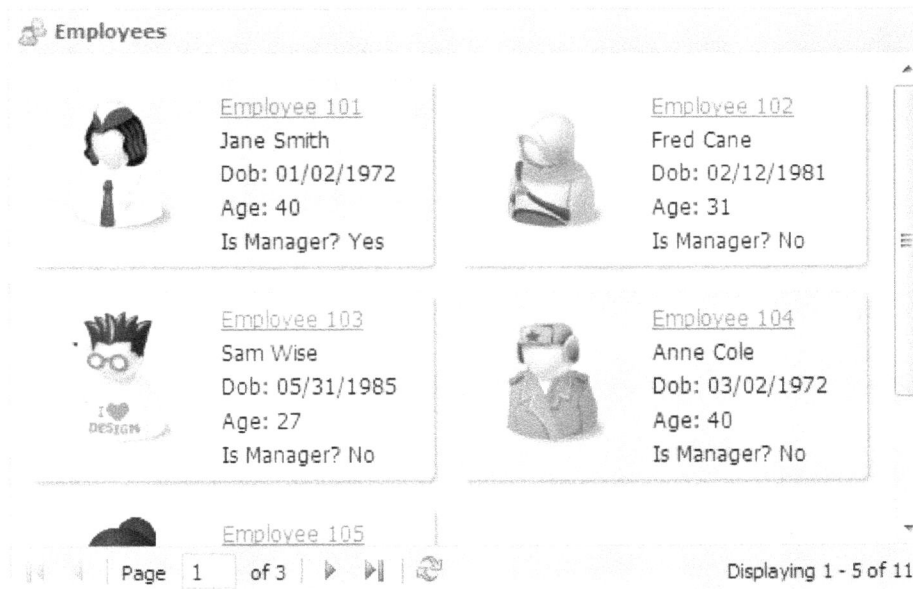

The icons are courtesy of Dante Michael Afrondoza (http://www.smashingmagazine.com/2008/11/05/dressup-avatars-icon-set/). Let's look at how this was achieved.

Preparing the data

First, we will use a simple class to present an employee as follows:

```
public class Employee
{
  public int Id { get; set; }
  public string FirstName { get; set; }
  public string LastName { get; set; }
```

```
public bool IsManager { get; set; }
public DateTime DateOfBirth { get; set; }
public int Age
{
  get { return DateTime.Today.Year - DateOfBirth.Year; }
}
}
```

We will also display this data in our XTemplate, using the following code:

```
<Tpl runat="server">
  <Html>
    <tpl for=".">
      <div class="info">
        <img src="/images/employees/{Id}.png" height="90"
             width="90" alt="Employee {Id}" />
        <p><a href="/details/{Id}">Employee {Id}</a></p>
        <p>{FirstName} {LastName}</p>
        <p>Dob: {DateOfBirth:date("m/d/Y")}</p>
        <p>Age: {Age}</p>
        <p>Is Manager? {IsManagerText}</p>
      </div>
    </tpl>
  </Html>
</Tpl>
```

Note that the date of birth line is written out using a date formatting function in the template itself. This is actually a shortcut to the `Ext.Date.format` function and is one of the various features of the XTemplate mentioned earlier.

In addition, notice that the `IsManagerText` property does not match any of the properties in the `Employee` class. This is because we can prepare the data for display using JavaScript, so we can dynamically augment a JavaScript instance of `Employee`. To demonstrate this, we will define a JavaScript function to prepare a given instance. We will see how it is used a little later:

```
var MyApp = {
  employee: {
    prepareData: function (data) {
      data.IsManagerText = data.IsManager === true ? 'Yes' : 'No';
      return data;
    }
  }
};
```

In the preceding code, a new property, `IsManagerText`, has been dynamically added to the data that has been passed in, based on the boolean `IsManager` property. This data will later be passed to the XTemplate for rendering so this new property can be used then.

The Store and Model in action

Now comes the part where we want to show a paged list. Our initial approach, to keep things simple, will be to bind a list of `Employee` instances to a component that can show them. As explained earlier, a Model defines the items that the Store will manage. So we will need to define a Model to represent the Employee and have the Store manage them:

```
<ext:Store ID="EmployeeStore" runat="server" PageSize="5">
  <Model>
    <ext:Model runat="server" IDProperty="Id">
      <Fields>
        <ext:ModelField Name="Id" />
        <ext:ModelField Name="FirstName" />
        <ext:ModelField Name="LastName" />
        <ext:ModelField Name="DateOfBirth" Type="Date" />
        <ext:ModelField Name="Age" Type="Int" />
        <ext:ModelField Name="IsManager" Type="Boolean" />
      </Fields>
    </ext:Model>
  </Model>
</ext:Store>
```

Note the following:

*   As no Proxy is defined explicitly, Ext.NET will default to `MemoryProxy`.

*   We have set `PageSize` to 5, so it will show five items at a time.

*   A Model is defined for the Store using `ModelField` to represent each item we want to show. As a minimum, we can set the `Name` property for the field. We can optionally set `Type` to one of `Auto` (default), `String`, `Int`, `Float`, `Boolean`, or `Date`. If set, the data will be converted accordingly.

*   Other properties can also be set, which we will look at later.

*   We have also told the Model that the `Id` field will act as the identifier for a given record. This is optional. If we don't have an identifier then the Store will manage one internally for you. Setting one is useful if you need to act on the ID or search the Store for records by an ID.

How will we populate this Store? One option is during the Load phase of the ASPX page:

```
protected void Page_Load(object sender, EventArgs e)
{
    this.EmployeeStore.DataSource = GetData();
    this.EmployeeStore.DataBind();
}

public List<Employee> GetData()
{
    // code to get the data…
}
```

A Store has a `DataSource` property, which can be set with the data we wish to bind. The type of `DataSource` is `System.Object`. Ext.NET checks if it is a bindable object, that is, something that implements any of the following:

* `System.ComponentModel.IListSource`
* `System.Collections.IEnumerable`
* `System.Web.UI.IDataSource`

In our example, it is `List<Employee>`. It could alternatively be a typed dataset, or an array or something else that implements one of the preceding interfaces. This means you can also reuse ASP.NET components as your data source, such as:

* `LinqDataSource`
* `ObjectDataSource`
* `SqlDataSource`
* `XmlDataSource`

> These data source controls can be defined separately on the page with their own `ID` property set. In that case, instead of setting the `DataSource` property on the Store, you set the `DataSourceID` property. Be sure to use just one. There are some examples at `http://examples.ext.net/#/search/datasource`.

A Store also has a `Data` property as we saw in the earlier XTemplate example. The difference with the `DataSource` property is that `Data` will just be serialized and sent to the client as it is. With the `DataSource` property the Store goes through all ModelFields and binds data accordingly ignoring any extra properties for which no ModelField is defined, assuming the Store `IgnoreExtraFields` is left with its default `true` value. (If `IgnoreExtraFields` is set to `false`, then all non-complex properties will be serialized.)

This means that Data can be hierarchical or deeply structured. When combined with the use of Associations, it can be used on the client in specialized cases. Visit http://examples.ext.net/#/Associations/HasMany/Simple/ for an example.

DataView to display the formatted data

Next, we put the Store inside a DataView control. DataView will basically watch for events from the Store (such as data being loaded) and pass the newly loaded data to the template for re-rendering. (In effect, DataView follows an MVC pattern, acting as a controller between the Store (which holds the model) and the template renderer (the view.) The following code shows how a DataView control can be declared:

```
<ext:DataView runat="server" ItemSelector=".info">
  <Store>
    <!--the Store we defined earlier goes here -->
  </Store>
  <Tpl runat="server">
    <!-- the template HTML we defined earlier goes here -->
  </Tpl>
  <PrepareData Fn="MyApp.employee.prepareData" />
</ext:DataView>
```

Notice the PrepareData property. We set its Fn property to point to our prepareData JavaScript function we defined earlier. This way whenever the DataView control is given new data by the Store, we get a chance to "prepare" it before passing it to the XTemplate.

Also note that DataView has a mandatory ItemSelector property, which is used if items are to be selected. We will shortly see an example of this.

Paging

So how do we enable paging? The DataView control doesn't come with an in-built pager; instead we re-use the PagingToolbar control from Ext.NET. We do this by declaring a DataView inside a container that can also contain such a toolbar, for example Panel:

```
<ext:Panel runat="server" Title="Employees" Icon="Group"
          AutoScroll="true">
  <Items>
    <ext:DataView runat="server" ItemSelector=".info">
      <!-- the DataView we defined earlier -->
    </ext:DataView>
  </Items>
  <BottomBar>
```

```
        <ext:PagingToolbar runat="server" StoreID="EmployeeStore" />
      </BottomBar>
   </ext:Panel>
```

Notice that `PagingToolbar` reuses the same Store we defined earlier by way of the `StoreID` property. The `PageSize` property from the Store will be passed to the `PagingToolbar` which will automatically respond to the Store's various events for you.

Putting it altogether

So putting the Ext.NET components all together it is quite a small amount of code:

```
<ext:Panel runat="server" Title="Employees" Icon="Group"
        AutoScroll="true" Height="330" Width="500">
   <Items>
     <ext:DataView runat="server" ItemSelector=".info">
       <Store>
         <ext:Store ID="EmployeeStore" runat="server" PageSize="5">
           <Model>
             <ext:Model runat="server" IDProperty="Id">
               <Fields>
                 <ext:ModelField Name="Id" />
                 <ext:ModelField Name="FirstName" />
                 <ext:ModelField Name="LastName" />
                 <ext:ModelField Name="DateOfBirth" Type="Date" />
                 <ext:ModelField Name="Age" Type="Int" />
                 <ext:ModelField Name="IsManager" Type="Boolean" />
               </Fields>
             </ext:Model>
           </Model>
         </ext:Store>
       </Store>
       <Tpl runat="server">
         <Html>
           <tpl for=".">
             <div class="info">
               <img
                 src="/images/employees/{Id}.png"
                 height="90" width="90" alt="Employee {Id}"
               />
               <p><a href="/details/{Id}">Employee{Id}</a></p>
               <p>{FirstName} {LastName}</p>
               <p>Dob: {DateOfBirth:date("m/d/Y")}</p>
               <p>Age: {Age}</p>
               <p>Is Manager? {IsManagerText}</p>
             </div>
           </tpl>
         </Html>
```

```
      </Tpl>
      <PrepareData Fn="MyApp.employee.prepareData" />
    </ext:DataView>
  </Items>
  <BottomBar>
    <ext:PagingToolbar runat="server" StoreID="EmployeeStore" />
  </BottomBar>
</ext:Panel>
```

Second attempt

The first attempt functions well. The client is loaded with all the employee data, and it is presented with paging and formatted, as we saw in the earlier screenshot.

Recall, however, that the default proxy was an in-memory proxy on the client side. This means the server has to get all the data to the client, even if some of it is not needed immediately. In some situations where the amount of data is relatively small, this can be efficient and prevent unnecessary round-tripping to the server. In many scenarios, however, we often deal with hundreds, if not thousands (or millions) of records of data. In those cases we would benefit from server-side paging.

Although our earlier example had 11 employees in total, we can still make use of server-side paging to see how the Store can be configured to retrieve extra data as required.

Generic ASHX handler for AJAX paging

As earlier chapters have shown, we can use many server-side approaches to retrieve data—MVC Controllers, ASMX, ASHX, and so on. Let us consider an ASHX handler:

```
public void ProcessRequest(HttpContext context)
{
    context.Response.ContentType = "application/json";

    var requestParams = new StoreRequestParameters(context);

    int start = requestParams.Start;
    int limit = requestParams.Limit;

    Paging<Employee> employees = GetData(start, limit);

    context.Response.Write(JSON.Serialize(employees));
}
```

Although this example is very small, there are a number of important things going on.

First, we create an instance of `StoreRequestParameters` with the current context. This is a simple Ext.NET class that exposes some useful Store-related properties, as follows:

- `int Start`: The starting record number to get (zero-based)
- `int Limit`: The number of records to get
- `int Page`: What page of data to get
- `DataFilter[] Filter`: A list of fields to filter on, including their values
- `DataSorter[] Sort`: A list of fields to sort on, including the sort direction
- `DataSorter[] Group`: A list of fields used for grouping

The first three are useful for our earlier example that we will be modifying. The `Filter` and `Sort` properties are also extremely useful and we will see them being used later. The `Group` property will be more easily demonstrated in *Chapter 6, Introducing GridPanels*.

In our example, we will make use of the `Start` and `Limit` properties, though we could alternatively have used the `Page` property—it depends on what data handling is needed. In our case, we modify our `GetData` from earlier to use a start and limit. The details of how `GetData` works are not important—you could call a database, a cache, whatever you need. For our purposes what is important is what to do with the data. In this example, we are returning an instance of a class called `Paging<T>` where `T` is of the `Employee` type.

`Paging<T>` is a simple class that contains two properties—`Data`, (of type `IEnumerable<T>`) which will be returned, and `TotalRecords` (an integer), which will let the PagingToolbar display the total number and calculate how much more paging to do. As long as you can get your data back like that then you are all set on the server side. Note, these are serialized into JSON as `data` (lowercase) and `total`.

Using an AjaxProxy

On the server side, the changes are quite simple. We do not need data-binding on `Page_Load`, so our earlier `Page_Load` method could be removed in its entirety. Instead, we simply add this Proxy to the Store, as follows:

```
<Proxy>
  <ext:AjaxProxy Url="EmployeesRetriever.ashx">
    <ActionMethods Read="GET" />
    <Reader>
      <ext:JsonReader Root="data" />
    </Reader>
  </ext:AjaxProxy>
</Proxy>
```

And that is it! So what is happening in the preceding code?

- We are making `AjaxProxy` work with `EmployeesRetriever.ashx`.

- We are setting the `ActionMethod` to be an HTTP `"GET"` request, rather than a `POST` request, as we are requesting a resource with a simple query.

- In addition, we are configuring a `Reader` to help it understand how to extract the data from the response. To see why, it is useful to see the JSON response our ASHX is sending back:

```
{
  "data":[{
    "Id":101,
    "FirstName":"Jane",
    "LastName":"Smith",
    "IsManager":true,
    "DateOfBirth":"1972-01-02T00:00:00",
    "Age":40
  },
  /* all the other records will appear here */
  ],
  "total":11
}
```

We are telling our JsonReader to read the data from the `data` property. The reader will, by default, find the total number of records in the `total` property. This configurability gives flexibility in cases where a `Paging<T>` result is not being used, or is not needed.

Filtering and sorting

In our ASHX example we saw the `Start`, `Limit`, and `Page` properties in the `StoreRequestParameters` object. It also had the `Filters` and `Sort` properties. Let's make use of them by adding a toolbar to the top of the Panel, which will let you filter on an employee's first name, and optionally sort on the last name, as follows:

```
<TopBar>
  <ext:Toolbar runat="server">
    <Items>
      <ext:ToolbarTextItem Text="Filter:" runat="server" />
      <ext:TextField ID="FilterText" runat="server"
                  EmptyText="Filter" />
      <ext:Button runat="server" Icon="Find">
        <Listeners>
          <Click Handler="MyApp.employee.filter(
```

```
                #{FilterText}.getValue(), #{EmployeeStore});" />
         </Listeners>
      </ext:Button>
      <ext:ToolbarSeparator runat="server" />
      <ext:Button runat="server" Icon="BulletArrowDown"
               Text="Sort by LastName Descending">
         <Listeners>
           <Click Handler=
            "#{EmployeeStore}.sort('LastName', 'DESC');"/>
         </Listeners>
      </ext:Button>
    </Items>
  </ext:Toolbar>
</TopBar>
```

The preceding code produces the following toolbar when added to the Panel:

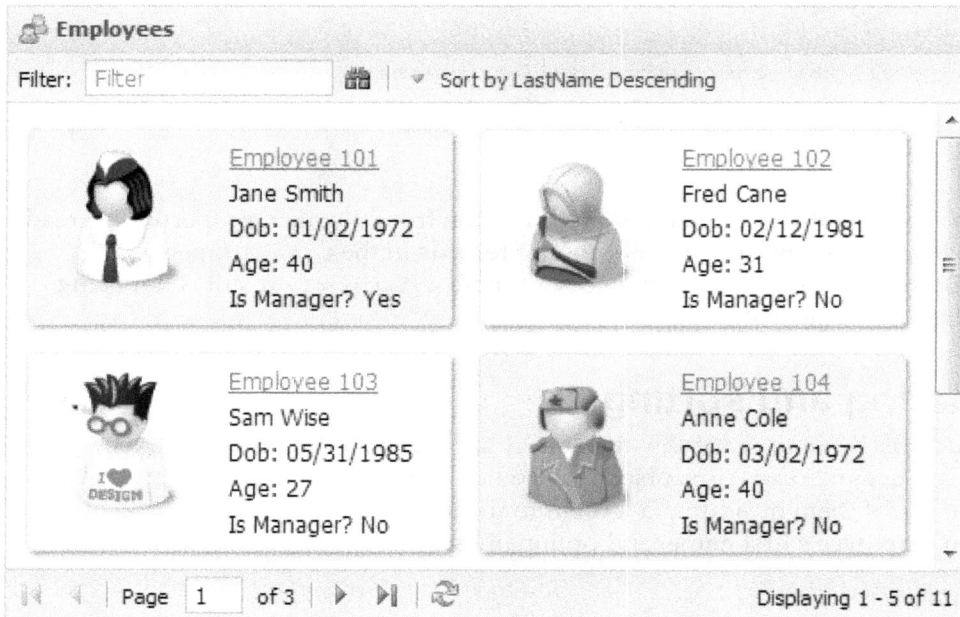

To enable the filtering and sorting to work remotely, we also need to tell the Store by setting the highlighted properties in the following line of code:

```
<ext:Store ID="EmployeeStore" runat="server" PageSize="5"
RemoteSort="true" RemoteFilter="true">
```

When the filter button is clicked, the client side instances of the TextField and Store are passed to our JavaScript function, `MyApp.employee.filter`, defined as follows:

```
filter: function (text, store) {
    store.filter('FirstName', text);
}
```

The client-side Store instance has a very simple and useful `filter` method where we can set the column to filter on and the value to filter with. In our contrived example, we've hardcoded it to filter on the first name. In a fuller example, we could have built more options into our toolbar to let the user choose.

The sort is also simple. We have called the Store's `sort` method when needed. The Store remembers the sort and filtering, so if you first filter and then press the sort button, it will send both items of data to the server and both those properties will be available on the `StoreRequestParameters` instance shown earlier. Then, it is up to your server handling code to pass the parameters to your business or data layer as required.

Handling selections in DataViews

So far, we have seen how data can be shown easily and quickly using a `DataView` control. We noted earlier that its `ItemSelector` property is mandatory. In this next example, we will show just the employee's image and name. Upon selecting a name, all the other data will be revealed. The following screenshot shows the screen after the initial load:

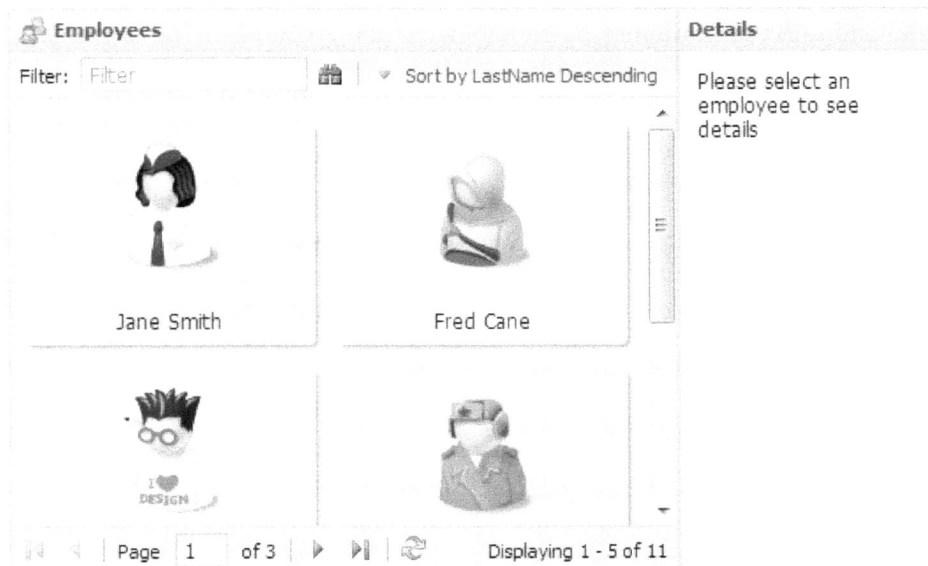

Once an employee is clicked on, the right-hand side **Details** panel will update to reveal more information. In the following screenshot **Jane Smith** has been clicked on:

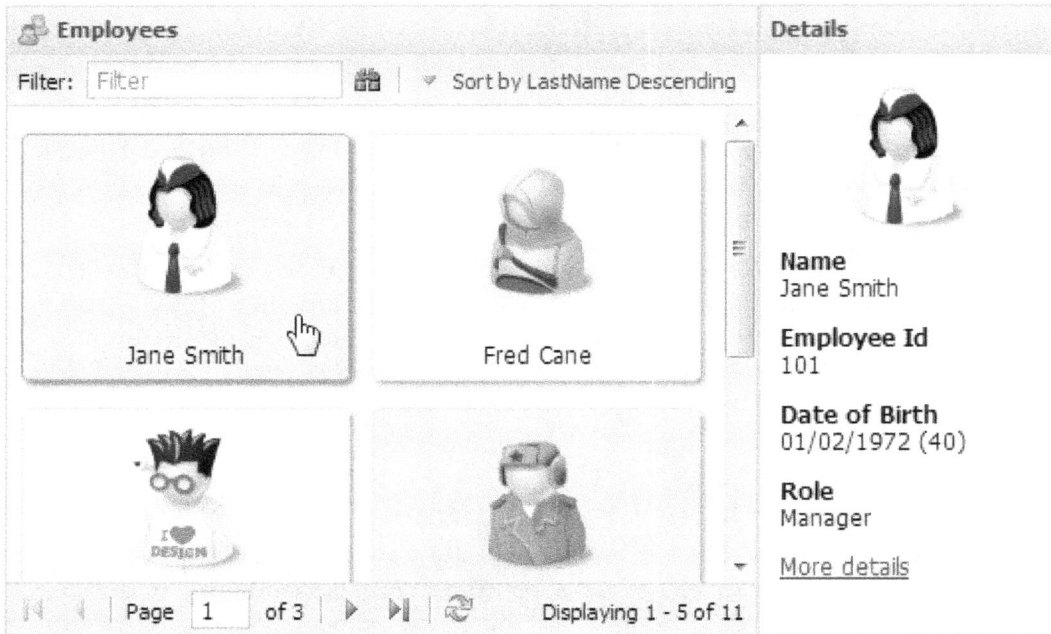

So how was this achieved? First, we put our Panel inside a lightweight Container and set the Layout to Border. We also moved the Width/Height dimensions out of the Panel and into the Container. The Panel was then given a Region of Center. And we finally introduced the East Panel to contain the details, as follows:

```
<ext:Container runat="server" Layout="Border" Width="530"
Height="330">
  <Items>
    <ext:Panel runat="server" Title="Employees" Icon="Group"
            AutoScroll="true" Region="Center">
      <!-- panel contents for the DataView goes here -->
    </ext:Panel>
    <ext:Panel
      ID="DetailsPanel"
      runat="server"
      Title="Details"
      BodyCls="details"
      Region="East"
      Width="150"
      Html="Please select an employee to see details">
```

```
    <!-- panel contents of employee details goes here -->
  </ext:Panel>
  </Items>
</ext:Container>
```

Next, for our Center Panel, almost everything is the same as before, except the following code snippet. We modify the template to show just the image and the name, as follows:

```
<Tpl runat="server">
  <Html>
    <tpl for=".">
      <div class="info">
        <img src="/images/employees/{Id}.png" height="90"
             width="90" alt="Employee {Id}" />
        <p>{FirstName} {LastName}</p>
      </div>
    </tpl>
  </Html>
</Tpl>
```

(The corresponding CSS is also adjusted as needed.) Recall, we set the `ItemSelector` property to `".info"`. It is a simple CSS selector that the `DataView` control will use to know what nodes to work with. It will also be used to map records with DOM nodes. In the template, there should be only one element that matches this CSS selector. Typically (though does not have to be) it is a `div` element with the required class, and the templates values go inside it.

So the other change needed is to handle the item selection event so that we can make the details appear on the right-hand side. To do this, we add a `SelectionChanged` listener to our Center region Panel, as follows:

```
<Listeners>
    <SelectionChange Handler="if (selections[0]) {
        App.DetailsPanel.loadRecord(selections[0]);
    }" />
</Listeners>
```

In the preceding code, we have just used an inline JavaScript handler. We test if there was a selection, and if so, we call the `loadRecord` method on `DetailsPanel` (our East region Panel). However, `loadRecord` is not available as a standard method on a `Panel` class. So let's see how the East Panel is put together.

This Panel is very simple as it just needs two parts—the template for the details to show and a way to define the `loadRecord` method mentioned earlier. The template can be added to the `Panel` control using the following code snippet:

```
<Tpl runat="server">
    <Html>
        <tpl for=".">
            <img src="/images/employees/{Id}.png" height="90"
                width="90" alt="Employee {Id}" />
            <h2>Name</h2>
            <p>{FirstName} {LastName}</p>

            <h2>Employee Id</h2>
            <p>{Id}</p>

            <h2>Date of Birth</h2>
            <p>{DateOfBirth:date("m/d/Y")} ({Age})</p>

            <h2>Role</h2>
            <p>
                <tpl if="IsManager === true">
                    Manager
                <tpl else>
                    Subordinate
                </tpl>
            </p>

            <p><a href="/Details/{Id}">More details</a></p>
        </tpl>
    </Html>
</Tpl>
```

Notice how we have been able to use properties of the prepared Employee data, such as `IsManager`. This is because when we first prepared the data, we added the property to the data that is maintained in the Store. That same data will be passed to this Panel for loading. We also used one of the XTemplate's many features, the conditional operator, to write out the correct role.

So now we need the `loadRecord` method to be defined on this `Panel` instance. There are a number of ways this can be done. One involves creating a `Panel` subclass in Ext JS and adding the method to that, followed by creating a corresponding subclass in Ext.NET and using that as our East region Panel. This is a good option but we will look at that in a later chapter. Another way, which is simpler for this example, and also shows the flexibility of Ext.NET is to simply add the function as a custom configuration property of this `Panel` instance:

```
<CustomConfig>
    <ext:ConfigItem
        Name="loadRecord"
```

```
            Value="function (employeeStore) {
                this.update(employeeStore.data);
            }"
            Mode="Raw"
            />
    </CustomConfig>
```

Recall that the `CustomConfig` collection can be used to store custom properties on your Ext.NET JavaScript component. As it is JavaScript, you can also dynamically add functions, not just data properties. Therefore, we can define a `loadRecord` method on this instance of the Panel which is called in our `SelectionChange` listener shown earlier. What this `loadRecord` method is doing is simply applying the template to the body of this Panel using the Store data that was passed in.

So there you have it; the server code (the ASHX to retrieve the Employee data) did not need modifying. Instead, we just slightly rearranged how the data would be displayed.

The preceding code could be optimized further as more data is being retrieved per Employee than what might be shown. In that case, we could do the following:

1. Make our Store Model much smaller by just defining the fields we need to show the name and picture (**First Name**, **Last Name**, **Employee Id**).

2. Modify the `loadRecord` method to invoke a DirectMethod to get the full details via an AJAX request.

3. Upon the success of that request, pass the AJAX response data to the East Panel's template to overwrite with this new data.

Example using a PageProxy

In the earlier example, we used an ASHX handler for an AjaxProxy and that is a great solution offering performance and flexibility for reuse. If you want to use a more familiar looking ASP.NET event model you can use the PageProxy instead.

In this approach you make use of the Store's `OnReadData` event, which is invoked when the Store is ready to receive data. The Store would then be configured, as follows:

```
<ext:Store ID="EmployeeStore" runat="server" PageSize="5"
        OnReadData="EmployeeStore_ReadData">
```

And instead of an AjaxProxy as the Store's `Proxy` property, you would use `PageProxy`:

```
<Proxy>
    <ext:PageProxy />
</Proxy>
```

Those two are the only differences to the Store configuration used for the AjaxProxy we used earlier. So what is left is to implement that event in our code-behind:

```
protected void EmployeeStore_ReadData(
    object sender, StoreReadDataEventArgs e)
{
    int start = e.Start;
    int limit = e.Limit;

    Paging<Employee> employees = GetData(start, limit);

    e.Total = employees.TotalRecords;

    EmployeeStore.DataSource = employees.Data;
    EmployeeStore.DataBind();
}
```

Notice how the code to get the data is exactly the same as the one in the ASHX handler used earlier. The Paging<T> object is useful because it contains the data we can pass to the Store's DataSource property but also the TotalRecords property (which is needed for the pager). Also note how TotalRecords is assigned a different way, using StoreReadDataEventArgs. This class is similar to StoreRequestParameters we saw earlier; it will also contain properties for the start of the page, the limit of how many to get, and any filtering information. But as we are using the PageProxy approach, it uses DirectEvents and ASP.NET event handling patterns to achieve the same end result.

Example using an ASP.NET data source control

If you are using one of the ASP.NET data source controls (or a custom one), such as ObjectDataSource, SqlDataSource, LinqDataSource, and so on, the setup of the Store is only slightly different. For example, let us consider ObjectDataSource:

```
<asp:ObjectDataSource
  ID="DataSource"
  runat="server"
  SelectMethod="GetData"
  TypeName="Data.DataViewExamples.Employee"
  OnSelected="DataSource_Selected">
  <SelectParameters>
    <asp:Parameter Name="start" DefaultValue="0" Type="Int32" />
    <asp:Parameter Name="limit" DefaultValue="5" Type="Int32" />
    <asp:Parameter Name="totalCount" Direction="Output"
                   Type="Int32" />
  </SelectParameters>
</asp:ObjectDataSource>
```

The corresponding `GetData` method signature might look like the following code:

```
public List<Employee> GetData(int start, int limit, out int
totalCount)
```

We won't show the implementation of that method; it would be whatever you need to get the data from your system. The key thing is that we can set this method to receive and return the type of information the Ext.NET Store would need, such as the starting record, how many to get, and the total count of all items which all help keep the pager in sync.

The `OnSelected` event handler will make sense once we see how to configure the Store. Compared to the earlier `PageProxy` example, we set `DataSourceID` as follows:

```
<ext:Store ID="EmployeeStore" runat="server" PageSize="5"
OnReadData="EmployeeStore_ReadData" DataSourceID="DataSource">
```

The `EmployeeStore_ReadData` event handler would, of course, be slightly different to our earlier example, too:

```
protected void EmployeeStore_ReadData(object sender,
    StoreReadDataEventArgs e)
{
    DataSource.SelectParameters["start"].DefaultValue =
        e.Start.ToString();
    DataSource.SelectParameters["limit"].DefaultValue =
        e.Limit.ToString();

    EmployeeStore.DataBind();
}
```

When the Store is ready to read the data, it adds a couple of extra parameters such as `Start` and `Limit` to the ObjectDataSource. It gets these from `StoreReadDataEventArgs`. This allows paged data to be returned.

However, we still need to get the total records so that the pager can display it and use it to calculate how many page numbers are possible. In our earlier example, Ext.NET's `Paging<T>` object contained a `TotalRecords` property. This time, however, we get it from the data source. Recall it was configured to have an out parameter. So this is where the `DataSource_Selected` event handler comes into play:

```
private void DataSource_Selected(object sender,
ObjectDataSourceStatusEventArgs e)
{
    ((PageProxy)EmployeeStore.Proxy[0]).Total =
        (int)e.OutputParameters["totalCount"];
}
```

Once the data has been read the out parameter is part of the event arguments sent to the Selected event; so in `DataSource_Selected`, we can simply update the Proxy's `Total` property to be `totalCount` that `GetData()` returned.

More about DataViews

DataViews are very rich and space in this chapter is unfortunately limited, so it is highly recommended to look at the Ext.NET Examples Explorer for more features of DataViews including multi-searching, multi-sorting, multi-filtering, and more at `http://examples.ext.net/#/search/dataview`.

ComboBox

While form controls will be covered in *Chapter 7, Forms and Validation*, it is worth investigating the ComboBox here. At first glance, it seems similar in functionality to a regular HTML `select` element, but in reality has more rich features akin to a desktop-like widget. In fact, it internally makes use of a `BoundList`, which is a subclass of DataView, hinting at the feature-rich options it potentially has, which we will touch upon.

Here we want to see how the idea of Stores and Models applies to a ComboBox. The reason these are reused here is that we are still binding data, but this time to the options of a ComboBox.

Define Store and Model with a ComboBox

Consider this following simple example that binds some data to a ComboBox. We will bind a list of five country names through the use of a Store:

```
<ext:ComboBox
    ID="ComboBox1"
    runat="server"
    Width="250"
    EmptyText="Select a country"
    DisplayField="name">
    <Store>
        <ext:Store runat="server">
            <Model>
                <ext:Model runat="server">
                    <Fields>
                        <ext:ModelField Name="name" />
                    </Fields>
                </ext:Model>
```

```
            </Model>
        </ext:Store>
    </Store>
</ext:ComboBox>
```

We have just defined a record with one field. We can then bind data to it; here we just bind an object array to keep the example simple, but in reality you may be getting this data from elsewhere:

```
protected void Page_Load(object sender, EventArgs e)
{
    var store = ComboBox1.GetStore();

    store.DataSource = new object[]
    {
        new object[] {"France"},
        new object[] {"Canada"},
        new object[] {"Germany"},
        new object[] {"Italy"},
        new object[] {"United Kingdom"},
        new object[] {"United States of America"}
    };

    store.DataBind();
}
```

And that is it. The following screenshot shows what we will see:

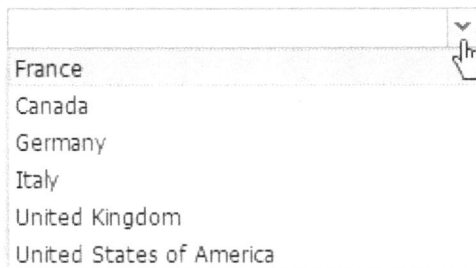

The ComboBox, by default, is a bit more functional than the HTML select element; it lets you type as well as pick and, therefore, acts as an autocomplete. You can configure whether to limit the ComboBox selection to the items in the drop-down list or allow free text entry to include items not bound to it. Many examples are available at http://examples.ext.net/#/search/ComboBox, but for our purposes here we want to see why Stores/Models, and even XTemplates are beneficial here.

Formatting the ComboBox with an XTemplate

Consider this example where we want to show extra information with each country. We will add a flag for each country and also some estimated population and GDP data.

First we will create a class to represent our data, as follows:

```
public class CountryInfo
{
    public string Name { get; set; }
    public double Gdp { get; set; }
    public int Population { get; set; }
    public Icon Icon { get; set; }
    public string IconClass
    {
        get { return ResourceManager.GetIconClassName(Icon); }
    }
}
```

To keep focus on the Ext.NET side of things, we will quickly add some static data to the preceding class. In reality this data may come from a database, for example:

```
private static readonly List<CountryInfo> Data = new List<CountryInfo>
{
    new CountryInfo { Icon = Icon.FlagCa, Name = "Canada", Gdp = 1.4,
Population = 34 },
    new CountryInfo { Icon = Icon.FlagFr, Name = "France", Gdp = 2.3,
Population = 63 },
    new CountryInfo { Icon = Icon.FlagDe, Name = "Germany", Gdp = 3.2,
Population = 83 },
    new CountryInfo { Icon = Icon.FlagGb, Name = "United Kingdom", Gdp
= 2.3, Population = 63 },
    new CountryInfo { Icon = Icon.FlagUs, Name = "United States of
America", Gdp = 15.0, Population = 313}
}
```

Next, we will now use it in our page by modifying our Page_Load method:

```
protected void Page_Load(object sender, EventArgs e)
{
    var store = this.ComboBox1.GetStore();
    store.DataSource = CountryInfo.Data;
    store.DataBind();

    var manager = ResourceManager.GetInstance();

    foreach (CountryInfo countryInfo in data)
    {
        manager.RegisterIcon(countryInfo.Icon);
    }
}
```

Note we are using the ResourceManager's `RegisterIcon` method to explicitly register the country flag icons that Ext.NET provides. This ensures the correct CSS and images are available to the code. If you have your own icons you do not need to do this. We will see how they are used shortly.

Next, we expand our Model to include the extra fields and declare types as needed:

```
<ext:Store runat="server">
  <Model>
    <ext:Model runat="server">
      <Fields>
        <ext:ModelField Name="icon" Mapping="IconClass" />
        <ext:ModelField Name="name" Mapping="Name" />
        <ext:ModelField Name="gdp" Mapping="Gdp" Type="Int" />
        <ext:ModelField Name="population" Mapping="Population"
                        Type="Float" />
      </Fields>
    </ext:Model>
  </Model>
</ext:Store>
```

The `Mapping` property shows that we can refer to a server property via a different name on the client if we want. This mapping happens on the client side after the data is received. There is also the option to do this mapping on the server side using the `ServerMapping` property. Visit the following link for examples:

http://examples.ext.net/#/GridPanel/Data_Presentation/Server_Mapping/

> The field has many other useful properties to control the sort direction, the sort data type (numeric sort, date sort, and so on), how to influence serialization, and more. It won't be possible to cover all of this in detail here due to constraints on this book's size, but the Sencha documentation has details worth studying:
>
> http://docs.sencha.com/ext-js/4-1/#!/api/Ext.data.Field

And finally to show this data, the ComboBox reuses the handy XTemplate features we have seen earlier via the `ListConfig` property, as follows:

```
<ListConfig>
  <ItemTpl runat="server">
    <Html>
      <div class="icon-combo-item {icon}">
        {name}
        <div class="details">
          <p>2011 Population (millions): {population}</p>
          <p>2011 GDP (trillions): ${gdp}</p>
        </div>
```

```
        </div>
      </Html>
    </ItemTpl>
  </ListConfig>
```

And assuming the CSS is formatted to your liking, you will get output, as follows:

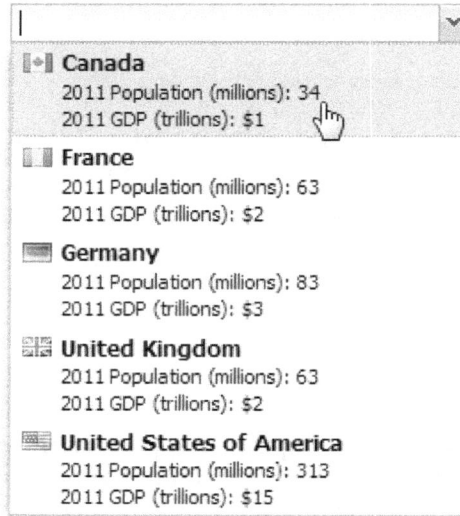

> In the preceding example, when a country is picked, the name is displayed in the ComboBox field. The following example shows how to display the icon as well: `http://examples.ext.net/#/Form/ComboBox/IconCombo/`.

This is quite powerful; you can format the ComboBox contents to show more data, richly formatted, improving the user experience and usability. But wait; it gets better!

Enabling store paging on a ComboBox

The preceding Stores do not have a Proxy defined. This means they get the in-memory Proxy by default, so all the data is shown in one go. Let us suppose that there was data for more countries (for our example we will say five more).

First we increase the size of our data (and register the additional icons accordingly). The code for that is the same as the first five countries shown earlier, so it is not repeated here. Next we simply update the Store to enable local paging using `IsPagingStore`:

```
<ext:Store runat="server" IsPagingStore="true" PageSize="5">
```

We also tell the ComboBox that paging is enabled so we add a similar `PageSize="5"` property there. And that is it. Our in-memory proxy is now paged, as follows:

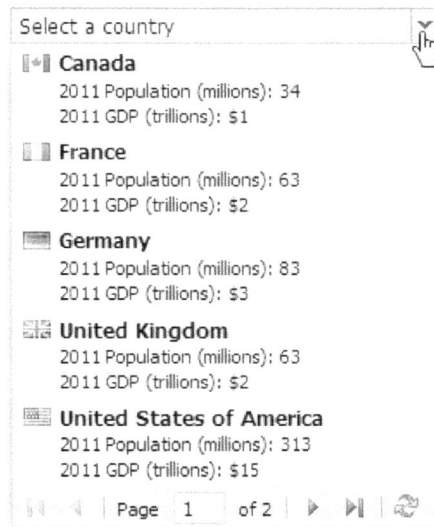

Selecting the second page simply replaces the data shown, as expected:

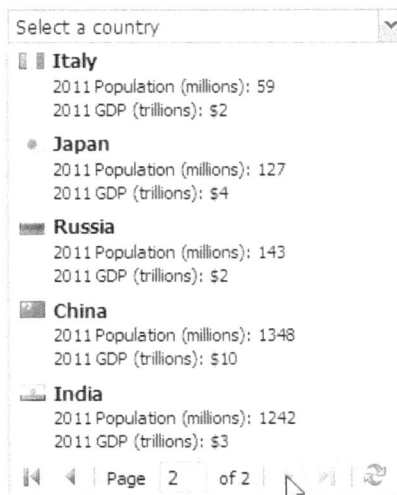

But we can still go further. A Store can be configured with other Proxies, so why not an AJAX-enabled one? This could be useful if showing hundreds of countries or other data.

Using a server-side Proxy for the Store

The only change we need to make to our ComboBox is to change the Store to use one of the server-side Proxies, such as AjaxProxy as this example shows:

```
<Proxy>
  <ext:AjaxProxy Url="CountryData.ashx">
    <ActionMethods Read="GET" />
    <Reader>
      <ext:JsonReader Root="Data" />
    </Reader>
  </ext:AjaxProxy>
</Proxy>
```

Finally the code in our Page_Load can be shifted into CountryData.ashx:

```
public void ProcessRequest(HttpContext context)
{
    context.Response.ContentType = "application/json";

    var requestParams = new StoreRequestParameters(context);

    int start = requestParams.Start;
    int limit = requestParams.Limit;

    var data = CountryInfo.GetData(start, limit);
    var total = CountryInfo.TotalDataCount;

    var countries = new Paging<CountryInfo>(data, total);

    context.Response.Write(JSON.Serialize(countries));
}
```

With paging enabled, the Start and Limit properties will be set. Assuming the CountryInfo example class has implemented the GetData() method and the TotalDataCount property, we can return the Paging<CountryInfo> instance as JSON.

And that is it; now the ComboBox is able to serve larger sets of data. The output would look the same as the paging screenshots earlier, except paging is now server side.

Summary

Data access is crucial in most applications. The architecture of Ext JS and Ext. NET's data access allows for a lot of flexibility. We looked at XTemplates that allow rich formatting of repeated data, and DataViews and ComboBoxes as examples where XTemplates are used. We also looked at Stores and Models, introduced with DataViews and ComboBoxes, which showed us how data-driven applications are modeled and how the architecture supports a clean separation of concerns.

Ext.NET is vast and would require volumes to write about all of its features! For example, a powerful new feature in Models is the ability to relate data to each other, much like how tables in a relational database can be related or how your data may be hierarchical. For example, a `Person` object may have a complex `Address` object. Ext. NET supports modeling data using Associations. It is worth studying some useful examples in the Ext.NET Examples Explorer at `http://examples.ext.net/#/search/associations`.

There are many other data-bound components that we have not had a chance to cover here, for example Charts (see `http://examples.ext.net/#/search/chart`) and TreePanels (see *Chapter 8, Trees and Tabs with Ext.NET*). One major data-bound component that we *can* devote an entire chapter to, however, is the GridPanel as it is also one of the more popular ones, so we will look at that next.

6
Introducing GridPanels

In the previous chapter, we were introduced to Stores, Models, and Proxies. They are a central part of Ext JS and Ext.NET's data architecture, providing a clean separation of concerns between presentation and data storage, retrieval and modeling. We looked at some components that make use of it in the previous chapter, but left the popular GridPanel to be covered in its own chapter here. The GridPanel is incredibly versatile, and although this chapter cannot cover all the possibilities here, we will look at the following:

- Overview of the GridPanel
- Simple GridPanels
- Column-types
- AJAX-based proxies
- Paging
- Filtering
- Sorting
- Grouping
- Column summaries
- Master detail
- Selection models
- Grid editing

By the end of this chapter, you will gain an appreciation for the versatility of the GridPanel, which enables a rich experience for end users.

GridPanel – overview

Although Stores handle data access and persistence, and Models define the data, the GridPanel is responsible for bringing them together with column management and other grid-related features.

Essentially, a GridPanel is made of two main parts as follows:

- A Store (and Model) to handle the data
- Columns to render the data into

In addition, a GridPanel can be augmented with many more capabilities, for example:

- A View, which handles rendering of each row. (By default, a GridPanel uses a View internally to render rows for you, but Ext.NET also exposes the View to be configured with more options if required)
- Paging, filtering, sorting, grouping
- Row expansion
- Controlling how data values are formatted for display
- Controlling how rows and cells might be selected
- Numerous options for editing grids, inline or per row
- A variety of ways to retrieve local or remote data by reusing the Store architecture described in *Chapter 5, Working with Data*, as well as using other data-bound controls, such as various DataSource controls
- A variety of ways to save data reusing the Store architecture and other APIs
- Extensibility through the use of custom features and plugins
- Flexible options to control paging and scrolling (for example, infinite scrolling with data loaded on demand)
- Commands that can be used to provide custom actions for a cell, a row, or a group of rows
- There is even the built-in drag-and-drop support for various operations (such as resizing and reordering columns)

The GridPanel is probably the most feature-rich of all components in Ext.NET, hence we have a full chapter for covering it. But even with its own chapter, it will not be possible to show everything! We will look at many core features here, but it is highly recommended to spend time looking at the Ext.NET Examples Explorer. The following link shows all grid-related functionality:

```
http://examples.ext.net/#/search/grid
```

Simple grid

We will start with a simple grid with just a Store and some basic column definitions. To show some different data types rendered, we will use the same dummy financial sample data used in some of Ext.NET's own Examples Explorer to produce the following:

Simple Grid					
Company	Price	Change	Change	Last Updated	
3m Co	$71.72	0.02	0.03%	2012-09-01 12:00am	▲
Alcoa Inc	$29.01	0.42	1.47%	2012-09-01 12:00am	
Altria Group Inc	$83.81	0.28	0.34%	2012-09-01 12:00am	≡
American Express Company	$52.55	0.01	0.02%	2012-09-01 12:00am	
American International Group, Inc.	$64.13	0.31	0.49%	2012-09-01 12:00am	
AT&T Inc.	$31.61	-0.48	-1.54%	2012-09-01 12:00am	
Boeing Co.	$75.43	0.53	0.71%	2012-09-01 12:00am	
Caterpillar Inc.	$67.27	0.92	1.39%	2012-09-01 12:00am	
Citigroup, Inc.	$49.37	0.02	0.04%	2012-09-01 12:00am	
E.I. du Pont de Nemours and Company	$40.48	0.51	1.28%	2012-09-01 12:00am	
Exxon Mobil Corp	$68.10	-0.43	-0.64%	2012-09-01 12:00am	
General Electric Company	$34.14	-0.08	-0.23%	2012-09-01 12:00am	▼

Let's have at a look at a breakdown of how we created the preceding grid. First we set up the data. For the purposes of this book, the sample data will be simply defined in the following `CompanyData` class with a static helper method to get the data:

```
public class CompanyData
{
    public int Id { get; set; }
    public string Name { get; set; }
    public double Price { get; set; }
    public double Change { get; set; }
    public double PercentChange { get; set; }
    public DateTime LastChange { get { return DateTime.Now; } }

    public CompanyData(int id, string name, double price,
        double change, double percentChange)
    {
        // code omitted for brevity; each argument is assigned
        // to corresponding property.
    }
```

```
public static List<CompanyData> GetData()
{
  return new List<CompanyData>
  {
    new CompanyData(1, "3m Co", 71.72, 0.02, 0.03),
    new CompanyData(2, "Alcoa Inc", 29.01, 0.42, 1.47),
    // The rest of the data omitted for brevity */
  }
}
}
```

Because GridPanels also work with Stores, we will bind the preceding code snippet to a Store that will be used by the GridPanel. We will assume the ID of the Store is set to Store1:

```
protected void Page_Load(object sender, EventArgs e)
{
  if (!X.IsAjaxRequest)
  {
    this.Store1.DataSource = CompanyData.GetData();
    this.Store1.DataBind();
  }
}
```

Similar to earlier examples in *Chapter 5, Working with Data*, we just assign the data to the DataSource which is assigned to the Store. We also do this once and only if it is not an AJAX request (that is during the page load without an AJAX PostBack). Now we set up the configuration of the GridPanel itself:

```
<ext:GridPanel runat="server" Title="Simple Grid">
  <Store>
    <!-- A store definition will go here -->
  </Store>
  <ColumnModel>
    <Columns>
      <!-- each column definition will go here -->
    </Columns>
  </ColumnModel>
</ext:GridPanel>
```

The following code snippet shows how the Store is defined:

```
<ext:Store ID="Store1" runat="server">
  <Model>
    <ext:Model runat="server" IDProperty="Id">
      <Fields>
        <ext:ModelField Name="Company" Mapping="Name" />
        <ext:ModelField Name="Price" Type="Float" />
```

```
        <ext:ModelField Name="Change" Type="Float" />
        <ext:ModelField Name="PctChange"
            Mapping="PercentChange" Type="Float" />
        <ext:ModelField Name="LastChange" Type="Date" />
      </Fields>
    </ext:Model>
  </Model>
</ext:Store>
```

For the Model, we have set the IDProperty to "Id". This indicates that this property will serve as the identifier for a record, even though we have not explicitly added a field declaration for it (because we are not going to do anything else with it).

We have also set specific data types for the rest of the fields, where necessary. The default is Auto, so the **Company** column doesn't need one explicitly set. Note, where Type is set to Date, you can also set a DateFormat property to tell the Store what format the expected data will be in. If omitted, the default will be the ISO-8601 sortable date format to which the JSON serializer will serialize. This just tells the Store which format to expect the data in, not which format to display it in (which we will see shortly).

> The DateFormat property uses .NET format strings, while Ext JS uses PHP-based date format strings. Ext.NET takes care of translating between the two for you.

For some of the fields, we have also set a mapping. This lets us map, if we want, a property in the underlying data to a different name that the Store (and in this case, the GridPanel too) will use.

Now that the Store is set, we need to define each column so that the ColumnModel and GridPanel can display the data from the Store appropriately:

```
<Columns>
  <ext:Column Text="Company" DataIndex="Company" Flex="1" />
  <ext:Column Text="Price" DataIndex="Price" Width="50">
    <Renderer Format="UsMoney" />
  </ext:Column>
  <ext:Column Text="Change" DataIndex="Change" Width="50">
    <Renderer Fn="change" />
  </ext:Column>
  <ext:Column Text="Change" DataIndex="PctChange" Width="50">
    <Renderer Fn="pctChange" />
  </ext:Column>
  <ext:DateColumn Text="Last Updated" DataIndex="LastChange"
Format="yyyy-MM-dd hh:mmtt" Width="130" />
</Columns>
```

There are many settings used in the preceding code snippet, explained as follows:

- `Flex="1"` will look familiar if you recall the HBox layout component in *Chapter 3, Layout with Ext.NET*. This is because columns are laid out using a special grid `ColumnLayout`, which is a subclass of the HBox layout. What it means for our columns is that the name column will take up any remaining space (as the others all have widths explicitly assigned to them).

- A `DataIndex` property has been assigned to each column to map the column to the corresponding field in the Store's Model. Note the `DataIndex` property matches the field name, not the mapping. Using a `DataIndex` property lets you swap the order of columns around, compared to the order they are defined in the Model or the order in which they are populated in the Store.

- Some of the columns also use a special `Renderer`, which calls a custom JavaScript function. This function will run for each cell in that column, so you have an opportunity to adjust the rendering of the cell value further. (This is how the **Change** columns in the earlier screenshot were formatted).

- The last column is a subclass of column; `DateColumn`. As a column for dates, it also has a `Format` property for the rendering format, so it can be independent of the format received by the Store.

The following is the JavaScript (and some associated CSS) for the renderers:

```
<style type="text/css">
  .positive { color: green; }
  .negative { color: red; }
</style>

<script>
  var template = '<span class="{0}">{1}</span>';

  var change = function (value) {
    return Ext.String.format(template,
        (value > 0) ? "positive" : "negative", value);
  };

  var pctChange = function (value) {
    return Ext.String.format(template,
        (value > 0) ? "positive" : "negative", value + "%");
  };
</script>
```

A value is passed to the `Renderer` function and is required to return a value. This value can be modified as we have done before, or it can return the original value if it does not need reformatting. The `Renderer` function is also passed additional parameters that we have not used here — metadata about the current cell, the current record, row and column indexes, the store, and the view. See the following link for more information about them:

```
http://docs.sencha.com/ext-js/4-1/#!/api/Ext.grid.column.Column-
cfg-renderer
```

Note that only two renderers are defined here. The renderer defined for the **Price** column is `UsMoney`, and uses the `Format` property instead of the `Fn` property. The `Format` property is a string name for a formatter function built into Ext JS.

> Other formatter functions can be found in the `Ext.util.`
> `Format` namespace in Ext JS, and is also documented at
> `http://docs.sencha.com/ext-js/4-1/#!/api/`
> `Ext.util.Format`. Ext.NET also adds `euroMoney`.

The default grid rendering has more than what a screenshot can show, for example:

- Scrolling is done on the data rows only, leaving the header fixed.
- By default, clicking on a row selects the entire row.
- You can sort by clicking on the column header.
- Each column has a column menu, where you can also pick the sort order you want. In addition, you can choose which columns to show/hide.
- Columns can be resized by default.
- Columns can be moved by dragging them to the preferred place.

The following are screenshots showing some of those features in action:

Simple Grid				
Company ▾	Price	Change	Change	Last Updated
Wal-Mart Stores, Inc.	$45.45	0.73	1.63%	2012-09-01 12:00am
Verizon Communications	$35.57	0.39	1.11%	2012-09-01 12:00am
United Technologies Corporation	$63.26	0.55	0.88%	2012-09-01 12:00am
The Procter & Gamble Company	$61.91	0.01	0.02%	2012-09-01 12:00am
The Home Depot, Inc.	$34.64	0.35	1.02%	2012-09-01 12:00am
The Coca-Cola Company	$45.07	0.26	0.58%	2012-09-01 12:00am
Pfizer Inc	$27.96	0.4	1.45%	2012-09-01 12:00am
Microsoft Corporation	$25.84	0.14	0.54%	2012-09-01 12:00am
Merck & Co., Inc.	$40.96	0.41	1.01%	2012-09-01 12:00am
McDonald"s Corporation	$36.76	0.86	2.4%	2012-09-01 12:00am
Johnson & Johnson	$64.72	0.06	0.09%	2012-09-01 12:00am
JP Morgan & Chase & Co	$45.73	0.07	0.15%	2012-09-01 12:00am
International Business Machines	$81.41	0.44	0.54%	2012-09-01 12:00am

In the preceding screenshot, the data has been sorted by clicking on the **Company** column heading. Also, one row has been selected. You can also resize columns:

Simple Grid				
Company	Price	Change ▲	Change ▾	Last Updated
AT&T Inc.	$31.61	-0.48	-1.54%	2012-09-01 12:00am
Exxon Mobil Corp	$68.10	-0.43	-0.64%	2012-09-01 12:00am
General Electric Company	$34.14	-0.08	-0.23%	2012-09-01 12:00am
Hewlett-Packard Co.	$36.53	-0.03	-0.08%	2012-09-01 12:00am
The Procter & Gamble Company	$61.91	0.01	0.02%	2012-09-01 12:00am

In the preceding screenshot, the **Change** column is sorted. The column also has the mouse cursor changed to a resize indicator as it hovers between its adjacent column. With the mouse hovered over the second column, a menu indicator is shown, as follows:

Simple Grid				
Company	Price	Change ▲	Change ▼	Last Updated
AT&T Inc.	$31.61	-0.48	-1.54%	A↓ Sort Ascending
Exxon Mobil Corp	$68.10	-0.43	-0.64%	Z↓ Sort Descending
General Electric Company	$34.14	-0.08	-0.23%	
Hewlett-Packard Co.	$36.	☑ Company		Columns ▷
The Procter & Gamble Company	$61.			
American Express Company	$52.	☑ Price		2012-09-01 12:00am
Citigroup, Inc.	$49.	☑ Change		2012-09-01 12:00am
3m Co	$71.			2012-09-01 12:00am
Honeywell Intl Inc	$38.	☑ Change		2012-09-01 12:00am
Johnson & Johnson	$64.	☑ Last Updated		2012-09-01 12:00am
JP Morgan & Chase & Co	$45.73	0.07	0.15%	2012-09-01 12:00am
Microsoft Corporation	$25.84	0.14	0.54%	2012-09-01 12:00am
The Coca-Cola Company	$45.07	0.26	0.58%	2012-09-01 12:00am

The default column menu allows you to sort the columns there as well, and even choose which columns you want to show/hide (by default they are all visible).

And you can also rearrange columns by dragging them, as follows:

Simple Grid				
Company	▼ Price	Change ▲	Change	Last Updated
AT&T Inc.	$31.61	-0.48	-1.54%	2012-09-01 12:00am
Exxon Mobil Corp	Last Updated		-0.64%	2012-09-01 12:00am
General Electric Company	$34.14	-0.08	-0.23%	2012-09-01 12:00am
Hewlett-Packard Co.	$36.53	-0.03	-0.08%	2012-09-01 12:00am

In the preceding screenshot, the **Last Updated** column is being dragged to appear after the **Company** column; and those are just the defaults. As we will see shortly, the column menu can also contain filtering options and grouping options. And the row selection model can be configured to be just the cell, or to go into editing mode, and more.

Column types

In the preceding section, we saw all but the **Last Updated** column defined using `<ext:Column />`. The **Last Updated** column was defined using `<ext:DateColumn />`. For the other numeric columns, we were happy to deal with them as strings, because the format functions were going to decorate the values with extra HTML anyway. Also, because our ModelField definition inside our Store for these columns had their Type set to Float, features such as sorting will be numeric sorting.

If you wanted a formatting specific to numbers, for example, rounding the first **Change** column to one decimal place, even though the raw data is in two decimal places, you could use NumberColumn, because its Format property takes a numeric format to use for display, for example:

```
<ext:NumberColumn Text="Change" DataIndex="Change" Width="50"
Format="0.0" />
```

BooleanColumn is also available that lets you set the "True" and "False" text to something else (such as, Yes and No) using the TrueText and FalseText properties.

Other types of columns include CheckColumn for a checkbox column, RatingColumn to create a column where you can see and enter ratings, and ComponentColumn, which lets you show components for each column, offering you flexibility for presentation. Visit http://examples.ext.net/#/search/column for examples.

In addition, CommandColumn, ImageCommandColumn, and ActionColumn allow you to set up columns with commands to apply custom actions. For more examples, go to http://examples.ext.net/#/search/command.

The following code enables a column of row numbers:

```
<ext:RowNumbererColumn runat="server" />
```

And you can even use `TemplateColumn` to take advantage of XTemplates per cell. For example, we could replace our percentage change column by using the following code:

```
<ext:TemplateColumn Text="Change" DataIndex="PctChange">
  <Template runat="server">
    <Html>
      <tpl for=".">
        <tpl if="PctChange &lt; 0">
          <span class="negative">{PctChange}% (Down)</span>
        <tpl elseif="PctChange === 0">
          (No change)
        <tpl else>
          <span class="positive">{PctChange}% (Up)</span>
        </tpl>
      </tpl>
    </Html>
  </Template>
</ext:TemplateColumn>
```

If we put the `RowNumbererColumn` as our first column as well as the previous `TemplateColumn`, it would result in the following screenshot:

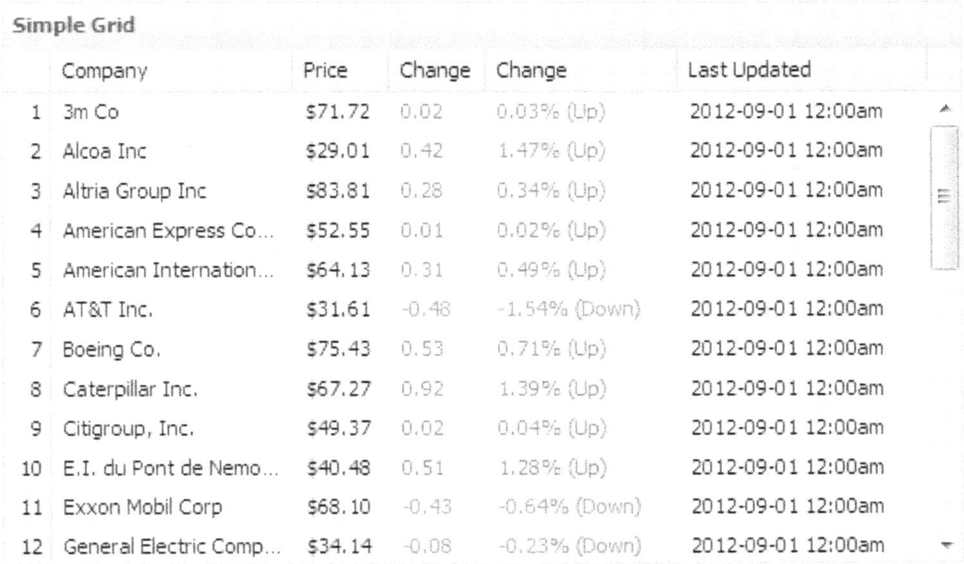

Simple Grid					
	Company	Price	Change	Change	Last Updated
1	3m Co	$71.72	0.02	0.03% (Up)	2012-09-01 12:00am
2	Alcoa Inc	$29.01	0.42	1.47% (Up)	2012-09-01 12:00am
3	Altria Group Inc	$83.81	0.28	0.34% (Up)	2012-09-01 12:00am
4	American Express Co...	$52.55	0.01	0.02% (Up)	2012-09-01 12:00am
5	American Internation...	$64.13	0.31	0.49% (Up)	2012-09-01 12:00am
6	AT&T Inc.	$31.61	-0.48	-1.54% (Down)	2012-09-01 12:00am
7	Boeing Co.	$75.43	0.53	0.71% (Up)	2012-09-01 12:00am
8	Caterpillar Inc.	$67.27	0.92	1.39% (Up)	2012-09-01 12:00am
9	Citigroup, Inc.	$49.37	0.02	0.04% (Up)	2012-09-01 12:00am
10	E.I. du Pont de Nemo...	$40.48	0.51	1.28% (Up)	2012-09-01 12:00am
11	Exxon Mobil Corp	$68.10	-0.43	-0.64% (Down)	2012-09-01 12:00am
12	General Electric Comp...	$34.14	-0.08	-0.23% (Down)	2012-09-01 12:00am

You can also disable a column menu by setting `DisableMenu="True"` for any column.

AJAX-based proxies

The same versatility we saw with Store Proxies in *Chapter 5, Working with Data*, applies to grids too, so that we can load the preceding financial data from an MVC Controller, ASMX Web Service, ASHX handler, and more. The following is an example of ASHX handler:

```
public void ProcessRequest(HttpContext context)
{
  context.Response.ContentType = "application/json";

  Paging<CompanyData> data = this.GetData();

  context.Response.Write(JSON.Serialize(data));
}

private Paging<CompanyData> GetData()
{
  var data = CompanyData.GetData();

  return new Paging<CompanyData>(data, data.Count);
}
```

And the following is the only modification needed to the Store to use the handler:

```
<ext:Store runat="server">
  <Model>
    <!-- as before -->
  </Model>
  <Proxy>
    <ext:AjaxProxy Url="../Shared/FinancialData.ashx">
      <Reader>
        <ext:JsonReader Root="data" />
      </Reader>
    </ext:AjaxProxy>
  </Proxy>
</ext:Store>
```

By adding AjaxProxy in this way, we can point to the handler we have created.

We can remove the initial Page_Load, which is no longer needed (so you could also remove ID off the Store because it is no longer used by anything, and everything else remains the same. The GridPanel will load and show the same data as per the earlier screenshots. With this in place, we can now look at some of the other features of the grid.

Paging

To show paging controls we reuse a `PagingToolbar`, as demonstrated in *Chapter 5, Working with Data*.

Client-side paging

To enable client-side paging, we just need to do two things. We add a `PagingToolbar` to the GridPanel. Because a GridPanel inherits a Panel, we just add it either to a docked item, or to one of the special properties such as `BottomBar`, `TopBar`, and so on. `BottomBar` is usually the typical option, so we add it to the GridPanel as follows:

```
<BottomBar>
    <ext:PagingToolbar runat="server" />
</BottomBar>
```

Next we simply need to initialize the Store with paging as follows:

```
<ext:Store runat="server" RemotePaging="false" PageSize="10">
```

The result will be a paging toolbar at the bottom, as shown in the following screenshot:

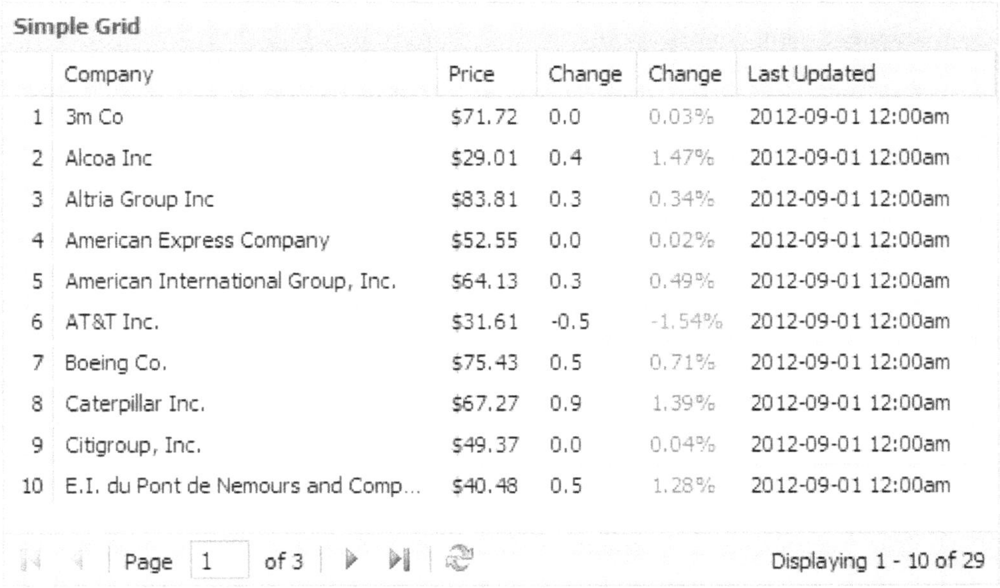

	Company	Price	Change	Change	Last Updated
Simple Grid					
1	3m Co	$71.72	0.0	0.03%	2012-09-01 12:00am
2	Alcoa Inc	$29.01	0.4	1.47%	2012-09-01 12:00am
3	Altria Group Inc	$83.81	0.3	0.34%	2012-09-01 12:00am
4	American Express Company	$52.55	0.0	0.02%	2012-09-01 12:00am
5	American International Group, Inc.	$64.13	0.3	0.49%	2012-09-01 12:00am
6	AT&T Inc.	$31.61	-0.5	-1.54%	2012-09-01 12:00am
7	Boeing Co.	$75.43	0.5	0.71%	2012-09-01 12:00am
8	Caterpillar Inc.	$67.27	0.9	1.39%	2012-09-01 12:00am
9	Citigroup, Inc.	$49.37	0.0	0.04%	2012-09-01 12:00am
10	E.I. du Pont de Nemours and Comp...	$40.48	0.5	1.28%	2012-09-01 12:00am

Page 1 of 3 ▶ ▶| ⟳   Displaying 1 - 10 of 29

If you are using a remote proxy such as the AjaxProxy shown earlier but with client-side paging, you need to set `RemotePaging` to `"false"` explicitly. Otherwise it will default to server-side paging. If you are using one of the client-side proxies, then `RemotePaging` would be `"false"` by default and would not need to be set.

Why would you want AJAX loading but just local paging? Admittedly, it is less likely a situation, though if you know the amount of data is small, you may want to keep your network activity down to a minimum and improve responsiveness for the end user.

Server-side paging

Despite the user experience benefit of paging locally, it of course has the drawback of needing to load all the data upfront, which in many cases would be too much. So we then use server-side paging, which we have seen with examples of DataViews and ComboBoxes. We will reuse those same techniques here.

First we set `RemotePaging="true"` on the Store (or omit it entirely because it is true by default for remote proxies). Next, we simply use the `StoreRequestParameters` to limit the data we retrieve to be just a page worth each time:

```
public void ProcessRequest(HttpContext context)
{
    context.Response.ContentType = "application/json";

    var requestParams = new StoreRequestParameters(context);

    int start = requestParams.Start;
    int limit = requestParams.Limit;

    Paging<CompanyData> data = GetData(start, limit);

    context.Response.Write(JSON.Serialize(data));
}

private Paging<CompanyData> GetData(int start, int limit)
{
    var data = CompanyData.GetData();

    int numberToGet = start + limit > data.Count
        ? data.Count - start : limit;

    return new Paging<CompanyData>(data.GetRange(start,
        numberToGet), data.Count);
}
```

Now that the paging is being done remotely as well, the grid will automatically show the loading mask when paging.

Filtering

Filtering on the grid is a common operation for rich applications. Each column is a potentially filterable column. Rich desktop applications often provide this quite easily, whereas for regular HTML-based tables implementing one yourself would require a fair bit of initial effort. Luckily a fair bit of effort has gone into building this functionality for us, so enabling filtering is a simple configuration.

Filtering can be configured to be client-side using the data already held by the Store, or server side, across all your data.

Client-side filtering

Filtering is defined as a "Feature" of the GridPanel. The GridPanel is quite complex compared to most other components. As a result, in addition to adding your own customizations via plugins that you can do to almost every component (which we will look at in a later chapter) some of the common components that were provided as plugins in previous versions are now included directly as features of the GridPanel to help them run with other features side-by-side more seamlessly.

So client-side filtering can be set up as follows:

```
<Features>
    <ext:GridFilters Local="true">
        <Filters>
            <ext:StringFilter DataIndex="Company" />
            <ext:NumericFilter DataIndex="Price" />
            <ext:NumericFilter DataIndex="Change" />
            <ext:NumericFilter DataIndex="PctChange" />
            <ext:DateFilter DataIndex="LastChange" />
        </Filters>
    </ext:GridFilters>
</Features>
```

Internally, filtering is really a feature of the Store. The Store knows the fields, which is why a DataIndex property is set. The GridPanel adds the visual presentation of filtering.

The following screenshot shows what the basic filter, the string filter, on the **Company** column looks like:

Simple Grid					
▽ *Company* ▾	Price	Change	Change	Last Updated
2 Alcoa Inc	A↓ Sort Ascending		.47%	2012-09-01 12:00am
3 Altria Group Inc	Z↓ Sort Descending		.34%	2012-09-01 12:00am
5 American International Group, Inc.			.49%	2012-09-01 12:00am
6 AT&T Inc.	▦ Columns ▸		1.54%	2012-09-01 12:00am
8 Caterpillar Inc.			.39%	2012-09-01 12:00am
9 Citigroup, Inc.	☑ Filters ▸	🎁 Inc		
15 Honeywell Intl Inc	$38.77	0.1	0.13%	2012-09-01 12:00am
21 Merck & Co., Inc.	$40.96	0.4	1.01%	2012-09-01 12:00am
23 Pfizer Inc	$27.96	0.4	1.45%	2012-09-01 12:00am
25 The Home Depot, Inc.	$34.64	0.3	1.02%	2012-09-01 12:00am
⏮ ◀ Page 1 of 2 ▶ ▶⏭ ↻				Displaying 1 - 10 of 11

Notice that the filtering is accessed from the column menu. As a string filter, it is showing a text field control as a menu item for your filter entry. When a filter is applied for a given column, its column header has a filter funnel icon added to it. To turn off filtering, simply pull down the menu and uncheck the **Filters** option.

As we are doing local paging here as well, it has filtered the original 29 records down to 11 matching ones, so the pager is updated for you automatically. This is because the actual filtering is simply done by the underlying Store, which raises the appropriate events for which the PagingToolbar is listening. The PagingToolbar then updates itself to reflect this new state.

> Local filtering and paging uses an Ext.NET JavaScript subclass of Store—Ext.data.PagingStore. This store provides useful features that help manage data across pages, so any filtering, sorting, and so on, is preserved as you page through the data. Even edited records won't be lost if paging. Of course, if you have lots of data all held locally, this would require more browser memory, and server-based approaches are better for larger data sets.

This means if the filtering was done on the server side, other than writing the code to do the filtering, the behavior on the grid would remain the same. We will look at server-side filtering shortly, but first some examples of the other filter columns.

The next screenshot shows how the **Price** filter column would render as a numeric filter:

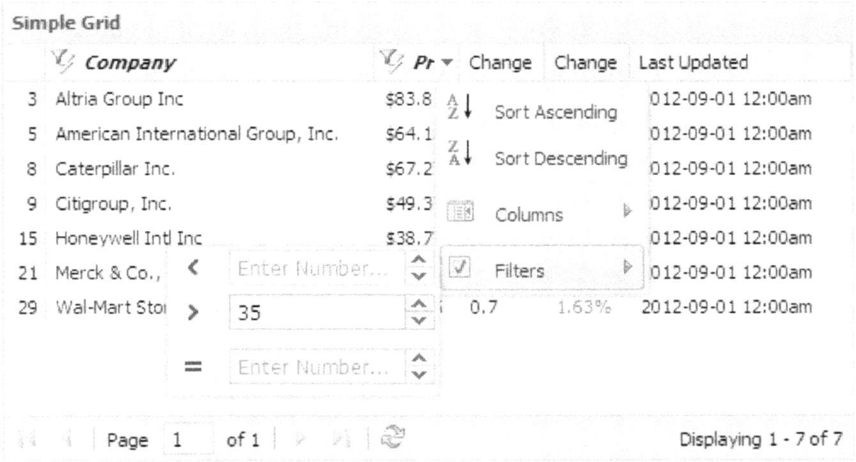

Notice that in the preceding screenshot, the **Company** column remains filtered too (from our previous example). This means that filters can be combined. As a numeric filter, we are offered with three numeric fields, so we can filter a range or an exact match.

The final column uses a date filter which can be seen in the following screenshot:

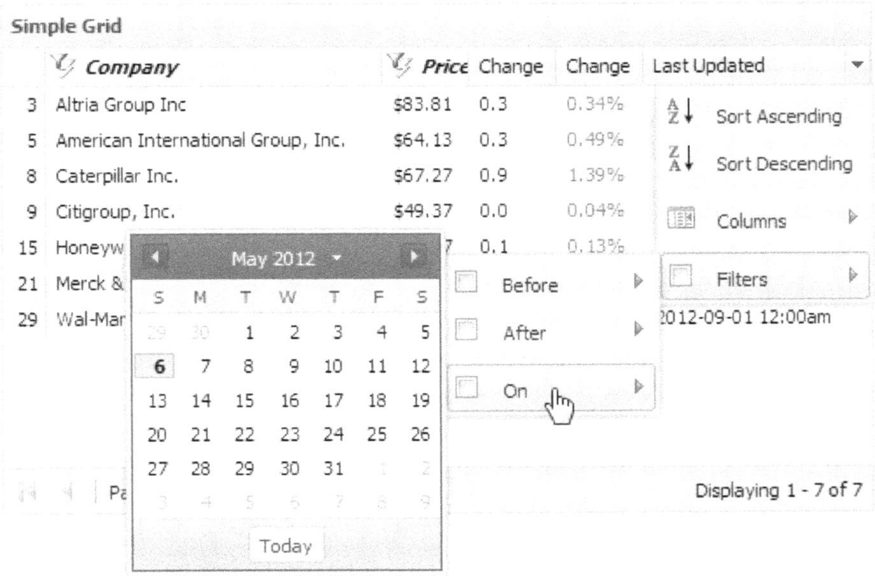

This time we have the same three options, but they are naturally labeled as **Before**, **After**, and **On**, and they render with a date picker instead of a number field. Other filtering options are as follows:

- `ListFilter`, which lets you filter by picking from a list of values
- `BooleanFilter`, which provides you a radio option menu

The following is an example of a `ListFilter`:

```
<ext:ListFilter DataIndex="Size" Options="extra
small,small,medium,large,extra large" />
```

The preceding code produces a column filter, as shown in the following screenshot:

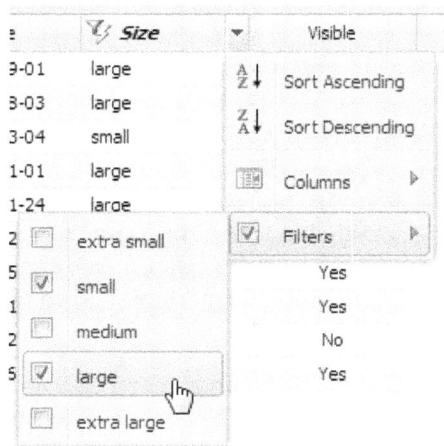

Note that you can pick more than one item.

A `BooleanFilter` is defined like this:

```
<ext:BooleanFilter DataIndex="Visible" />
```

It would render as follows:

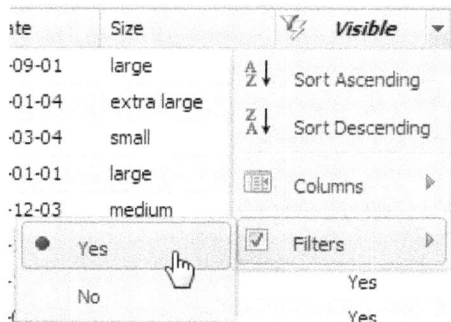

Server-side filtering

For server-side filtering, the same GridPanel configuration is used earlier, except you set `Local="false"`, or you can remove it altogether as `false` is the default:

```
<ext:GridFilters>
```

Then, you need to handle it on the server, where a little bit more effort is needed.

Earlier, when we looked at Stores with DataViews, we introduced the `StoreRequestParameters` class and we noted it had a property named `Filter`, which was an array of `DataFilter` classes. This is fine when being used with the DataView. However, `GridFilters` is a feature of the GridPanel, not the Store. It adds support for conditions (such as less than, greater than), which the underlying Store does not have. This means the `Filter` property on the `StoreRequestParameters` instance is not enough. However, the filter data that is submitted can still be accessed.

Taking the ASHX example we had earlier for server-side paging, let's look at what gets sent via HTTP to the ASHX from the grid when doing a filter. Using Firebug or similar, we can see that if we filter the grid on the **Price** column where the value is between $30 and $70, the following is sent to the server:

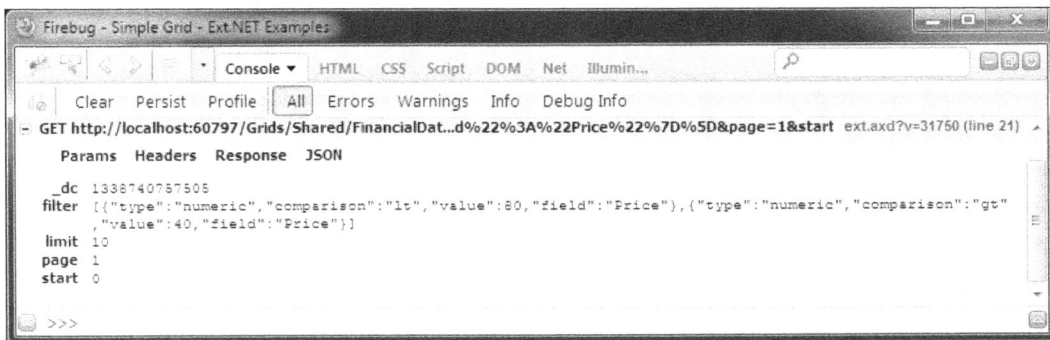

We can see a parameter named `filter`. If we format it for easier reading, we will see the following:

```
[{
    "type"       : "numeric",
    "comparison" : "lt",
    "value" : 80,
    "field" : "Price"
}, {
    "type"       : "numeric",
    "comparison" : "gt",
```

```
        "value" : 40,
        "field" : "Price"
}]
```

It is basically a JSON structure. Ext.NET provides a useful `FilterConditions` class, which can parse such a JSON string and convert it into a structured class for you. Using the ASHX example earlier, this is how we might modify it:

```
public void ProcessRequest(HttpContext context)
{
    context.Response.ContentType = "application/json";

    var requestParams = new StoreRequestParameters(context);

    int start = requestParams.Start;
    int limit = requestParams.Limit;

    string filters = context.Request["filter"];
    FilterConditions conditions = null;

    if (!string.IsNullOrWhiteSpace(filters))
    {
        conditions = new FilterConditions(filters);
    }

    Paging<CompanyData> data = GetData(start, limit, conditions);

    context.Response.Write(JSON.Serialize(data));
}
```

In the preceding code snippet, we get the filters off the request and create an instance of the `FilterConditions` class. It is then passed to the `GetData()` method, which would work with your underlying data access components extracting the filter information as your data access layer needs it.

Note, if you are not using an ASHX, ASMX, or MVC Controller as your proxy but instead are using a PageProxy, the filter parameters are still available, but in the event's `Parameters` collection.

Let us consider an example. First the subtle modification to our Store code, to replace the `AjaxProxy` with `PageProxy`:

```
<ext:Store ID="Store1" runat="server" PageSize="10"
OnReadData="Store1_ReadData">
  <Model>
    <ext:Model runat="server" IDProperty="Id">
```

```
    <Fields>
      <ext:ModelField Name="Company" Mapping="Name"  />
      <ext:ModelField Name="Price" Type="Float" />
      <ext:ModelField Name="Change" Type="Float" />
      <ext:ModelField Name="PctChange"
          Mapping="PercentChange" Type="Float" />
      <ext:ModelField Name="LastChange" Type="Date" />
    </Fields>
  </ext:Model>
</Model>
<Proxy>
  <ext:PageProxy />
</Proxy>
</ext:Store>
```

As well as replacing the Proxy, we have wired up the OnReadData event so we know when to run our code to get the data. (Another option is to use the DirectFn property on PageProxy to invoke a DirectMethod for this, as described at the following link:

http://examples.ext.net/#/GridPanel/Paging_and_Sorting/DirectMethod/

In addition, the Store was given an explicit ID, so we can use it in our event handler:

```
protected void Store1_ReadData(object sender,
                          StoreReadDataEventArgs e)
{
    int start = e.Start;
    int limit = e.Limit;

    string filters = e.Parameters["filter"];
    FilterConditions conditions = null;

    if (!string.IsNullOrWhiteSpace(filters))
    {
        conditions = new FilterConditions(filters);
    }

    Paging<CompanyData> data = GetData(start, limit, conditions);

    e.Total = data.TotalRecords;

    this.Store1.DataSource = data.Data;
    this.Store1.DataBind();
}
```

Sorting

Sorting on GridPanels is done by either clicking on the column header, or by using the **Sort** option in the column menu.

Sorting therefore involves knowing two pieces of information — the column you want to sort, and the direction to sort in.

> Sorting by multiple fields is supported by the Store but not the GridPanel.
>
> Natively, the GridPanel itself doesn't support the ability to sort by multiple columns. The underlying Store, however, does.
>
> Given that the GridPanel uses a Store, you can build a custom implementation to sort by more than one column. It would likely require a lot more Ext JS JavaScript to be written. An example is provided in Ext.NET's Examples Explorer at http://examples.ext.net/#/GridPanel/Paging_ and_Sorting/Multiple_Sorting_Local/.

Like paging and filtering, sorting can also be done either client side or server side.

Client-side sorting

Sorting is actually a feature of the Store, which the GridPanel takes advantage of. It is enabled by default. To turn off sorting on particular columns, simply set that column's Sortable property to false, as follows:

```
<ext:DateColumn Text="Last Updated" Sortable="false"
DataIndex="LastChange" Format="yyyy-MM-dd hh:mmtt" Width="130" />
```

Pre-configuring a grid to be sorted by a particular column simply involves configuring the Store to say which field to sort by, as follows:

```
<Sorters>
    <ext:DataSorter Property="Company" Direction="ASC" />
</Sorters>
```

The preceding two examples together would show that the first column is loaded already in a sorted form, and the last column has sort disabled:

```
Simple Grid

        Company  ▲                      Price    Change   Change   Last Updated              ▼
   1    3m Co                          $71.72   0.0      0.03%      A↓   Sort Ascending
                                                                    Z
   2    AT&T Inc.                      $31.61   -0.5     -1.54%
                                                                    Z↓   Sort Descending
   3    Alcoa Inc                      $29.01   0.4      1.47%      A
   4    Altria Group Inc               $83.81   0.3      0.34%      ▦    Columns            ▷
   5    American Express Company       $52.55   0.0      0.02%
   6    American International Group, Inc.  $64.13  0.3   0.49%     ☐    Filters            ▷
   7    Boeing Co.                     $75.43   0.5      0.71%      2012-09-01 12:00am
   8    Caterpillar Inc.               $67.27   0.9      1.39%      2012-09-01 12:00am
   9    Citigroup, Inc.                $49.37   0.0      0.04%      2012-09-01 12:00am
  10    E.I. du Pont de Nemours and Comp...  $40.48  0.5  1.28%    2012-09-01 12:00am

  ⏮  ◀  │ Page   1   of 3 │  ▶  ▶│  ⟳                          Displaying 1 - 10 of 29
```

Server-side sorting

To enable server-side sorting, simply set the `RemoteSort` property to `true` on the Store. For example;

```
<ext:Store runat="server" RemoteSort="true" PageSize="10">
```

You then need to handle this on the server. Again, Ext.NET helps to convert the Store sorting configuration into a structured object for you, via the `StoreRequestParameters` object we saw earlier.

For example, in our ASHX handler we could do the following:

```
public void ProcessRequest(HttpContext context)
{
    context.Response.ContentType = "application/json";

    var prms = new StoreRequestParameters(context);
    // use prms.Sort[0].Property and prms.Sort[0].Direction
}
```

The `StoreRequestParameters` object processes the current `HttpContext` and provides an initialized Sort array for you. (Recall this is an array because the underlying Store supports multiple sorts; but the grid supports single column sorting only.) You can use that in your server implementation to get data sorted how you need.

You could mix things up—get data from the server but sort locally. Practically speaking, this normally only makes sense if you know you have one page of data to sort, otherwise the user would have to go to each page and sort, which is not usually expected!

It may be an optimization to detect that the store is reloaded with data that fits within the page, so knowing that there cannot be paging, you might be tempted to switch the store into local sorting mode, programmatically. This may avoid some extra HTTP traffic, but it may lead to subtly different results if your server's sorting configuration is different from how JavaScript will do the sorting. For example, your database may have a particular collation setting that impacts how sorting is done in various cases, which may not be supported by JavaScript. So beware of micro-optimization!

Grouping

The GridPanel also comes with a feature to allow grouping the data by a column, as shown in the following screenshot:

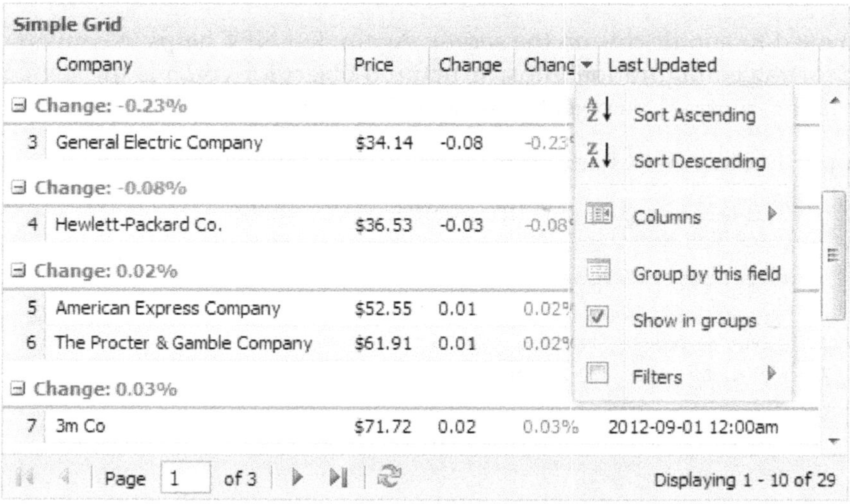

Notice the menu now provides two extra options — to enable grouping at all (**Show in Groups**) and whether to group by the current column whose menu is being shown.

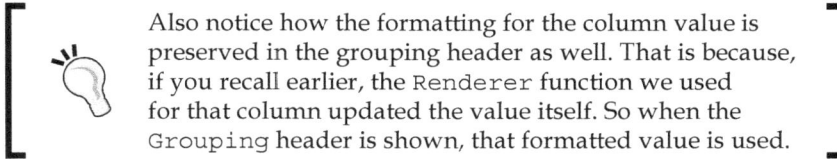

> Also notice how the formatting for the column value is preserved in the grouping header as well. That is because, if you recall earlier, the `Renderer` function we used for that column updated the value itself. So when the `Grouping` header is shown, that formatted value is used.

To set this up we simply add another "Feature" to the GridPanel as follows:

```
<Features>
    <ext:GridFilters Local="true">
        <!-- Filter options go here -->
    </ext:GridFilters>
    <ext:Grouping />
</Features>
```

The preceding example shows the bare minimum configuration needed; just the `Grouping` feature. Note, as a client-side feature on the GridPanel, it is independent of the underlying Store. So, if more data is retrieved, (for example, when paging or sorting on the server), the grouping is still applied. Sorting, for example, will sort within each group.

There are numerous other configuration options possible. For example, to start the grid in a collapsed state, you can use `StartCollapsed="true"` on the `Grouping` property. To disable grouping for some columns (for example, in the preceding screenshot, the company name is going to be unique, so doesn't make sense to allow grouping for it), simply set `Groupable="false"` on the column, as follows:

```
<ext:Column Text="Company" DataIndex="Company" Flex="1"
Groupable="false" />
```

You can also customize the grouping header text. The default is the format as shown in the preceding screenshot — the column name followed by the grouped value. That is the equivalent of the following line of code:

```
<ext:Grouping GroupHeaderTplString="{columnName}: {name}" />
```

The template string reuses the XTemplate component, so all the formatting and syntax capabilities offered by XTemplates can be used here. To use a different value you can provide a different header template, for example:

```
<ext:Grouping
  GroupHeaderTplString=
    "{columnName}: {name} {[MyApp.formatGroupSummary(values)]}"
/>
```

In the preceding example, recall that anything inside square brackets in a template string is evaluated as JavaScript code. So the preceding code snippet calls a `formatGroupSummary` method, which may look like the following:

```
var App = {
  formatGroupSummary: function (values) {
    var rows = values.rows,
      numRows = rows.length,
      prefix = rows.length > 1 ? "Items" : "Item";

    return Ext.String.format("({0} {1})", numRows, prefix);
  }
};
```

The preceding method is simply appending `Item` or `Items` to the grouping summary text, which we can see, as shown in the following screenshot:

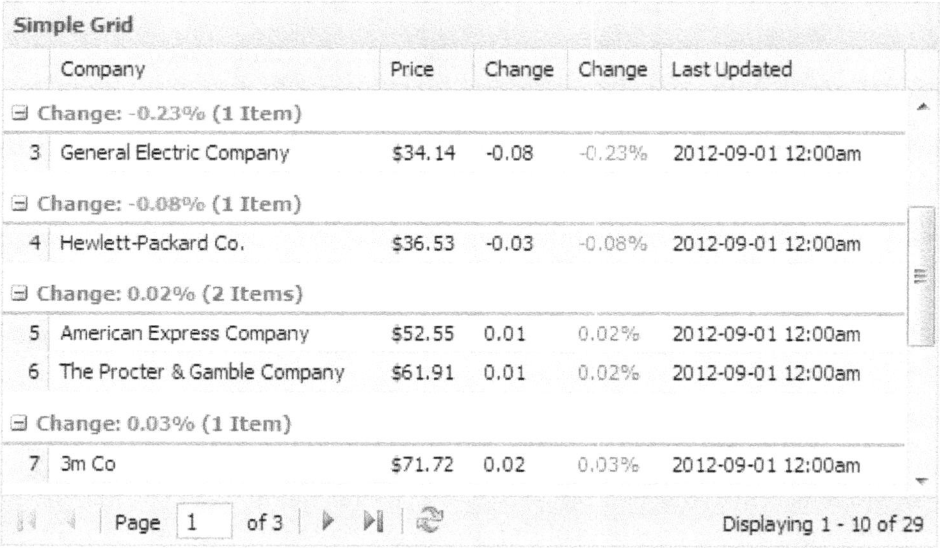

Simple Grid					
Company	Price	Change	Change	Last Updated	
⊟ Change: -0.23% (1 Item)					▲
3 General Electric Company	$34.14	-0.08	-0.23%	2012-09-01 12:00am	
⊟ Change: -0.08% (1 Item)					
4 Hewlett-Packard Co.	$36.53	-0.03	-0.08%	2012-09-01 12:00am	
⊟ Change: 0.02% (2 Items)					
5 American Express Company	$52.55	0.01	0.02%	2012-09-01 12:00am	
6 The Procter & Gamble Company	$61.91	0.01	0.02%	2012-09-01 12:00am	
⊟ Change: 0.03% (1 Item)					
7 3m Co	$71.72	0.02	0.03%	2012-09-01 12:00am	
◄◄ ◄ Page 1 of 3 ► ►◄ 🔄				Displaying 1 - 10 of 29	

Column summaries

You can also make the grid calculate totals for you. To do this we use another feature of the GridPanel—`summary`. At its simplest, it involves the following two steps:

1. Declare the feature.
2. Set up the columns to be summarizable columns, if needed.

To declare the feature, we can extend our earlier example with the following code:

```
<Features>
    <ext:GridFilters Local="true">
        <!-- Filter options go here -->
    </ext:GridFilters>
    <ext:Grouping />
    <ext:Summary />
</Features>
```

Next, we need to configure each column to support summarizing. Until now, we have used the Column class or <ext:Column /> to define each column. Now we will use a subclass, SummaryColumn or <ext:SummaryColumn />. Let's look at this, a few columns at a time:

```
<ext:RowNumbererColumn />
<ext:SummaryColumn Text="Company" DataIndex="Company" Flex="1"
Groupable="false" SummaryType="Count">
    <SummaryRenderer Handler="return '(' + value +' Companies)';" />
</ext:SummaryColumn>
```

Notice that for the row numbering column a summary doesn't make sense, so we leave that as it is. For the **Company** column we could also leave that as it is, but here we will just summarize how many we want to show. To do that after setting it to be a SummaryColumn, we set the SummaryType property to be Average. SummaryType can have a number of preset values, such as Average, Count, Min, Max, None, or Sum.

We also provide a custom SummaryRenderer, which is a JavaScript function that will have a parameter of the value that will be shown. Here we append the 'Companies' string after the value. (The SummaryRenderer function also provides parameters for summaryData (containing all raw summary values for the row) and field (to provide the name of the field currently being calculated).

Next we change the various number columns we had as follows:

```
<ext:SummaryColumn Text="Price" DataIndex="Price" Width="50"
Groupable="false" SummaryType="Average">
    <Renderer Format="UsMoney" />
    <SummaryRenderer Fn="Ext.util.Format.usMoney" />
</ext:SummaryColumn>

<ext:SummaryColumn Text="Change" DataIndex="Change" Width="50"
SummaryType="Average" />

<ext:SummaryColumn Text="Change" DataIndex="PctChange" Width="50"
SummaryType="Average">
    <Renderer Fn="pctChange" />
    <SummaryRenderer Fn="pctChange" />
</ext:SummaryColumn>
```

In the preceding examples, we opt to show averages. For the **Price** and **Change** (percentage) columns, we use a `SummaryRenderer` function to render the summary value in the same way the column value is rendered.

Note, that by changing from `NumberColumn` to `SummaryColumn`, we may lose some formatting information. For example, in `NumberColumn`, there is a property named `Format`. It can take a value such as `0.00` to tell the grid to render this column with two decimal places. By switching to a `SummaryColumn`, the `Format` property is lost. So, we can modify the `pctChange` function to apply the same rounding:

```
var pctChange = function (value) {
    var renderer = Ext.util.Format.numberRenderer('0.00');

    return Ext.String.format(template, (value > 0)
        ? "positive" : "negative", renderer(value) + "%");
};
```

In the preceding JavaScript formatter, we have used the same underlying `numberRenderer` function factory method that the GridPanel uses behind the scenes when we set the `Format` property of `NumberColumn`. This factory method returns a function that we then use to format the final display value.

Finally, the date column we have chosen to leave as it is, without any summary:

```
<ext:DateColumn Text="Last Updated" DataIndex="LastChange"
Format="yyyy-MM-dd hh:mmtt" Width="130" />
```

The final result then looks like the following screenshot:

	Company	Price	Change	Change	Last Updated
1	3m Co	$71.72	0.02	0.03%	2012-09-01 12:00am
2	Alcoa Inc	$29.01	0.42	1.47%	2012-09-01 12:00am
3	Altria Group Inc	$83.81	0.28	0.34%	2012-09-01 12:00am
4	American Express Company	$52.55	0.01	0.02%	2012-09-01 12:00am
5	American International Group, Inc.	$64.13	0.31	0.49%	2012-09-01 12:00am
6	AT&T Inc.	$31.61	-0.48	-1.54%	2012-09-01 12:00am
7	Boeing Co.	$75.43	0.53	0.71%	2012-09-01 12:00am
8	Caterpillar Inc.	$67.27	0.92	1.39%	2012-09-01 12:00am
9	Citigroup, Inc.	$49.37	0.02	0.04%	2012-09-01 12:00am
10	E.I. du Pont de Nemours and Com...	$40.48	0.51	1.28%	2012-09-01 12:00am
	(10 Companies)	**$56.54**	**0.254**	**0.42%**	

Simple Grid — Page 1 of 3 — Displaying 1 - 10 of 29

Also note that the summary applies, even if you filter the data, or sort it (or both). The following screenshot shows an example where the **Price** column has been filtered for any values greater than $70 and sorted by company name:

	Company ▲	Price	Change	Change	Last Updated
1	3m Co	$71.72	0.02	0.03%	2012-09-01 12:00am
2	Altria Group Inc	$83.81	0.28	0.34%	2012-09-01 12:00am
3	Boeing Co.	$75.43	0.53	0.71%	2012-09-01 12:00am
4	International Business Machines	$81.41	0.44	0.54%	2012-09-01 12:00am
	(4 Companies)	**$78.09**	**0.3175**	**0.41%**	

Simple Grid

Page 1 of 1   Displaying 1 - 4 of 4

Column summaries per group

If you try to group the columns when the Summary feature is enabled using just the preceding changes, then things are not quite right. The following is a screenshot where the grid (having had the filters and sort reset) is grouped by the **Change** column:

	Company	Price	Change	Change	Last Updated
	Change: -0.23% (1 Item)				
3	General Electric Company	$34.14	-0.08	-0.23%	2012-09-01 12:00am
	(10 Companies)	**$50.94**	**-0.0...**	**-0.2...**	
	Change: -0.08% (1 Item)				
4	Hewlett-Packard Co.	$36.53	-0.03	-0.08%	2012-09-01 12:00am
	(10 Companies)	**$50.94**	**-0.0...**	**-0.2...**	
	Change: 0.02% (2 Items)				
5	American Express Company	$52.55	0.01	0.02%	2012-09-01 12:00am
6	The Procter & Gamble Company	$61.91	0.01	0.02%	2012-09-01 12:00am
	(10 Companies)	**$50.94**	**-0.0...**	**-0.2...**	

Simple Grid

Page 1 of 3   Displaying 1 - 10 of 29

The modification for this is really simple. There is another feature of the GridPanel that we can use—`GroupingSummary`. We simply remove the previously declared `Grouping` feature and the `Summary` feature, and replace them by this one composite feature:

```
<Features>
    <ext:GridFilters Local="true">
        <!-- Filter options go here -->
    </ext:GridFilters>
    <ext:GroupingSummary GroupHeaderTplString="{columnName}: {name}
{[App.formatGroupSummary(values)]}" />
</Features>
```

The `GroupHeaderTplString`, which was part of the `Grouping` class, is also available as a property of the `GroupingSummary` class. The next screenshot shows the improvement:

Simple Grid					
	Company	Price	Change	Change	Last Updated
⊟ Change: -0.23% (1 Item)					
3	General Electric Company	$34.14	-0.08	-0.23%	2012-09-01 12:00am
	(1 Companies)	**$34.14**	**-0.08**	**-0.2...**	
⊟ Change: -0.08% (1 Item)					
4	Hewlett-Packard Co.	$36.53	-0.03	-0.08%	2012-09-01 12:00am
	(1 Companies)	**$36.53**	**-0.03**	**-0.0...**	
⊟ Change: 0.02% (2 Items)					
5	American Express Company	$52.55	0.01	0.02%	2012-09-01 12:00am
6	The Procter & Gamble Company	$61.91	0.01	0.02%	2012-09-01 12:00am
	(2 Companies)	**$57.23**	**0.01**	**0.02%**	
⏮ ◀ Page 1 of 3 ▶ ⏭ ⟳					Displaying 1 - 10 of 29

In the preceding screenshot, we have filtered the **Company** column for any value containing the word "Company". We have then sorted it in descending order (note the grouping means that it sorts within each group). The summary for each group is recalculated each time, so it always reflects the visible data.

Row expanding

A common use of grids is to show related data. Often it will be to expand details, or show some data related to the current row. A typical design pattern for this is the master-detail pattern. In a grid context, a grid row is the master, and then the detail can be shown in a number of ways. Sometimes it can be done by expanding a row; other times it might be to show details in a side panel (similar to e-mail readers such as Outlook that have a reading pane below or to the side of the list of e-mails).

We saw an example of the master-detail pattern with the DataView in *Chapter 5, Working with Data*, where we selected an employee and saw more details to the side. Similar techniques can be used with the GridPanel. This is because the row of data is held by the Store, which is common to the DataView and GridPanel. Here we will look at expanding a grid row as a way to show more details.

Row expanding using templates

Consider the financial data example we have been using earlier. Suppose we want to expand each row to see more information about a company. For now, we will just show some additional company data, such as a description about the company and maybe a chart image showing the company's recent stock performance.

The following data is made up for demonstration purposes, and you should not use it to determine whether you want to buy stock in that company!

We will expand our data model to include a new field — a Description field to hold the company's description. We will also assume we can render the image based off the company's stock symbol, so we will add a field for that, too:

```
<ext:ModelField Name="Description" />
<ext:ModelField Name="Symbol" />
```

Next we make use of the RowExpander plugin as follows:

```
<Plugins>
  <ext:RowExpander runat="server">
    <Template runat="server">
      <Html>
        <div class="company-details">
          <div class="perf">
            <h2>Recent Stock Performance</h2>
            <img
              alt=""
              src="/images/perf/{Symbol}.png"
              width="160"
              height="160" />
          </div>
```

```
        <h2>Company:</h2>
        <p>{Company}</p>

        <h2>Description:</h2>
        <p>{Description}</p>
      </div>
    </Html>
  </Template>
  </ext:RowExpander>
</Plugins>
```

The `RowExpander` plugin uses an XTemplate via the `Template` property, giving you the flexibility to format the data how you want. And that is it (assuming our data now returns this additional information). The grid will have a small expand icon in the first column:

		Company	Price	Change	Change	Last Updated
⊞	1	3m Co	$71.72	0.0	0.03%	2012-09-01 12:00am
⊞	2	Alcoa Inc	$29.01	0.4	1.47%	2012-09-01 12:00am
⊞	3	Altria Group Inc	$83.81	0.3	0.34%	2012-09-01 12:00am
⊞	4	American Express Company	$52.55	0.0	0.02%	2012-09-01 12:00am
⊞	5	American International Group, ...	$64.13	0.3	0.49%	2012-09-01 12:00am
⊞	6	AT&T Inc.	$31.61	-0.5	-1.54%	2012-09-01 12:00am
⊞	7	Boeing Co.	$75.43	0.5	0.71%	2012-09-01 12:00am
⊞	8	Caterpillar Inc.	$67.27	0.9	1.39%	2012-09-01 12:00am
⊞	9	Citigroup, Inc.	$49.37	0.0	0.04%	2012-09-01 12:00am
⊞	10	E.I. du Pont de Nemours and ...	$40.48	0.5	1.28%	2012-09-01 12:00am

Simple Grid

Page 1 of 3 ▶ ▶| ↻   Displaying 1 - 10 of 29

When a row is expanded, the grid will show the data defined in the template, as follows:

You can also add custom JavaScript handlers for the `Expand` and `Collapse` events if you need by adding the following to the `RowExpander` plugin's `Listeners` property:

```
<Listeners>
    <Collapse Handler="console.log(arguments);" />
    <Expand Handler="console.log(arguments);" />
</Listeners>
```

In the preceding example, we are simply writing out the arguments passed to the handler into the browser console.

Of course, sometimes it may be more optimal to get this additional data on demand, rather than always load it, especially if many of the rows will never get expanded. So we can handle the `Expand` event and make an AJAX request to get more data. This also presents an opportunity to introduce some additional Ext.NET features.

Row expanding using Ext.NET components

In our previous example, we added two new fields—Description and Symbol. We will keep Symbol, as it will act as a useful key. But we will remove the Description field. This is the large field that we want to get via AJAX. We will do this via a DirectMethod call defined on the page like the following code snippet:

```
[DirectMethod]
public static string GetCompanyDescription(string symbol)
{
    // your code to get the description given a symbol
}
```

So our general approach will be as follows:

1. When the row is expanded, we invoke the JavaScript handler.
2. The JavaScript handler sees if we already have the description cached.
3. If so, we have nothing to do; let the row expander carry on expanding and showing the previously fetched data.
4. If no data, then we get it from the server by invoking the DirectMethod.
5. Once the server has returned the description, we cache it by applying the description to the rest of the Store data and applying the updated data to an XTemplate that will be used to show the new data.

To achieve this, we will change our RowExpander. We can't use the Template property, but we can reuse the HTML we defined for it and use our own XTemplate declaration.

There are at least two ways to do this. One way is to declare the XTemplate outside of the GridPanel (and outside any of its containers, for example, defining XTemplate just inside the HTML body element). However, as it is just used for this GridPanel, defining it outside makes it appear more like an orphaned control. Ext.NET has a feature to help us address this. All components have a Bin property, which can contain an arbitrary collection of Ext.NET components. The Ext.NET Examples Explorer looks at this in more detail at http://examples.ext.net/#/search/htmlbin. For our purposes we just need one item, our XTemplate:

```
<Bin>
    <ext:XTemplate ID="CompanyDetailsTemplate" runat="server">
        <Html>
            <div class="company-details">
                <div class="perf">
                    <h2>Recent Stock Performance</h2>
                    <img src="/images/perf/{Symbol}.png"
                        alt="" width="160" height="160" />
                </div>
```

```
                <h2>Company:</h2>
                <p>{Company}</p>

                <h2>Description:</h2>
                <p>{Description}</p>
            </div>
        </Html>
    </ext:XTemplate>
</Bin>
```

Now with the XTemplate in place, we can see what our RowExpander will look like:

```
<ext:RowExpander runat="server">
    <Listeners>
        <Expand Handler="onExpand(
            record.data,
            #{CompanyDetailsTemplate},
            #{CompanyDetailsContainer});"
        />
    </Listeners>
    <Component>
        <ext:Container ID="CompanyDetailsContainer" />
    </Component>
</ext:RowExpander>
```

Notice, that in place of the Template property we have used the Component property, which allows any Ext.NET component to be placed inside the RowExpander so that we can pass data to it to display. We will be using a lightweight (and parent of the Panel class) Container.

The JavaScript event handler is given the data for the current row, a pointer to the XTemplate that the data will apply to, and a pointer to the container that will be updated with the applied XTemplate. The following is the event handler:

```
var onExpand = function (data, template, container) {
    if (data.Description != undefined)
        return;

    App.direct.GetCompanyDescription(
        data.Symbol,
        {
            success: function (description) {
                data.Description = description;
                template.overwrite(container.getEl(), data);
            },
            eventMask : { showMask : true }
        }
    );
};
```

The preceding code snippet checks if we already have `Description` set on the current data that came from the Store. If we do, by returning we let the `RowExpander` continue expanding the row. We know that if we had `Description`, it must have been retrieved earlier and the row will have been populated with the description and chart already, so returning allows rendering to carry on as usual. This saves unnecessary AJAX requests.

Next, if we do need to get data from the server, we make the `DirectMethod` request to `GetCompanyDescription`, passing the symbol and a `DirectMethod` configuration. The configuration has two settings—a success handler and an event loading mask to show the user while the data is being retrieved. For the success handler, we update the original data with the description, thus caching it on the client. We then overwrite the template with the full data (so we can make use of other bits of the data, such as the symbol and company name), and we finally apply it to the container's DOM element.

The `Component` property of the `RowExpander` plugin is powerful. You are not limited to a `Container` class as in the earlier example, but many other controls, such as a Panel, TabPanel, TreePanel, or a custom component of your own could be used.

It is also worth noting that the `RowExpander` plugin has a `SingleExpand` property, which is `true` by default. This means only one row is expanded at a time; when you expand another row, the previously expanded row will collapse. Setting `SingleExpand` to `false` will allow you to keep many rows expanded. The example given on the following link for the Ext.NET Examples Explorer demonstrates this:

```
http://examples.ext.net/#/GridPanel/RowExpander/Shared_Component/
```

The `RowExpander` plugin demonstrates just one of many ways to implement a master-detail pattern. Other examples, in addition to what was shown in *Chapter 5, Working with Data*, are shown here in the Ext.NET Examples Explorer:

```
http://examples.ext.net/#/search/details
```

Selection models

The row expander examples are nice; they provide you an extra column with a small expansion icon. Other times you might want to let the user select the whole row, select many rows, or select a particular cell so that you can then perform some action on those selected rows. Ext.NET's selection models help us here.

Default row selection

In all the grid examples we have covered so far, we have not explicitly defined how a row is selected. So the default, known as the RowSelectionModel, is used. This lets you click anywhere on a row to select it. You can also enable multirow selection, so a user can select multiple rows like they would on a desktop application, using *Ctrl* and click, or *Shift* and click. So, omitting a selection model is equivalent to the following code snippet:

```
<GridPanel>
    <!-- all the other declarations go here as before -->
    <SelectionModel>
        <ext:RowSelectionModel runat="server" />
    </SelectionModel>
</GridPanel>
```

To enable multirow selection it is simply a matter of adding Mode:

```
<GridPanel>
    <!-- all the other declarations go here as before -->
    <SelectionModel>
        <ext:RowSelectionModel runat="server" Mode="Multi" />
    </SelectionModel>
</GridPanel>
```

This will let you select multiple rows, as shown in the following screenshot:

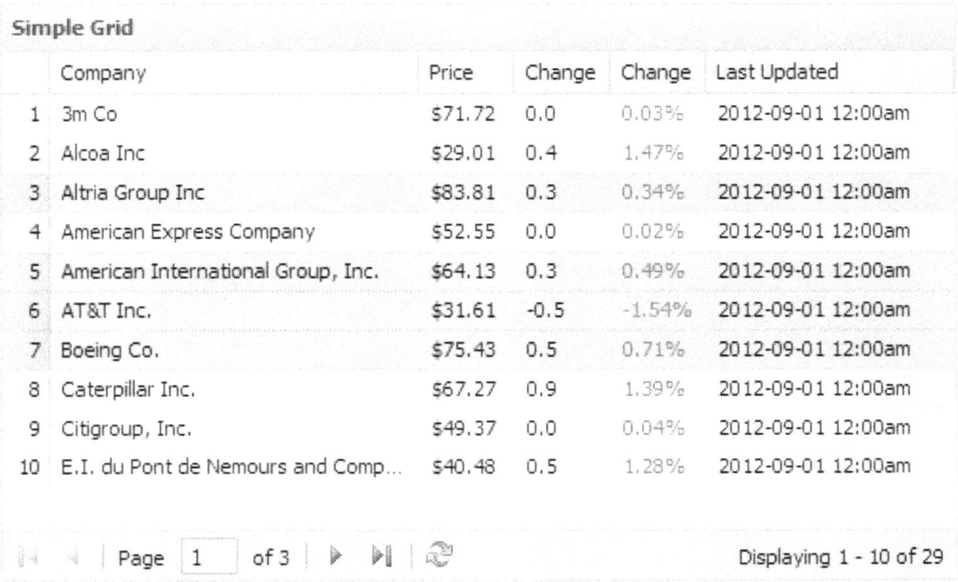

Simple Grid					
	Company	Price	Change	Change	Last Updated
1	3m Co	$71.72	0.0	0.03%	2012-09-01 12:00am
2	Alcoa Inc	$29.01	0.4	1.47%	2012-09-01 12:00am
3	Altria Group Inc	$83.81	0.3	0.34%	2012-09-01 12:00am
4	American Express Company	$52.55	0.0	0.02%	2012-09-01 12:00am
5	American International Group, Inc.	$64.13	0.3	0.49%	2012-09-01 12:00am
6	AT&T Inc.	$31.61	-0.5	-1.54%	2012-09-01 12:00am
7	Boeing Co.	$75.43	0.5	0.71%	2012-09-01 12:00am
8	Caterpillar Inc.	$67.27	0.9	1.39%	2012-09-01 12:00am
9	Citigroup, Inc.	$49.37	0.0	0.04%	2012-09-01 12:00am
10	E.I. du Pont de Nemours and Comp...	$40.48	0.5	1.28%	2012-09-01 12:00am

Page 1 of 3 ▶ ▶| Displaying 1 - 10 of 29

You use the Ext.NET JavaScript API to access the selections on the client, or use DirectEvents to access them on the server.

The following is a client-side example, which accesses the selected rows and submits them to a static `DirectMethod` for removal. First we add a button to the grid's top bar:

```
<TopBar>
  <ext:ToolBar>
    <Items>
      <ext:Button Icon="Delete" Text="Remove Selected">
        <Listeners>
          <Click Handler="MyApp.remove(#{GridPanel1});" />
        </Listeners>
      </ext:Button>
    </Items>
  </ext:ToolBar>
</TopBar>
```

Notice that to refer to #{GridPanel1}, we also need to add and set the GridPanel's ID to GridPanel1 and add runat="server". Next, we define the client-side remove method:

```
var MyApp = {
  remove: function (grid) {
    var selModel = grid.getSelectionModel(),
        selectedRecords = selModel.getSelection(),
        data = [];

    Ext.each(selectedRecords, function (item) {
      data.push(item.data.Name);
    });

    App.direct.Remove(data,
    {
      success: function(result) {
        MyApp.removeSuccess(result, grid, selectedRecords);
      }
    });
  },

  removeSuccess: function(result, grid, selectedRecords) {
    grid.getStore().remove(selectedRecords);

    grid.getView().refresh();
  }
};
```

In essence, we get the selected records from the selection model. Then we extract just the data's Name property of each one and add that to an array, which will be the input to our DirectMethod. Once the DirectMethod has succeeded, our success handler — removeSuccess will be called. This will remove the records from the grid on the client side and refresh the view so the RowNumbererColumn will be updated with the correct row numbers. The DirectMethod itself will look something like the following code:

```
[DirectMethod]
public static void Remove(string values)
{
    var data = JSON.Deserialize<List<string>>(values);

    // Delete code goes here
}
```

In this code snippet, the values are JSON strings for each row selected, so we deserialize them first. This gives us our list of company names to key off for the removal.

The Mode property of RowSelectionModel also supports two other values — Single, which enables only a single row to be selected, and Simple, which is similar to Multi, except the user simply has to click on each row to select it. Use of *Shift* or *Ctrl* along with a click is not required.

Checkbox selection

Similar to the RowSelectionModel, CheckboxSelectionModel creates a column of checkboxes to select rows. This is useful if you have other columns that are clickable themselves (for example, hyperlinks). The following code shows how it is declared:

```
<SelectionModel>
    <ext:CheckboxSelectionModel runat="server" Mode="Multi" />
</SelectionModel>
```

Everything else is the same. Using our example earlier, we can use the same Button and JavaScript handler to call the same `DirectMethod`. The only difference is the rendering:

		Company	Price	Change	Change	Last Updated	
☐	1	3m Co	$71.72	0.0	0.03%	2012-09-01 12:00am	
☐	2	Alcoa Inc	$29.01	0.4	1.47%	2012-09-01 12:00am	
☐	3	Altria Group Inc	$83.81	0.3	0.34%	2012-09-01 12:00am	
☑	4	American Express Company	$52.55	0.0	0.02%	2012-09-01 12:00am	
☐	5	American International Gro...	$64.13	0.3	0.49%	2012-09-01 12:00am	
☑	6	AT&T Inc.	$31.61	-0.5	-1.54%	2012-09-01 12:00am	
☑	7	Boeing Co.	$75.43	0.5	0.71%	2012-09-01 12:00am	
☐	8	Caterpillar Inc.	$67.27	0.9	1.39%	2012-09-01 12:00am	
☐	9	Citigroup, Inc.	$49.37	0.0	0.04%	2012-09-01 12:00am	
☐	10	E.I. du Pont de Nemours a...	$40.48	0.5	1.28%	2012-09-01 12:00am	

Simple Grid

⊖ Remove Selected

Page 1 of 3 ▶ ▶| ⟳   Displaying 1 - 10 of 29

Cell selection

You can also act on specific cells being clicked, too. The following is an example of invoking a DirectEvent when a cell is clicked using the `CellSelectionModel`:

```
<SelectionModel>
  <ext:CellSelectionModel runat="server">
    <DirectEvents>
      <Select OnEvent="Cell_Click" />
    </DirectEvents>
  </ext:CellSelectionModel>
</SelectionModel>
```

And the following is an example of an event handler on the server:

```
protected void Cell_Click(object sender, DirectEventArgs e)
{
  var sm = GridPanel1.GetSelectionModel() as CellSelectionModel;
  X.Msg.Notify("Cell selected",
    string.Format("RecordID: {0}<br />Name: {1}<br />Value: {2}<br
/>Row: {3}<br />Column: {4}",
```

```
        sm.SelectedCell.RecordID,
        sm.SelectedCell.Name,
        sm.SelectedCell.Value,
        sm.SelectedCell.RowIndex,
        sm.SelectedCell.ColIndex)).Show();
}
```

In the preceding example, a notification of the selected cell's properties is created.

Grid editing

A popular feature of the grid is its inline editing capability. There are two main ways that the grid can be edited inline as follows:

- Cell editing
- Row editing

Cell editing lets you click onto a cell and start editing. You have keyboard support to tab to additional fields, which will then switch into editing mode automatically (assuming the fields in those columns are also editable). This can be useful if you want to allow many cells from many rows to be edited and then update in one pass. (You also have the option to save each edit as you go, if you want.)

Row editing lets you make an entire row go into edit mode with **Update** and **Cancel** buttons that appear below the highlighted row. This can be useful if your server accepts a row of edits at any one time.

Both are enabled in two general steps as follows:

1. Configure the columns you want to be editable.
2. Use the appropriate plugin based on the editing style you need.

We will first look at how to configure columns for editing, and then look at each plugin in turn.

Configuring columns to be editable

Not all columns need to be editable. For those columns you require editing, the `Editor` property can be configured. This holds the configuration for a field to be shown when the cell goes into editing mode and enables data entry. The field can be any `TextField` type, `ComboBox`, `DateField`, or a custom (and richer) control, if needed.

> The editor field is applied to a column and is not duplicated per row. Instead, the same editor instance is reused and shown in the right place when the grid switches into editing mode. This is important to note so as not to expect the editor field to cache a particular cell's value. The Store tracks changed values for you.

The financial data we have been using so far can have its column definition modified in the following way:

```
<Columns>
  <ext:Column Text="Id" DataIndex="Id" Width="25" />
  <ext:Column Text="Company" DataIndex="Company" Flex="1">
    <Editor>
      <ext:TextField runat="server" />
    </Editor>
  </ext:Column>
  <ext:NumberColumn Text="Price" DataIndex="Price" Width="75">
    <Renderer Format="UsMoney" />
    <Editor>
      <ext:NumberField runat="server" />
    </Editor>
  </ext:NumberColumn>
  <ext:NumberColumn Text="Change" DataIndex="Change" Width="60">
    <Renderer Fn="change" />
    <Editor>
      <ext:NumberField runat="server" />
    </Editor>
  </ext:NumberColumn>
  <ext:NumberColumn Text="Change" DataIndex="PctChange" Width="60">
    <Renderer Fn="pctChange" />
    <Editor>
      <ext:NumberField runat="server" />
    </Editor>
  </ext:NumberColumn>
  <ext:DateColumn Text="Last Updated" DataIndex="LastChange"
                  Format="yyyy-MM-dd hh:mmtt" Width="130">
    <Editor>
      <ext:DateField runat="server" />
    </Editor>
  </ext:DateColumn>
</Columns>
```

What we have done can be explained as follows:

1. We have added the **Id** column, which we did not show before. This is just to demonstrate that not all columns need to be editable.

2. For the **Company** column we have added a simple `TextField`.

3. The **Price**, **Change** (in amount), and **Change** (in percentage) columns use a `NumberField` editor (like a `TextField` but only accepts numeric input).

4. Finally for the **Last Updated** column, we have used a `DateField`. This will produce a date picker (for the purposes of this example we will assume all times are 12:00 a.m. and the column formatter will take of this for us).

> It is possible to set up multiple editors per column and use various strategies to decide which one to use. Due to limitations on this book's size, these are not covered here, but Ext.NET's Examples Explorer demonstrates how to use it:
>
> `http://examples.ext.net/#/TreePanel/Basic/Editors/`
>
> Although the example is using editors on a TreePanel (to edit nodes), the same techniques apply to GridPanel column editors.

Now the columns are set up, let's enable editing.

Cell editing

To enable cell-based editing, it is simply a matter of using the following plugin:

```
<Plugins>
    <ext:CellEditing runat="server">
</Plugins>
```

Now we have an editable grid. The following are some examples of what can be done. If we double-click on one of the fields from the **Company** column, then that cell becomes editable using the `TextField` we configured, as shown in the following screenshot:

Simple Grid					
Id	Company	Price	Change	Change	Last Updated
1	3m Co	$71.72	0.02	0.03%	2012-09-01 12:00am
2	Alcoa Inc	$29.01	0.42	1.47%	2012-09-01 12:00am
3	Altria Group Inc	$83.81	0.28	0.34%	2012-09-01 12:00am
4	American Express Company	$52.55	0.01	0.02%	2012-09-01 12:00am
5	American International Gr…	$64.13	0.31	0.49%	2012-09-01 12:00am
6	AT&T Inc.	$31.61	-0.48	-1.54%	2012-09-01 12:00am
7	Boeing Co.	$75.43	0.53	0.71%	2012-09-01 12:00am
8	Caterpillar Inc.|	$67.27	0.92	1.39%	2012-09-01 12:00am
9	Citigroup, Inc.	$49.37	0.02	0.04%	2012-09-01 12:00am
10	E.I. du Pont de Nemours a…	$40.48	0.51	1.28%	2012-09-01 12:00am

Page [1] of 3 ◁ ◀ ▶ ▶▏ ⟳   Displaying 1 - 10 of 29

If we edit one of the numeric columns (either by tabbing to it, or double-clicking on it), such as **Price**, or one of the **Change** columns, we get the `NumberField` editor:

Simple Grid					
Id	Company	Price	Change	Change	Last Updated
1	3m Co	$71.72	0.02	0.03%	2012-09-01 12:00am
2	Alcoa Inc	$29.01	0.42	1.47%	2012-09-01 12:00am
3	Altria Group Inc	$83.81	0.28	0.34%	2012-09-01 12:00am
4	American Express Company	$52.55	0.01	0.02%	2012-09-01 12:00am
5	American International Gr…	$64.13	0.31	0.49%	2012-09-01 12:00am
6	AT&T Inc.	$31.61	-0.48	-1.54%	2012-09-01 12:00am
7	Boeing Co.	$75.43	0.53	0.71%	2012-09-01 12:00am
8	Caterpillar	$67.27	0.92 ⏶⏷	1.39%	2012-09-01 12:00am
9	Citigroup, Inc.	$49.37	0.02	0.04%	2012-09-01 12:00am
10	E.I. du Pont de Nemours a…	$40.48	0.51	1.28%	2012-09-01 12:00am

Page [1] of 3 ◁ ◀ ▶ ▶▏ ⟳   Displaying 1 - 10 of 29

Each edited cell will have a "dirty" (or edited) marker on it. Any edited value is also passed to any defined rendering function again. Therefore, if we edit a value which is positive and make it negative, our formatter function (which makes it red for negative and green for positive) will run, so that the new value will be correctly colored. The next example shows this as well as it shows another row entering into editing mode:

Id	Company	Price	Change	Change	Last Updated
1	3m Co	$71.72	0.02	0.03%	2012-09-01 12:00am
2	Alcoa Inc	$29.01	0.42	1.47%	01/09/2012
3	Altria Group Inc	$83.81	0.28	0.	
4	American Express Company	$52.55	0.01	0.	
5	American International Gr...	$64.13	0.31	0.	
6	AT&T Inc.	$31.61	-0.48	-1	
7	Boeing Co.	$75.43	0.53	0.	
8	Caterpillar	$67.27	-0.08	1.	
9	Citigroup, Inc.	$49.37	0.02	0.	
10	E.I. du Pont de Nemours a...	$40.48	0.51	1.	

September 2012 calendar showing dates from 26–31 (prior month) through 30 and next month, with Today button.

Page 1 of 3

In the preceding screenshot, we have edited the **Change** amount for **Caterpillar** to be negative, which now becomes red. At the same time we also see the DateField editor for another row. Note, if we pick another date, it will automatically display as 12:00 a.m. of that date, because this DateColumn formatter property was explicitly configured to show the date and time, and a date object's default time is 12:00 a.m.

> The dirty indicator in the corner can be disabled using the MarkDirty property on the GridPanel's view and setting it to false.
>
> The number of clicks required to enter editing mode can be configured using the ClicksToEdit property on the CellEditing plugin. Setting the value to 1 means you just need a single click on a cell value to enter editing mode.

Committing changes

There are numerous ways in which changes can be handled by Ext.NET. From a user perspective there are two broad ways this will be done as follows:

- Automatic updating
- Manual committing

Automatic updating involves the application updating the system automatically for the user while he/she is editing; they don't need to explicitly press a **Save** button, for example. This gives a good user experience. But it can have server-side penalties. For example, if each edit updates the server and many updates are being performed, it may not scale. On the other hand, such small updates could be more efficient than larger bulk updates, depending on numerous backend factors.

Manually committing changes involves the user pressing **Save** (or similar), and then submitting the changes in bulk to be updated by the backend of the system.

With Ext.NET both approaches are quite similar.

Automatically updating as you edit

To autoupdate as you edit, you set the Store's `AutoSync` property to `true`. This will tell the Store to sync any committed change with the underlying Proxy automatically (in effect, update the backend system).

To enable this we follow a few steps. First we set the `AutoSync` property on the Store:

```
<ext:Store runat="server" PageSize="10" AutoSync="true">
```

Next, we need something with which our Store can sync. The proxies we have seen so far have all used readers. We now introduce a writer as follows:

```
<Proxy>
  <ext:AjaxProxy Url="../Shared/FinancialData.ashx">
    <Reader>
      <ext:JsonReader Root="data" />
    </Reader>
    <Writer>
      <ext:JsonWriter Root="data" Encode="true"
                      WriteAllFields="false" />
    </Writer>
    <API Update="../Shared/FinancialDataUpdate.ashx" />
  </ext:AjaxProxy>
</Proxy>
```

In the preceding code snippet, we have added a `JsonWriter` and set the following:

- The `Root` property that will contain the updated values.
- A flag to indicate the data should be encoded (so that it is part of a form `POST` parameter, rather than making up the entire body of `POST`).
- A flag to tell the proxy to only send the updated fields (and the record identifier), not all fields for the modified record. This helps to keep the HTTP traffic down.

The `API` property is optional. It has properties for all **CRUD** operations (**Create**, **Read**, **Update**, and **Delete**), so you could specify different URLs to handle each. If you do not configure the `Url` property, each request is sent to the URL defined on the proxy itself. `API` also has a `Sync` property used to set a common URL for the server to handle the Create, Update, and Delete operations where a particular operation is not explicitly declared.

With just those changes, autosynced editing is now in place; as soon as you complete editing a cell, it will be submitted to the server. It is submitted as a JSON array of key/value pairs, which can be deserialized on the server side as a list of `Dictionary<string, object>`.

A useful class from Ext.NET — `StoreDataHandler` can help to extract the data for you. For example, this is what `FinancialDataUpdate.ashx` might look like:

```
public void ProcessRequest(HttpContext context)
{
    var response = new StoreResponseData();
    var dataHandler = new StoreDataHandler(context);

    List<Dictionary<string, object>> data =
        dataHandler.ObjectData<Dictionary<string, object>>();

    foreach (Dictionary<string, object> list in data)
    {
        try
        {
            // update system with list values

            // return the data as response
            response.Data = JSON.Serialize(data);
        }
        catch (Exception e)
        {
            // logging, etc.
```

```
            response.Success = false;
            response.Message = e.Message;
        }
    }

    response.Return();
}
```

The `StoreDataHandler` takes care of deserializing the JSON update for you. To do this, it makes the assumption that the `Root` property defined on the `JsonWriter` has the value of `data`. This is why we had to use that value in our `JsonWriter`. If you have used another value, you can use an overload on the constructor:

```
new StoreDataHandler(context.Request['griddata'])
```

If the operation is successful, a return value is required for any created or updated records. So in our case, we can return the `data` instance.

Also note that if we had not used `WriteAllFields="false"`, but instead sent all data for a row back, we could have used the more strongly typed `CompanyData`:

```
List<CompanyData> data = dataHandler.ObjectData<CompanyData>();
```

Explicitly saving changes by letting the user click on a Save button

To have the changes saved at the press of a button (or any other event you may want), the preceding `JsonWriter` can still be reused. On the Store configuration, we remove `AutoSync="true"`. Then we have a button that, when clicked, will do the saving for us, for example:

```
<ext:Button runat="server" Text="Save" Icon="Disk">
    <Listeners>
        <Click Handler="#{Store1}.sync();" />
    </Listeners>
</ext:Button>
```

In the preceding code snippet, we are explicitly calling the Store's `sync()` method. This allows the user to make many changes in one pass before saving, giving the him/her the time to change his/her mind if he/she so wishes. The Store can even help here—another button can wire up to a `rejectChanges()` method on the Store to revert any edits and clear the dirty/edited marker in the corner of each edited field.

Paging while rows have been edited

What happens if you now change pages (or apply a filter or sort) on the server side? You would lose any changes if you do not commit them first. It might be easy to forget if the commit is not automatic.

Fortunately the Store has a property to detect changes to the data when there are uncommitted edits:

```
<ext:Store runat="server" PageSize="10" RemoteSort="true"
WarningOnDirty="true">
```

In the preceding code, we have not set the AutoSync property, but we have set a flag on the Store to warn if there are still uncommitted changes, or dirty records, when there is a request to reload the Store with new data (for example from sorting, filtering, and so on).

In such a case, a warning appears asking if you want to lose changes, and carry on or not:

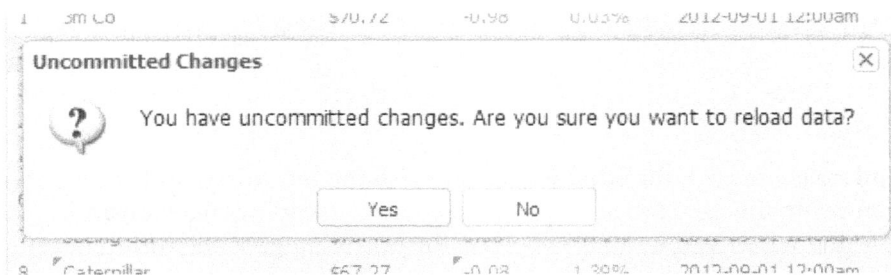

Row editing

To edit one row at a time, we can simply switch from the CellEditing plugin to the RowEditing plugin as follows:

```
<ext:RowEditing runat="server">
```

The way the row editor works is that as you double-click anywhere on a row, you get an editing bar. As with the CellEditing plugin, you can use the ClicksToEdit property to configure the number of clicks required to enter row editing mode.

You click on **Update** or **Cancel** once done. **Update** will update the local store by default. The following screenshot shows the `RowEditor` plugin in action:

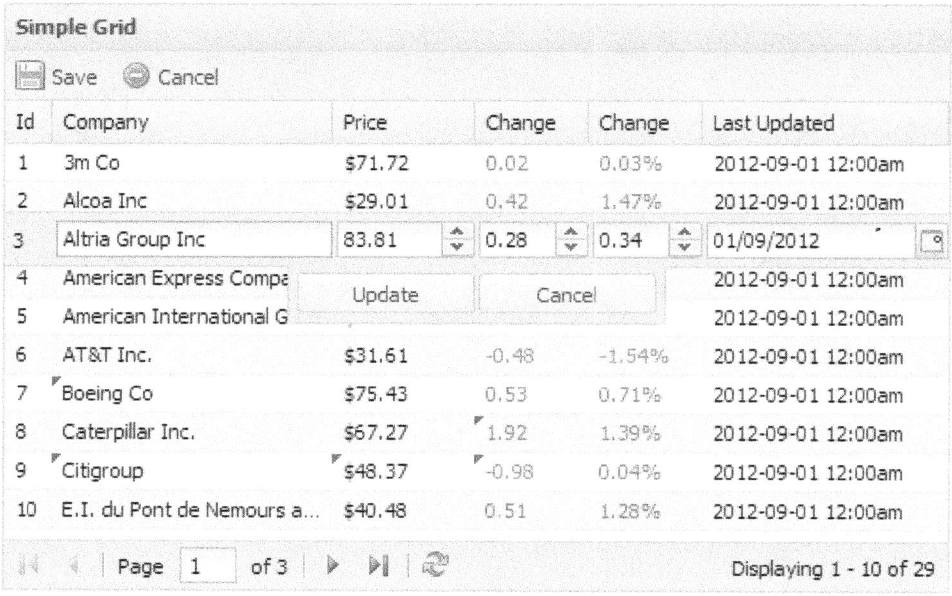

Simple Grid					
🖫 Save ⟲ Cancel					
Id	Company	Price	Change	Change	Last Updated
1	3m Co	$71.72	0.02	0.03%	2012-09-01 12:00am
2	Alcoa Inc	$29.01	0.42	1.47%	2012-09-01 12:00am
3	Altria Group Inc	83.81 ⬍	0.28 ⬍	0.34 ⬍	01/09/2012 ⌕
4	American Express Compa		Update	Cancel	2012-09-01 12:00am
5	American International G				2012-09-01 12:00am
6	AT&T Inc.	$31.61	-0.48	-1.54%	2012-09-01 12:00am
7	Boeing Co	$75.43	0.53	0.71%	2012-09-01 12:00am
8	Caterpillar Inc.	$67.27	1.92	1.39%	2012-09-01 12:00am
9	Citigroup	$48.37	-0.98	0.04%	2012-09-01 12:00am
10	E.I. du Pont de Nemours a...	$40.48	0.51	1.28%	2012-09-01 12:00am
⏮ ◀ Page 1 of 3 ▶ ⏭ ⟳					Displaying 1 - 10 of 29

Once **Update** is pressed, the edited cells get the same red "dirty" indicator as we saw when using the `CellEditing` plugin. As the underlying mechanism for syncing to the writer is the same as before, the only change is the different plugin for editing. You can also handle the **Update** button click on the server, as demonstrated by Ext.NET:

```
http://examples.ext.net/#/GridPanel/Plugins/RowEditor_Remote/
```

Other editing options

A combination of cell and row editing options are also available using the `ComponentColumn` approach. This type of column has a property called `Component` inside which you can put components such as various fields used to let users edit that cell. You can control when these components will appear (for example always show the editing components, or only when the mouse is hovered, and so on). You can use this to make your grid always in edit mode with all cells being form fields of various kinds, or achieve a similar effect with the `RowEditing` plugin. As space in this book is constrained, it won't be possible to cover this here. However, Ext.NET provides some very clear and useful examples demonstrating this capability:

```
http://examples.ext.net/#/search/componentcolumn
```

Many more GridPanel capabilities not covered here

As long as this chapter is, it only touches the surface of what can be done with GridPanels. For more examples, it is worth spending time browsing Ext.NET's Examples Explorer, as the GridPanel section is perhaps the largest of all the examples:

```
http://examples.ext.net/#/search/grid
```

Also to learn more about the inner workings at the Ext JS level, Sencha's own documentation and examples are very valuable to explore, too:

- `http://docs.sencha.com/ext-js/4-1/#!/api/Ext.grid.Panel`
- `http://www.sencha.com/products/extjs/examples/`

Summary

This has been quite a long chapter, because it is one of the most crucial ones. Yet, we've only touched the surface of what Ext.NET can do with data. We looked at paging, filtering, sorting, and grouping. We saw how data can be obtained from the server. We also looked at how columns can be configured for display in different ways. Features and plugins that enhance the GridPanel experience were also introduced. Finally we looked at ways to edit data in-line and how updates can be saved back to the server.

Data processing is core to most web applications, and we have seen Ext.NET has covered this very well. Having got a glimpse of some form fields during grid editing, we will look at these, as well as forms and validation more generally, next.

Forms and Validation

7

Forms are essential to most rich applications. Up to now we have seen a few form elements used to demonstrate other concepts, but here we will look at the following:

- Form fields available in Ext.NET
- Arranging form fields together
- Form field validation
- Data-bound forms

By the end of this chapter, you will have an understanding of how to create desktop-like, rich, and usable forms fit for the complex needs of business applications.

Form fields – overview

Ext.NET's fields are a useful abstraction over HTML-based inputs, but also very rich.

We start with the simple `TextField`, because it introduces many features common to other fields. It is not possible to list every possible feature and combination that Ext.NET and Ext JS support, so it is also highly recommended to refer to their documentation and examples to see the full set of options available.

TextField

A `TextField` class represents a textbox input field, but comes packed with features.

Controlling field labels

All fields have a `FieldLabel`. In addition, you can control aspects of it through a number of properties. For example, the `LabelSeparator` property lets you change the string to another value (including empty string for no separator) to appear after the label (colon is the default). The `LabelAlign` property lets you control where the field label appears. Allowed values are `Top`, `Left`, and `Right`.

> **Usability implications of different form label placement options**
>
> For small forms, alignment to the top (that is above the field) has often been shown to increase the speed with which people complete forms.
>
> In scenarios where far more fields are required (for example, complex business applications that may require 50 or even a few hundreds of fields), there is less research and data to be more definitive. Some evidence suggests that right alignment can help very large forms compared to top or left alignment.

The following screenshot shows three alignment samples for comparison:

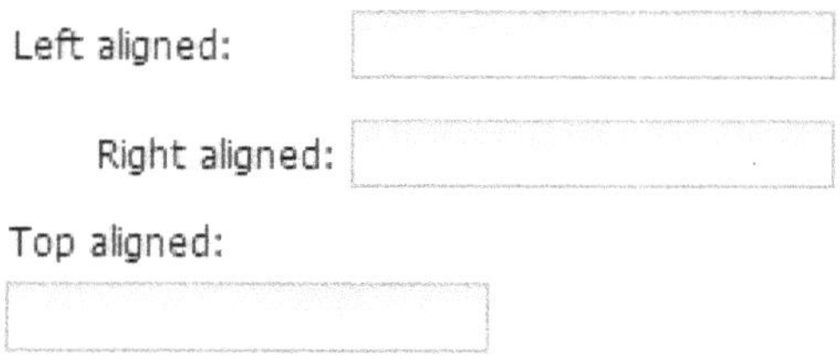

Left aligned:

Right aligned:

Top aligned:

If using `Left` or `Right` `LabelAlign`, the `LabelWidth` property lets you set a width on just the field label. Note, if for example, you have `FieldWidth` of 300px and `LabelWidth` is set to 100px, the remaining width for the input field will be 200px.

Many other label features can be controlled and are described in Sencha's documentation:

```
http://docs.sencha.com/ext-js/4-1/#!/api/Ext.form.Labelable
```

Field icon

You can add a field icon to many fields. For TextField, the icon will appear just inside the text field, but padded so that editing starts after the icon.

Consider the following example:

```
<ext:TextField runat="server" FieldLabel="Text field" Icon="Pencil" />
```

The preceding line of code will produce the following. Note the cursor is automatically positioned just after the icon:

Text field:

Default empty text

You can set some default text to appear if the field is empty. For example:

```
<ext:TextField runat="server" FieldLabel="Text field" EmptyText="Empty
text" />
```

The preceding line of code will render the following:

Text field: Empty text

> **Careful with empty text and no field label!**
>
> Some may use placeholder text as a substitute for a label for aesthetic reasons or due to some constraint. The main usability problem is (depending on the browser) the empty text disappears once the field has focus or if it is not empty, whereas a label remains permanent. The empty text should augment rather than replace the field label.

Field notes

You can also supply field notes, above or below a field. For example:

```
<ext:TextField
    runat       = "server"
    FieldLabel = "Text field"
    Note        = "This is a note"
    NoteAlign   = "Down"
    />
```

The preceding code snippet produces the following:

Text field:

This is a note

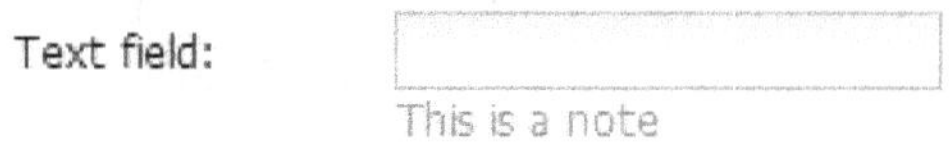

You can also align the note to appear above the field using `NoteAlign="Top"`.

Field indicator

Similar to the field note is an indicator, for example:

```
<ext:TextField
    runat = "server"
    FieldLabel = "Text field"
    IndicatorIcon = "Lightbulb"
    IndicatorText = "Tip: make it short and sweet!"
    />
```

The preceding code snippet produces the following:

Text field: Tip: make it short and sweet!

Custom icons

Icon-based properties, such as `IndicatorIcon` and `Icon` can use one of the 1700 plus included icons, which the following Examples Explorer section summarizes:

```
http://examples.ext.net/#/Miscellaneous/Icon/Icon_Summary/
```

You can always customize and add your own icon using similar properties that end in `Cls`. Because they are class names, any CSS can be applied.

Initial value

You can set a `TextField` element's `Text` property to an initial value, for example:

```
<ext:TextField
    runat="server"
    FieldLabel="Text field"
    Text="Initial text"
    />
```

The preceding code snippet produces the following:

Text field: Initial text

> Although there is a common Value property (of type Object) on all fields, each Field type, such as TextField, will have a type-specific property unique to that field. For example, the Text property should be used for a TextField, NumberField has Number, DateField has SelectedDate, and so on. These properties automatically update the Value property.

NumberField

NumberField is a descendant class of the TextField class. It has a spinner to show up and down arrows to help the user change the field value. NumberField also constrains the input to be numeric values only. The following is an example:

```
<ext:NumberField
    runat="server"
    FieldLabel="Number"
    MinValue="0"
    MaxValue="100"
    AllowDecimals="true"
    DecimalPrecision="1"
    Step="0.5"
    Number="3"
    />
```

The preceding code snippet produces the following:

Number: 3

In the preceding screenshot, we have set the initial value to **3**, via the Number property. We have also set an allowed range, from a minimum of 0 to a maximum of 100. To allow decimals the precision is set to one decimal place. The Step property defines the amount by which the arrows buttons will increase/decrease the value. So, if the increment arrow is pressed, the value would update to 3.5 in the preceding example. You can also hide the up and down buttons by setting the HideTrigger property to true.

TextArea

As with HTML, `TextArea` allows for multiline input. In addition to the settings possible for `TextField`, a `TextArea` can also be configured to grow automatically as you type using `Grow="true"`. `GrowMin` can be used to control the minimum height to allow, and `GrowMax` can define the largest height to allow. For example:

```
<ext:TextArea
    runat      = "server"
    FieldLabel = "Text area"
    LabelAlign = "Top"
    Width      = "450"
    Grow       = "true"
    GrowMax    = "250"
    />
```

This TextArea has been set to grow automatically, but only to a maximum of 250 pixels. When that is reached, scrollbars will appear. Consider the following screenshot:

Text area:

Text area:

Lorem ipsum dolor sit amet, consectetur adipiscing elit. Nunc a nunc ipsum, id varius erat. Phasellus mattis pulvinar orci, eget euismod neque aliquet vitae. Proin commodo pretium metus, in lacinia ipsum ornare et. Nam quis justo massa. Phasellus aliquet ante sit amet augue auctor et laoreet tellus mollis. Nam sodales egestas ante, non varius sapien euismod scelerisque. Nullam bibendum leo hendrerit mi vehicula consequat.

Text area:

tellus tincidunt sit amet lacinia ligula luctus. Nunc eu turpis a diam ultricies malesuada at quis dolor. Nunc posuere eros ut sapien facilisis cursus. Aliquam rutrum, est non rhoncus porttitor, orci sem eleifend lorem, nec bibendum purus leo vitae est. Nam laoreet felis ut nulla elementum sit amet bibendum eros tristique. Mauris facilisis adipiscing venenatis. Phasellus pulvinar ultrices nisl vestibulum sollicitudin. Fusce justo est, pharetra vitae vehicula vehicula, ullamcorper ut nibh. Vivamus non erat dui, ac mattis leo.

Curabitur est magna, sodales id gravida eu, viverra vitae lacus. Fusce nulla orci, sollicitudin a molestie sit amet, dignissim a urna. Aenean sit amet enim elit. Nulla cursus orci sit amet risus egestas id tempor diam feugiat. Donec cursus quam congue libero vulputate a sagittis velit lacinia. Sed vitae purus metus, sit amet viverra dolor. Etiam pellentesque pharetra nibh eu fringilla. Proin lacus nibh, aliquet id volutpat a, faucibus et quam.

In the preceding screenshot, the TextArea is initially at its default height. As text is entered, the TextArea will automatically grow. When entered text grows beyond the maximum grow height, scrollbars appear. Note the `Grow` properties can also be used on a TextField, which will grow in width, but not in height.

HtmlEditor

HtmlEditor is a very lightweight WYSIWYG editor for an end user to provide rich content in HTML. The following is an example:

```
<ext:HtmlEditor
    runat       = "server"
    FieldLabel  = "HTML Editor"
    LabelAlign  = "Top"
    Width       = "450"
    Text        = "<h2>Heading</h2><p>Some text goes here</p>"
    />
```

The preceding code snippet will produce the following:

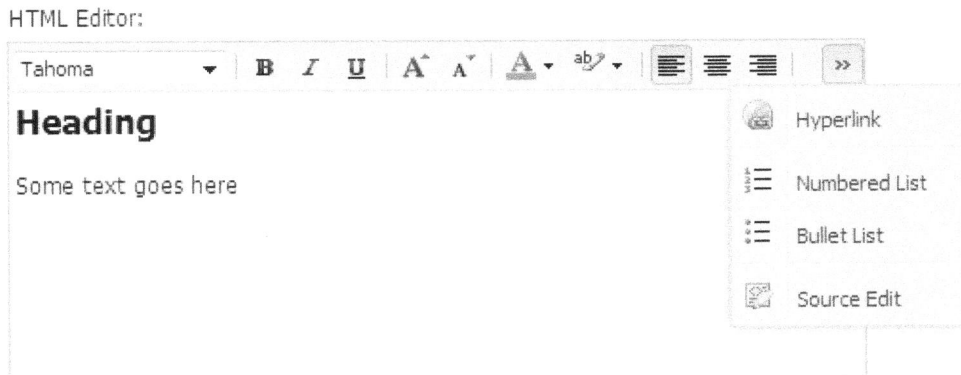

Note, the HtmlEditor is quite lightweight. Various features shown previously can be enabled and disabled. However, the control is browser dependent, so not all features will show for all browsers. Sencha's client-side documentation covers this in detail:

`http://docs.sencha.com/ext-js/4-1/#!/api/Ext.form.field.HtmlEditor`

Be aware that the toolbar options in the HtmlEditor do not necessarily offer the best semantic markup options (for example, there are unfortunately no heading tags that can be created by the user unless they switch to Source Edit mode, which is likely to be very rare). This can be an issue for accessibility of content, or if the content is used as part of a public-facing website, it may make consistent sitewide branding/formatting harder to do.

As a lightweight editor that is dependent on the functionality offered by the browser, be aware that different browsers can produce different HTML. Being a lightweight editor, these issues are not really addressed by the Sencha Ext JS component. Other third-party HTML editors do fill these gaps quite well, but are often larger components and would need integrating into Ext JS manually, and as such is not in the scope of this book.

ComboBox

In *Chapter 5, Working with Data*, we saw how ComboBox works as a data-bound control, using the Store/Proxy/Model architecture with formatting via XTemplates. You can also define values in-line, for example:

```
<ext:ComboBox
    runat="server"
    Editable="false"
    FieldLabel="Country"
    LabelAlign="Top"
    EmptyText="Select a country...">
    <Items>
        <ext:ListItem Text="Canada" Value="CA" />
        <ext:ListItem Text="United States" Value="USA" />
    </Items>
    <SelectedItems>
        <ext:ListItem Value="USA" />
    </SelectedItems>
</ext:ComboBox>
```

The preceding code snippet will produce the following:

The items are defined inline using the `Items` collection. Note that using the optional property, `Editable="false"`, disables manual editing, making it behave similar to an HTML select box, forcing you to choose only from the drop-down list items. Otherwise it behaves similar to an autocomplete list with the option to type your own value.

The `SelectedItems` collection lets you access or set any selected items. In our example we pre-select the **United States** item. You can also select an item by its index if you know it using the following alternative inside the `SelectedItems` collection:

```
<ext:ListItem Index="1" />
```

`ComboBox` also has a boolean `MultiSelect` property to allow multiple selection. This will allow more than one item in the drop-down list to be selected, and the value will be a comma-delimited list of selected items. `ComboBox` has many more features which are described at `http://examples.ext.net/#/search/combobox`.

For a richer multiselection UI, there is also a similar control named `MultiSelect`, which has many examples demonstrated at `http://examples.ext.net/#/Form/MultiSelect/Overview/`.

`SelectBox` mimics an HTML select box even more closely, which you can find at `http://examples.ext.net/#/Form/ComboBox/SelectBox/`.

TimeField

`TimeField` lets users pick a time value. The following is an example:

```
<ext:TimeField
    runat        = "server"
    MinTime      = "9:00"
    MaxTime      = "18:00"
    Increment    = "30"
    SelectedTime = "10:00"
    Format       = "hh:mm tt"
    />
```

The preceding code snippet creates a TimeField, autopopulated with values from 9 a.m. – 6 p.m., in half-hour increments. 10 a.m. is preselected. Note that the display format is independent of the min/max/selected time properties (which, when set in code behind are the `TimeSpan` instances). The following screenshot shows what is rendered:

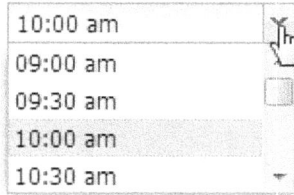

DateField

`DateField` provides a flexible date picker as we saw when it acted as an editor in an editable grid. The following shows `DateField` being used with a few additional options:

```
<ext:DateField
    ID          = "DateField1"
    runat       = "server"
    Format      = "yyyy-MM-dd"
    FieldLabel  = "Enter Date"
    />
```

The `Format` property is a format string that .NET supports, which is internally converted by Ext.NET into a format that the Ext JS `DateField` will support. The `MinDate`, `MaxDate`, and `SelectedDate` properties are of type `System.DateTime`:

```
var today = DateTime.Today;
DateField1.SelectedDate = today;
DateField1.MinDate = today.AddDays(-5);
DateField1.MaxDate = today.AddDays(5);
```

The following screenshot shows what is rendered:

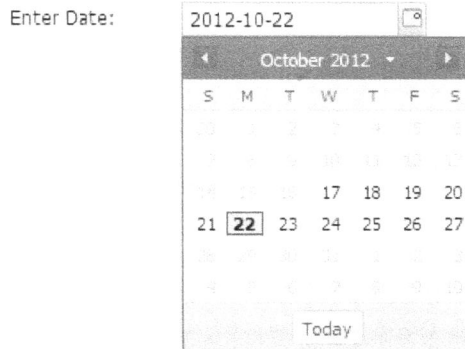

Note, when these properties are populated via markup, they are string values of any .NET parseable date format. You can also set the `Type` property to `Month` (default is `Date`) and the picker that appears will be a month picker. The month that is picked will represent the first day of that month if you choose to use a format string that displays a day portion.

TriggerField

A trigger field is a general-purpose input field that can be configured with one or more trigger buttons. Many fields we have looked at are descendent classes of `TriggerField`. For example, `PickerField` is a useful abstract subclass of `TriggerField`, which provides the ability to pick things from a more complex control. `ComboBox`, `TimeField`, `DropDownField`, and `DateField` controls all inherit from this `PickerField`.

You can also custom-code your own triggers with or without subclassing. The following is an example of using `TriggerField` without subclassing:

```
<ext:TriggerField runat="server">
    <Triggers>
        <ext:FieldTrigger
            Icon="Clear"
            Tag="clear"
            Qtip="<h2>Title</h2><p>Custom title</p>"
            />
        <ext:FieldTrigger Icon="Search" Tag="search" />
    </Triggers>
    <Listeners>
        <TriggerClick Fn="MyApp.onTriggerClick" />
    </Listeners>
</ext:TriggerField>
```

In the preceding sample, we added two field triggers to a trigger field. The first uses a built-in trigger icon for "clear" and uses a `Qtip`, which is a shorthand for an Ext JS tool tip (which allows HTML). The second trigger is for performing a search. Trigger button clicks have to be handled. So our handler for the preceding example is as follows:

```
var MyApp = {
    onTriggerClick: function (field, trigger, index, tag) {
        switch (tag) {
            case 'clear':
                field.setValue('');
                break;
            case 'search':
                // do search
        }
    }
};
```

Each tag is available as one of the event handler arguments, so we switch on it to perform the appropriate action. In our case, for clearing the search term we simply call `setValue` on the field with empty string as the argument. In the case of search we can write the code needed to perform the search:

You can use your own icons, or a variety of inbuilt icons. You can also choose to hide or show triggers at different times, for example, we could have initially hidden the clear trigger until something is actually typed. These and other examples are detailed at `http://examples.ext.net/#/search/triggerfield`.

DropDownField

`DropDownField` is a useful subclass of `PickerField` (which is a subclass of `TriggerField`) implemented by Ext.NET. It provides a handy way to put complex panels as contents of the drop-down list, so you are not limited to `ComboBox` style interfaces (which are rich via XTemplates, nonetheless). Instead you can put Panels in there, which also means GridPanels, TreePanels, or any ASP.NET web control if placed within the `<Content>` region of a container, making this a rich and flexible tool.

Consider the following as a general pattern for using a `DropDownField`:

```
<ext:DropDownField runat="server">
  <Component>
    <!-- Ext.NET component goes here -->
  </Component>
</ext:DropDownField>
```

Inside `Component` we could put the GridPanel defined in the following example:

```
<ext:GridPanel runat="server" Height="150">
  <Store>
    <ext:Store ID="Store1" runat="server" PageSize="3">
      <Model>
        <ext:Model runat="server">
          <Fields>
            <ext:ModelField Name="Symbol" />
            <ext:ModelField Name="Company" />
          </Fields>
        </ext:Model>
      </Model>
    </ext:Store>
  </Store>
  <ColumnModel runat="server">
    <Columns>
      <ext:Column Text="Symbol" DataIndex="Symbol" Width="60" />
      <ext:Column Text="Company" DataIndex="Company" Flex="1" />
      <ext:CommandColumn Align="Center" OverOnly="true" Width="25">
        <Commands>
          <ext:GridCommand Icon="Accept" CommandName="pick" />
        </Commands>
        <Listeners>
          <Command Handler="this.grid.dropDownField.setValue(record.
data.Symbol);" />
        </Listeners>
      </ext:CommandColumn>
    </Columns>
  </ColumnModel>
  <BottomBar>
    <ext:PagingToolbar runat="server" />
  </BottomBar>
</ext:GridPanel>
```

The preceding GridPanel might be populated with some data, for example:

```
protected void Page_Load(object sender, EventArgs e)
{
  if (!X.IsAjaxRequest)
  {
    this.Store1.DataSource = new object[]
    {
      new object[] { "AXP", "American Express Company" },
      new object[] { "BA", "Boeing Co." },
```

```
            new object[] { "CAT", "Caterpillar Inc." },
            new object[] { "ABC", "Blah" };
        };

        this.Store1.DataBind();
    }
}
```

The preceding code snippet produces the following:

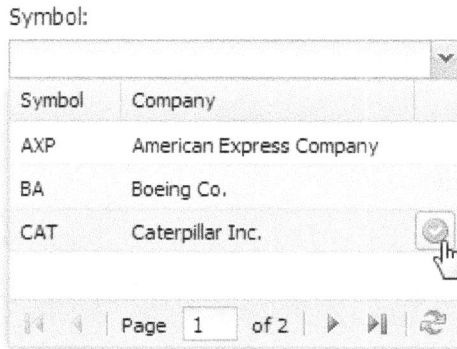

In the preceding GridPanel we have used a command column to show a button when hovered over a particular row. When clicked, the symbol on that row is assigned as the `DropDownField` control's value.

The Ext.NET examples at `http://examples.ext.net/#/search/dropdownfield` are worth studying further for additional examples.

Checkbox

Ext.NET's `Checkbox` lets you hide field labels or reserve space:

```
<ext:Checkbox BoxLabel="Dog" FieldLabel="Favorite Animals" />
<ext:Checkbox BoxLabel="Cat" HideEmptyLabel="false" />
<ext:Checkbox BoxLabel="Monkey" Checked="true"
              HideEmptyLabel="false" />
```

The preceding code snippet produces the following:

Radio buttons

Radio buttons are defined much like checkboxes, except you use the `Radio` class instead of the `Checkbox` class (or `<ext:Radio>` in markup). You also set the `Name` property, because HTML requires so the browser knows which radio buttons to associate with each other.

FileUploadField

A useful field to upload files is `FileUploadField`. As Sencha explains in their documentation, there is no secure cross-browser way to set the value of a file input programmatically, so the `setValue` method usually available on all fields is not implemented by this widget. In addition, `getValue` will return a browser-specific value (some will have path, some will not). See the following for more information:

`http://docs.sencha.com/ext-js/4-1/#!/api/Ext.form.field.File`

Also note file upload does not use AJAX. Behind the scenes, a separate iframe is used to submit the entire form. See the following website for further examples:

`http://examples.ext.net/#/Form/FileUploadField/Basic/`

Many more form fields

Due to the limited space in this book, we can't cover every form field available in Ext.NET. Just a few not covered include `HyperLink`, `Slider`, `SpinnerField`, and `DisplayField`. Be sure to study the examples for even more controls as well as more options on controls that have been introduced here at the following website:

`http://examples.ext.net/#/search/Form`

Form layout

Ext.NET provides a number of ways in which you can arrange form fields.

Checkbox and Radio button grouping

Checkboxes and Radio buttons can be configured to show in a variety of ways, for example, rendered in rows, or a column, or multiple columns. For example, using a simple container to hold a RadioGroup:

```
<ext:RadioGroup runat="server" Width="400">
    <Items>
        <ext:Radio BoxLabel="Item 1" />
```

```
            <ext:Radio BoxLabel="Item 2" Checked="true" />
            <ext:Radio BoxLabel="Item 3" />
            <ext:Radio BoxLabel="Item 4" />
            <ext:Radio BoxLabel="Item 5" />
        </Items>
    </ext:RadioGroup>
```

The preceding code snippet will produce the following:

⦿ Item 1　　○ Item 2　　○ Item 3　　○ Item 4　　○ Item 5

Using a `RadioGroup` means you do not need to set a radio `Name`. You can set the number of columns you want and how they render, vertically or horizontally. For example, `<ext:RadioGroup ColumnsNumber="3" Vertical="true">` will produce this:

○ Item 1　　　　○ Item 3　　　　○ Item 5
⦿ Item 2　　　　○ Item 4

Checkboxes can also be grouped using the similar `CheckboxGroup` class (or `<ext:CheckboxGroup>` in markup).

Fieldsets

Ext.NET's fieldsets render like HTML `fieldset` elements, but can optionally be expanded or collapsed using the `Collapsed` and `Collapsible` properties. For example:

```
<ext:FieldSet Collapsed="false" Collapsible="true" Title="Name">
    <Items>
        <ext:TextField FieldLabel="First name" />
        <ext:TextField FieldLabel="Last name" />
    </Items>
</ext:FieldSet>
```

The preceding code will initially render as follows:

┌─ ▲ Name ─────────────────────────┐
│ First name: [   ] │
│   │
│ Last name: [   ] │
└──────────────────────────────────┘

Once collapsed, it will then look like the following screenshot:

▼ Name

FormPanel

FormPanel is a subclass of Panel. It acts as a container for form fields (although you are not forced to use a FormPanel). It also provides some layout management for your fields. The default is an Anchor layout, which will stretch fields within the FormPanel when given the appropriate anchor values. Other layouts are also possible. The following is an example using VBoxLayout:

```
<ext:Window runat="server" Layout="FitLayout" Width="300"
        Height="250" Title="Enter values"
        Icon="ApplicationForm">
  <Items>
    <ext:FormPanel runat="server" BodyPadding="5" Border="false"
              ButtonAlign="Right" Layout="VBoxLayout">
      <LayoutConfig>
        <ext:VBoxLayoutConfig Align="Stretch" />
      </LayoutConfig>
      <Defaults>
        <ext:Parameter Name="LabelWidth" Value="90" Mode="Raw" />
      </Defaults>
      <Items>
        <ext:TextField FieldLabel="First Name" />
        <ext:TextField FieldLabel="Last Name" />
        <ext:TextArea FieldLabel="Profile" LabelAlign="Top"
                Flex="1" />
      </Items>
    </ext:FormPanel>
  </Items>
  <Buttons>
    <ext:Button runat="server" Text="Save" />
    <ext:Button runat="server" Text="Cancel" />
  </Buttons>
</ext:Window>
```

In the preceding code, we are placing a FormPanel inside a Window. We set the default label width to be 90 pixels for any form fields in the FormPanel and we are stretching the TextArea (via Flex="1") to fit the remaining space. When we resize the Window, the form fields automatically stretch, as shown in the following screenshot:

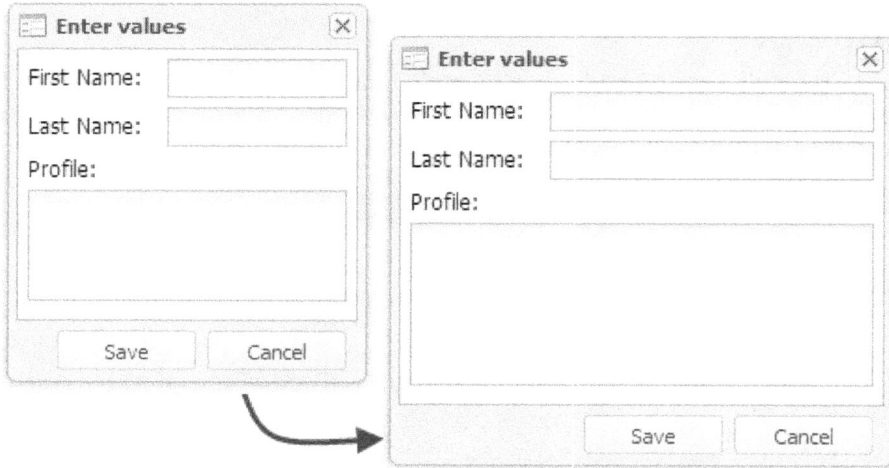

There are a number of useful examples from Ext.NET worth studying further, as follows:

- http://examples.ext.net/#/Layout/VBoxLayout/VBox_Form/
- http://examples.ext.net/#/Layout/FormLayout/Overview/
- http://examples.ext.net/#/Layout/AnchorLayout/Anchor_With_Form/
- http://examples.ext.net/#/Layout/AbsoluteLayout/Absolute_Layout_Form/

FieldDefaults

In the earlier example, we set the default label width for all fields by adding a parameter to the Defaults property of the FormPanel. This can also be done on a FieldContainer, which is another way to group fields, which we will see shortly. If we wanted to set more than one default this way, we would add another parameter. However, there are many properties that can be defaulted, so there is a useful property named FieldDefaults to let you set properties more succinctly. The following is an example:

```
<FieldDefaults
    LabelAlign="Right" LabelWidth="90" MsgTarget="side"
    />
```

In this example, three default properties are being set for all fields that will be inside the `FormPanel` or the `FieldContainer` control to which this declaration belongs.

Each individual field could of course override the default if needed. For a list of properties that can be set this way, see the following documentation from Ext JS:

`http://docs.sencha.com/ext-js/4-1/#!/api/Ext.form.Labelable`

FieldContainer

`FieldContainer` is a more general-purpose container for grouping fields. You can provide a single label for those fields or combine field error messages (when we look at validation we will cover error messages, too). Consider the following example:

```
<ext:FieldContainer runat="server" Width="350"
                    Layout="HBoxLayout" FieldLabel="Full Name"
                    DefaultMargins="0 5 0 0">
  <Items>
    <ext:ComboBox Width="50">
      <Items>
        <ext:ListItem Text="Mr" Value="mr" />
        <ext:ListItem Text="Mrs" Value="mrs" />
        <ext:ListItem Text="Miss" Value="miss" />
      </Items>
      <SelectedItems>
        <ext:ListItem Value="mr" />
      </SelectedItems>
    </ext:ComboBox>
    <ext:TextField Flex="1" />
    <ext:TextField Flex="1" />
  </Items>
</ext:FieldContainer>
```

Using a `FieldContainer` with an `HBox` layout, the two text fields will stretch to fill the remaining space after the title ComboBox, which has been given an explicit width:

We can also show the labels of each field if we want. In addition, some fields can have formatting display text using `DisplayField`. The following is a more involved example:

```
<ext:FormPanel runat="server" BodyPadding="10" Width="450"
DefaultAnchor="100%">
  <Items>
    <ext:FieldContainer FieldLabel="Full Name"
                        Layout="HBoxLayout"
                        DefaultMargins="0 5 0 0">
      <FieldDefaults LabelAlign="Top" />
      <Items>
        <ext:ComboBox Width="50" FieldLabel="Title">
          <Items>
            <ext:ListItem Text="Mr" Value="mr" />
            <ext:ListItem Text="Mrs" Value="mrs" />
            <ext:ListItem Text="Miss" Value="miss" />
          </Items>
          <SelectedItems>
            <ext:ListItem Value="mr" />
          </SelectedItems>
        </ext:ComboBox>
        <ext:TextField Flex="1" FieldLabel="First Name" />
        <ext:TextField Flex="1" FieldLabel="Last Name"
                        Margins="0" />
      </Items>
    </ext:FieldContainer>

    <ext:TextField FieldLabel="Favourite sport" />

    <ext:FieldContainer FieldLabel="Phone"
                        Layout="HBoxLayout"
                        DefaultMargins="0 5 0 0">
      <Items>
        <ext:DisplayField Text="(" Margins="0" />
        <ext:TextField Width="29" Margins="0" />
        <ext:DisplayField Text=")" />
        <ext:TextField Width="29" />
        <ext:DisplayField Text="-" />
        <ext:TextField Width="48" />
      </Items>
    </ext:FieldContainer>
  </Items>
</ext:FormPanel>
```

In the preceding code, we have removed the width from the `FieldContainer` and introduced another container, a `FormPanel`. Note we've also overridden the default margin for the **Last Name** field (as it doesn't need a 5-pixel margin to its right-hand side, and therefore will line up nicely with other fields in other rows). In addition, for the **Full Name** field, we have decided to show each field's individual label, and using the `FieldDefaults` property, we've set labels to show above their fields by default.

We've also added a text field without a container (because it will stretch as part of the default `FormPanel` layout. Below that we've then shown a phone number field using `DisplayField` classes to put some text around the different fields.

The preceding code will produce the following screenshot:

Form validation

Ext.NET provides support for both client-side and server-side (remote) validation. Here we provide an overview of available constraints, validation message appearance configuration, some of the different validation types, and custom validators.

Constraining and guiding input

Some fields allow defining the range of acceptable values. `TextField` and `TextArea` have `MinLength`/`MaxLength`. `NumberField` has `MinValue`/`MaxValue`. `DateField` has `MinDate`/`MaxDate` as well as options to disable specific dates. These properties help to alert the user if the entered value is beyond these bounds.

`TextField` also has the additional property, `EnforceMaxLength`, which can be set to `true` to set `maxlength` on the underlying HTML input to constraint what you type.

In addition, text fields have a `MaskRe` property for configuring a regular expression used to filter keystrokes that do not match. It does not, however, filter characters already in the input. There is a similar property called `StripCharsRe`, which is a regular expression used to strip unwanted content from the value during input.

The boolean property `AllowBlank` can also be set to `true` (default) or `false` for a field.

As two examples of useful guided input features, the `InputMask` plugin helps constrain input to a specified format, and the `PasswordMask` plugin shows the typed symbol temporarily before being replaced by a bullet. These examples demonstrate those plugins:

- `http://examples.ext.net/#/Form/TextField/InputMask/`
- `http://examples.ext.net/#/Form/TextField/Password_Mask/`

Customizing the appearance of validation messages

Consider these two TextFields of which one is configured not to allow blank values:

```
<ext:FormPanel runat="server" BodyPadding="10">
  <Items>
    <ext:TextField FieldLabel="First Name" AllowBlank="false" />
    <ext:TextField FieldLabel="Last Name" />
  </Items>
</ext:FormPanel>
```

When you focus onto the **First Name** field, nothing special happens. Once it loses focus (for example, tabbing or clicking onto **Last Name**), then a red underline appears because of the `AllowBlank` setting. Hovering over the field will result in the following tool tip:

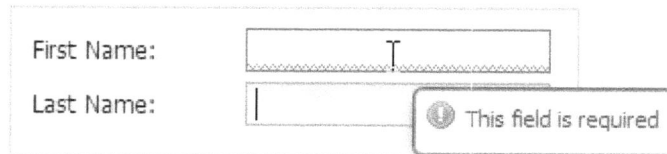

The default text can be changed by setting the `BlankText` property on the field. If we add `MaxLength` of 10 to the **Last Name** field (not realistic, but just to demonstrate!) as we start typing, the validation starts checking the length. As soon as you go over you start to see a similar message (which can be overridden using the `MaxLengthText` property).

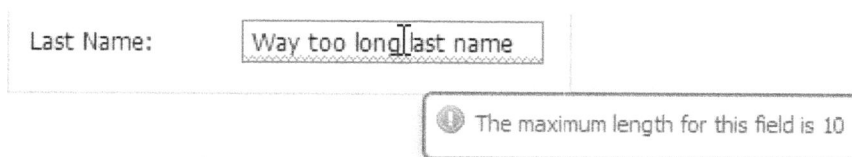

The same applies for the `MinLength`/`MinLengthText` and `RegEx`/`RegExText` properties. The latter lets you test the input against a JavaScript-compatible regular expression.

The following properties let you change the appearance and placement of messages:

- `ErrorMsgCls` to format the error message.
- `InvalidItemCls` to change how an invalid field looks (the default being the red squiggly lines you see in the preceding screenshot).
- `MsgTarget` to define how the message is shown. A tool tip (known as a `Qtip`) is the default as above. Other options are `Under` and `Side` to place the message on the screen, an HTML ID for a custom location, `Title` (for a regular HTML tool tip rather than an Ext JS `Qtip` tool tip), or `None`.

Consider the following example:

```
<ext:TextField
    FieldLabel="Enter a value"
    AllowBlank="false"
    InvalidCls="custom-err"
    MsgTarget="Under"
    />
```

The class name when the field is invalid has been set to a custom value, but the target for the message, rather than being a tool tip (the default) has been set to `Under` to appear below the field. The following CSS has been used:

```
.custom-err-field { background:#fdd; border-color:#a88; }
.custom-err .x-form-item-label { font-weight:bold; }
```

Note that the custom class is applied to the container of the field, not the field itself. By convention, Ext JS puts `-field` after the class name, so we can target the field and change the background color and border color for example. In case you are seeing the following screenshot in black and white, the field label has been made bold too:

Validation messages using FieldContainers

With FieldContainers you can combine messages to appear together. For example:

```
<ext:FieldContainer
  runat="server"
  Width="350"
  FieldLabel="Full Name"
  Layout="HBoxLayout"
  DefaultMargins="0 5 0 0"
  DefaultFlex="1"
  CombineErrors="true"
  MsgTarget="Under">
  <FieldDefaults AllowBlank="false" LabelAlign="Top" />
  <Items>
    <ext:TextField FieldLabel="First Name" />
    <ext:TextField FieldLabel="Last Name" />
  </Items>
</ext:FieldContainer>
```

The use of `CombineErrors` and `MsgTarget` means the messages will appear as below:

Validation types

Ext JS provides validation types which it calls **VTypes**. Each type of validation is a VType. Default VTypes from Ext JS are `alpha`, `alphanum`, `email`, and `url`. These are explained further in Sencha's documentation:

http://docs.sencha.com/ext-js/4-1/#!/api/Ext.form.field.VTypes

Ext.NET supports those but also provides some additional useful VTypes for password validation, date range validation, and IP address validation.

Consider the following code:

```
<ext:TextField FieldLabel="Enter a value" Vtype="alphanum" />
<ext:TextField FieldLabel="Email" Vtype="email" />
```

The `alphanum` (and `alpha`) are examples of VTypes that apply as you type. If you type a non-alphanumeric character in the preceding example (underscore is also allowed), the value is rejected and not allowed in the field. In the case of the `email` VType, each keystroke results in validation occurring and showing an appropriate message, as follows:

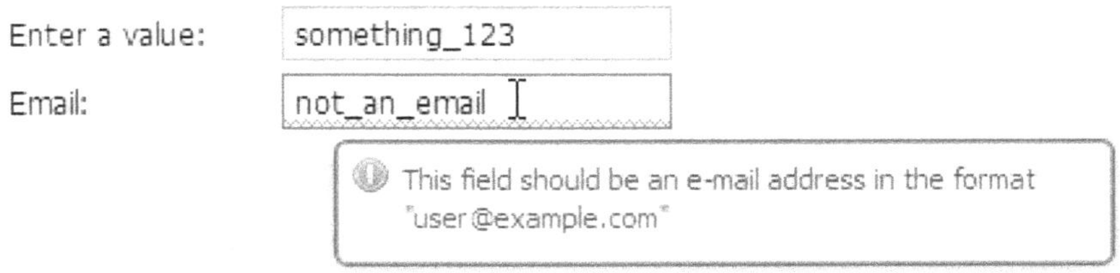

The following is an example of a date range validator:

```
<ext:DateField
    ID="StartDate" runat="server" FieldLabel="Start"
    Vtype="daterange" EndDateField="EndDate"
    />

<ext:DateField
    ID="EndDate" runat="server" FieldLabel="End"
    Vtype="daterange" StartDateField="StartDate"
    />
```

The preceding code produces the following screenshot:

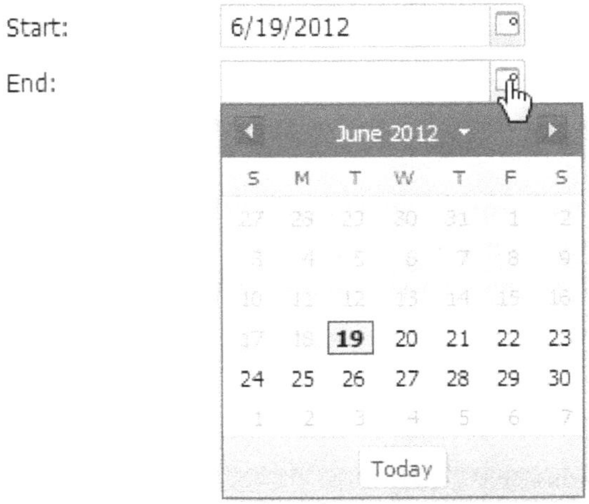

In this case, your input has been constrained. The moment you pick a start date, the end date cannot start before it. While the picker helps, you can still type an earlier date manually in which case you would see the following screenshot:

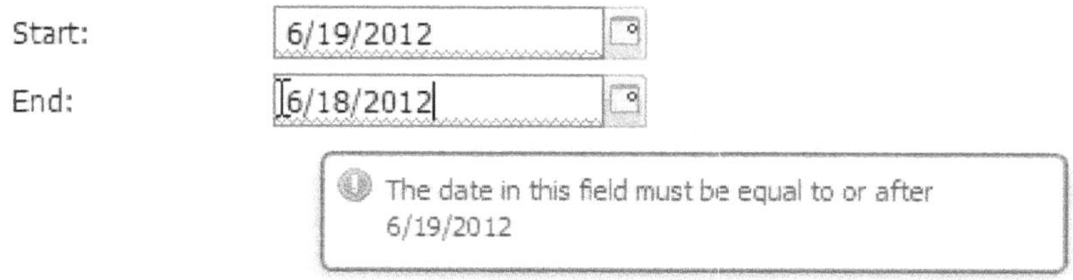

Start: 6/19/2012

End: 6/18/2012

The date in this field must be equal to or after 6/19/2012

The same of course applies to the start date.

Custom validation VTypes

Creating your own VType validator is a matter of writing some Ext JS JavaScript. Ext. NET's own additional ones are such examples. Here is their current implementation of the password validation VType, which compares two password fields to make sure they are the same. It is nice and simple, and illustrates well how to create your own:

```
Ext.apply(Ext.form.VTypes, {
    password : function (val, field) {
        if (field.initialPassField) {
            var pwd = Ext.getCmp(field.initialPassField);
            return pwd ? (val === pwd.getValue()) : false;
        }

        return true;
    },

    passwordText : "Passwords do not match"
});
```

The VType is defined by simply declaring a function (password in this case), which accepts two parameters; the value to compare and an instance of the field. This function is added to Ext JS's own Ext.form.VTypes singleton via Ext.apply. Consider its usage:

```
<ext:TextField
  ID="PasswordField"
  runat="server"
  FieldLabel="Password"
  InputType="Password"
  />
```

```
<ext:TextField
  runat="server"
  Vtype="password"
  FieldLabel="Confirm Password"
  InputType="Password">
  <CustomConfig>
    <ext:ConfigItem Name="initialPassField"
                    Value="PasswordField" Mode="Value" />
  </CustomConfig>
</ext:TextField>
```

JavaScript is a dynamic language, so you can just add another property to an instance of a password field without having to subclass the password field to do this. Ext.NET provides a CustomConfig collection where any custom property can be set, initialPassField in this case. The validator will then automatically handle the logic:

This is one example where being familiar with Ext JS will help. More information on how to create custom VTypes can be found at following links:

- http://docs.sencha.com/ext-js/4-1/#!/api/Ext.form.field.VTypes
- http://examples.ext.net/#/Form/Validation/Custom_VType/

You can also override the default validation process by providing a Validator property on a field. This is a JavaScript function that will be called first during field validation and returns a boolean true if the value being validated is valid, or a string for an error message. See the following URL for more information:

http://docs.sencha.com/ext-js/4-1/#!/api/Ext.form.field.Text-cfg-validator

Remote validation

Remote validation lets you reuse business functionality. Various Ext.NET approaches are available, from DirectEvents to calling ASMX services or ASHX handlers. For example:

```
<form runat="server">
    <ext:TextField ID="UserName" runat="server"
            FieldLabel="Username" IsRemoteValidation="true">
        <RemoteValidation OnValidation="CheckUserName" />
    </ext:TextField>
</form>
```

The corresponding DirectEvent can be defined like the following in code behind:

```
protected void CheckUserName(object sender,
                        RemoteValidationEventArgs e)
{
    var field = (TextField)sender;
    if (IsValid(field.Text))
    {
        e.Success = true;
    }
    else
    {
        e.Success = false;
        e.ErrorMessage = field.Text + " is not available";
    }
}
```

In the preceding code, we have assumed `IsValid` can implement business logic to determine if the user is valid. The event arguments parameter is updated based on the success, and has an error message if unsuccessful. By default, an animated loading icon renders next to the field while remote validation is occurring, as the following shows:

If the value is invalid, the standard error highlighting will apply (red squiggly lines and a tool tip with the error message set on the DirectEvent handler).

To use a web service or another URL to do the remote validation, you would change the `RemoteValidation` property in preceding section to use its `Url` property instead and tell it to expect the request parameters to be in JSON format, like this:

```
<RemoveValidation Url="MyService.ashx" Json="true" />
```

See the following Ext.NET example for more details:

```
http://examples.ext.net/#/Form/Validation/Remote_Validation/
```

Note that we need the `<form>` element if we need the field's state to be posted back to the same page. If you are using a URL for remote validation, then you do not need it.

Validation events

In addition to the remote validation events seen earlier, there are a number of other events related to validation. For example, most fields have the following Listeners and DirectEvents, whose names are quite self explanatory:

- `BeforeRemoteValidation`
- `RemoteValidationFailure`
- `RemoteValidationInvalid`
- `RemoteValidationValid`
- `ValidityChange`

In addition, you can control when a field does its validation using the boolean properties `ValidateOnChange` and `ValidateOnBlur`.

There is also the JavaScript function on a field named `isValid`, which can be used at any time to check the validity programmatically. An example of this is shown a bit later.

The FormPanel has some useful validation-related events. For example, the `FieldValidityChange` event tells you which field in the form changed, and the `ValidityChange` event notifies you if any fields in that FormPanel have changed the overall validity of the form. You could use this to enable/disable a **Save** or **Submit** button for example, shown in the example at the following URL:

```
http://examples.ext.net/#/Form/Validation/Remote_Validation/
```

In addition, there is also a `ValidationStatus` plugin that hooks into the `StatusBar` and automatically monitors the validation status of any fields in the associated FormPanel. This is demonstrated on Ext.NET's Examples Explorer:

```
http://examples.ext.net/#/Toolbar/StatusBar/Advanced/
```

Manually submitting a form

With Ext.NET, developers have a lot of control over the submission of a `<form>` element or FormPanel, even if not using the standard ASP.NET `<form runat="server">`. The basic principle for manually submitting a form to the server is the Ext JS FormPanel `getForm` method, which returns the underlying form manager, the BasicForm associated with the FormPanel. It has a `getValues` method, which returns values as a dictionary of name/value pairs that can be submitted to the server using Ajax, for example:

```
<ext:Button runat="server" Text="Save">
  <DirectEvents>
    <Click OnEvent="SaveData"
           Before="return #{FormPanel1}.isValid();">
      <ExtraParams>
        <ext:Parameter
          Name="values"
          Value="#{FormPanel1}.getForm().getValues()"
          Mode="Raw"
          Encode="true"
          />
      </ExtraParams>
    </Click>
  </DirectEvents>
</ext:Button>
```

In the preceding code, notice that before the click handler fires, we call the `isValid` method on a FormPanel instance. If it is not valid, returning `false` will cancel the event. We pass the data via a `DirectEvent` parameter. So using `getForm().getValues()`, we assign it to a parameter named `values`. Then in the code behind you can use it like this:

```
protected void SaveData(object sender, DirectEventArgs e)
{
    var values = JSON.Deserialize<Dictionary<string, string>>(e.
ExtraParams["values"]);

    // process the values
}
```

In the preceding code, we have simply extracted the `values` parameter which is a JSON string, and we deserialize it into `Dictionary<string, string>`.

The Button in the above code is not defined inside an ASP.NET `<form runat="server">`. If it was, the DirectEvent request (which is a POST to the server) would submit the rest of the form values too, so the above would then lead to a bit of duplication. To avoid that you can also use `Type="Load"` in the DirectEvent, as we saw in *Chapter 4*, *AJAX with Ext.NET*, or use the `submit` function on the client-side to submit the form to another URL.

> It is important to note that for this to work, each field being submitted should have a `Name` property assigned, as this will be the key in each dictionary item. If you do not set the Name property yourself, Ext.NET will use the `ClientID` of the field as the `Name`. For example, if you have
>
> `<ext:TextField ID="TextField1" Name="MyTextField" />`
>
> Then the key submitted is "MyTextField".

The FormPanel also has a JavaScript `submit` method to submit a form programmatically. There is also the `Url` property to submit the form to a different location, such as an MVC Controller, another ASPX page, or an ASHX handler. Here is an example:

```
<ext:FormPanel ID="FormPanel1" runat="server" BodyPadding="5"
Url="HandleForm.ashx">
  <Items>
    <ext:TextField Name="Fname" FieldLabel="First Name" />
    <ext:TextField Name="Lname" FieldLabel="Last Name" />
  </Items>
</ext:FormPanel>
<ext:Button runat="server" Text="Save">
  <Listeners>
    <Click Handler="#{FormPanel1}.submit();" />
  </Listeners>
</ext:Button>
```

Assuming the above code is inside the HTML body (with no other form declarations), the `Fname` and `Lname` values will be all that is posted to `HandleForm.ashx` which can request these values from the HttpRequest collection and process them as needed.

Binding Stores and Records to a form

In *Chapter 5, Working with Data*, we saw Stores working with Models and Fields. These are then bound to data-bound controls. A grid column, for example, used a `DataIndex` property to associate a column with a Store's Fields. With a form, the `Name` can serve the same purpose. With a grid, it automatically loaded the store's records into the grid for you. But you can also reuse a store with a form, with a small manual step to load a record into a form. This means you can achieve this kind of UI if you want:

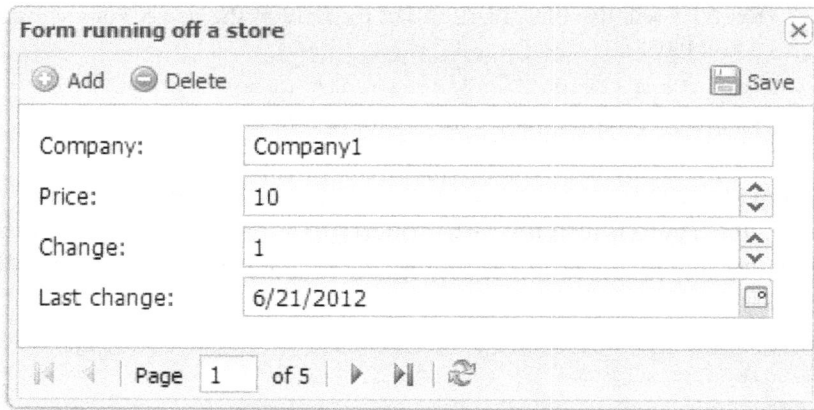

To create the above, we first create a store, as we have seen in many previous examples:

```
<ext:Store ID="Store1" runat="server" OnReadData="FetchRecord"
PageSize="1">
  <Proxy>
    <ext:PageProxy />
  </Proxy>
  <Model>
    <ext:Model runat="server">
      <Fields>
        <ext:ModelField Name="ID" />
        <ext:ModelField Name="Company" />
        <ext:ModelField Name="Price" Type="Float" />
        <ext:ModelField Name="Change" Type="Float" />
        <ext:ModelField Name="LastChange" Type="Date" />
      </Fields>
    </ext:Model>
  </Model>
```

```
    <Listeners>
     <DataChanged Handler="
       var record = this.getAt(0) || {};
       #{FormPanel1}.getForm().loadRecord(record);
       #{FormPanel1}.clearInvalid();" />
    </Listeners>
  </ext:Store>
```

Three things are highlighted:

1. A server method (`FetchRecord`, called via a DirectEvent) will be invoked each time a record has to be read.
2. The PageSize is set to 1, as a form will only show 1 record at a time.
3. We use the Store's own `DataChanged` event handler to update the form with the new record. The `loadRecord` method is just a standard Ext JS method.

`FetchRecord`, on the server, binds data to the Store:

```
protected void FetchRecord(object sender, StoreReadDataEventArgs e)
{
    this.Store1.DataSource = GetData(e.Start);
    this.Store1.DataBind();
    e.Total = GetCount();
}
```

By now, the above code should look familiar, as it uses a Window, a Toolbar with buttons, and a PagingToolbar using techniques we have already covered. The above example is a cut down version from Ext.NET's own example, which is worth studying:

```
http://examples.ext.net/#/Form/Miscellaneous/Edit_Form_View/
```

This technique also makes it easy to create master-detail UI patterns. For example, if you have a GridPanel bound to a Store, upon a row selection event, you could load a details form with that selected record. Ext.NET has an example of this, too:

```
http://examples.ext.net/#/Form/FormPanel/Basic/
```

Summary

We covered a number of form related features. We looked at many examples of form fields: TextField, NumberField, TextArea, HtmlEditor, ComboBox, TimeField, DateField, TriggerField, DropDownField, Checkbox, Radio buttons, and FileUploadField. We also saw how forms can be laid out, validated, and submitted. We also saw how stored and records can be bound to a form.

A great thing about Ext.NET and Ext JS when it comes to forms is that they do not try to reinvent conventions. The field class hierarchy means many features are reused and easily available to subclasses, making common tasks easier. Forms can also load records, thus reusing the store architecture.

There are many more field types and layout options which were not covered here, so be sure to look at the Ext.NET examples explorer for more fields and more examples on how to use them. Two very popular and rich controls we can look at further in the next chapter are the TreePanel and TabPanel.

8
Trees and Tabs with Ext.NET

Tree and tab controls are popular controls within rich web applications. Tree controls are useful for managing a hierarchy of data, while tabs are useful for grouping related data further. In Ext.NET, these controls are known as the **TreePanel** and **TabPanel**. This chapter will provide an overview of their capabilities and cover the following:

- TreePanel
    - TreePanel – overview
    - Asynchronous tree node loading
    - Data binding with TreeStore and ColumnModel

- TabPanel
    - TabPanel – overview
    - Asynchronous tab loading
    - Useful tab features

TreePanel

`TreePanel` inherits from `TablePanel`, which is also the abstract parent class of `GridPanel`. This means that trees can get many features that GridPanels do (for example, multiple columns). A `TreePanel` can also work with a subclass of `Store`—the `TreeStore`—which is especially useful for AJAX-based tree interactions. These useful architectural changes from previous versions of Ext.NET increase familiarity and code reuse, while making TreePanels quite rich.

TreePanel – overview

We will leave the Store aspect for a later part of this chapter. In this section we will have a look at the basic mechanics of putting a TreePanel together.

A TreePanel is made up of nodes. A node may have children, which are more nodes. If a node does not have any child nodes it is referred to as a **leaf node**. A TreePanel has a single **root node** (which is optional to display). Tree nodes can be loaded upfront when the page is loaded (or when the TreePanel is constructed), or nodes can be expanded and populated locally or via the result of an AJAX request (remote loading). You can store additional data on each node through the use of custom attributes.

To illustrate, we will convert a folder containing icons in many subfolders into a TreePanel. This screenshot shows two types of TreePanel. The left-hand side shows the default look, while the right-hand side hides the root node and uses custom icons:

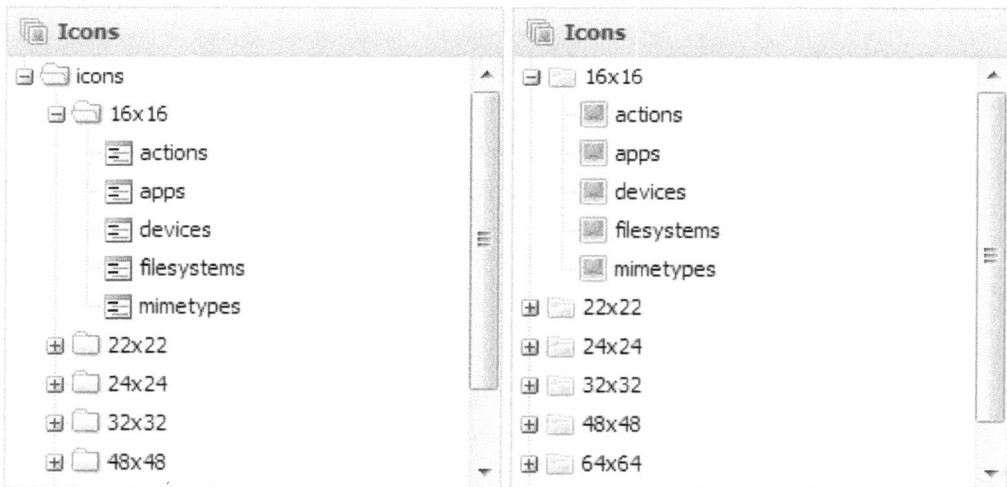

To produce the left hand TreePanel we can create the nodes manually as follows:

```
<ext:TreePanel runat="server" Width="250" Height="250"
               Icon="Pictures" Title="Icons" AutoScroll="true">
  <Root>
    <ext:Node Text="icons" Expanded="true">
      <Children>
        <ext:Node Text="16x16" Expanded="true">
          <Children>
            <ext:Node Text="actions" Leaf="true" />
```

```
              <ext:Node Text="apps" Leaf="true" />
              <ext:Node Text="devices" Leaf="true" />
              <ext:Node Text="filesystems" Leaf="true" />
              <ext:Node Text="mimetypes" Leaf="true" />
            </Children>
          </ext:Node>
          <!-- all the other sizes go here -->
        </Children>
      </ext:Node>
    </Root>
  </ext:TreePanel>
```

As a descendent class of `Panel`, you can set properties such as `Title`, `AutoScroll`, `DockedItems`, and more. By default, leaf node icons are different from non-leaf nodes. These can be set via the `Icon` or `IconCls` property as we have seen throughout Ext.NET. You can also hide the root node by setting `RootVisible="false"` on the TreePanel. These two techniques were used to produce the TreePanel on the right, shown earlier.

In this next example, the nodes are populated by reading the directory structure recursively from the filesystem. The following is a method we will invoke from code-behind to create the tree nodes:

```
public Node CreateTreeNode(string path)
{
  int lastSeparatorPos =
      path.LastIndexOf(Path.DirectorySeparatorChar) + 1;
  string directoryName = path.Substring(lastSeparatorPos);

  var dirs = new DirectoryInfo(path).GetDirectories()
    .OrderBy(info => info.Name, new NaturalOrderComparer());

  var node = new Node
  {
    Text = directoryName,
    Leaf = !dirs.Any()
  };

  foreach (DirectoryInfo subDir in dirs)
  {
    node.Children.Add(CreateTreeNode(subDir.FullName));
  }

  return node;
}
```

The preceding method works by creating a node for the current path. All its subdirectories are added to it by recursively calling itself.

> .NET's implementation does not sort directories in the same name order as Windows Explorer does (as can be seen in the earlier screenshot). A custom `NaturalOrderComparer` has, therefore, been used, but its implementation is not important for the purposes of this example.

We can then modify our initial code example. The markup now looks like this:

```
<ext:TreePanel ID="IconFolderTree" runat="server" Width="250"
  Height="250" Icon="Pictures" Title="Icons" AutoScroll="true"
  />
```

Note, we explicitly set the TreePanel's ID, so we can refer to it in the code-behind:

```
protected void Page_Load(object sender, EventArgs e)
{
  Node rootNode = CreateTreeNode(StartingPath);
  rootNode.Expanded = true;
  rootNode.Children[0].Expanded = true;
  this.IconFolderTree.Root.Add(rootNode);
}
```

We assume `StartingPath` has been set to the location of the images. Then it simply sets the root node of the TreePanel to be the result of the `CreateTreeNode` method we defined earlier. The end result is the same as the earlier screenshot.

Asynchronous tree node loading

In the earlier examples the tree nodes are all loaded up front. In some cases this is not practical; it may be too much to load up front for the server or just a waste if many nodes are not going to be opened. We may, therefore, want to create the tree nodes on demand when the user (or other code) opens the tree.

`TreePanel` supports remote loading by reusing the Store architecture. In addition, nodes created asynchronously are just normal tree nodes so closing/expanding them again does not require another call to the server, when they have already been fetched.

Consider the following modification of our earlier example to show the Store approach:

```
<ext:TreePanel ID="IconFolderTree" runat="server" Width="250"
Height="250" Icon="Pictures" Title="Icons" AutoScroll="true">
  <Root>
    <ext:Node NodeID="Root" Text="icons" Expanded="true" />
  </Root>
  <Store>
    <ext:TreeStore runat="server">
      <Proxy>
        <ext:AjaxProxy Url="/IconTree/GetSubDirectories"/>
      </Proxy>
    </ext:TreeStore>
  </Store>
</ext:TreePanel>
```

In the preceding code snippet, the following are worth looking at further:

- The NodeID property for the root node and for asynchronous requests
- The use of a TreeStore to create nodes on the server
- The implications of Expanded="true"

NodeID for asynchronous node requests

The server needs an identifier for the node being expanded so it can get the appropriate data. That is defined by the NodeID property and is, therefore, required for remote loading.

In our example, each node is a directory path, so we could just use the full file path as it will be unique. However, we don't want to leak the full path to the outside world. So we will just use "Root" as the starting point, as we know it will not be the name of any child folders. The server can map that to the actual file path.

Using TreeStore to create nodes on the server

TreeStore is a subclass of AbstractStore, which is a base class for the Store as well. Hence, we get to reuse the same Proxy mechanisms we have seen earlier for other data-bound items. We will cover TreeStore a bit later to see other data-related features.

In this example, we have opted to call an ASP.NET MVC Controller:

```
//
// GET: /IconTree/GetSubDirectories
//
public StoreResult GetSubDirectories(string node)
{
  var path = node == "Root"
    ? StartingPath
    : Path.Combine(StartingPath, node);

  var dirs = new DirectoryInfo(path).GetDirectories()
    .OrderBy(info => info.Name, new NaturalOrderComparer());

  var nodes = new NodeCollection(false);

  foreach (DirectoryInfo subDir in dirs)
  {
    var childNode = new Node
    {
      NodeID = subDir.FullName.Substring(StartingPath.Length + 1),
      Text   = subDir.Name,
      Leaf   = subDir.GetDirectories().Length == 0
    };
    nodes.Add(childNode);
  }

  Return this.Store(nodes);
}
```

The preceding controller has code similar to the earlier `CreateTreeNode` method, but we have taken out the recursion as we are now creating nodes on demand.

The `node` parameter contains the value of the node ID. The first line checks that if the node ID passed in is the root (`"Root"`), it will use the internally known `StartingPath`. Otherwise, they are combined. When looping through the subdirectories, new nodes are created with node IDs so we also strip out the `StartingPath` of the path there.

Note the controller is returning an instance of `StoreResult` instead of the typical `JsonResult`, which is normally used for a JSON result.

Expanding tree nodes

A node can be set to appear expanded or collapsed, via the Expanded property. The TreePanel just invokes the expand method internally if needed. Therefore, if remote loading is enabled and Expanded is true for the root node, it will automatically make the AJAX request to fetch its immediate child nodes for you when the tree is rendered.

For the root node, Expanded="true" has been set to expand just the next level. You can also hide the root node itself by using RootVisible="false". This also has the effect of forcing the root node to be expanded. This can be changed by setting the AutoLoad property on the TreeStore to false.

In our controller we do not set the Expanded property on any of the generated nodes (so it will be false by default). If we did set any of those nodes to Expanded="true" and they were not initialized with child nodes already, they too would automatically load their child nodes via additional AJAX requests when added to the tree. If nodes were set to be expanded in our preceding code, it would mean you would actually recursively open all nodes. This would not be an optimal way to load all nodes because of the excessive number of AJAX requests. The earlier examples would be better for this purpose, instead. However, if you know some conditions when to auto-expand and when not to, in your server code, then this could be a useful trick.

Data binding with TreeStore and ColumnModel

TreePanel is quite rich as it inherits from TablePanel, which is what GridPanel inherits from, while TreeStore inherits from Store. This makes data binding familiar, but it also allows us to use multiple fields and columns to represent additional data.

Custom node attributes and explicit TreeStore Models

You may want to store an additional state on each node. In our earlier example, we only have the node's ID holding some path information and the text representing the path name. Suppose when a tree's node is clicked, we will show the number of files in that directory, the number of subdirectories, and when that directory was last modified. This can be done by adding additional data to each node's CustomAttributes collection. Each item in the collection is of the type ConfigItem, which we have seen before.

We then need the tree's store to know about these additional items. The `TreeStore` examples up to now have not defined any fields as seen with other Stores, so an implicit model is created internally. By defining fields explicitly, the tree and its `TreeStore` will map the custom attributes to the correct fields for you, as follows:

```
<ext:TreeStore runat="server">
  <Model>
    <ext:Model>
      <Fields>
        <ext:ModelField Name="numFiles" Type="Int" />
        <ext:ModelField Name="numSubDirs" Type="Int" />
        <ext:ModelField Name="lastMod" Type="Date"
                          DateFormat="yyyy-MM-dd HH:mm:ss" />
      </Fields>
    </ext:Model>
  </Model>
  <Proxy>
    <ext:AjaxProxy Url="/IconTree/GetSubDirectories" />
  </Proxy>
</ext:TreeStore>
```

Note the node ID itself doesn't need mapping; it is mapped to the Store Model's `IDProperty`, which is `id` by default (and a Node's `NodeID` serializes to `id`). Also note that `TreePanel` has a `Fields` property, which is shorthand for the `Fields` collection in the TreeStore Model.

To show additional information when a node is clicked we will add a static helper method to the `IconTreeController` which will add the custom attributes as follows:

```
public static void SetNodeCustomAttributes(
  Node node, DirectoryInfo dirInfo)
{
  string lastMod = dirInfo.LastWriteTime.ToString("yyyy-MM-dd
HH:mm:ss");
  string numFiles = dirInfo.GetFiles().Length.ToString();
  string numSubDirs = dirInfo.GetDirectories().Length .ToString();

  var attrs = new[]
  {
    new ConfigItem("lastMod", lastMod, ParameterMode.Value),
    new ConfigItem("numFiles", numFiles, ParameterMode.Raw),
    new ConfigItem("numSubDirs", numSubDirs, ParameterMode.Raw)
  };
  node.CustomAttributes.AddRange(attrs);
}
```

A shorthand to the `CustomAttributes` collection is to use `AttributesObject`:

```
node.AttributesObject = new { lastMod, numFiles, numSubDirs };
```

The controller's `GetSubDirectories` method calls it before adding the child nodes:

```
SetNodeCustomAttributes(childNode, subDir);
nodes.Add(childNode);
```

In addition we will also call that method for the root node of the tree:

```
protected void Page_Load(object sender, EventArgs e)
{
  if (!X.IsAjaxRequest)
  {
    var dirInfo = new DirectoryInfo(StartingPath);
    var rootNode = this.IconFolderTree.Root[0];
    this.IconTreeController.SetNodeCustomAttributes(rootNode,
                                                    dirInfo);
  }
}
```

Next, we add a panel to the docked item of the tree and handle the node selection event:

```
<ext:TreePanel ID="IconFolderTree" runat="server" Width="250"
Height="250" Icon="Pictures" Title="Icons" AutoScroll="true">
  <!-- Root and Store declared as before -->
  <DockedItems>
    <ext:Panel Dock="bottom" Height="70">
      <Tpl>
        <Html>
          <p>Last Modified: <strong>{lastMod}</strong></p>
          <p>Number of files: <strong>{numFiles}</strong></p>
          <p>Number of subdirectories: <strong>{numSubDirs}</strong></
p>
        </Html>
      </Tpl>
    </ext:Panel>
  </DockedItems>
  <Listeners>
    <Select Handler="MyApp.showInfo.call(
      #{IconFolderTree}, record);" />
  </Listeners>
</ext:TreePanel>
```

The select handler updates the docked panel with the record data for the current node:

```
var MyApp = {
  showInfo: function (record) {
    var panel = this.getDockedItems("panel[dock=bottom]")[0];
    panel.update(record.data);
  }
};
```

When all of that is put together, you will see the following once a tree node is selected:

Multiple fields and tree grids

Like the GridPanel, the TreePanel also supports a column model because they both inherit the abstract `TablePanel`. This enables another type of tree-based UI, the tree grid, whereby you can show additional columns of data for each node. By default a `TreePanel` uses a single column. However, we can explicitly add columns:

```
<ext:TreePanel ID="IconFolderTree"
  runat="server" Width="300" Height="250"
  Icon="Pictures" Title="Icons" AutoScroll="true">
  <ColumnModel>
    <Columns>
      <ext:TreeColumn Text="Folder" Flex="1" DataIndex="text" />
      <ext:TemplateColumn Text="Last Modified" Width="150"
        DataIndex="lastMod">
        <Template>
          <Html>
```

```
            {lastMod:date("F j, Y, g:i a")}
        </Html>
      </Template>
    </ext:TemplateColumn>
  </Columns>
 </ColumnModel>
 <!-- everything else as before -->
</ext:TreePanel>
```

We have added two columns to our TreePanel, TreeColumn and TemplateColumn. TreeColumn provides the indentation and folder structure which is required for any tree grid approach. The other column is a regular column that we also see on grids. Note for TreeColumn, the DataIndex property has been set to "text". Like id, this is one of the default properties for a given store record of a node. The text value is the display text for each node. This gives us the following screenshot:

What else can you do with TreePanels?

It is highly recommended to visit the Ext.NET Examples Explorer to see features such as, filtering, checkbox nodes, editing nodes, submitting selected nodes, reordering nodes, drag-and-drop between trees and other components, loading an XML file, and more:

```
http://examples.ext.net/#/search/tree
```

TabPanel

TabPanel is a subclass of Panel which has an Items collection used to add many other Container type components, each of which will become a tab. TabPanel overrides how this Items collection is rendered because internally TabPanel uses a CardLayout layout manager allowing it to hide each child item until it is activated. A tab bar shows the tabs. The title and icon of each item in the Items collection is also used to set the tab's title and icon. Therefore, unlike normal panels, a tab item won't render a header.

With a TabPanel, you can programmatically add tabs. You can add some at the moment a TabPanel is created while adding others later if needed. The contents of the tabs can be configured to render immediately, or when the tab is activated (the default action). This is controlled by the DeferredRender property on the TabPanel class, which defaults to true. In addition, AJAX techniques can be used to load tab contents on demand.

TabPanel also provides numerous features to handle many tabs, such as scrolling and paging through tabs. The tab bar also allows other items to be added to it which can be useful as we will see. Each tab can also be configured to have a close button. A context menu can be configured, to provide common tab management options without taking up too much of the screen's real estate.

TabPanel – overview

Like Panel, the default type of component that goes into the TabPanel's Items collection is Panel. But other types can also be added, such as various subclasses of Panel and components such as the lightweight Container. This also means that if you want a grid or tree to be a child item of a TabPanel you do not need to wrap it in a Panel. The following is a simple example of TabPanel with two tabs:

```
<ext:TabPanel runat="server" Border="false" DefaultBorder="false">
  <Items>
    <ext:Panel Html="<p>First tab</p>" BodyPadding="5"
Title="Panel as tab" Icon="Application" />
    <ext:TreePanel Html="<p>First tab</p>" Closable="true"
      Title="Tree as tab" Icon="ApplicationSideTree">
      <Root>
        <ext:Node Text="Root" Expanded="true">
          <Children>
            <ext:Node Text="Child 1" Leaf="true" />
            <ext:Node Text="Child 2" Leaf="true" />
            <ext:Node Text="Child 3" Leaf="true" />
```

```
                <ext:Node Text="Child 4" Leaf="true" />
            </Children>
          </ext:Node>
        </Root>
      </ext:TreePanel>
    </Items>
  </ext:TabPanel>
```

In the preceding code snippet, we added two items to be the tabs—a `Panel` and a `TreePanel`. As they are panels we are able to set their title and icon as we would with normal panels but they will be rendered into the tab. The `TreePanel` also has `Closable` set to `true`. This will provide a close icon on the tab, which when clicked will close that tab. We can also put this tab panel inside another container. For example, if we put it inside a Window with a layout of `fit`, the TabPanel will take up the full Window content and automatically adjust when the Window is resized. The following is produced when the preceding code is rendered inside a Window with a layout of `fit`:

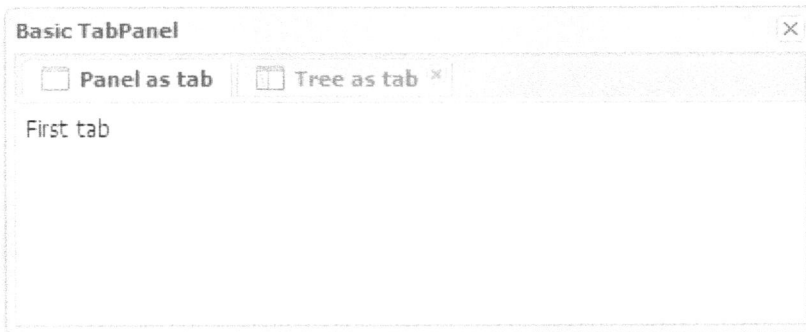

In the next screenshot, we have switched to the second tab and resized the window to show the auto adjustment and the TreePanel then getting scrollbars:

We can also add a GridPanel directly to a TabPanel too, as follows:

```
<ext:TabPanel runat="server" Border="false" DefaultBorder="false">
  <Items>
    <ext:Panel Html="<p>First tab</p>" BodyPadding="5"
      Title="Panel as tab" Icon="Application" />
    <ext:TreePanel Html="<p>First tab</p>" Closable="true"
      Title="Tree as tab" Icon="ApplicationSideTree">
      <Root>
        <!-- As before -->
      </Root>
    </ext:TreePanel>
    <ext:GridPanel Title="Simple Grid" Icon="Table">
      <!-- Rest of grid definition goes here -->
    </ext:GridPanel>
  </Items>
</ext:TabPanel>
```

This then gives us the following screenshot:

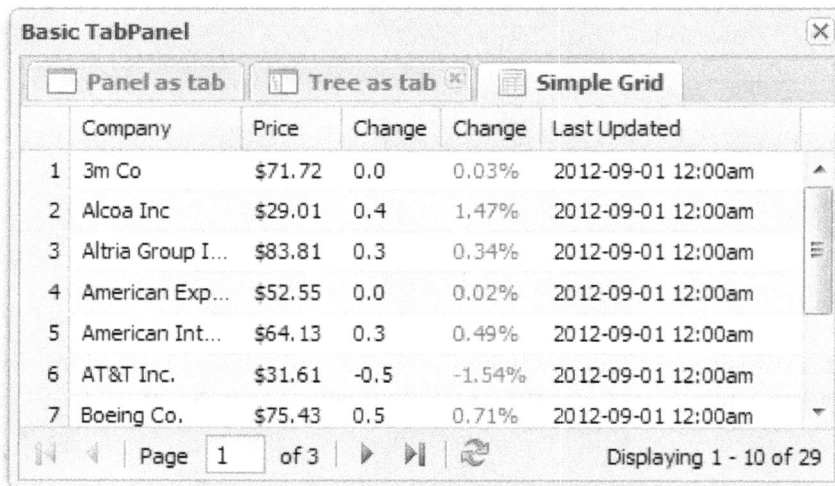

You can add additional nested tabs, or additional panels with their own layout such as accordions. The following is an example of a `border` layout panel:

```
<ext:Panel Layout="border" Title="Border"
        Icon="ApplicationSideList">
  <Items>
```

```
    <ext:Panel Region="West" Width="150" Title="West"
      Collapsible="true" Split="true" />
    <ext:Panel Region="Center" Title="Center" />
  </Items>
</ext:Panel>
```

We can add this as the fourth item in the `Items` collection to produce the following:

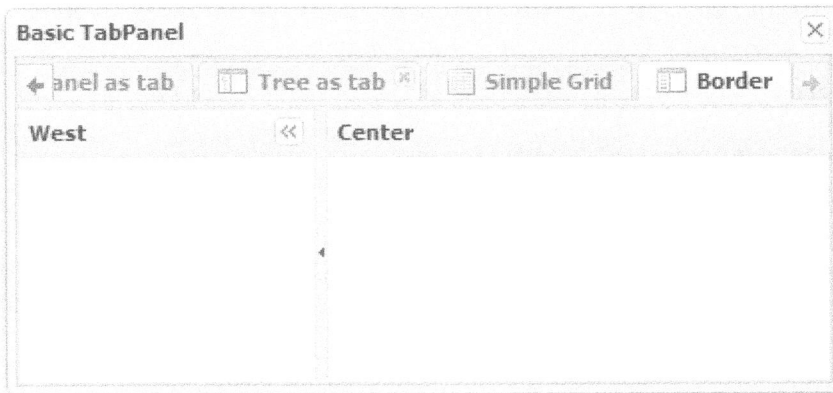

Notice the `TabPanel` automatically added scroll handles to each side of the tab bar when it detected that the tabs would overflow the visible tab strip area.

Asynchronous tab loading

Sometimes it is useful to make the loading of the tab asynchronous. This can help us make the initial page load a bit lighter and, therefore, quicker to load for the end user. Dynamically loading a tab allows you to respond to other changes happening to the page by passing additional parameters to the AJAX request.

In *Chapter 4, AJAX with Ext.NET*, we saw an example of using `ComponentLoader` to dynamically load tabs. In this example we will use a DirectEvent to dynamically populate the second tab when first activated. First, the markup (assuming it will go inside a window as with earlier examples):

```
<ext:TabPanel ID="TabPanel1" runat="server" Border="false"
            DefaultBorder="false">
  <Items>
    <ext:Panel Html="<p>First tab</p>" Title="Tab 1" />
    <ext:Panel ID="Tab2" runat="server" Title="Tab 2"
              Layout="fit">
      <DirectEvents>
```

```
            <Activate OnEvent="Tab2_Activate" Single="true">
              <EventMask ShowMask="true" Target="This" />
            </Activate>
          </DirectEvents>
        </ext:Panel>
      </Items>
    </ext:TabPanel>
```

The DirectEvent `Tab2_Activate` method handler for the `Activate` event is
as follows:

```
protected void Tab2_Activate(object sender, DirectEventArgs e)
{
    TreePanel panel = BuildTreePanel();
    panel.AddTo(this.Tab2);
}
```

In the preceding code, we are generating a new `TreePanel` in code-behind (that
method is not important to show for our purpose here). We then add it to **Tab 2**,
as follows:

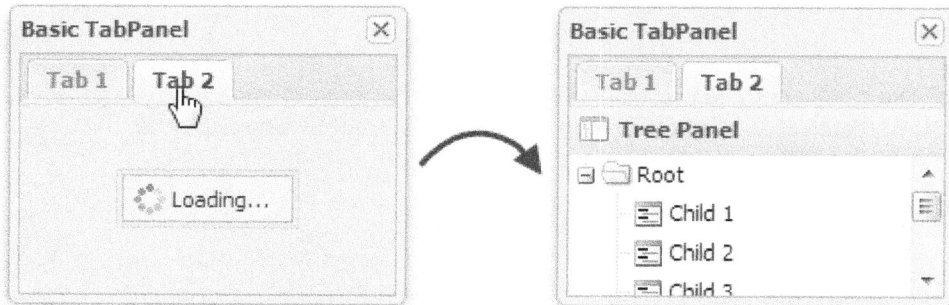

Because we added an `EventMask` to the DirectEvent if the server takes a while to
respond, the user will see the loading mask before seeing the server-rendered panel.

You can also use panel loaders as we saw briefly in the AJAX chapter. Ext.NET
has a useful example on this at `http://examples.ext.net/#/TabPanel/Basic/
Ajax_Load/`.

Useful tab features

The next sections give an overview of some other TabPanel features to consider.

Tabs rendered at the bottom

You can position the tab bar at the bottom by simply using `TabPosition="Bottom"` on a `TabPanel`. Applying it on an earlier example will render the following:

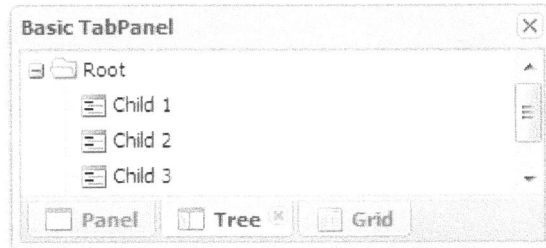

Tab scrolling works for bottom-positioned tabs too.

Plain tabs

The colored background behind the tabs can also be removed for a plainer look, using `Plain="true"` on a `TabPanel` to give the following effect:

TabScrollerMenu plugin

If you render many tabs inside a `TabPanel`, the `TabScrollerMenu` plugin, as its name suggests, provides a menu for the tabs next to the tab scroller, as follows:

The preceding result is achieved by simply declaring the plugin, as follows:

```
<ext:TabPanel ID="TabPanel1" runat="server" Width="420" Height="180">
  <Plugins>
    <ext:TabScrollerMenu PageSize="5" />
  </Plugins>
</ext:TabPanel>
```

You set the PageSize property to control how the tabs are grouped by the plugin.

Tab menus

Ext.NET provides a useful plugin called TabMenu. This allows each tab to have its own menu items. A default set of menu items can be applied to all tabs, or custom tab menus can be defined for specific tabs as the following example shows:

```
<ext:TabPanel runat="server" Height="150" Width="400">
  <DefaultTabMenu>
    <ext:Menu>
      <Items>
        <ext:MenuItem Text="Close" Icon="TabDelete">
          <Listeners>
            <Click Fn="MyApp.onClose" />
          </Listeners>
        </ext:MenuItem>
        <ext:MenuItem Text="Close Other Tabs" />
        <ext:MenuSeparator />
        <ext:MenuItem Text="Move To Previous">
          <Listeners>
            <Click Fn="MyApp.onTabMovePrevious" />
          </Listeners>
        </ext:MenuItem>
        <ext:MenuItem Text="Move To Next">
          <Listeners>
            <Click Fn="MyApp.onTabMoveNext" />
          </Listeners>
        </ext:MenuItem>
        <ext:MenuSeparator />
        <ext:TriggerField Text="New title"
          StyleSpec="margin-left:33px;"
          FieldLabel="Rename Tab" LabelAlign="Top">
          <Triggers>
            <ext:FieldTrigger Icon="Empty" />
          </Triggers>
          <Listeners>
            <TriggerClick Fn="MyApp.onTriggerClick" />
          </Listeners>
```

```
            </ext:TriggerField>
          </Items>
        </ext:Menu>
    </DefaultTabMenu>
    <Items>
      <ext:Panel Title="Default Menu 1" Html="Tab 1" />
      <ext:Panel Title="Default Menu 2" Html="Tab 2" />
      <ext:Panel Title="Custom Menu" Html="Tab 3" >
        <TabMenu>
          <ext:Menu>
            <Items>
              <ext:MenuItem Text="Custom" />
            </Items>
          </ext:Menu>
        </TabMenu>
      </ext:Panel>
    </Items>
    <Listeners>
      <BeforeTabMenuShow Fn="MyApp.onBeforeTabMenuShow" />
    </Listeners>
  </ext:TabPanel>
```

The preceding code shows a TabPanel with three inner panels as tabs. The first two tabs get their menu items defined by DefaultTabMenu, while the last tab defines its own TabMenu. The following screenshot shows the menu options for the first tab:

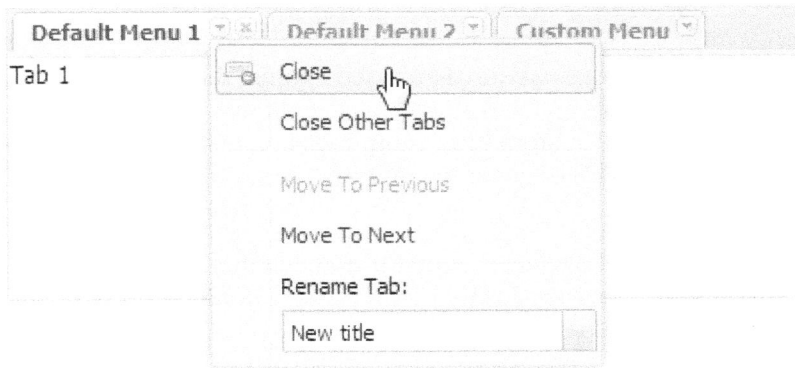

If you want an individual tab not to have menus but you have defaults defined, you can set TabMenuHidden="true" on any tab to hide menus for that tab.

We defined some event handlers to close, rename, and move tabs, as well as disable the previous and next menu items when appropriate.

The tab is closed once we get the menu instance that holds a reference to the tab:

```
onClose: function () {
  this.up('menu').tab.close();
}
```

To rename a tab we simply update the tab's title, as follows:

```
onTriggerClick: function () {
  var menu = this.up('menu');
  menu.tab.setTitle(this.getValue());
  menu.hide();
}
```

If any items need disabling we can do that in the `BeforeTabMenuShow` event, as follows:

```
onBeforeTabMenuShow: function (tabPanel, tab, menu) {
  var menuPrev = menu.items.get(3),
      menuNext = menu.items.get(4);

  if (menuPrev !== undefined) {
    menuPrev.setDisabled(tabPanel.items.first() === tab);
  }

  if (menuNext !== undefined) {
    menuNext.setDisabled(tabPanel.items.last() === tab);
  }
}
```

In the preceding code snippet, we have guarded against the menu items not being found in case the tab we are on has its own custom menus. (Normally relying on an index is not enough as a custom menu could also have items in these positions. We could use menu item IDs or custom configurations, but we have left it out here for brevity.)

In the preceding code, we have also set the disabled status to `true` or `false` each time this event handler is invoked rather than just at initialization time, in case the tabs are moved, which is what the next methods do:

```
onTabMovePrevious: function () {
  MyApp.moveTab.call(this, -1);
},

onTabMoveNext: function () {
  MyApp.moveTab.call(this, 1);
},

moveTab: function (position) {
```

```
var menu = this.up('menu'),
  tabItem = menu.tab,
  tab = tabItem.tab,
  tabPanel = tabItem.ownerCt,
  tabBar = tabPanel.tabBar,
  newPosition = tabBar.items.indexOf(tab) + position;

tabBar.items.remove(tab);
tabPanel.items.remove(tabItem);

tabBar.items.insert(newPosition, tab);
tabPanel.items.insert(newPosition, tabItem);

tabPanel.setActiveTab(tabItem);
tabBar.doLayout();
}
```

In the preceding code, we are removing the tab item and the tab inside the tab bar itself from their respective collections and inserting them again into the new position. We issue a call to `doLayout` of `tabBar` only to redisplay the new order.

Using TabBar to add custom toolbar items

As well as holding each tab, `TabBar` can also hold additional items. For example, you can provide an "Add tab" button, as this next example shows:

```
<ext:TabPanel ID="TabPanel1" runat="server" Width="300" Height="150">
  <TabBar>
    <ext:ToolbarFill />
    <ext:Button Id="Add" Flat="true" Icon="Add">
      <DirectEvents>
        <Click
          OnEvent="AddTab"
          Success="MyApp.onTabAddSuccess.call(
                  #{Help},
                  #{TabPanel1});" />
      </DirectEvents>
    </ext:Button>
    <ext:Button ID="Help" Flat="true" Icon="Help">
      <Listeners>
        <Click Fn="MyApp.showHelp" />
      </Listeners>
    </ext:Button>
  </TabBar>
  <Items>
    <ext:Panel Title="Tab 1" />
  </Items>
</ext:TabPanel>
```

The preceding code snippet produces the following result:

The tab bar supports any item you can put in a menu collection, so it could also contain rich menus. When enough tabs are added, the tab scrolls are shown, as follows:

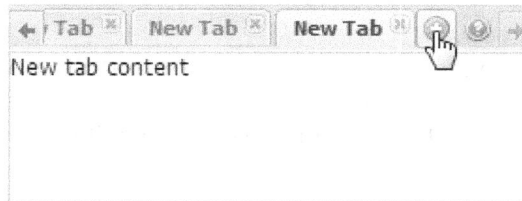

This is achieved by a bit of manual intervention. In the preceding code we have used a DirectEvent to get a new tab from the server. To prevent those buttons from scrolling out of the visible area of the tab strip, the DirectEvent's success event handler is used to call the following client method to keep the buttons in view:

```
onTabAddSuccess: function (tabPanel) {
    tabPanel.tabBar.layout.overflowHandler.scrollToItem(this);
}
```

In the preceding code we scrolled to the item in the current context. Note, by default the current context would be the button that invoked this method (the "Add tab" button) but that would mean any other items after it would be scrolled out of view, so we switched context to the last item—the "Help" button—thus keeping all those items in view.

More TabPanel examples

The Ext.NET Examples Explorer also demonstrates other features of the TabPanel:

http://examples.ext.net/#/search/tabpanel

They include demonstrations of the GroupTabPanel, which allows for tabs on the side with tabs grouped by an outer tab; TabStrip, which allows a lightweight tab strip to be added to any position within a toolbar; and more.

Summary

We have seen that the `TreePanel` and `TabPanel` classes are quite versatile and powerful. They also share features common to their parent class, `Panel`. We had an overview of some TreePanel features including, asynchronous tree node loading, and data binding using TreeStore and ColumnModel. We also had an overview of the TabPanel and looked at asynchronous tab loading, as well as other useful tab features.

The Ext.NET Examples Explorer is highly recommended to discover additional features, such as renaming a tree node inline by reusing editors (similar to what we saw for editing inside grid cells inline), enabling dragging/dropping nodes from one tree to another tree, grouping tabs, using tab strips, and more.

Up to now, all the chapters have introduced various features in Ext.NET. In the next chapter we will look at how you can create your own reusable custom components and incorporate some of those features.

Extending Ext.NET – Custom Controls and Plugins

As rich as the Ext.NET and Ext JS controls are, you often want to create custom variations for your own applications for reuse. As well as componentizing a server control, you may also need to package associated CSS and JavaScript with it so you know they are always available. In addition, you may want to support both ASP.NET Web Forms and ASP.NET MVC, including the Razor template. There are a number of ways in which this can be done. This chapter will compare a few approaches as follows:

- Basic control builder
- Extending Ext.NET controls
- Plugins
- Plugin or extend

By the end of this chapter you will gain an understanding of how to extend components and have an idea of how to decide whether to extend a component or use a plugin.

Basic control builder

This option to create custom components is the most basic approach and can work for simple, lightweight cases. The basic idea is as follows:

1. Create a factory or builder class to create an instance of your component.

2. Provide decorators or similar methods to add features for different uses.

3. Your component is not an extension of an Ext.NET control, but just a code-behind representation of what you might build using ASP.NET Web Forms markup or the MVC template.

4. Any JavaScript handlers go into a JavaScript file that you include manually.

Example

Consider our earlier financial data grid we used in *Chapter 6, Introducing GridPanels,* for the server-side paging example. We will create the same component in code-behind:

```
public class FinancialGridBuilder
{
    private const int InitialPageSize = 10;
    private const string GridId = "FinancialGrid";

    public GridPanel Build()
    {
        return new GridPanel
        {
            ID = GridId,
            Title = "Simple Grid",
            Store = { BuildStore() },
            ColumnModel =
            {
                Columns = { BuildColumnModel() }
            },
            SelectionModel =
            {
                new RowSelectionModel()
            },
            BottomBar = { new PagingToolbar() }
        };
    }
}
```

In the preceding code, we are building the same grid as we did with markup. The
Store and Columns properties are built inside separate methods, though it is up
to you how to organize the code. Your class could offer additional properties and
methods to govern how the component will be built, for example. Those additional
methods are as follows:

```
private Store BuildStore()
{
  return new Store
  {
    PageSize = InitialPageSize,
    Model =
    {
      new Model
      {
        Fields =
        {
          new ModelField("Company") { Mapping = "Name" },
          new ModelField("Price", ModelFieldType.Float),
          new ModelField("Change", ModelFieldType.Float),
          new ModelField("PctChange", ModelFieldType.Float)
                      { Mapping="PercentChange" },
          new ModelField("LastChange", ModelFieldType.Date),
          new ModelField("Symbol")
        }
      }
    },
    Proxy =
    {
      new AjaxProxy
      {
        Url = "~/Shared/FinancialData.ashx",
        Reader =
        {
          new JsonReader { Root = "data" }
        }
      }
    }
  };
}

private IEnumerable<ColumnBase> BuildColumnModel()
{
  return new ItemsCollection<ColumnBase>
  {
    new RowNumbererColumn(),
    new Column {Text="Company",DataIndex="Company",Flex=1},
```

```
new Column
{
  Text = "Price",
  DataIndex = "Price",
  Width = 50,
  Renderer = { Format = RendererFormat.UsMoney }
},
new Column { Text="Change", DataIndex="Change", Width=50,
            Renderer = { Fn = "MyApp.change" } },
new Column { Text="Change", DataIndex="PctChange",
    Width=50, Renderer = { Fn = "MyApp.pctChange" } },
new DateColumn { Text = "Last Updated", DataIndex =
    "LastChange", Format="yyyy-MM-dd hh:mmtt",
    Width=130 }
  };
}
```

The preceding code produces the same server-side paging grid as we saw in *Chapter 6, Introducing GridPanels*. The following is a simple example of how it can be used:

```
<%@ Page Language="C#" %>

<script runat="server">
protected void Page_Load(object sender, EventArgs e)
{
    var grid = new FinancialGridBuilder().Build();
    grid.Width = 450;
    grid.Height = 300;

    this.PlaceHolder1.Controls.Add(grid);
}
</script>

<!DOCTYPE html>
<html>
    <head runat="server">
        <title>Custom Component Example</title>
        <link rel="stylesheet" type="text/css"
              href="Resources/style.css" />
        <script src="Resources/grid.js"></script>
    </head>
    <body>
        <ext:ResourceManager runat="server" />
        <asp:PlaceHolder ID="PlaceHolder1" runat="server" />
    </body>
</html>
```

This example uses a very small amount of markup, with just the resource manager being declared. We build our grid in code-behind and add it straight to the page, via the ASP.NET PlaceHolder's `Controls` collection. (If we had a Viewport or another panel or container, we would add it to that component's `Items` collection).

The JavaScript can be put in its own file, and would look something like this:

```
var MyApp = {
  template: '<span class="{0}">{1}</span>',

  change: function (value) {
    return Ext.String.format(MyApp.template, (value > 0)
      ? "positive" : "negative", value);
  },

  pctChange: function (value) {
    return Ext.String.format(MyApp.template, (value > 0)
      ? "positive" : "negative", value + "%");
  }
};
```

And the CSS would be as before in the earlier chapter:

```
.positive { color: green; }
.negative { color: red; }
```

The preceding example would produce this:

Simple Grid

	Company	Price	Change	Change	Last Updated
1	3m Co	$71.72	0.02	0.03%	2012-09-01 12:00am
2	Alcoa Inc	$29.01	0.42	1.47%	2012-09-01 12:00am
3	Altria Group Inc	$83.81	0.28	0.34%	2012-09-01 12:00am
4	American Express Compa...	$52.55	0.01	0.02%	2012-09-01 12:00am
5	American International G...	$64.13	0.31	0.49%	2012-09-01 12:00am
6	AT&T Inc.	$31.61	-0.48	-1.54%	2012-09-01 12:00am
7	Boeing Co.	$75.43	0.53	0.71%	2012-09-01 12:00am
8	Caterpillar Inc.	$67.27	0.92	1.39%	2012-09-01 12:00am
9	Citigroup, Inc.	$49.37	0.02	0.04%	2012-09-01 12:00am
10	E.I. du Pont de Nemours ...	$40.48	0.51	1.28%	2012-09-01 12:00am

Page 1 of 3   Displaying 1 - 10 of 29

Benefits of this approach

This approach can be useful to quickly build simple, reusable components. By putting the building code into a class, it can be invoked easily without copy-pasting.

Drawbacks to this approach

Reuse of these types of components is limited; for example it is not easy to use in markup or MVC templates; you would have to instantiate them in code-behind and add them to the correct container collection. This could make it more cumbersome to use.

The JavaScript is written like a large singleton or set of static functions. Over time as the application grows, the JavaScript code would grow and be harder to manage and reuse. If you are attempting to dynamically include the right JavaScript code at the right time (rather than all of it every time any page is loaded), this can become tedious or require a custom solution. Similar concerns would apply to CSS associated with a component.

Extending Ext.NET controls

We can take the earlier example and improve on it considerably. It would feel quite natural to subclass the grid panel. Ext JS encourages this, and Ext.NET provides excellent support for this concept. The basic approach involves the following:

- Subclassing the component on the .NET side
- Subclassing the component on the Ext JS side (optional)
- Adding custom CSS (optional)
- Defining custom events (optional)
- Adding MVC support (optional)

Let's see how this might work. To keep things simplified, we will extend the GridPanel to become a reusable financial grid panel.

Extending the Ext.NET class

In this approach we will do the following, while extending the GridPanel:

1. Initialize the `Store`, `Columns`, and various other properties.
2. Define the Ext JS component and instance type (optional).
3. Include associated CSS and JavaScript as embedded resources (optional).

The reason behind the final two points being optional is that for very simple components, a corresponding Ext JS subclass may not be needed. In addition, we can use JavaScript listeners in our earlier example.

We will look at an initial version that does not have its own JavaScript subclass and CSS, and add them in later. For now, we will assume the same JavaScript and CSS are used as in the previous example. The following code shows the resulting Ext. NET component:

```
public class FinancialGrid : GridPanel
{
    protected override void OnInit(EventArgs e)
    {
        Title = string.IsNullOrWhiteSpace(Title)
            ? "Simple Grid" : Title;
        Store.Add(BuildStore());
        ColumnModel.Columns.Add(BuildColumnModel());
        SelectionModel.Add(new RowSelectionModel());
        BottomBar.Add(new PagingToolbar());

        base.OnInit(e);
    }
}
```

We use the `OnInit` override so if this control is posted back by a Page or a DirectEvent on this control, any controls and items we add here are recreated correctly on the server side avoiding any errors with invalid ViewState (if enabled).

The `BuildStore()` and `BuildColumnModel()` methods are exactly the same as the previous example so are not shown here.

In the preceding example, the `Title` property has a default if not explicitly set. We leave out other properties where we don't have our own defaults (for example, `Height` and `Width`).

The following code shows how it might be used on a WebForms page:

```
<%@ Page Language="C#" %>
<%@ Register TagPrefix="cc1"
    Namespace="CustomControlsAndPlugins.Components"
    Assembly="CustomControlsAndPlugins" %>

<!DOCTYPE html>
<html>
  <head runat="server">
    <title>Custom Component Example</title>
    <link rel="stylesheet" type="text/css"
        href="Resources/style.css" />
```

```
      <script src="Resources/grid.js"></script>
    </head>
    <body>
      <ext:ResourceManager runat="server" />

      <cc1:FinancialGrid runat="server" Width="550" Height="300" />
    </body>
  </html>
```

Other than registering and adding the new `FinancialGrid` component, the remainder of the markup is virtually the same as the previous example.

This component is quite reusable. However, we can go further; the JavaScript itself is not very well encapsulated and you have to ensure that you have included the script (and CSS) on the page that includes the control. Fortunately, Ext.NET provides a way to load these resources as and when these components are needed.

Extending the Ext JS class

We will create a JavaScript class to be the counterpart of the server-side `FinancialGrid` class. On the Ext JS side, the grid that we need to subclass is `Ext.grid.Panel`.

In our earlier example, we defined static-like functions in the `MyApp` namespace. We will use the `MyApp` namespace to define our custom grid, as follows:

```
Ext.define('MyApp.FinancialGrid', {
    extend   : 'Ext.grid.Panel',
    alias    : 'widget.financialgrid',
    template : '<span class="{0}">{1}</span>',

    change: function (value) {
        return this.formatChange(value);
    },

    pctChange: function (value) {
        return this.formatChange(value, '%');
    },

    formatChange: function (value, suffix) {
        return Ext.String.format(
            this.template,
            (value > 0) ? 'positive' : 'negative',
            value,
            suffix || '');
    }
});
```

As a starting point, the preceding code could go inside `grid.js`, which the earlier markup example was including.

Although it is out of the scope of this book to explain Ext JS conventions as well in depth, to help you get started, the preceding code snippet also shows the `change` and `pctChange` functions refactored slightly to call another instance method.

Specific Ext JS classes such as widgets (or controls), plugins, and features have an `alias` property, which is an alias to their class names. They also have corresponding `xtype`, `ptype`, and `ftype` properties, which are short names for those components. The `alias` property is, therefore, a unified way to refer to these different types of objects and allows for a more feature-rich API, for example helpful methods to find components by alias, regardless of what type of object it might be.

While `alias` is typically used when defining the class definition, `xtype`, `ftype`, and `ptype`, are powerful because they can be used to instantiate those classes using a JavaScript configuration object (a JavaScript object literal) rather than an explicitly created object instance. This allows Ext JS to choose when to instantiate components (lazy instantiation) which can help to improve performance and flexibility.

So, in our JavaScript code, we define `alias`. By default Ext JS will automatically make the `xtype` property of that class the same as `alias` but without the `widget.` part. When creating an object through lazy instantiation in JavaScript we set the `xtype` property. For custom controls in Ext.NET, we set the `xtype` property so Ext. NET can generate the optimal initialization JavaScript. You can read more about xtype at the following URL:

http://docs.sencha.com/ext-js/4-1/#!/api/Ext.AbstractComponent-cfg-xtype

So we now need to update our server component in the following way:

1. Override the `InstanceOf` and `XType` properties so that the correct instance and `xtype` values are generated by the Ext.NET initialization JavaScript.

2. Change our column `Renderer` code to invoke instance methods.

Our grid component would then look like the following code snippet:

```
public class FinancialGrid : GridPanel
{
    public override string InstanceOf
    {
        get { return "MyApp.FinancialGrid"; }
    }

    public override string XType
    {
```

```
        get { return "financialgrid"; }
    }

    protected override void OnLoad(EventArgs e)
    {
        Title = "Simple Grid";
        Store.Add(BuildStore());
        ColumnModel.Columns.Add(BuildColumnModel());
        BottomBar.Add(new PagingToolbar());

        base.OnLoad(e);
    }
}
```

And inside the `BuildColumnModel` method, the two columns using the `Renderer` property would change from using the function pointer to using an inline handler that can invoke the instance methods:

```
new Column
{
  Text="Change",
  DataIndex="Change",
  Width=50,
  Renderer =
  {
    Handler = "return this.change.apply(this, arguments);"
  }
},
new Column
{
  Text="Change",
  DataIndex="PctChange",
  Width=50,
  Renderer =
  {
    Handler = "return this.pctChange.apply(this, arguments);"
  }
},
```

Note, by using the JavaScript `apply` method, and setting the context to `this` and passing the handler's own method arguments as the arguments to the `change` or `pctChange` method, we are in effect doing a call-forward in JavaScript. This can help us eliminate the need to go back to your server-side component any time you tweak your event definition to add/remove event arguments.

Embedding the resources

At this point the preceding code works reasonably well; the server side has a client-side counterpart. The example web page uses an instance of that server-side class, which will generate appropriate JavaScript that, in turn, will instantiate the client-side counterpart.

One limitation still remains; if we stop here for every place you use the server-side component, you would need to remember to include the associated JavaScript and CSS.

You could put the JavaScript and CSS into your main site's JavaScript and CSS files (or use an automated process to combine/minify these to reduce HTTP requests). However, this may not always be enough. For example:

- If you have a large application where some pages may not use this component while others might do, you may not always want to download this code unnecessarily

- If you want to package up your components to be used in more than one project, then you may wish to minimize the effort that users of your component have to go through to get set up

Ext.NET supports using ASP.NET's embedded resources for your JavaScript, CSS, and other resources (such as images that might be used by your CSS, for example). To use it in our example, there are just a few additions to be made to our project as follows:

- Mark various resources such as JavaScript, CSS, and image files as embedded resources in Visual Studio

- Use the ASP.NET `WebResource` attribute in your project so that ASP.NET can help you create links to these resources from your HTML pages

- Tell the Ext.NET component which embedded resources your class needs

Once these steps are done, you do not need to add the resources to your own pages manually; Ext.NET will load them on demand, if they are not already loaded on the page. And the ASP.NET web resource handler deals with caching to minimize HTTP traffic.

There is no strict file naming convention for your embedded JavaScript and CSS components, but one possibility is to name them based on your Ext.NET component. As our example class is called `FinancialGrid`, the associated JavaScript and CSS files could be called `FinancialGrid.js` and `FinancialGrid.css`, respectively.

So the following section shows an example.

Declaring your embedded web resources

After marking your JavaScript and CSS as embedded resources in Visual Studio, we can declare them as web resources. You could define them in at least one of two places — in your project's `AssemblyInfo.cs` file, or (if that gets too big over time) in the same file as your component, above the namespace declaration (as `WebResource` is an attribute at the assembly level). Regardless of where you choose to put it, this is what it would look like for our `FinancialGrid`:

```
[assembly: WebResource("CustomControlsAndPlugins.Components.Resources.
FinancialGrid.js", "text/javascript")]
[assembly: WebResource("CustomControlsAndPlugins.Components.Resources.
FinancialGrid.css", "text/css", PerformSubstitution = true)]
```

The namespace to the embedded resource will need to match your location in your own assembly. The preceding code is an example based on the sample code for this chapter.

Notice, for the CSS web resource, we've used `PerformSubsitution=true`. This lets us use background images that are themselves links to ASP.NET `WebResources` following standard ASP.NET conventions for embedded resources, if we need.

Adding your embedded resources to your Ext.NET component

To ensure our Ext.NET component loads these resources, we simply override the `Resources` property of our component as follows:

```
protected override List<ResourceItem> Resources
{
    get
    {
        const string ns =  "CustomControlsAndPlugins.Components.
Resources.FinancialGrid.";

        List<ResourceItem> baseList = base.Resources;
        baseList.Capacity += 2;

        baseList.Add(new ClientScriptItem(
            typeof(FinancialGrid), ns + "js", ""));

        baseList.Add(new ClientStyleItem(
            typeof(FinancialGrid), ns + "css", ""));

        return baseList;
    }
}
```

The preceding code overrides the Resources property to add a ClientScriptItem and a ClientStyleItem. For each one, the embedded resource path has been set.

The third parameter is a URL path that could be used if you do not want to embed the resources (though you would lose the self-contained nature of the component). As we are not doing that here we can leave it as an empty string. Some overloads for the resource item constructors also take additional values, such as the path for a debug version of the file. So if you have your own process for minifying your production JavaScript while using a full readable version for debugging, for example, then you would use one of the overloads to mention all of these as needed.

> If you have embedded images to be used as background CSS images, Ext.NET does not need to know about them; instead, you use normal ASP.NET techniques in CSS for loading the web resources as CSS background images from within your CSS file. Just be sure to mark your required images as embedded web resources for your project.
>
> The following Ext.NET forum post has further information about embedding JavaScript and CSS, and how to use CSS images:
>
> http://forums.ext.net/showthread.php?7946

The final step is in our HTML example page that uses our component; we can simply remove the reference to the CSS and JavaScript in the HTML head.

Custom events

When writing your own components in JavaScript, you can define and use custom events. You can do the same for your Ext.NET components, too. Furthermore, you can define both client-side Listeners and server-side DirectEvents on your components, providing flexibility for users of your component on how to consume these events.

Let us take the grid example we have seen so far. If a user selects a row, we normally get the GridPanel's row selection event—select. In our client-side custom class, we will internally subscribe to the select event and raise a more component/business-oriented event, such as companyselected. In this event we will only send the current grid and the selected record as additional data, not all the other information in the select event.

This may be overkill as a user of our financial grid can just as easily subscribe to the `select` event, but as a simple example it demonstrates the main technique. This also gives us the opportunity to raise the same event in other scenarios in the future if the need ever comes up, and users of this component would not need to change which event they subscribe to. A custom event also gives us the chance to do further internal processing of the `select` event before or after our custom event is raised, if needed.

Defining the event in the JavaScript class

We first define the custom event in JavaScript using standard Ext JS conventions, so we add the following code to our client-side class:

```
initEvents: function () {
    this.addEvents('companyselected');
    this.on('select', this.onSelect, this);
    this.callParent();
},

onSelect: function (row, record) {
    this.fireEvent('companyselected', this, record);
}
```

This makes our custom event available on the client side. With JavaScript, once we have an instance of our grid control, we can attach to the `companyselected` event as needed.

Defining the client-side event on the server side

You could stop here as this works as it stands; you could use the Ext.NET component to create a `FinancialGrid` instance, and you could attach to the `companyselected` event using Ext JS code and deal with it purely in JavaScript.

However, one drawback is that you cannot declaratively use the `companyselected` event via Ext.NET's markup or server-side capability. This is because the server-side Ext.NET component doesn't know this event exists. With a few small steps, we can make this event available to instantiate on the server side (but it will still run on the client side).

If you look at the source code of any of the Ext.NET classes, you will see that for each list of supported events for a given component, there is an associated listeners class where these events are actually listed. An instance of this associated listeners class is then added as a property of the component and the property is called `Listeners`.

Similarly, we can create our own custom listeners by performing the following steps:

1. Define your own custom listeners class by extending the listeners class of the parent component you are extending.

2. In this class you define your custom events.

3. Override ConfigOptions to ensure these custom events get serialized.

4. In your component subclass, create a property called Listeners with a getter, whose type is this new listeners class. Ensure the property is serialized to Ext JS as listeners by overriding ConfigOptions and adding the custom listener to it.

Let's see this in action.

Defining your custom listeners class

The following is an example that covers the first three steps:

```
public class FinancialGridListeners : GridPanelListeners
{
  private const string CompanySelectedJs = "companyselected";

  private ComponentListener _companySelected;

  [ListenerArgument(0, "grid")]
  [ListenerArgument(1, "record")]
  [TypeConverter(typeof (ExpandableObjectConverter))]
  [PersistenceMode(PersistenceMode.InnerProperty)]
  [NotifyParentProperty(true)]
  public virtual ComponentListener CompanySelected
  {
    get { return _companySelected ??
        (_companySelected = new ComponentListener()); }
  }

  [Browsable(false)]
  [EditorBrowsable(EditorBrowsableState.Never)]
  [DesignerSerializationVisibility(
    DesignerSerializationVisibility.Hidden)]
  [XmlIgnore]
  [JsonIgnore]
  public override ConfigOptionsCollection ConfigOptions
  {
    get
    {
      ConfigOptionsCollection list = base.ConfigOptions;
```

```
        list.Add(CompanySelectedJs,
          new ConfigOption("CompanySelected",
            new SerializationOptions(CompanySelectedJs,
              typeof(ListenerJsonConverter)),
            null,
            CompanySelected));

        return list;
    }
  }
}
```

The first property, CompanySelected, is the server-side representation of our custom event. It has various attributes to help with the serialization process. The TypeConverter, PersistenceMode, and NotifyParentProperty attributes help with ASP.NET and the visual designer. The ListenerArgument attributes are the names of the arguments passed to the handler function. This helps Ext.NET generate an appropriate JavaScript when this listener is used via Handler. It may be easier to visualize this by considering the following markup:

```
<cc1:FinancialGrid runat="server" Width="450" Height="300">
    <Listeners>
        <CompanySelected Handler="console.log(arguments);" />
    </Listeners>
</cc1:FinancialGrid>
```

The preceding code snippet will produce the following as part of the Ext.NET-generated initialization script (pretty printed):

```
listeners: {
    companyselected: {
        fn: function (grid, record) {
            console.log(arguments);
        }
    }
}
```

The ListenerArgument attributes generate the correct function arguments (in bold).

The second property is ConfigOptions. This basically extends the parent listener class's ConfigOptions property by adding our custom events to that list.

> When adding the item to the list, the first argument to the ConfigOption constructor should match a server property name.

Using the custom listener in your custom component

If you look at the definition of GridPanel in Ext.NET's source code, you will see that the `Listeners` property is defined as follows:

```
public GridPanelListeners Listeners
{
    // getter defined here
}
```

In C# it is not possible to override the `Listeners` property to return our own custom `FinancialGridListeners` (an issue of covariance and contravariance in overriding).

The Ext.NET team faced this problem creating their own component hierarchy and came up with a solution that involved splitting their component (such as GridPanel) into two types of classes—a parent or base class that defined all the properties and functionality, and a child or final class to contain the listeners (and DirectEvents and other overrides related to event handling).

This means supporting custom listeners in custom components requires that `FinancialGridPanel` must inherit from GridPanel's own parent class, GridPanelBase:

```
public class FinancialGrid : GridPanelBase
```

We can then add the additional properties to support the custom listener. This involves the following two steps itself:

1. Define the `Listener` property.

2. Add Ext.NET serialization support to generate the right JavaScript for our custom listener.

Let's see how this will work. First, we define the additional event listener property:

```
private FinancialGridListeners _listeners;

[NotifyParentProperty(true)]
[PersistenceMode(PersistenceMode.InnerProperty)]
[DesignerSerializationVisibility(DesignerSerializationVisibility.
Visible)]
public FinancialGridListeners Listeners
{
    get
    {
        return _listeners
            ?? (_listeners = new FinancialGridListeners());
    }
}
```

Recall that the GridPanelBase class itself does not have a Listeners property (only the child class GridPanel does) so we are not overriding it as we are extending GridPanelBase. Through convention we are calling this property Listeners but returning a different type. This helps to create consistency and familiarity with other Ext.NET components.

The NotifyParentProperty, PersistenceMode, and DesignerSerializationVisibility attributes are for ASP.NET design time support.

The second step is to ensure the custom listener is serialized correctly when the entire component becomes JavaScript code. To do this we override the ConfigOptions property to add our new listener property as the listener serialization:

```
[Browsable(false)]
[EditorBrowsable(EditorBrowsableState.Never)]
[DesignerSerializationVisibility(DesignerSerializationVisibility.
Hidden)]
[XmlIgnore]
[JsonIgnore]
public override ConfigOptionsCollection ConfigOptions
{
    get
    {
        ConfigOptionsCollection list = base.ConfigOptions;

        list.Add("listeners",
            new ConfigOption("Listeners",
                new SerializationOptions("listeners",
                    JsonMode.Object),
                null,
                Listeners));

        return list;
    }
}
```

> The serialization option here is subtly different from the one used inside the listener's ConfigOptions override. This is because the Listeners property here will be serialized into a JavaScript object (using JavaScript object literal syntax), whereas for the listeners class, the serialization will be a custom ListenerJsonConvertor (which generates different JavaScript based on how you use the listener, for example, whether you use Handler, Fn, Scope, or various other ComponentListener properties).

There is a useful `ConfigOptionsExtractions` property you could optionally override. It returns an enum to control configuration option serialization. If you returned `ConfigOptionsExtraction.Reflection`, the serialization process will use reflection to find all properties with a `ConfigOption` attribute. This means you could use separate properties with a `ConfigOption` attribute instead of a `ConfigOptions` collection, which is what the default extraction option is (`ConfigOptionsExtraction.List`). For this book, we will concentrate on the default way and not override this property.

With that in place, our custom `FinancialGrid` class is now ready to be used and the custom listener is available via IntelliSense:

```
<ext:Viewport runat="server">
    <Items>
        <cc1:FinancialGrid Id="Grid" runat="server">
            <Listeners>
                <
            </Lis
        </cc1:Fin
    </Items>
</ext:Viewport>
ody>
```

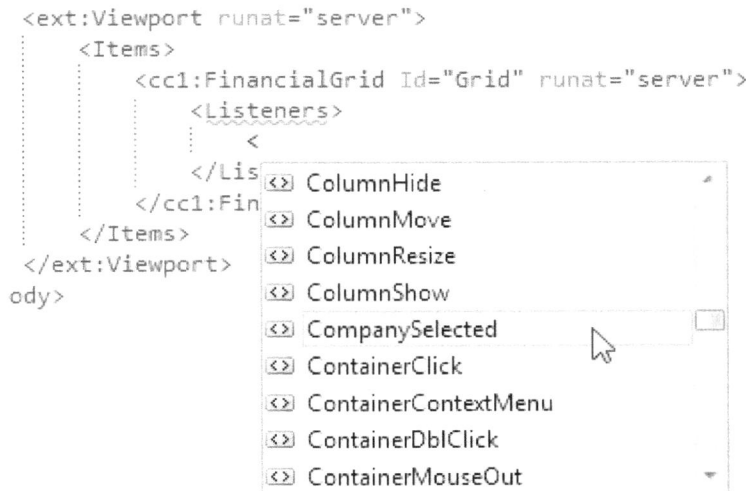

Notice that because we simply extended the `GridPanelListeners` class we see all the other events as well as our custom event, `CompanySelected`.

Creating a custom DirectEvent

The same approach to create client-side listeners can be used to create DirectEvents:

1. Create a `DirectEvents` class that subclasses the `DirectEvents` class that your parent component uses.
2. Use that in your component as the `DirectEvents` property.
3. Update your `ConfigOptions` property to include the `DirectEvents` property so that it is also serialized to the client side.

The following shows a `CompanySelected` DirectEvent:

```
public class FinancialGridDirectEvents : GridPanelDirectEvents
{
  public FinancialGridDirectEvents() { }

  public FinancialGridDirectEvents(Observable parent)
  {
    Parent = parent;
  }

  private ComponentDirectEvent _companySelected;

  [TypeConverter(typeof(ExpandableObjectConverter))]
  [PersistenceMode(PersistenceMode.InnerProperty)]
  [NotifyParentProperty(true)]
  public virtual ComponentDirectEvent CompanySelected
  {
    get
    {
      return _companySelected ??
        (_companySelected = new ComponentDirectEvent(this));
    }
  }

  [Browsable(false)]
  [EditorBrowsable(EditorBrowsableState.Never)]
  [DesignerSerializationVisibility(
    DesignerSerializationVisibility.Hidden)]
  [XmlIgnore]
  [JsonIgnore]
  public override ConfigOptionsCollection ConfigOptions
  {
    get
    {
      ConfigOptionsCollection list = base.ConfigOptions;

      list.Add("companyselected",
        new ConfigOption("CompanySelected",
          new SerializationOptions("companyselected",
            typeof(DirectEventJsonConverter)),
          null,
          CompanySelected));

      return list;
    }
  }
}
```

In the preceding code, the pattern is almost exactly as it is for creating listeners, except the class is a subclass of `GridPanelDirectEvents`. There are also a couple of constructors to help in the serialization process that are needed.

Another difference is that the `CompanySelected` property in the `DirectEvents` class also does not have the `ListenerArgument` attributes (if they are there, they are just ignored). This is because DirectEvents do not pass back custom event arguments automatically to the server. To pass events you use the `ExtraParams` collection, as explained in *Chapter 4, AJAX with Ext.NET.*

Once we have defined the class we now need to add it to our `FinancialGrid`:

```
private FinancialGridDirectEvents _directEvents;

[NotifyParentProperty(true)]
[PersistenceMode(PersistenceMode.InnerProperty)]
[DesignerSerializationVisibility(
    DesignerSerializationVisibility.Visible)]
public FinancialGridDirectEvents DirectEvents
{
    get
    {
        return _directEvents
            ?? (_directEvents =
                    new FinancialGridDirectEvents(this));
    }
}
```

This is also similar to what was needed for the `Listeners` property. The final step is to update our `ConfigOptions` override property in `FinancialGrid` and add the DirectEvent serialization configuration option:

```
public override ConfigOptionsCollection ConfigOptions
{
    get
    {
        ConfigOptionsCollection list = base.ConfigOptions;

        list.Add("listeners",
            new ConfigOption("Listeners",
                new SerializationOptions("listeners",
                    JsonMode.Object),
                null,
                Listeners));

        list.Add("directEvents",
            new ConfigOption("DirectEvents",
```

```
            new SerializationOptions("directEvents",
                JsonMode.Object),
            null,
            DirectEvents));

        return list;
    }
}
```

The custom DirectEvent is now available in IntelliSense, for example:

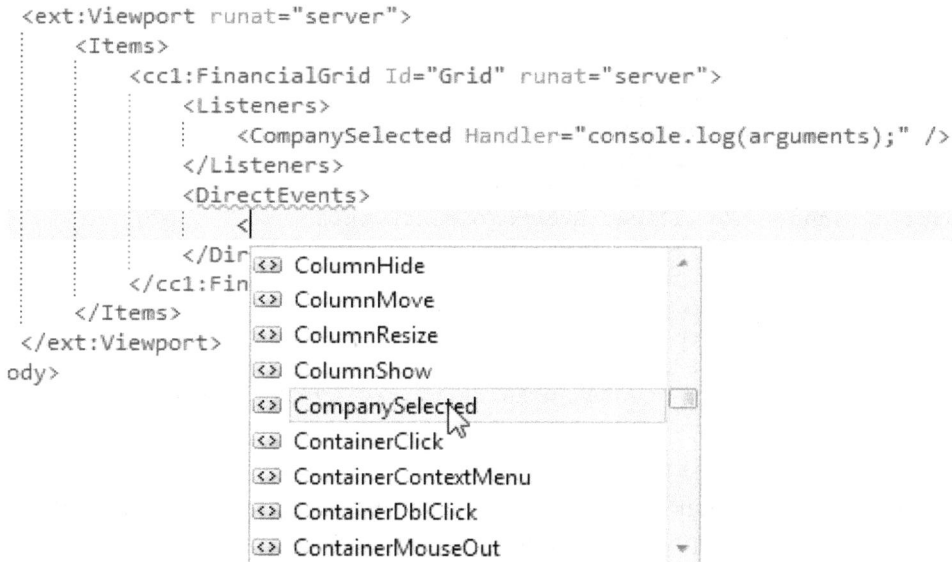

```
<ext:Viewport runat="server">
    <Items>
        <cc1:FinancialGrid Id="Grid" runat="server">
            <Listeners>
                <CompanySelected Handler="console.log(arguments);" />
            </Listeners>
            <DirectEvents>
                <|
            </Dir
        </cc1:Fin|       ColumnHide
    </Items>              ColumnMove
</ext:Viewport>          ColumnResize
ody>                     ColumnShow
                         CompanySelected
                         ContainerClick
                         ContainerContextMenu
                         ContainerDblClick
                         ContainerMouseOut
```

Passing properties to your JavaScript class

We can also use the ConfigOptions override to add other properties that will be passed to the JavaScript class, not just Listeners and DirectEvents.

For example, if you have a string property on your custom component called MyProperty and want to pass it through to your JavaScript class, you can use something similar to this inside the ConfigOptions override property we saw earlier:

```
list.add("myProperty", null, "", this.MyProperty);
```

For simple types like string, date, boolean, and various numeric types, the null serializer argument is used because Ext.NET will serialize those values into correct JavaScript types automatically. The empty string for the third argument in the preceding code, is an example of a default value. If the property value is equal to this default value, the property is not serialized nor sent to the client. The source code for Ext.NET has many examples of how different types of properties can be set like this.

> **ConfigOptions or CustomConfig?**
>
> As noted in *Chapter 2, Ext.NET Controls Overview*, you can add custom configuration options to controls via the CustomConfig property. So why use ConfigOptions? Inside your own control, you should use ConfigOptions, as this is the most efficient technique for serializing the values. Users of your control will use CustomConfig (which can also be used to override corresponding configuration options in ConfigOptions, if needed).

Using the custom component on an ASP.NET Web Form

To use the custom component in our example page, we can use one or both of the events, for example:

```
<%@ Page Language="C#" %>
<%@ Register TagPrefix="cc1" Namespace="CustomControlsAndPlugins.
Components" Assembly="CustomControlsAndPlugins" %>

<script runat="server">
protected void Grid_CompanySelected(object sender, DirectEventArgs e)
{
  X.MessageBox.Alert("Company selected", e.ToString()).Show();
}
</script>

<!DOCTYPE html>
<html>
  <head runat="server">
    <title>Custom Component Example</title>
  </head>
  <body>
    <ext:ResourceManager runat="server" />

    <ext:Viewport runat="server">
```

```
          <Items>
            <cc1:FinancialGrid ID="Grid" runat="server">
              <Listeners>
                <CompanySelected
                  Handler="console.log(arguments);" />
              </Listeners>
              <DirectEvents>
                <CompanySelected
                  OnEvent="Grid_CompanySelected" />
              </DirectEvents>
            </cc1:FinancialGrid>
          </Items>
        </ext:Viewport>
    </body>
  </html>
```

In the preceding example, if a row is selected, two events will actually fire — the client-side `CompanySelected` listener (which will log the arguments to the browser console) and the server-side `CompanySelected` DirectEvent (which just alerts out the event).

> Recall from *Chapter 4, AJAX with Ext.NET*, with DirectEvents if you want to access other features of the grid during the event you may want to put the page in `<form runat="server">` so that when the DirectEvent causes a postback, another control state is also posted back.

Using your custom component in ASP.NET MVC (Razor)

The custom component, as it stands, can be used in a Razor template. If we see the earlier web forms example, we can recreate the same page in a Razor template (showing just the relevant portion of the Razor template):

```
<body>
    @Html.X().ResourceManager().Theme(Theme.Gray)

    @Html.X().Viewport().Items(items => items.Add(new
FinancialGrid()))
</body>
```

A basic control renderer

The preceding code is nice and covers many use cases (as our `FinancialGrid` may often be used inside a layout or a Viewport if we are trying to create an application feel). However, other times you need to be able to create a custom component directly. For example, you may have subclassed the Viewport and want to load that as the first component. Or you may just simply want to insert your custom component onto a page directly. In our `FinancialGrid` example we might want to be able to do this:

```
@Html.FinancialGrid().Height(300).Width(500)
```

But there is no extension method for `FinancialGrid`. So how can we support this?

The main thing to consider is that when creating extension methods for the Razor template, most methods return a string. We have seen that many Ext.NET components have an ancestor class that exposes methods such as `ToScript()` or `SelfRender()`, which return such strings. However, Ext.NET's own processing pipeline is such that not all components will necessarily return fully executable scripts this way; they may return templates that will still be processed further. So, ASP.NET MVC has an interface we can take advantage of called `IHtmlString`. Any class implementing this interface must implement `ToHtmlString()`. So a common and repeatable pattern for your subclasses may be the following:

```
public class ControlRender : IHtmlString
{
    public ControlRender(BaseControl control)
    {
        Control = control;
    }

    public BaseControl Control { get; private set; }

    public string ToHtmlString()
    {
        return Control.SelfRender();
    }

    public ControlRender Height(int height)
    {
        Control.Height = height;
        return this;
    }

    public ControlRender Width(int width)
    {
        Control.Width = width;
        return this;
    }
}
```

The preceding code is a general control renderer that will render any `BaseControl` class (and all Ext.NET controls are derived from this class). We can expose various methods and properties here to be used in our Razor template, and if we do, they return an instance of themselves, which also allows chaining.

The class implements `IHtmlString` so we use it when creating an MVC helper method that adds an extension method to the ASP.NET MVC `HtmlHelper` class:

```
public static class FinancialGridBasicMvcExtensions
{
    public static IHtmlString FinancialGridBasic(
        this HtmlHelper helper, int height, int width)
    {
        return new ControlRender(new FinancialGrid
        {
            Height = height,
            Width = width
        });
    }

    public static ControlRender FinancialGridBasic(
        this HtmlHelper helper)
    {
        return new ControlRender(new FinancialGrid());
    }
}
```

There are two extension methods in the preceding example, though you could create as many as you need. With that example in place, you can use it in an MVC Razor template and do something like the following example:

```
@Html.FinancialGridBasic().Height(300).Width(500)
```

Or you can use the overload like this next example:

```
@Html.FinancialGridBasic(300, 500)
```

Reusing Ext.NET's builder pattern for a richer custom MVC framework for your own application

The earlier example is very powerful and can be expanded as needed. However that is also where its drawback lies; you have to manually extend it to support the different properties you want to set. But if you look at Ext.NET's own MVC code, they have a rich framework to expose all their properties.

It would be useful if our class could somehow tap into that and expose those, too. After all, our `FinancialGrid` inherits `GridPanelBase`, so all the properties there should ideally show up in our Razor code IntelliSense, too. It would also be nice to provide a namespace for all our components (similar to how Ext.NET provides for its own components so you can use `@Html.X()` and then access all its components under `X()`). Then, we could do the following:

```
@Html.MyApp().FinancialGridBasic().Height(300).Width(500)
```

This is very similar to the earlier Razor example, except it has `MyApp()`, which we could eventually extend with more of our custom components we need for our application.

Fortunately with a small bit of effort, it is possible. Ext.NET provides a class called `BuilderFactory` for all its components. They are spread out using partial classes but that gives them good organization to separate MVC from core ASP.NET functionality.

The basic process (at a high level) is as follows:

1. First, make your component a partial class (unless you want to put all your code into one file).

2. Next make another partial class with the same name.

3. In this class define two nested classes — `Builder` to tap into Ext.NET's framework and `Config` to expose any custom configuration.

4. You then build a `BuilderFactory` class (this is mimicking Ext.NET's pattern because we cannot add our own implementation into their `BuilderFactory` class as partial classes cannot span multiple projects).

5. Add appropriate constructors and a `ToBuilder` method to return your builder from your component.

6. Expose your component to the MVC Razor template through extension methods.

Applying this to the `FinancialGrid` component, we make our component a partial class (unless you want to keep all the MVC code in the same file, too). The classes `Builder` and `Config`, the `ToBuilder()` method and supporting constructors are set as follows:

```
public partial class FinancialGrid
{
    public FinancialGrid() { }

    public FinancialGrid(Config config)
    {
        Apply(config);
    }
```

```csharp
        public Builder ToBuilder()
        {
            return new BuilderFactory().FinancialGrid(this);
        }

        public class Builder : Builder<FinancialGrid, Builder>
        {
            public Builder() : base(new FinancialGrid()) { }

            public Builder(FinancialGrid component) :
                base(component) { }

            public Builder(Config config) :
                base(new FinancialGrid(config)) { }
        }

        new public class Config : GridPanelBase.Config
        {
            public static implicit operator Builder(Config config)
            {
                return new Builder(config);
            }

            private FinancialGridListeners listeners;

            public FinancialGridListeners Listeners
            {
                get
                {
                    return _listeners ?? (this.listeners =
                        new FinancialGridListeners());
                }
            }

            private FinancialGridDirectEvents directEvents;

            public FinancialGridDirectEvents DirectEvents
            {
                get
                {
                    return _directEvents ?? (this.directEvents =
                        new FinancialGridDirectEvents());
                }
            }
        }
    }
}
```

In the preceding code, an empty constructor is followed by one that can take a
`Config` class, which itself is defined as a nested class, as is the `Builder` class.
The `Builder` class extends `GridPanelBase.Builder<TGridPanelBase, TBuilder>`
to follow Ext.NET's builder framework. The various constructors are used within
that framework.

The `Config` class is a new implementation of the `GridPanelBase.Config` class
so that custom listeners (and any other custom properties) can be exposed as
configuration properties to MVC.

Now the basic component additions are in place, how do we enable MVC Razor for
our components?

Mimicking Ext.NET's approach we create our own `BuilderFactory` class, as follows:

```
public partial class BuilderFactory
{
    public HtmlHelper HtmlHelper { get; set; }
}
```

This class is a partial class in our project added to each custom component we have.
For our `FinancialGrid` component we would then add the following methods:

```
public partial class BuilderFactory
{
    public FinancialGrid.Builder FinancialGrid()
    {
        return FinancialGrid(new FinancialGrid
        {
            ViewContext = HtmlHelper != null
                ? HtmlHelper.ViewContext : null
        });
    }

    public FinancialGrid.Builder FinancialGrid(
        FinancialGrid component)
    {
        component.ViewContext = HtmlHelper != null
            ? HtmlHelper.ViewContext : null;

        return new FinancialGrid.Builder(component);
    }
}
```

The preceding code adds the `FinancialGrid()` factory methods to the `BuilderFactory` class so we can eventually use it in our Razor template. By returning a `FinancialGrid.Builder` instance this enables method chaining, for example, `FinancialGrid().Height(100)`. However, we are still not done; we need to be able to expose this via an `HtmlHelper` extension for MVC.

As noted earlier, Ext.NET has used `X()` as an extension method of `Html` and exposed all its components from there (for example, `@Html.X().ViewPort()`). Similarly, we will use `MyApp` (as that was also the client-side namespace we chose) so that we can call `@Html.MyApp()`. To do this, we expose our builder factory so we can chain together `@Html.MyApp().FinancialGrid()` and so on. First, we create the `MyApp` class:

```
public class MyApp
{
}
```

At this stage the class is empty; it is just a holder. Next, we add an extension method to extend `HtmlHelper` as follows:

```
public static class MyAppExtensions
{
    public static BuilderFactory MyApp(this HtmlHelper helper)
    {
        return new BuilderFactory { HtmlHelper = helper };
    }
}
```

And there we have it. The following is a summary of the steps:

1. We add `MyApp` as an extension of `HtmlHelper` enabling `@Html.MyApp()`.

2. The extension method returns our `BuilderFactory` class.

3. Our `BuilderFactory` class has a `FinancialGrid()` factory method on it allowing us to do `@Html.MyApp.FinancialGrid()`.

4. Because the factory method returns a `FinancialGrid.Builder` class, it supports the ability to chain other methods such as `.Height()` and `.Width()`, which come from the parent classes Ext.NET has provided for us, and we manage to reuse without duplicating their efforts.

With all that in place we can use this in a Razor template, for example:

```
@Html.MyApp().FinancialGridBasic().Height(300).Width(500)
```

> We have only scratched the surface of Ext.NET's MVC and Razor support and how we can tap into it. The Ext.NET team is continually improving it too, so be sure to look at their forums and blogs for more announcements and capabilities.

Recap of steps to create a custom component

It has taken a while to explain how to create a custom component. Once you are used to it, hopefully you will agree that it is a lot simpler to do it than explain it! Here is a summary of the steps needed:

1. Extend a base Ext.NET component (required, other steps optional).

2. Define a counterpart JavaScript extension.

3. In the Ext.NET component, indicate the instance and alias (xtype) of the JavaScript counterpart using the `InstanceOf` and `XType` properties.

4. Mark the JavaScript, CSS, and any image resources as embedded.

5. Mark JavaScript and CSS as web resources.

6. Override the `Resources` property in your component to register custom JavaScript and CSS.

7. Define custom `Listener` and `DirectEvent` classes. Use those in the custom component by implementing the `Listeners` and `DirectEvents` properties.

8. For ASP.NET MVC Razor support, create a supporting class that implements `IHtmlString`.

This gives you an encapsulated component. You may not need to perform all of these steps. In particular, if you do not require custom events, you can safely inherit the "final" class (for example, `GridPanel` instead of `GridPanelBase`). This saves redefining the `Listeners` and `DirectEvents` properties and associated configuration overrides.

The following flowchart summarizes the steps to take, based on your scenario:

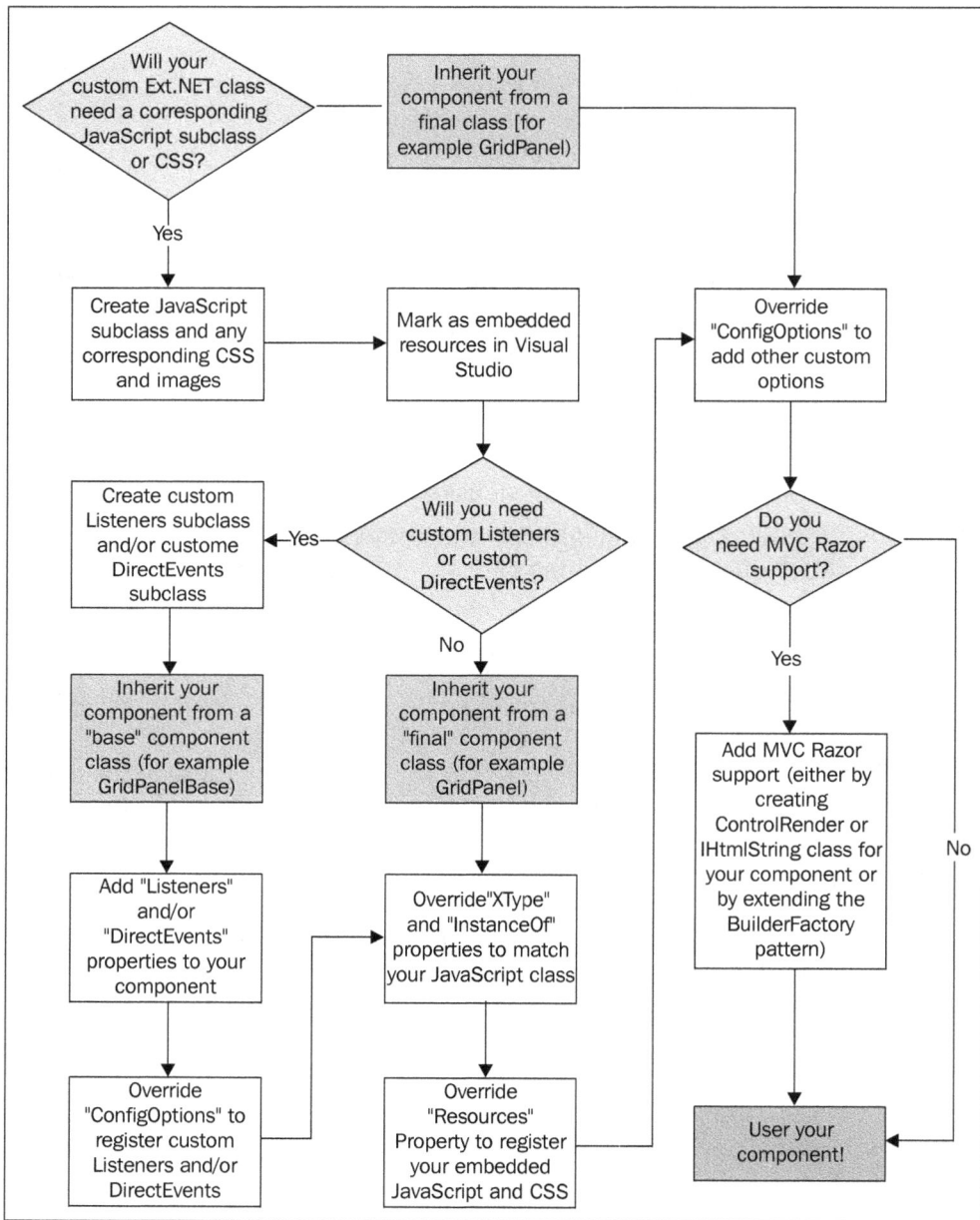

As the flowchart shows, overall there are three scenarios.

Scenario 1 – simple subclass, no custom events, no custom JavaScript or CSS

In this scenario, you simply need to subclass a "final" non-base class such as `GridPanel`. If your subclass internally needs to subscribe to events from subcomponents that make up the `GridPanel` class, then you have to manage the location of the JavaScript handlers yourself. Users of your component can still subscribe to all `GridPanel` events as normal.

Scenario 2 – simple subclass, no custom events, but with custom JavaScript or CSS

Similar to the first scenario, you can subclass a "final" class such as `GridPanel`. But you also need to override the `XType` and `InstanceOf` properties to return the Ext JS xtype and the name of your JavaScript class.

Although you don't need to, you may benefit from also embedding your JavaScript class and associated CSS (and any CSS-related images). To do this do the following:

1. Mark your resources as embedded in your Visual Studio project.
2. Use the `WebResource` attribute in Visual Studio to register your JavaScript, CSS, and any CSS images with the assembly.
3. Override the `Resources` property in your custom component to register/add your component's own JavaScript and CSS-embedded files.

Scenario 3 – subclass with custom Listeners and/or DirectEvents, and custom JavaScript/CSS

This is a fuller scenario where your component is much richer. Here are the steps:

1. Subclass the "base" class rather than a "final" class; for example, the `GridPanelBase` subclass instead of `GridPanel`.
2. Define a JavaScript class to extend the client-side component.
3. Embed resources such as JavaScript, CSS, and any associated CSS images.
4. Define any custom `Listeners` property in a class that subclasses your main component's own `listeners` class.
5. Define any custom `DirectEvents` property in a class that subclasses your main component's own `DirectEvents` class.
6. In your own component subclass, override `ConfigOptions` to add custom `Listeners`, `DirectEvents`, or other properties so they get serialized.

One possible future-proofing tip is if you are thinking of following scenario 1, consider opting for scenario 2 instead. By creating a JavaScript subclass—even if you don't think you need it now—it may save time in the future if you will extend client-side behavior.

Component design considerations

As your custom controls become more complex, it is more and more likely that you will need (or benefit from) scenarios 2 or 3.

Building more complex controls through composition

An example of where scenarios 2 or 3 help is in composite controls. For example, suppose you have a Panel with a BorderLayout that contains a TreePanel and a GridPanel to create a look and feel commonly seen with e-mail or file browser applications.

A common pattern for component design is for the containing component (the Panel in this case) to coordinate its contained items by reacting to events. For example, if a TreePanel node is selected, you may want to reload the GridPanel with some new data.

Instead of directly calling methods on the GridPanel, the TreePanel would raise appropriate events. The containing Panel would subscribe to these so it can then tell the GridPanel to reload its data, thus coordinating between the two components. This is "separation of concerns" in action; the GridPanel and TreePanel are acting independently for all they know, allowing reuse of these components elsewhere independently or with totally different components.

This pattern can be achieved in Ext.NET by creating the appropriate subclasses of `Panel` and even `GridPanel` and `TreePanel` on both the server and JavaScript sides. The `Panel` subclass on the JavaScript side could subscribe to the appropriate events from the TreePanel and GridPanel that it contains and coordinate the appropriate actions between them. By making `Panel` a subclass on the server and client sides, all this wiring up of events happens internally; users of your component don't need to care, making it easier for them to use the composite component in many places in many ways.

GenericComponent<T> – a quick alternative to wrap Ext JS ready Components

One useful technique Ext.NET provides is the ability to wrap custom components that are pure JavaScript. Typically these would be Ext JS components. Perhaps you or a community member has written one before and want to make it available quickly in Ext.NET applications. The following simple example shows the general approach:

```
Panel1.Items.Add(new GenericComponent<Toolbar>
{
  GenericXType = "acceptdecline",
  GenericInstanceOf = "Ext.net.AcceptDecline",
  Component =
  {
    FieldLabel = "Question 1"
  }
});
```

Declaring DirectMethods on custom components

In *Chapter 4, AJAX with Ext.NET*, we saw how DirectMethods can be declared in a user control. Similarly you can define DirectMethods in custom components. This can further help ensure your component is as self-contained as possible. Note these DirectMethods must be non-static, just as they must be in user controls. In addition, you have to register these DirectMethods with the `ResourceManager` attribute as explained in the Ext.NET forum post at `http://forums.ext.net/showthread.php?15060`.

The following Examples Explorer sample also shows the same:

`http://examples.ext.net/#/Combination_Samples/Applications/Simple_Tasks/`

Supporting ASP.NET Web Forms IPostBackDataHandler

A benefit of Ext.NET in ASP.NET Web Forms is that you can often avoid the ASP.NET PostBack model as virtually all server interactions can be done with AJAX. However, if you are using DirectEvents or still need to do a traditional ASP.NET Web Forms PostBack to the server, you may need to obtain some client-side state for your custom control. With traditional ASP.NET controls you can implement the `IPostBackDataHandler` interface. This can also be used for Ext.NET components, if needed. For further information, the following URL may be useful:

`http://msdn.microsoft.com/en-us/library/system.web.ui.ipostbackdatahandler.aspx`

The Ext.NET forum post at the following URL also demonstrates how it may be used:

```
http://forums.ext.net/showthread.php?14973
```

Benefits of extending Ext.NET controls

By extending Ext.NET controls, your product component that are highly reusable in a variety of ways; from markup, from MVC views, from code-behind. As our example extends a grid, wherever you would normally add `GridPanel` you can use this class to behave as a grid. This means it can be added to a container's `Items` collection, for example. It also means you set various grid properties and add other grid features as well as plugins to the customized subclass, if needed.

Another benefit of this approach is the familiarity over time. If you study the Ext. NET source code itself, you will see this is how they also create most of their server-side counterparts to the Ext JS components from Sencha, and how they create their own extensions. This means you benefit from their practices.

Lastly, if you have your own or some third-party components written in Ext JS, only this pattern gives you good guidance on how to make it compatible with Ext.NET.

Drawbacks of this approach

The main drawback of this approach is perhaps the slightly extra work needed to create the component in the first place. In addition more JavaScript and understanding of Ext JS is needed. However, this drawback is just an initial hurdle to overcome. In the long run it encourages knowing Ext JS which is a good thing as mentioned before in this book!

Using plugins

Extending Ext.NET controls is immensely powerful and flexible. Over time you can build solid applications with reusable components very easily.

However, there are times where you need reusable snippets of code that augment your components (or the existing Ext.NET ones) without needing to subclass them.

JavaScript is a very dynamic language, meaning you could even write parts of a class or plugin that can be added to components that are unrelated to each other.

Consider our `FinancialGrid` component. We might want to let the user change the page size and present options inside the paging toolbar, as per the following screenshot:

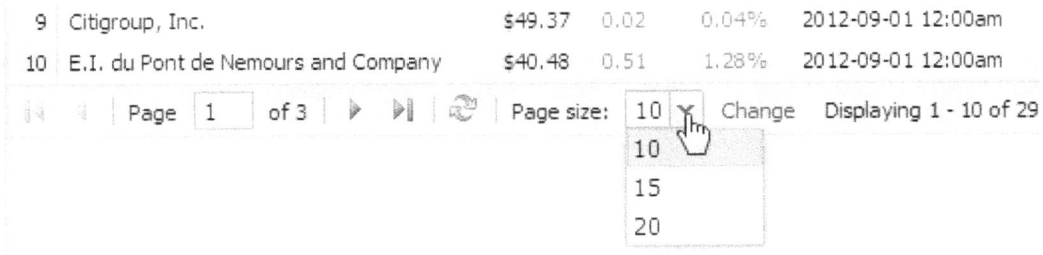

| 9 | Citigroup, Inc. | $49.37 | 0.02 | 0.04% | 2012-09-01 12:00am |
| 10 | E.I. du Pont de Nemours and Company | $40.48 | 0.51 | 1.28% | 2012-09-01 12:00am |

Page 1 of 3 ▶ ▶| ↻ Page size: 10 ▼ Change   Displaying 1 - 10 of 29

10
15
20

One way to achieve this is to simply modify our custom `FinancialGrid` component, where we set the toolbar before as follows:

```
BottomBar.Add(new PagingToolbar());
```

We could replace it with something like the following line of code:

```
BottomBar.Add(BuildBottomBar());
```

The `BuildBottomBar` method is defined as follows::

```
private PagingToolbar BuildBottomBar()
{
  return new PagingToolbar
  {
    Items =
    {
      new ToolbarSeparator(),
      new ComboBox
      {
        FieldLabel = "Page size",
        Width = 100,
        LabelWidth = 55,
        Value = Convert.ToString(InitialPageSize),
        Items =
        {
          new ListItem("10"),
          new ListItem("15"),
          new ListItem("20")
        }
      },
      new Button
      {
```

```
            Text = "Change",
            Listeners =
            {
              Click =
              {
                Handler =
                 "var grid = this.up('financialgrid')," +
                 "   pageSize = this.prev().getValue();" +
                 "grid.changePageSize.call(grid,pageSize);"
              }
            }
          }
        }
      };
  }
```

Assume `InitialPageSize` is a constant or property initially set to `10`. The button click handler finds the `financialgrid` xtype and calls `changePageSize`, defined as follows:

```
changePageSize: function (pageSize) {
    var store = this.getStore();
    store.pageSize = pageSize;
    store.load();
}
```

While the preceding code works, it is limited. For example, it is custom coded into the `FinancialGrid` class. Clearly other uses of the GridPanel may benefit.

One option may be to subclass `PagingToolbar` and use that where needed. That is a lot better. However, that too may be limited — some scenarios for the same component may not require the page size changer. This could be done with flags on the custom paging toolbar subclass. But if the paging toolbar has lots of other optional functionality like this, your sub class would get quite bloated to manage what is turned off and on.

Converting this into a plugin may be better. It is mostly Ext JS work and then using it in Ext.NET. Following Ext JS conventions, here is what the plugin code might look like:

```
Ext.define('Ext.ux.plugin.PageSizeChanger', {
    extend: 'Ext.AbstractPlugin',

    alias: 'plugin.PageSizeChanger',

    labelText: 'Page size:',
```

```
    pageSizes: [10, 15, 20],

    changeButtonLabel: 'Change',

    init: function (pager) {
        if (!(pager instanceof Ext.PagingToolbar)) {
            throw "This plugin needs a paging toolbar";
        }

        this.store = pager.getStore();
        this.initComboBox();
        this.initChangeButton();

        var insertOffSet = pager.displayInfo === true ? 2 : 0;

        function getPosition() {
            return pager.items.getCount() - insertOffSet;
        }

        pager.insert(getPosition(), '-');
        pager.insert(getPosition(), { xtype: 'tbtext', text: this.
labelText });
        pager.insert(getPosition(), this.comboBox);
        pager.insert(getPosition(), this.changeButton);
    },

    destroy: function () {
        delete this.comboBox;
        delete this.changeButton;
        delete this.store;
    },

    initComboBox: function () {
        var pageSizeRecords = [];

        Ext.each(this.pageSizes, function (item) {
            pageSizeRecords.push([item, item]);
        });

        this.comboBox = new Ext.form.ComboBox({
            width: 45,
            value: this.store.pageSize,
            typeAhead: false,
            forceSelection: true,
            editable: false,
            valueField: "value",
            store: new Ext.data.SimpleStore({
```

```
                              fields: ["text", "value"],
                              data: pageSizeRecords
                          }),
                          listeners: {
                              select: { fn: this.select, scope: this }
                          }
                      });
              },

              initChangeButton: function () {
                  this.changeButton = new Ext.Button({
                      disabled: true,
                      text: this.changeButtonLabel,
                      listeners: {
                          click: {
                              fn: this.click,
                              scope: this
                          }
                      }
                  });
              },

              select: function () {
                  this.changeButton.enable();
              },

              click: function () {
                  var size = this.comboBox.getValue();
                  this.store.pageSize = size;
                  this.store.load();
                  this.changeButton.disable();
              }
          });
```

Here's a quick explanation. After the alias and custom configuration defaults (the labels and the page sizes to show), the standard `init` method for plugins initializes our plugin. Inside this method, we initialize the combobox and the change button. Then we work out whether to insert it into the end of the toolbar or just before the paging information.

To initialize the combobox we simply make a non-editable combobox (for simplicity here). As a usability enhancement we've also added a select handler so that it enables the change button once a selection is made. When the change button is clicked, as well as reloading the store with the new page size, the change button is disabled.

To use this plugin from our Ext.NET FinancialGrid custom component, we can modify our BuildBottomBar() method to simply be the following:

```
private PagingToolbar BuildBottomBar()
{
  return new PagingToolbar
  {
    Plugins =
    {
      new GenericPlugin
      {
        InstanceName = "Ext.ux.plugin.PageSizeChanger",
        Path = "~/Plugins/Resources/PageSizeChanger.js"
      }
    }
  };
}
```

We simply created GenericPlugin and used the Path property so Ext.NET will generate a script tag to load that path. Our JavaScript plugin had custom/default properties, labelText and pageSizes. These can easily be overridden as follows:

```
new GenericPlugin
{
  InstanceName = "Ext.ux.plugin.PageSizeChanger",
  Path = "~/Plugins/Resources/PageSizeChanger.js",
  CustomConfig =
  {
    new ConfigItem("labelText", "Custom label:",
                   ParameterMode.Value)
  }
}
```

Another technique is to extend the Plugin class. The following is an example:

```
[assembly: WebResource("CustomControlsAndPlugins.Plugins.Resources.
PageSizeChanger.js", "text/javascript")]

namespace CustomControlsAndPlugins.Plugins
{
  public class PageSizeChangerPlugin : Plugin
  {
    protected override List<ResourceItem> Resources
    {
      get
      {
        const string resourcePath = "CustomControlsAndPlugins.Plugins.
Resources.PageSizeChanger.js";
```

```
      List<ResourceItem> baseList = base.Resources;
      baseList.Capacity += 1;

      baseList.Add(new
        ClientScriptItem(typeof(PageSizeChangerPlugin),
        resourcePath, ""));

      return baseList;
    }
  }

  public override string InstanceOf
  {
    get { return "Ext.ux.plugin.PageSizeChanger"; }
  }
 }
}
```

With this approach the embedded JavaScript resource is served by ASP.NET's
`WebResource` mechanism, so any caching and other techniques used are consistent
with the custom components approach. For brevity we have omitted setting
custom properties for `labelText` and `pageSizes`. Doing this would be similar
to techniques described earlier. The code for using it is a bit simpler than that for
using `GenericPlugin`:

```
private PagingToolbar BuildBottomBar()
{
  return new PagingToolbar
  {
    Plugins = { new PageSizeChangerPlugin() }
  };
}
```

With the `GenericPlugin` declaration, each use would require setting the
`InstanceName` and `Path` properties. By extending Plugin, you achieve
better encapsulation.

Benefits of this approach

This plugin is now standalone to be used wherever needed and the plugin code
doesn't need to know about any other plugins that may, or may not have, also
been used on the paging toolbar. Another advantage of this plugin code being in
JavaScript is you can also reuse this plugin in scenarios where you are creating
components directly in JavaScript.

Drawbacks of this approach

As with the drawbacks listed for extending controls, the main drawbacks are perhaps there is a bit more JavaScript to write (which, as also mentioned previously, is actually a good thing!), and it may require a bit more effort and, learning curve to get over initially. However, the dividends should pay off so it may be a worthwhile investment to make!

Plugins versus extending components

There is no one right answer to the question of whether you should use plugins or extend components. In reality you are likely going to need both in the right circumstance. If you extend components too much, you might have a hard time refactoring or reusing bits of functionality elsewhere. If you have too many plugins, it may be hard to handle specific features of controls in a manageable way.

If you are likely to use components such as Windows, TabPanels, GridPanels, Panels (perhaps with specific layouts) repeatedly to show very specific information, then that could be a candidate for subclass.

In object-oriented terms, if what you build "is a" component you are extending, then that is a good fit for extending. If you are repeatedly composing components by including others, then you can make that composing component into a subclass of whatever it is and internalize the composition. If, on the other hand, you are augmenting functionality and want to package it for uses in many places, a plugin is likely to be your best bet.

If you want to build a grid where you can sort rows using drag-and-drop, you would likely do this as a plugin so it can be used by most types of grids. If you subclassed GridPanel just to add this, you are forcing all grids to be one of these (or a subclass) just to get this functionality. The drag-and-drop itself does not fit the "is a" grid test, so it is not an extension itself; it is more appropriately a plugin. (You could argue that you would name your subclass GridPanelWithDraggableRows, but that is stretching it! "With" hints that it is an additional feature of the grid, not that the grid has really been extended.)

Consider this example of extending a component. If you create an application look by using a Viewport but you have a fixed header and/or footer area, you could subclass the Viewport to define this. Then on your pages you could always start off with this Viewport subclass and insert your items into it. This could mean you don't need master pages, or if you do have them, they could be very simple and just contain things that go into the HTML head, or above/below where the Viewport goes.

Summary

We can extend and organize our Ext.NET-based components in various ways, as follows:

- Using a control builder approach to wrap common code
- Extending Ext.NET controls
- Using plugins

The first approach, while quick, may not be flexible enough. The other two, however, are immensely powerful and although we might wonder which one we should use, in reality both extending and creating plugins are needed in complex applications.

All options are likely to require JavaScript, but the extending and plugin approaches encourage better JavaScript code and organization by following Ext JS conventions. As stated before, getting the most out of Ext.NET involves embracing and learning Ext JS rather than shying away from it, and Ext.NET's approach to extending controls and using plugins helps you with that very much.

We also spent some time specifically looking at ways in which you can extend Ext.NET components based on scenarios, such as whether you will have custom JavaScript/CSS, custom Listeners/DirectEvents and other properties, and whether you need MVC Razor support or not. It may seem complex at first, but after a few attempts, it will hopefully make creating reusable components easier which helps increase the productivity of building applications on top of them.

Another aspect to increase productivity of application building is troubleshooting, which we turn to next.

10
Troubleshooting and Debugging

Web applications can get complicated quickly. In addition, Ext.NET is packed with features and the team is constantly adding more capabilities. If your components span the browser and server then different tools and techniques are needed to troubleshoot any issues that arise. This chapter covers the following:

- Debugging and troubleshooting Ext.NET applications
- Browser developer tools
- Getting support from Ext.NET

By the end of this chapter, you will gain an understanding of how to troubleshoot your application and how to request further assistance from the Ext.NET team.

Debugging and troubleshooting Ext.NET applications

For any server-side Ext.NET-based code, usual debugging techniques apply. This typically involves using the Visual Studio debugger and attaching it to your web process as needed. Debugging Ext.NET server-side controls is not any different from debugging any other ASP.NET based controls.

As mentioned in *Chapter 1*, *Getting Started with Ext.NET*, Ext.NET source code is available for download. This also means that if you really need to, you can build and debug or browse the code to learn more about how it works.

If you are using the NuGet package, the Ext.NET team has helpfully included the debugging symbols in Ext.Net.pdb to help with debugging in Visual Studio.

However, because Ext.NET offers tight integration with Ext.NET's JavaScript and Ext JS JavaScript, troubleshooting usually involves knowing how to find out information about your components once they are rendered and running on the browser. The tips in this section are mostly about configuring your application to help debug the JavaScript layer of your Ext.NET application.

> In addition, it may be worth spending some time on the Sencha website for more on debugging Ext JS based applications. Two useful starting points are:
>
> `http://www.sencha.com/learn/extjs/?4x`
>
> `http://www.sencha.com/learn/debugging-ext-js-applications`

Enabling debug mode scripts

By default, Ext.NET outputs minified versions of both Ext.NET and Ext JS JavaScript. The minified versions are stripped of any whitespace and have other optimizations to ensure the download speed and size are as optimal as possible as this is the preferred approach when a site is live.

Enabling the non-minified versions can be useful to help debug the client-side JavaScript more easily. You can enable debug mode scripts in a variety of ways:

- Enable it globally using the `<extnet>` settings in `Web.config`
- Enable it in a ResourceManager for your page or master template
- Enable it conditionally based on compilation flags or other conditions

Debug mode can be set in `Web.config` using `<extnet scriptMode="Debug" />`.

The following code shows how to set it using the ResourceManager on a page:

```
<ext:ResourceManager ID="Mgr" runat="server" ScriptMode="Debug" />
```

> Notice the case difference. In `Web.config`, properties of the `<extnet>` configuration settings are in CamelCase, whereas in ASP.NET control, ASP.NET MVC and in code-behind it is in PascalCase.

You can programmatically set the `ScriptMode` property in code-behind too. For example, using the above ResourceManager in code-behind, you would do the following:

```
Mgr.ScriptMode = ScriptMode.Debug;
```

Notice in the code-behind version the value is assigned a `ScriptMode` enum, not a string.

Doing this programmatically may give you control over when you want to switch into debug mode. For example, if your code is compiled with a flag such as the `DEBUG` flag then you could set it to `Debug`. Or, you may have your own mechanism to trigger it.

> Be sure that you have a process in place to turn off the debug scripts when the code is deployed into production!

Controlling Source Formatting

Similar to enabling/disabling debug mode scripts, you can also use the ResourceManager to indicate how the initialization JavaScript (the script rendered to the page) should be formatted; either minified or not. This too can help with debugging.

By default, initialization scripts are minified. Consider the generated HTML source of the `Ext.Net.Default.aspx` page that comes with Ext.NET's NuGet package install:

```
<!DOCTYPE html>
<html>
<head>
    <link type="text/css" rel="stylesheet" href="/extjs/resources/css/ext-all
    <link type="text/css" rel="stylesheet" href="/extnet/resources/css/extnet
    <script type="text/javascript" src="/extjs/ext-all-js/ext.axd?v=43109"></
    <script type="text/javascript" src="/extnet/extnet-all-js/ext.axd?v=43109
    <script type="text/javascript" src="/extnet/locale/ext-lang-en-GB-js/ext.

    <title>Ext.NET Example</title>

    <script type="text/javascript">
    //<![CDATA[
        Ext.net.ResourceMgr.init({id:"ctl03",aspForm:"ctl01",theme:"gray",icc
    //]]>
    </script>
</head>
<body>
    <form method="post" action="Ext.NET.Default.aspx" id="ctl01"><a href="htt
```

Notice the initialization JavaScript section has one line (not wrapped in the screenshot). In more complex pages, this initialization script line can get very long. This means it is hard to read. Ext.NET's ResourceManager has a boolean property called `SourceFormatting` to indicate whether to format the source or not. Enabling it (setting the value to `true`) means the same initialization script is now generated like this:

```
1  <!DOCTYPE html>
2  <html>
3  <head>
4      <link type="text/css" rel="stylesheet" href="/extjs/resources/css/ext-all
5      <link type="text/css" rel="stylesheet" href="/extnet/resources/css/extnet
6      <script type="text/javascript" src="/extjs/ext-all-js/ext.axd?v=43109"></
7      <script type="text/javascript" src="/extnet/extnet-all-js/ext.axd?v=4310
8      <script type="text/javascript" src="/extnet/locale/ext-lang-en-GB-js/ext.
9
10     <title>Ext.NET Example</title>
11
12     <script type="text/javascript">
13     //<![CDATA[
14         Ext.net.ResourceMgr.init({
15  id: "ctl03",
16  aspForm: "ctl01",
17  theme: "gray",
18  icons: ["Accept"]
19  });Ext.onReady(function(){Ext.create("Ext.window.Window",{
20  height: 180,
21  hidden: false,
22  renderTo: Ext.get("ctl01"),
23  width: 350,
24  defaultAnchor: "100%",
25  defaultButton: "0",
26  items: [
27      {
28  id: "TextArea1",
```

The script section is not on a single line any more. While not indented perfectly, any JavaScript debugger you use can now more accurately report the line number for any problem you are trying to figure out.

> As with the `ScriptMode` property, be sure to turn off `SourceFormatting` on your production servers to optimize downloading.
>
> Whether you use the `SourceFormatting` option or not, for readability you can copy this initialization script into a JavaScript beautifier, such as
>
> http://jsbeautify.com/

Browser developer tools

Most modern browsers such as IE9, Firefox, Chrome, Safari, and Opera provide developer tools including console tools, CSS/HTML/DOM inspectors, a JavaScript debugger, a network or HTTP traffic inspector and more. Many of these are useful for Ext.NET applications as well.

Most development tools are native to their browser. Being native means they generally perform quite well even on complex web application pages. Firefox has the well-known Firebug extension. It is very rich and powerful. Although Firefox has recently started providing native tools, as of writing they do not match Firebug fully. Firebug is also perhaps the most powerful for Ext.NET debugging. So, although it could be a bit slower to run if your page is extremely heavy or you leave Firebug on all the time, it is usually fine, but it may be something to be aware of especially if your development machine is old or doesn't have enough CPU or memory.

> Firebug has to be installed manually. More information can be found here: http://getfirebug.com/

Cross-browser considerations

The Ext.NET and Ext JS teams put a lot of effort into cross-browser compatibility saving you a lot of work. However, as you build your applications and add your own HTML, CSS and JavaScript, it is still important to cross-browser test your application as different browsers of course may have different capabilities and different bugs! So even if you have a preferred browser for its developer tools, it is worth getting to know the development tools available in all the browsers you aim to support.

As a general guide (though there could always be exceptions) it is best to test in the most modern or standard compliant browsers first, followed by the older ones. This will reduce the effort you put in to make your application work cross-browser. Although it seems counter-intuitive this should hold even if you expect your target audience to primarily use another browser. For example, if you have a business application deployed to a corporate environment that is still mostly on IE6 and IE7, you should still test your code on Firefox, Chrome, Opera, Safari, and IE9 first (IE10 may be out around the time this book goes to print—a note about this is further discussed below). Then test with IE8, followed by IE7 and IE6.

Of course, there will be variations; you might decide you are not going to actively spend time and resources supporting some browsers if you can be sure they won't be used. However, consider the browser landscape does change so testing on newer browsers first helps improve future compatibility of your applications to a reasonable extent. In our earlier example where your app may have a current target audience of IE6 and IE7 users, you may not know when they upgrade. Or, if another customer wishes to buy your application and they are all on more modern operating systems and use other browsers instead, then developing with those in mind means your application is ready for them, too. With web technologies such as CSS and even JavaScript and, increasingly HTML5, this can be quite important; you would most likely write less code to start with by targeting a newer browser first, and only add in additional code if, and when, needed.

HTML doc types

As we saw earlier, the default `Ext.Net.Default.aspx` page that comes with the NuGet package, Ext.NET supports the HTML5 doctype:

```
<!DOCTYPE html>
```

This will help browsers (including old browsers such as IE6) render as close to W3C standards as those browsers support. This helps reduce JavaScript, DOM, and CSS discrepancies (though there still will be some). Ext JS and Ext.NET handles any differences that still result for you, though of course in your application if you have custom CSS and JavaScript you may need to be careful in your cross-browser testing.

Other standard-compliant doc types will also be okay, such as XHTML 1.0 Strict, or HTML 4.01 Strict (or Transitional) as long as they are written out in full. Partial doctype declarations or unknown ones may make some browsers render in what is known as Quirks mode (the browser's own interpretation of various features which may differ from the W3C specifications making your site harder to maintain across different browsers).

Setting IE rendering mode

As of writing, IE9 is the latest browser from Microsoft and, therefore, has the latest developer tools. Since IE7, Microsoft has tried to provide some developer tools that let you switch the rendering modes of the browser to show the site in various modes. These indicate whether the site should render by following a strict implementation of W3C standards or its own interpretation—Compatibility View.

It is important to note that if your application is running in an Intranet environment quite often (depending on settings) IE may run your application in Compatibility View by default. However, Compatibility View offers up its own problems and Ext JS has decided to support only standards-compliant browser modes which is, therefore, what Ext.NET will support. You can enforce this in your applications. For example, in `Web.config` you can set a custom header in the `system.webServer` section:

```
<configuration>
  <system.webServer>
    <httpProtocol>
      <customHeaders>
        <clear />
        <add name="X-UA-Compatible" value="IE=IE9" />
      </customHeaders>
    </httpProtocol>
  </system.webServer>
</configuration>
```

> Although you can also set it via an HTML meta tag, it is better to place this in Web.config as explained in MSDN:
> http://msdn.microsoft.com/en-us/library/cc288325%28v=vs.85%29.aspx

IE developer tools and taking advantage of rendering modes

When it comes to IE cross-browser testing, you generally have two options:

- Create different virtual machines for each operating system and IE version combination you want to support
- Use IE developer tools to support IE7, and above, on your development environment and install IE6 on Windows XP in a virtual machine

Ideally, do both! This of course depends on your testing regime, budget, priorities, and so on. There are other options, but these two are perhaps more stable than others.

It is important to note that using different Virtual Machines is probably the most reliable option but, of course, this may have license and budget implications. Be aware that with IE9, the JavaScript engine has changed and as Microsoft has warned, there might be subtle differences between older IEs via IE9's developer toolbar and running an older IE via a Virtual Machine. Generally speaking these issues can be rare (Ext JS and Ext.NET have done a lot of IE testing for us), but it is important to be aware of it. For further information the following are useful:

- `http://blogs.msdn.com/b/ie/ archive/2011/03/24/ie9-s-document-modes- and-javascript.aspx`
- `http://coding.smashingmagazine. com/2011/09/02/reliable-cross-browser- testing-part-1-internet-explorer/`

The first option should be reasonably self-explanatory, so we will focus on the second option here for a moment. As IE9 is the latest official release of Internet Explorer as of writing, you can browse your application in IE9 and use its developer tools to show how your application will look in IE8 and IE7, as the following screenshot demonstrates:

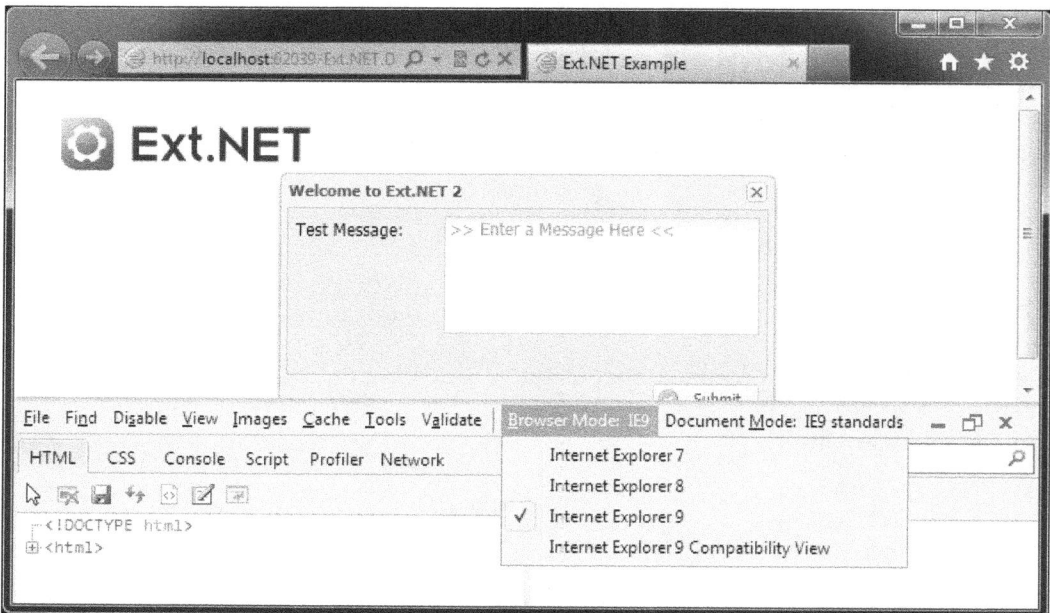

In the preceding screenshot the **Browser Mode** menu shows the available browser modes. The default shows **Internet Explorer 9** as the browser mode with the **Document Mode** as **IE9 standards** mode. The **Document Mode** will look similar to this:

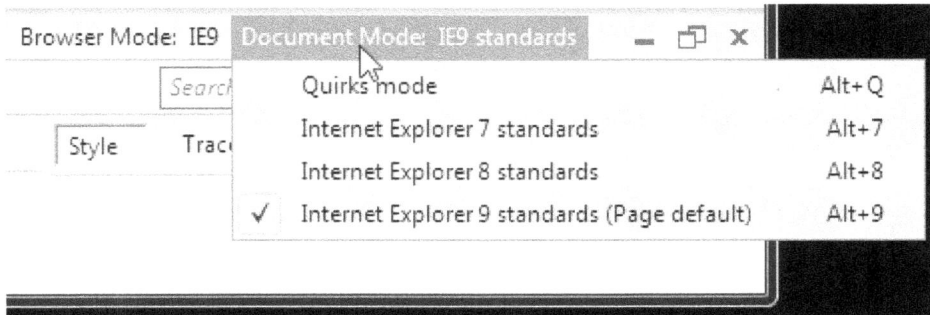

> The **Browser Mode**, **Compatibility View**, **Document Mode**, and **Quirks mode**, are not supported in Ext.NET and Ext JS. Normally, you do not need to select the **Document Mode** manually. When you change **Browser Mode**, the **Document Mode** usually updates to the corresponding value. In cases where it does not, you change it manually. Changing these values will also cause the page to reload. The versions in the Browser and Document Modes must match to be supported by Ext JS and Ext.NET. Variations such as IE8 Browser Mode with Internet Explorer 7 standards Document Mode are not supported.

IE10 support

IE10 comes with Windows 8. As of writing, Windows 8 has only just been released and IE10 has not yet been released for Windows 7 but is expected to be at some point.

As has happened with previous versions of Ext JS and Ext.NET, once a new version of IE is officially released, the Sencha team quickly gets to work to fix or update any affected code and then release an update to Ext JS. After that, Ext.NET can quickly incorporate the update and provide any of their own changes if needed. A new build of Ext.NET is then released and provided for download.

It is, therefore, advisable to use the latest known version of IE (currently IE9) in the X-UA-Compatible header mentioned earlier, even though IE=edge means the latest version. If your application is already deployed before a newer version of IE comes out, but your users start upgrading their browser before you have a chance to update your application, your users can still use a functioning application as the newer browser will render using the **IE9 standards** Document Mode, thus giving you some breathing room to upgrade.

IE 6 support

If you require IE6 support (many business environments in particular still use Windows XP and may have IE6), you can install a DOM Inspector and use Microsoft's Script Debugger. Although the experience is not great, at least there are some tools!

For an IE6 DOM Inspector, see this (admittedly old) article from MSDN:

http://blogs.msdn.com/b/ie/archive/2005/05/10/416156.aspx

And for Microsoft's Script Debugger see this:

http://www.microsoft.com/en-gb/download/details.aspx?id=22185

Do note, that these tools may no longer be supported or only work on Windows XP. In addition, there may be some third-party tools available as alternatives. Windows XP is the last Windows operating system to support IE6, so it may be worth investing in a virtual machine with Windows XP on it where you can install these tools, if you require IE6 support. As an additional bonus, past and current versions of Ext JS and Ext.NET have put a lot of effort into IE6 support so you do not need to spend as much time on this antiquated browser as you may otherwise need.

There is no guarantee IE6 will be officially supported in the future based on Microsoft's support policy. Some popular websites have dropped official support for IE6, though in the business world IE6 is more represented than in the consumer application space. So if your application is a line of business application then this is worth keeping in mind.

Browser console

The browser console outputs any JavaScript errors, warnings, or other messages produced by your application. You can also use it to evaluate your own JavaScript on the fly which is useful for inspection and debugging. For example, we can inspect the App namespace while browsing the **Ext.Net.Default.aspx** page:

By simply entering `App` into the console area and clicking on **Run**, we see output on the left hand side. If you then click on the console output you can drill into the object:

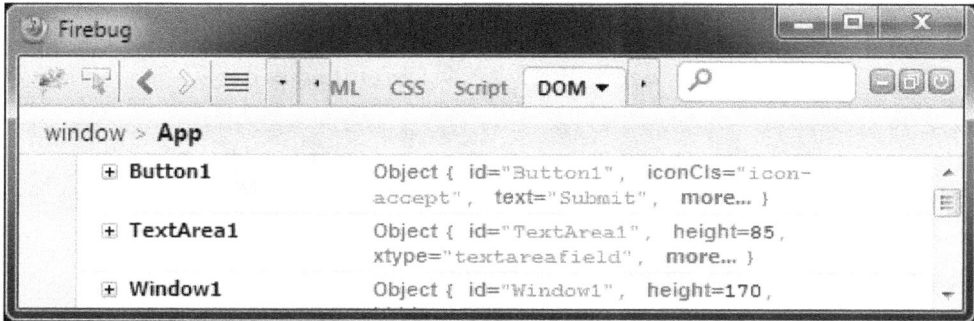

This is a list of the properties of the `App` object. You can expand each property to see their individual values and you can run any JavaScript code in the console. Here we log the `TextArea1` component from the earlier Window example:

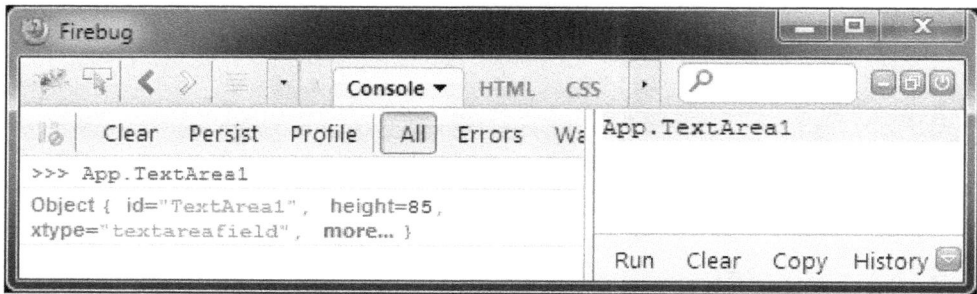

It can also be obtained using Ext JS code, such as `Ext.getCmp('TextArea1')`.

You can then drill into the result by clicking the output to see something like this:

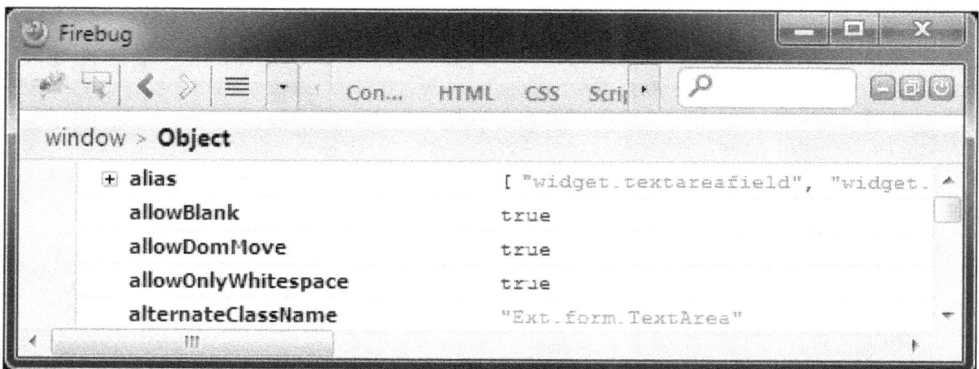

This is a good way to discover the many properties of components and see if that matches your expectation. If you are troubleshooting in your application, you can often attach to a given event and in your method include some logging to the console.

You can also manipulate various components. For example, using the **Window1** reference we can get the parent Window and show or hide it:

In the preceding screenshot, the `hide` method has been invoked so the Window is no longer visible. You can also do more advanced things, such as attach to events at run time. We could, for example, issue a command such as:

```
App.window1.on('show', function() {
    console.log('On Show: ', this);
});
```

Now, if we show the Window, this event handler will output information to the console (in this case just the Window again, but you could output other information as needed).

This lets you see what is happening without having to necessarily modify your code.

> The above techniques can be used in other browser tools such as the console tool for IE, Chrome, Safari, and Opera.

Remember to remove `console` calls in your production code because older browsers, in particular IE6 and IE7 do not have a native console, so that code would cause JavaScript errors in those browsers. Failing that there are techniques to create a console polyfill object for those browsers if you prefer. An Internet search on this will reveal many techniques to deal with this.

> Also note that `log` is not the only function on the `console` object. The Firebug Console API documentation lists many useful cross-browser supported methods:
>
> `https://getfirebug.com/wiki/index.php/Console_API`

Illuminations for Developers

There is an additional extension to Firebug that may also be very useful. It is called *Illuminations for Developers* and is written by *Steven Roussey*, a volunteer on the Firebug team. It lets you inspect Ext JS-based components (including Ext.NET components) in a more friendly way.

> You can find more information about how *Illuminations for Developers* works, how to get it and how to use it (including videos and blog posts) at this website:
> `http://www.illuminations-for-developers.com/`.

Illuminations for Developers lets you inspect parts of the screen by clicking on nodes but instead of seeing the HTML inspection panel open, you see an Illuminations inspection panel open which lets you inspect your components rather than the underlying HTML. This helps understand complex component frameworks such as Ext JS and Ext.NET.

Illuminations for Developers explicitly supports Ext JS, which means Ext.NET is implicitly supported. This means it can provide specialized views for inspection inside the Firebug panel. For example, consider the following screenshot:

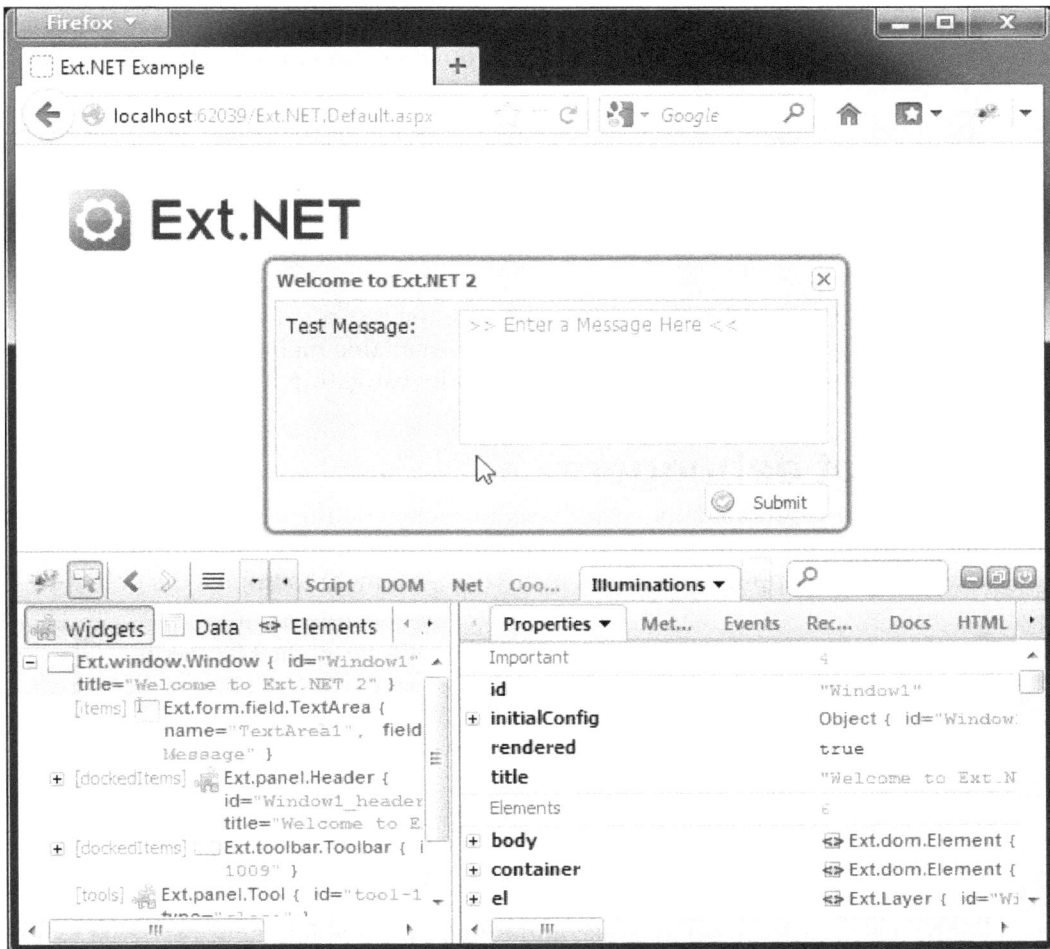

In the preceding screenshot, you can see an **Illuminations** tab added to Firebug. The inspection toggle button has been turned on and the Window has been selected with a mouse-click. The **Illuminations** tab then shows information about that component.

The right-hand side shows various properties grouped by importance and class inheritance, which can be very useful. For the purposes of the screenshots the right-hand pane looks like it does not use the available space very well, but further down there are some properties with longer names. In addition, the screenshots are taken at a screen size suitable for this book, but in reality your windows are likely to be wider and, thus, more information is visible in these useful Firebug panels.

> The properties tab is a useful tool to see if the component you want to debug is an Ext.NET JavaScript component or Ext JS component as it will show properties in order of their Ext JS class hierarchy. This can be a quick way to know which source code to look at to learn more about that component.

Illuminations for Developers also lets you browse the records of any Store objects you might be inspecting. You can also look at the available methods, events, documentation and more, so it is certainly worth investigating further.

JavaScript debuggers

The browser tools mentioned above all have JavaScript debuggers that work like any other debugger, using breakpoints, conditional breakpoints, watch windows and so on. JavaScript itself supports the useful `debugger` statement to invoke the debugger.

> A useful tip for debugging IE is to use Visual Studio's JavaScript debugger as explained here:
> * http://weblogs.asp.net/scottgu/
>   archive/2007/07/19/vs-2008-javascript-
>   debugging.aspx
> * http://www.asp.net/web-forms/videos/
>   aspnet-35/visual-studio-editor/javascript-
>   debugging-in-visual-studio-2008

With Ext.NET `ScriptMode` set to `Debug` and optionally enabling `SourceFormatting` the debugger is more usable because you can easily search for the code you want to breakpoint. The other benefit is you can step into Ext.NET's own JavaScript, as well as Sencha's Ext JS JavaScript to see what is happening. This can be a useful way to understand the underlying framework.

Debugging requests

There may be times where you need to look at data being transferred from the server to the client or see why some resources are not loading as you might expect. Web developer tools in most browsers offer network/HTTP traffic inspection. In Firebug for example, this is found in the **Net** tab, as the following screenshot shows:

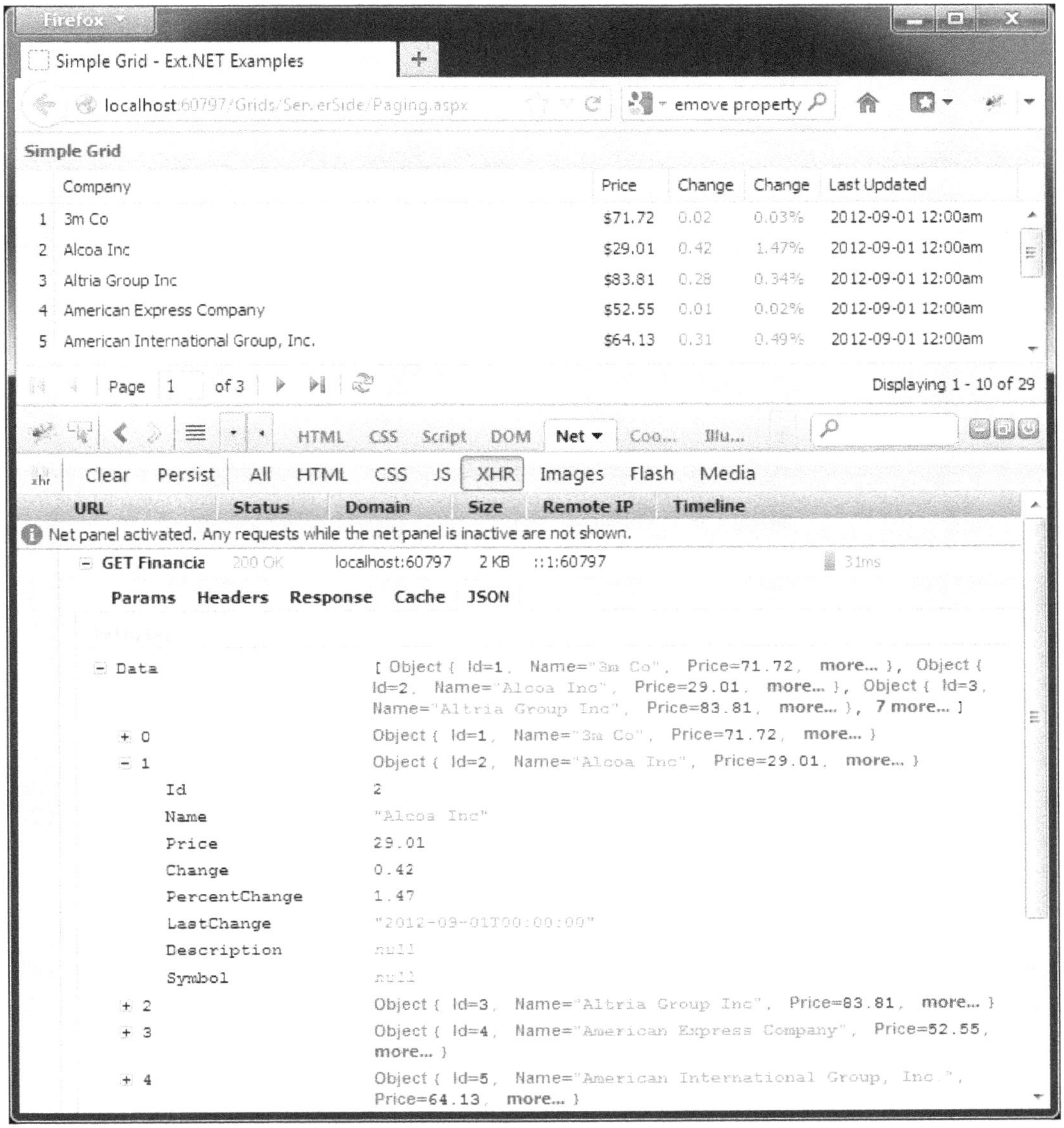

In the preceding screenshot, a GridPanel is using an AjaxProxy which calls an ASHX handler which in turn returns the Store data. The **JSON** tab shows a formatted version of what can be seen in the **Response** tab, which allows additional inspection, if needed. Notice also, the **Net** tab has been further filtered to show only XHR requests (XHR standards for XmlHttpRequest, the underlying mechanism used to make AJAX requests).

Another useful aspect of the **Net** tab is to inspect Ext.NET components generated during an AJAX request. Consider the following screenshot:

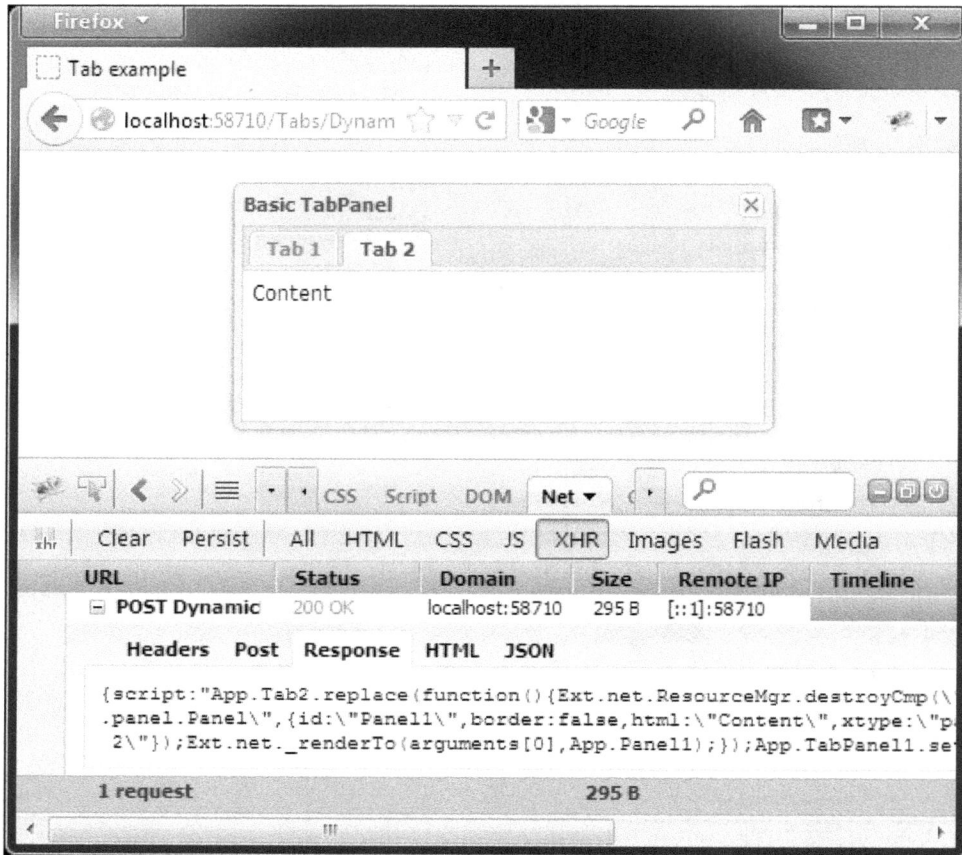

In the preceding screenshot, when **Tab 2** is activated, an AJAX request is issued to generate its contents (an Ext.NET Panel) on the server and load it inside this tab.

The **Response** in the Firebug **Net** tab shows a simple JSON result which has a `script` property. The value of the script is a string (which will be evaluated into JavaScript). As a string, you can see quotes are escaped using `\"`.

Although the above example is rendering a simple Panel with just **Content** as the content, realistically you may be generating far more complex controls, such as GridPanels or DataViews. If they are not rendering quite how you expect, it can be worth seeing what JavaScript is being generated to see if it matches your expectation. So with the above response, you can quickly pretty-print it using the following steps:

1. Copy the Response body (right-click anywhere in the response for short-cut options) into a text editor.
2. Remove the starting { `script:`" and trailing "}.
3. Replace the remaining \" with ".
4. Paste into a JavaScript pretty-print tool, such as `http://jsbeautifier.org/`.

Using the earlier tab example here is what you may see:

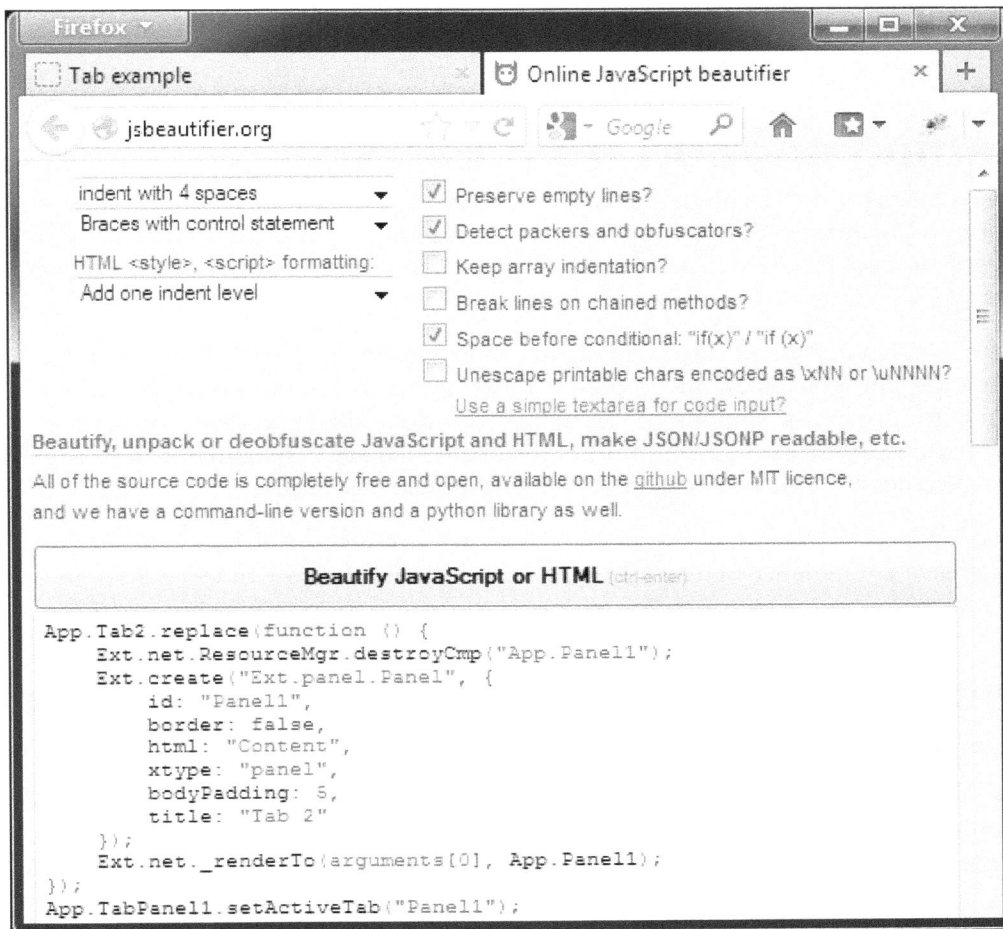

In the preceding screenshot the single long line of response script has been pretty-printed into a more readable format. With more complex controls there will be more code to look at, but it can be a useful start to see if/why something is not as you expected.

> A powerful browser-independent tool for HTTP debugging is Fiddler:
>
> http://www.fiddler2.com

Another problem you may occasionally come across is blank pages. This could be caused by a JavaScript error during initialization (in which case the earlier techniques to view the source and get pretty-printed output can help), or a request could have failed (in which case earlier described HTTP tools can help). It may also be that Web.config has not been set up correctly. Comparing to the NuGet-installed Web.config may help in that case to ensure various Ext.NET resources remain correctly registered.

Getting support from Ext.NET

One of the great non-technical aspects of Ext.NET is their support. If, after all your efforts, you cannot get something to work, or you think you have found a bug, you can get support from Ext.NET by asking questions or raising bugs in their forums, at http://forums.ext.net.

There is also a dedicated forum if you have a Premium Support Subscription where questions asked are given high priority and usually answered well within 24 hours, usually hours, sometimes minutes. If you do not have a Premium Support Subscription, there are still community forums which are very active. The Ext.NET team also answers questions there, often very quickly as well.

How can Ext.NET respond so quickly? There are a number of things you can do to increase your chance of a rapid response, which also helps you learn more in the process!

The overall principle–reproduce the problem in small, standalone code

The overall principle is to first reproduce your problem in a standalone environment, completely independent of your production code. If you successfully recreate the problem, using this code in the forums makes it easier for everyone to understand.

Use a test project independent of your production code

To achieve this small reproducible example, you should create a separate web project that is completely independent of your main production code. This one-off step will also let you explore, learn and prototype Ext.NET-based solutions and ideas very quickly.

Examples of what to cut from your sample

When creating a cut-down sample, you should try to remove all extraneous things. For example, suppose your production code has a problem with a GridPanel that is inside a TabPanel which is inside a ViewPort with a BorderLayout.

When recreating the problem in a standalone page, try to create a page with a GridPanel only. Do not recreate the ViewPort with BorderLayout and TabPanel. This way you hone in on the problem. (Also, if you need to send this to the Ext.NET team, it is easier for them to narrow down the problem, improving your chances for a quicker response).

It is even worth removing properties of the GridPanel that are not part of the problem. For example, if you are having a problem formatting the rows, then your GridPanel probably does not need the `Title` property to be set. Anything that cuts your code down to its bare minimum helps. Use dummy data to quickly populate a Store, for example.

Remove any non-essential CSS or JavaScript. Place any relevant CSS and JavaScript onto the single ASPX page (in relevant `style` and `script` blocks). This keeps as much of the code as possible in one file which is easier to copy/paste into a forum request.

Try to avoid code-behind too. You can often use a `<script runat="server">` block on the top of your stand-alone ASPX page.

For ASP.NET MVC pages, if possible, use an extremely simple View. If help is needed with the Controller code, create a very reduced scenario to narrow down the problem area.

If your code interacts with third-party services or components, try to mock those up for your stand-alone sample. Make it as easy as possible for the Ext.NET team to run the sample straight away without spending time configuring/installing other components. This can also be a good learning exercise for componentization and reduced coupling.

If you cannot reproduce the problem

If you still struggle to reproduce the problem look at the Examples Explorer for similar scenarios, or see if your real solution includes interactions with third party components.

Of course, if you do not find a problem after doing this, then slowly add more features that mimic more behavior of your production code until you can reproduce the problem.

At this point your working sample can be pasted directly into an Ext.NET forum post.

> When posting samples to the forums, just the simplified ASPX code is required, not the whole test project. The Ext.NET support team should be able to copy/paste your code sample into their local test project without having to make modifications to your code.
>
> To ensure your code is formatted correctly wrap it with [CODE] and [/CODE].
>
> The following guidelines for posting help requests include further tips and tricks to format your code and increase the chances for a speedy response:
>
> http://forums.ext.net/showthread.php?3440
>
> http://forums.ext.net/showthread.php?10205

Effort should pay off in other ways

Although it seems like a bit of an effort, spending a bit of time recreating the problem like this has a number of additional benefits:

1. You do not need to divulge sensitive information or implementation if you need to report a problem to the Ext.NET team.

2. The Ext.NET team (or even other forum members) should then have all the information they need to reproduce the problem and respond accordingly.

3. In the process of building up separate test pages like this, you get an environment to explore and prototype Ext.NET solutions.

4. Often, in trying to recreate the issue, as you simplify it down to just the problem area, you may often find the solution presents itself without having to post in the forums. This can be a useful self-learning exercise while saving you some time from posting a forum question and waiting for an answer.

5. The Ext.NET team can get to the problem quickly so you get a faster response.

6. Posting your samples and following up may help others in the future looking for a solution to the same questions

Helping the Ext.NET team in these ways increases your chance for a faster response, but it also means they save time themselves, which they can use making an awesome product even more awesome! Who would not want that?

Summary

In this chapter we had a look at how you might troubleshoot an Ext.NET application. On the server side, there is nothing special you have to do compared to normal; Visual Studio debugging for Ext.NET is as it would be for any other ASP.NET-based application.

On the client side, as we have to consider multiple browsers we looked at a number of options to help troubleshoot. We saw how Ext.NET provides the ability to load debug versions of their JavaScript and of Ext.NET for easier debugging. We also reviewed tools, such as the Console to analyse HTTP requests and format responses for easier reading.

Finally, we looked at how you can try to reproduce any problems you are having in a standalone solution to try and isolate the issue as much as possible from the rest of your code. We saw an additional advantage of this approach is that you can post this isolated code sample directly into the Ext.NET forums if you need further help and support from the Ext.NET team. This helps them see your problem quickly and hopefully results in a speedy response while giving them more time to continue developing Ext.NET further.

Index

Symbols

<extnet> settings 356
<form> element 282

A

Absolute Layout 97
AbstractComponent 157
AbstractStore 291
Accordion layout
  about 84, 85
  combinations 87, 88
  panel subclasses, as accordion items 86, 87
ActionColumn 210
AddToServerTime() method 129
AJAX 99
AJAX-based proxies 212
AJAX Control Toolkit 99
AjaxProxy
  about 173
  using 182, 183
AJAX requests
  types 103
AJAX requests, types
  in-page 103
  off-page 103
AJAX, with ASP.NET
  about 99
  page methods 102, 103
  UpdatePanel 100, 101
alias property 319
AllowBlank property 273
Anchor Layout 97
App client-side namespace 113

appearance
  customizing, for validation
    messages 274, 275
apply method 320
ArrayStore class 172
ASHX 125
ASHX handler
  about 166, 212
  example 212
  for AJAX paging 181, 182
ASMX 99
ASMX Web Service
  about 103, 146, 212
  JSON Serialization considerations 146-149
ASP.NET 99
ASP.NET data source control
  example 190, 191
ASP.NET Empty Web project 16
ASP.NET MVC
  and Ext.NET 8
ASP.NET MVC 3 Web Application
    project 23
ASP.NET MVC Controller
  about 125
  calling 144
  invoking 123, 124
ASP.NET MVC (Razor)
  custom components, using in 334-336
ASP.NET MVC Razor Project
  creating, with Ext.NET enabled 23
ASP.NET project
  creating, with Ext.NET enabled 16
ASP.NET Web Form
  and Ext.NET 8
  custom components, using on 333, 334
ASPX 125

parameters
  passing, to events 106, 107
PasswordMask plugin 274
pctChange function 319
PersistenceMode attribute 328
PickerField 263
plain tabs 303
Plugin class 351
plugins
  benefits 352
  drawbacks 353
  using 346-352
  versus extending components 353
Premium Support Subscription 374
PrepareData property 179
prerequisites, Ext.NET 2 12
properties
  adding, to JavaScript class 332
Proxies
  about 173
  types 173
Proxies, types
  client-side 173
  server-side 173

R

Radio button
  about 267
  configuring 267, 268
RadioGroup 268
records
  binding, to forms 284, 285
regions 72
RegisterIcon method 195
rejectChanges() method 248
relativeTime parameter 121
RemoteSort property 223
remote validation 280
RemoteValidationFailure event 281
RemoteValidationInvalid event 281
RemoteValidation property 280
RemoteValidationValid event 281
Renderer function 207
Renderer property 320
requests
  debugging 371-374
ResourceManager attribute 345

ResourceManager object 135
resources
  embedding 321
Resources property 322
RestProxy 173
Result property 167
RethrowException property 137
root node 288
row
  expanding 231
  expanding, Ext.NET components
    used 234-236
  expanding, templates used 231-233
row editing
  about 241, 249
  enabling 249, 250
  options 250
RowEditing plugin 249
RowExpander plugin 232, 233
row expansion feature 231
RowNumbererColumn 211
RowSelectionModel 237

S

Safari 359
Script Debugger 364
ScriptManager 104
scriptMode property 22
ScriptMode property 356, 358
ScriptService attribute 145
SelectBox 261
SelectedDate property 262
SelectedItems collection 261
select event 323
SelectionChanged listener 187
selection models
  about 236
  cell selection 240, 241
  checkbox selection 239
  default row selection 237-239
selections
  handling, in DataViews 185-189
SelfRender() method 335
Sencha
  URL, for official website 7
Sencha Ext JS component 260

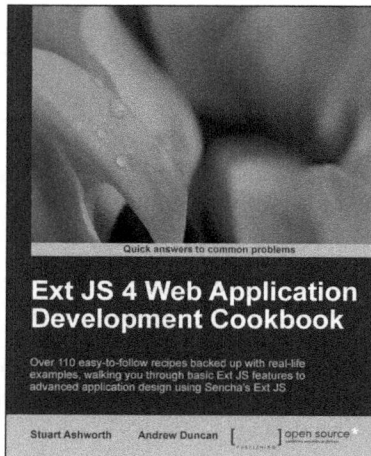

Ext JS 4 Web Application Development Cookbook

ISBN: 978-1-849516-86-0   Paperback: 488 pages

Over 110 easy-to-follow recipes backed up with real-life examples, walking you through basic Ext JS features to advanced application design using Sencha's Ext JS

1. Learn how to build Rich Internet Applications with the latest version of the Ext JS framework in a cookbook style

2. From creating forms to theming your interface, you will learn the building blocks for developing the perfect web application

3. Easy to follow recipes step through practical and detailed examples which are all fully backed up with code, illustrations, and tips

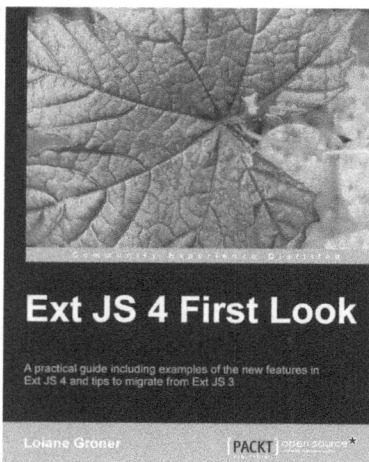

Ext JS 4 First Look

ISBN: 978-1-849516-66-2   Paperback: 340 pages

A practical guide including examples of the new features in Ext JS 4 and tips to migrate from Ext JS 3

1. Migrate your Ext JS 3 applications easily to Ext JS 4 based on the examples presented in this guide

2. Full of diagrams, illustrations, and step-by-step instructions to develop real word applications

3. Driven by examples and explanations of how things work

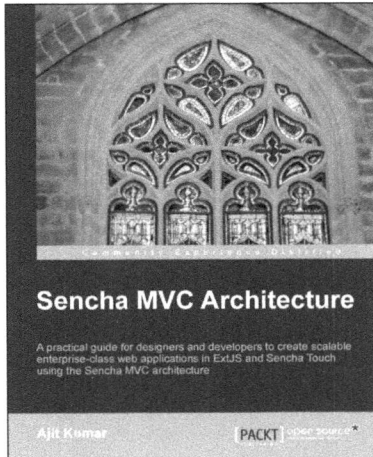

Sencha MVC Architecture

ISBN: 978-1-849518-88-8   Paperback: 126 pages

A practical guide for designers and developers to create scalable enterprise-class web applications in ExtJS and Sencha Touch using the Sencha MVC architecture

1. Map general MVC architecture concept to the classes in ExtJS 4.x and Sencha Touch

2. Create a practical application in ExtJS as well as Sencha Touch using various Sencha MVC Architecture concepts and classes

3. Dive deep into the building blocks of the Sencha MVC Architecture including the class system, loader, controller, and application

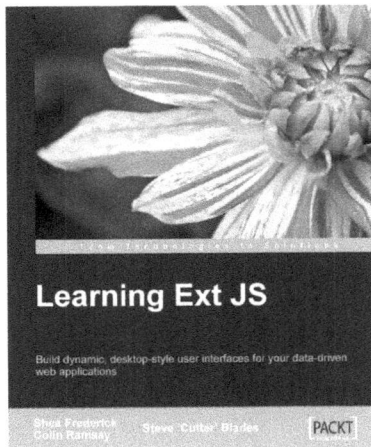

Learning Ext JS

ISBN: 978-1-847195-14-2   Paperback: 324 pages

Build dynamic, desktop-style user interfaces for your data-driven web applications

1. Learn to build consistent, attractive web interfaces with the framework components.

2. Integrate your existing data and web services with Ext JS data support.

3. Enhance your JavaScript skills by using Ext's DOM and AJAX helpers.

4. Extend Ext JS through custom components.

Please check **www.PacktPub.com** for information on our titles

* 9 7 8 1 8 4 9 6 9 3 2 4 0 *